PLO IN LEBANON

PLO IN LEBANON
SELECTED DOCUMENTS

Edited by
Raphael Israeli

Weidenfeld and Nicolson
London

Raphael Israeli is a Senior Lecturer at the Insitute of Asian and African Studies, a Fellow of the Truman Research Institute and Director of the Centre for Pre-Academic Studies, all at the Hebrew University in Jerusalem. He has written several books and articles on the Middle East, Islam and Islam in China, and has edited two other works on Islam in Asia.

Dr. Israeli completed his undergraduate studies in History and Arabic at the Hebrew University in 1963. He received an M.A. degree in East Asian History in 1970 and a Ph.D. in Islamic and Chinese History in 1974, both at the University of California at Berkeley.

First published in Great Britain by
George Weidenfeld & Nicolson Limited
91 Clapham High Street, London SW4

ISBN 0 297 78259 2

Printed in Great Britain by
Butler & Tanner Limited
Frome and London

Table of Contents

MAPS OF LEBANON

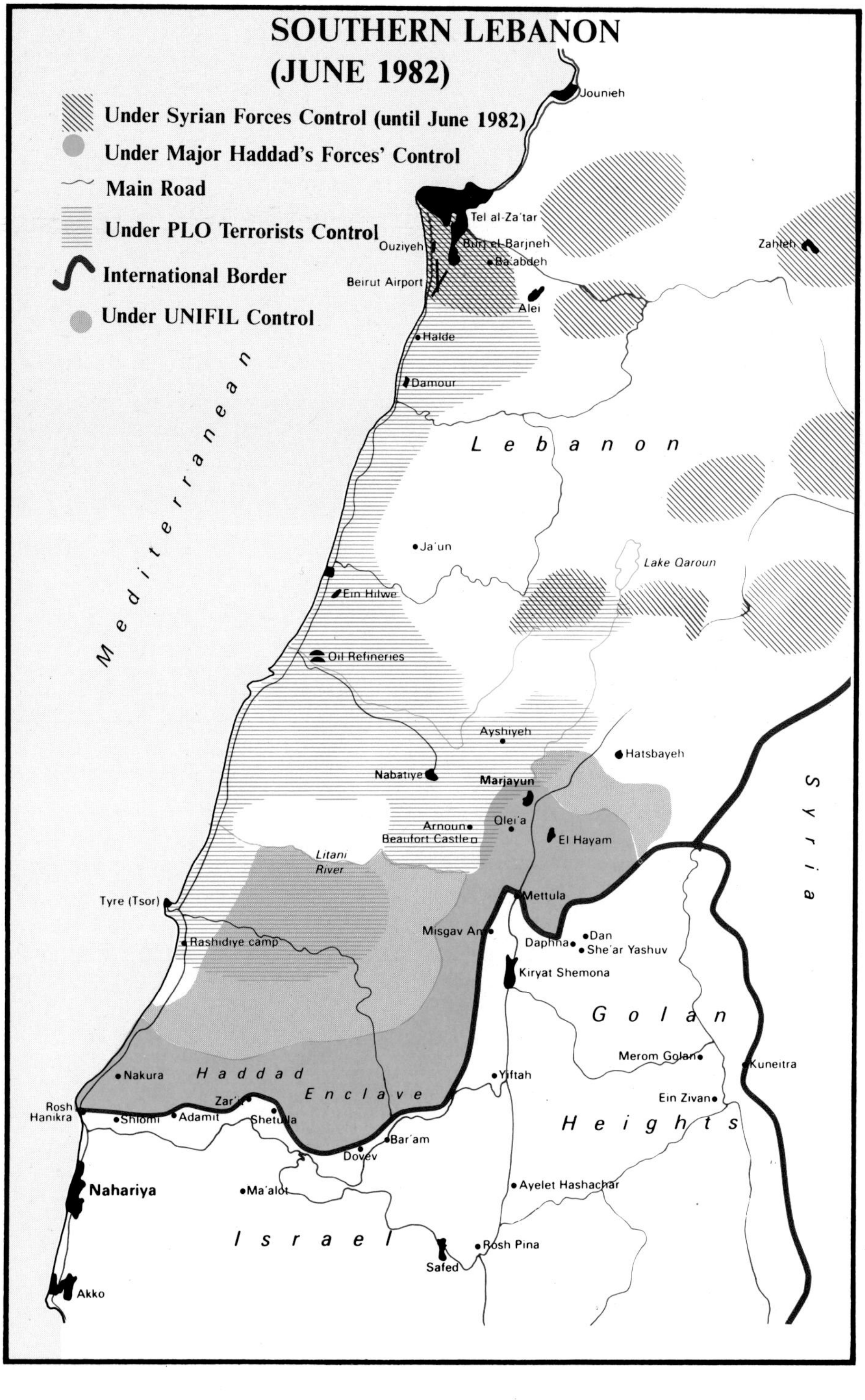

SOUTHERN LEBANON
(JUNE 1982)
Under Syrian Forces Control (until June 1982)
Under Major Haddad's Forces' Control
Main Road
Under PLO Terrorists Control
International Border
Under UNIFIL Control
Jounieh
Tel al-Za'tar
Ouziyeh
Burj el-Barjneh
Ba'abdeh
Zahleh
Beirut Airport
Alei
Halde
Damour
Mediterranean
Lebanon
Ja'un
Lake Qaroun
Ein Hilwe
Oil Refineries
Ayshiyeh
Hatsbayeh
Nabatiye
Marjayun
Syria
Arnoun
Qlei'a
Beaufort Castle
El Hayam
Litani River
Tyre (Tsor)
Mettula
Misgav Am
Dan
Daphna
She'ar Yashuv
Rashidiye camp
Kiryat Shemona
Golan
Merom Golan
Kuneitra
Nakura
Haddad Enclave
Yiftah
Rosh Hanikra
Zar'it
Ein Zivan
Shlomi
Adamit
Shetula
Heights
Bar'am
Dovev
Nahariya
Ma'alot
Ayelet Hashachar
Israel
Safed
Rosh Pina
Akko

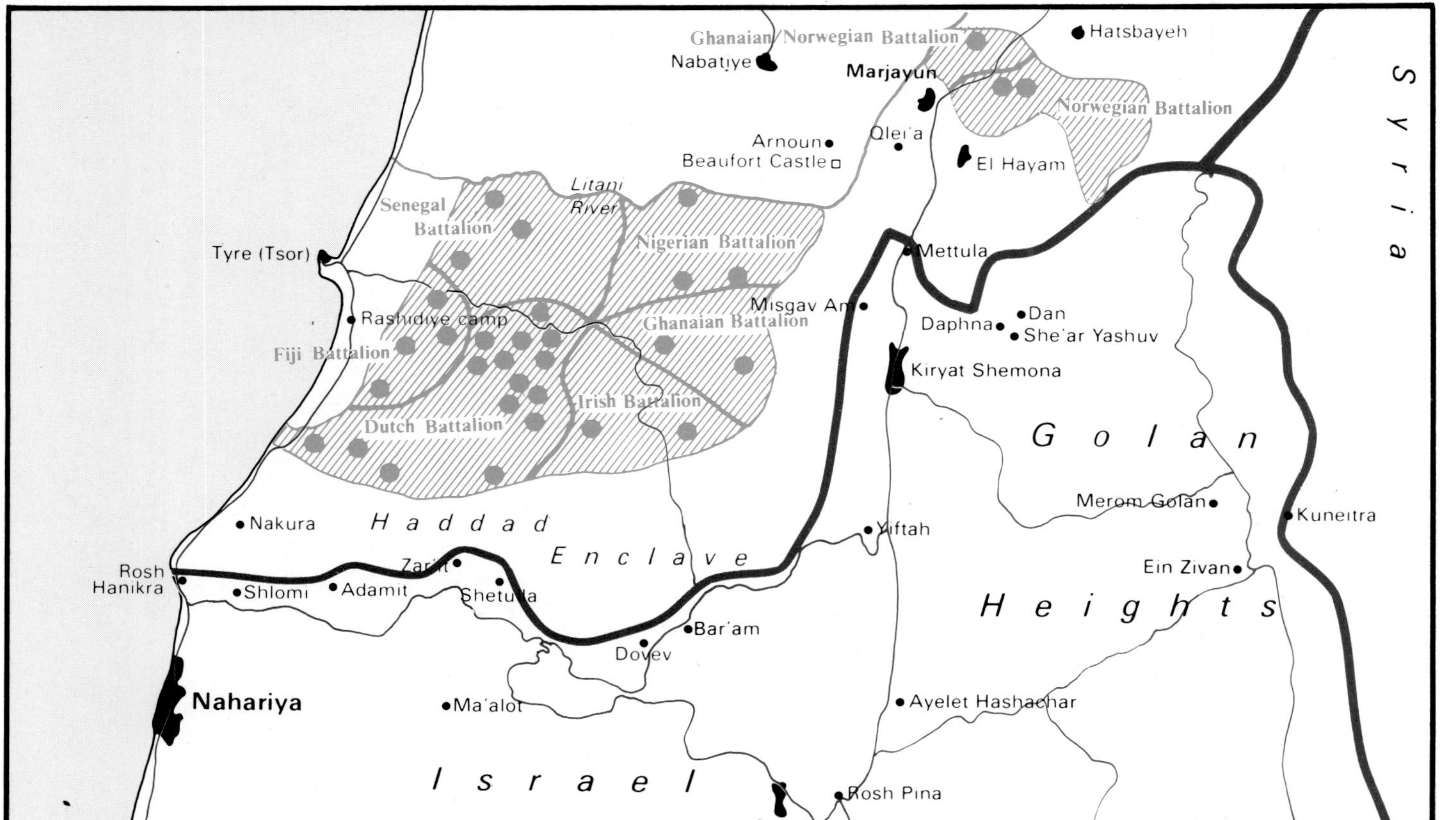

PLO BASES WITHIN UNIFIL AREAS (JUNE 1982)

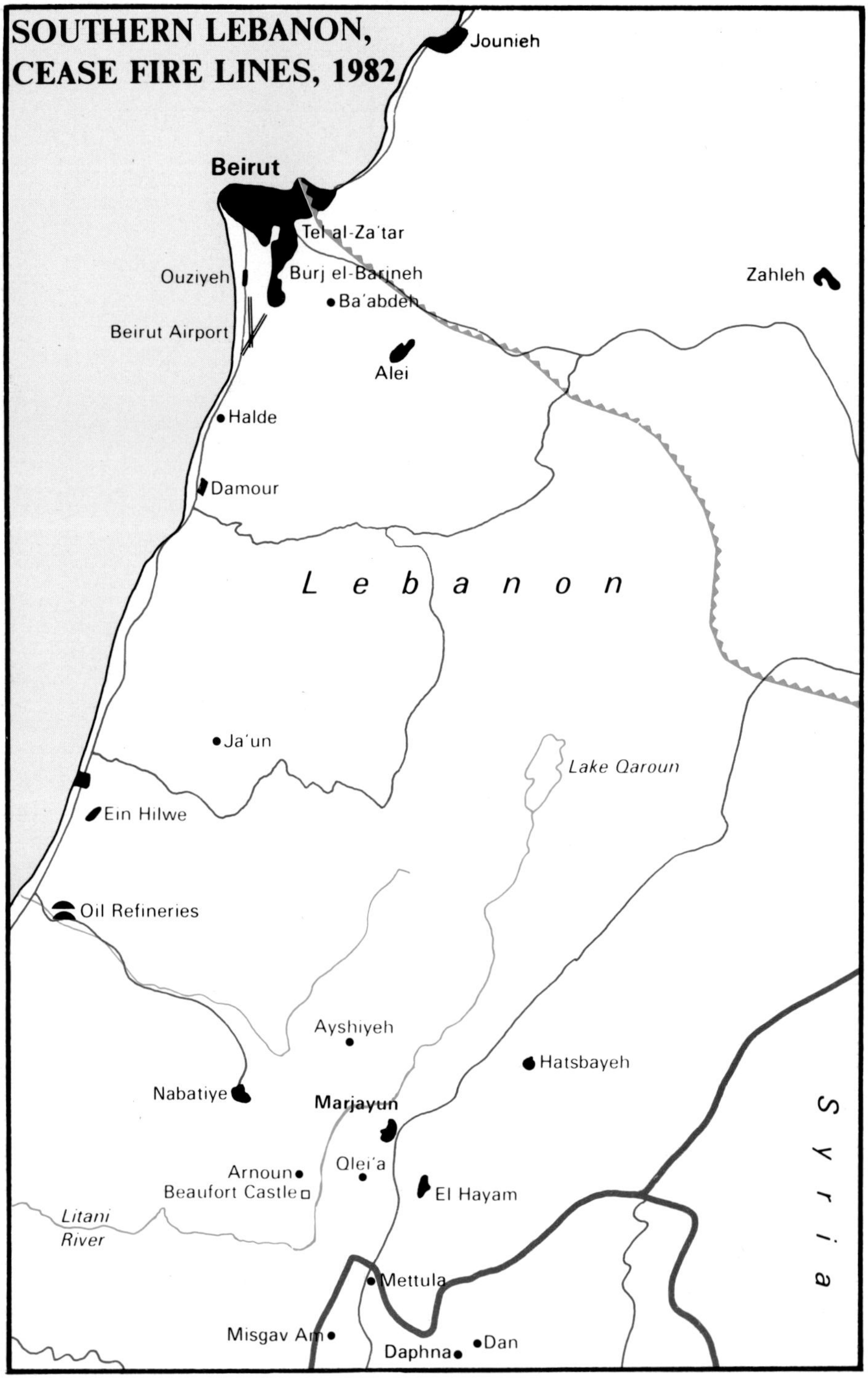
SOUTHERN LEBANON, CEASE FIRE LINES, 1982
Jounieh
Beirut
Tel al-Za'tar
Burj el-Barjneh
Zahleh
Ouziyeh
Ba'abdeh
Beirut Airport
Alei
Halde
Damour
Lebanon
Ja'un
Lake Qaroun
Ein Hilwe
Oil Refineries
Ayshiyeh
Hatsbayeh
Nabatiye
Marjayun
Syria
Arnoun
Qlei'a
Beaufort Castle
El Hayam
Litani River
Mettula
Misgav Am
Dan
Daphna

I. FOREWORD

When Israel launched Operation Peace for Galilee on 6 June 1982, all eyes, in Israel and the world, turned to the battles in which Israel's troops engaged the full Palestine Liberation Organization (PLO) military array for the first time. Few suspected the extent of the PLO hold on southern Lebanon, or imagined the amount of military hardware which the organization had accumulated over the years on Lebanese territory. Still more surprising, however, was the myriad of documents seized in the local and regional headquarters of the various PLO factions. In the city of Nabatiye alone, some 22 different headquarters, representing as many groups within the PLO, were captured and destroyed. In practically all of them, files were seized which illuminated the ideological and operational aims of the PLO with regard to Israel, revealed the ramified connections between that organization and the Eastern bloc countries in support of international terror and exposed other activities, such as trading in drugs and meddling in other countries' affairs.

As the fighting in Lebanon subsided the destitute people who had been driven from their towns and villages by PLO terror since 1975 began to return. For example, Nabatiye in the south which had been evacuated by its inhabitants after prolonged PLO terror and repeated massacres, began to reabsorb thousands of families as soon as the PLO was expelled. The repatriated refugees told horrifying stories of expulsion, rape, intimidation and murder suffered at the hands of PLO members. They expressed their joy that the PLO was gone, and their hope that they could now rebuild their homes.

Both the written documents seized at PLO offices and the eye-witness evidence attesting to PLO behaviour towards the Lebanese population should be instructive for both the general public and specialists. They constitute part of the tragic recent history of that part of the Middle East. The editor, who found the task of collecting documents and interviewing returning refugees quite daunting, received generous assistance from many individuals and institutions. Much of the material reproduced here was made available by the Israel Defence Forces (IDF). The Israel Broadcasting Authority, and especially the Arabic television department, were very helpful in transcribing some of the interviews. I am also grateful to the officers of the IDF Civilian Aid Unit who assisted me in the interviews I conducted in various parts of Lebanon, to the Ministry of Foreign Affairs for arranging my trip through the war-affected zones of Lebanon and to the Israel Information Centre which provided the technical facilities for the publication of this volume.

Jerusalem, 30 August 1982

III. INTRODUCTION

Israel's incursion into Lebanon in June 1982 aimed at freeing its civilian population of the northern Galilee, from the threat of Lebanese-based PLO artillery attacks and guerrilla raids. It was the culmination of a long series of events which had made a shambles of Lebanese unity and sovereignty. Lebanon's plight was not the result of Syrian and PLO occupation alone. The country's long history of disunity ultimately led to its dismemberment and foreign intervention.

Indeed the ethnic, cultural and religious make-up of Lebanon is so varied as to defy the conventional definitions of nationhood. Each ethno-cultural-religious group is not only subdivided among itself (Sunnis and Shi'ites among Muslims; Maronites, Greek Orthodox and Greek Catholic among Christians), but these subdivisions tend to be further exacerbated by family and clan rivalries and controversies, which at times take on the appearance of "political" differences (for example, the "socialist" Druze led by the Jumblatt clan as against the conservative Druze led by the Arselan clan). Add regional antagonism (south against north; Mt. Lebanon against the coastal cities), the Palestinian influx in 1948 and then again in 1970, and the amazingly complex residential patterns (Druze within Christian areas; Christians within Muslim areas; etc.), and you have a recipe for constant clashes, bickering, competition and one-upmanship.

Between 1945, when Lebanon became independent from the French, and 1975, successive governments were able to preserve the country's independence and territorial integrity. Nearly all the Arabs recognized Lebanon's separate identity and its title as an Arab state which it won through membership in the Arab League. Syria, however, never recognized the Lebanese polity, and is the only Arab country which has never established regular diplomatic relations with Beirut. Its claims to "Greater Syria" have of necessity limited its contacts with the Lebanese to talks between leaders of the two countries — or to military occupation.

Lebanon's distinctive situation was reflected in its modest military structure on the one hand and the phenomenal growth of its economy on the other. Indeed, a large-scale army, which Lebanon could have economically afforded, would have brought into focus its domestic inter- and intra-communal dissensions and created chaos instead of stability. Thus, Lebanon left its defences to the "guarantees" of France and the Arab League members, and adopted a very low profile on the Arab-Israeli conflict. The Lebanese channelled their energy, creativity and enterprising spirit into business, trading and banking. The country became a major clearing house for Arab oil money. Lebanon continued to survive as an island of free political discourse in the Arab world, while attempting to maintain the delicate, uneasy balance between its various communities.

In 1958, Nasserist sentiment led to public support among some Lebanese Muslims for the incorporation of Lebanon into the United Arab Republic of Egypt and Syria. President Camille Chamoun felt incapable of toning down Muslim fervour; he feared that full-fledged intervention by his Christian-dominated army in the disturbances could end in civil war. Pierre Jemayel's Christian forces tried to take on the battle in "private," but they proved inadequate to tackle the Muslim-inspired rising which signalled the first cracks in the country's fragile political structure.

President Chamoun called in the United States Marine Corps, which eventually left Lebanon when a new president, Fouad Chihab, was elected. Stability seemed to be restored.

PALESTINIAN INTERVENTION

Until the 1967 Six-Day War, at least some of the 200,000 or so Palestinian refugees in Lebanon were well on their way to assimilating into the existing political system. The refugees' presence both within and outside their camps hardly posed a problem to the Lebanese authorities. After the mid-1960's, however, when the Fatah group began to take the lead in the PLO, the Palestinian refugee camps in Lebanon became the setting for paramilitary training, political propaganda, mass mobilization, social radicalization and arms stockpiling.

The Syrians, who had grudgingly witnessed the Lebanese state grow and prosper outside their grip, now saw a golden opportunity to arm, train, finance and dominate the PLO armed groups as possible surrogates in Lebanon. Despite their discontent at the sight of growing PLO power in Lebanon, the Lebanese felt impotent to arrest the process, much less undo it, for fear of Syrian intervention or renewed civil disturbances or both. PLO groups began to surface in Lebanon's major cities and towns to operate in the full light of day, and use their Lebanese base to launch worldwide acts of terror, such as plane hijackings, bombings and killings.

By the 1970's, a PLO state-within-a-state had emerged in Lebanon, with its own administrative and military services. The PLO systematically encroached upon Lebanese sovereignty, and provoked Israeli reprisal raids against its forces inside Lebanon. The Lebanese had no choice but to provide it with political and diplomatic shelter. Lebanon desperately sought to accommodate PLO wishes while preserving what remained of its sovereignty, but all attempts to limit Palestinian raids against Israel from Lebanese territory ended in failure. At times Israel reacted violently against attacks on its civilian population centres, airlines and embassies, as when it raided the Beirut airport in December 1968, or launched the April 1973 commando operation against PLO headquarters inside the Lebanese capital.

As early as 1968, the Lebanese Army had, in practical terms, renounced its supervision of those areas of Lebanon which had come directly under PLO rule: the Palestinian refugee camps and the southeastern region of the country. "Fatahland," at the foot of Mount Hermon, was a particularly important sanctuary for the PLO because of its contiguity with Syria, which enabled the Ba'ath regime in Damascus to provide logistic backing to the Palestinians. Remote and isolated, especially in view of the firm Syrian refusal to allow operations from Syrian territory, the PLO began to cultivate "revolutionary" myths and symbols drawn from a wide range of communist and anti-Western ideologies from Mao to Castro, Guevara and Ho Chi-minh. "Guerrilla warfare," "Arafat trail," and the "revolution growing from the barrel of the gun" became household words in the PLO. The now familiar unshaven faces, the acts of terror, the repeated hijackings and the much-publicized training in such monstrosities as tearing apart live chickens, drinking the enemy's blood or mutilating their prisoners, added much impetus to the glorification of the "Palestinian revolution," which was solidifying its launching base in southern Lebanon.

In October 1969, serious clashes broke out in southern Lebanon between the Lebanese Army, which was fighting a rear-guard battle for the restoration of some semblance of order in the country, and the PLO, which was unwilling to accept any limitations on its activities against Israel. President Charles Helou of Lebanon urged Nasser to restrain the PLO and its patrons — the Syrians — only to succumb to a new "compromise solution" under which the Lebanese government would facilitate PLO incursions from Lebanon into Israel, in return for a Palestinian commitment to refrain from interfering in the domestic affairs of its host country. However, after "Black September" in 1970, when the main base of PLO activity was eradicated in Jordan, Lebanon became the one country where the Palestinian squads could secure a political, military and logistic base. The Lebanese Army desperately attempted to prevent the PLO military takeover of southern Lebanon and even ventured, at the price of all-out military clashes, to disarm PLO militants travelling outside their camps. The Syrians, however, openly backed the PLO, both politically and logistically, until finally the Beirut government resigned itself to a new "agreement" with the PLO.

A long string of skirmishes, negotiations and compromises followed one another during the years 1970-77, but they could not stabilize the situation for any length of time. Any such "agreement" to yield authority and sovereignty to a foreign body was, by definition, detrimental to the central government. When open clashes broke out in Sidon in April 1975 between the PLO and the Christian forces, who could no longer bear the central government's impotence, they soon spread all over Lebanon. Although the fighting took place mainly between Lebanese Christians (now dubbed "rightists" or "conservatives" by the media) and a coalition of the PLO and the Muslims (who won the new epithets of "leftists" and "progressives"), it also exposed internecine quarrels between various factions within each major division. In any case, the war was long and cruel and its main victims were Lebanese civilians. In the capital city of Beirut alone some 50,000 people lost their lives, 200,000 others were wounded and many hundreds of thousands, mainly Christians, were uprooted from their homes and lands by the PLO and the Muslim left, and forced to either migrate to other parts of Lebanon or leave the country.

In the process, the Lebanese Army was dismantled, with its various communal components joining their respective co-religionists, or simply deserting. The Lebanese government could no longer function, despite the election in 1976, under Syrian guns, of a new president, Elias Sarkis, by the hurriedly-convened parliament. The president and his cabinet barely controlled the vicinity of the presidential palace, while the rest of the country was carved up between the belligerent groups (see map). Many attempts were made by various Arab conferences to settle the Lebanese crisis, but all they yielded were dozens of "cease-fire agreements" which were violated as soon as they were signed. The "all-Arab" troops brought to Beirut in June 1976 to supervise the cease-fire, in accordance with the resolutions of a conference in Cairo, soon proved inadequate for the task, while the internal Lebanese conflict, in which the PLO now took an increasingly crucial part, kept raging.

THE SYRIAN TAKEOVER

Events in Lebanon took a new turn in the summer of 1976, when Syria decided to move in directly and stop pretending it was merely implementing "all-Arab" resolutions. While, in April 1975, Syria had made no secret of its support for Muslim PLO and other pro-Syrian elements in Lebanon, a year later it attempted to create a new order in Lebanon, which would perpetuate the communal divisions in Lebanese politics and would place the Lebanese state under a *de facto* Syrian protectorate. The Christians, who feared extermination at the hands of the PLO and other "leftists," reluctantly consented to the proposed arrangement, thus pulling the rug out from underneath the "natural allies" of the Syrians — the PLO and the left. The latter rejected the offer as no longer reflecting the new demographic balance in Lebanon and renewed the fighting. Syria, fearing that the PLO-leftist coalition would take over Lebanon and set it onto a separate course, sent in troops in May 1976 to take over the major cities and roads. The Christians joined in the fighting on the Syrian side and, in August 1976, conquered Tel al-Za'tar, the PLO stronghold in Beirut, thus signalling what they thought would be the beginning of the end of PLO domination in Lebanon. By late summer, Lebanon was divided into three *de facto* areas of control: the Syrians in the north and east controlled some two-thirds of the country; the Christians in the north now dominated East Beirut, the northern part of Mt. Lebanon and parts of the littoral around the port of Jounieh; and the PLO-Muslim coalition now ran West Beirut, the Tripoli area and southern Lebanon. In September 1976, the Syrian and Christian forces launched a combined offensive against the PLO-Muslim coalition in both Mt. Lebanon and the south which resulted in the military collapse of the PLO.

In October 1976, at the Riyadh Summit, a new cease-fire was agreed upon, restoring the situation in Lebanon to its pre-April 1975 shape. The Cairo Agreement of November 1969 was invoked to limit PLO activities within Lebanon but to "permit" the Palestinians to channel their terrorist operations against Israel. At the summit, whose terms were reaffirmed by the second Cairo Conference of October 1976, it was agreed that the Syrians would henceforth make up the bulk of the "all-Arab peace-keeping force" in Lebanon. The Syrians also proceeded to disarm the various parties. In 1977, the level of violence escalated once again into a full-fledged war between the Christians and the PLO, especially following the murder of leftist leader Kamal Jumblatt in March. The Shtura Conference in Lebanon, in July 1977, at which new attempts were made to work out an arrangement between the parties, also ended, in effect, in deadlock, although an "agreement" was announced between Syria, Lebanon and the PLO.

When the PLO-Muslim coalition had been subdued and stripped of its previous formidable military clout, the Syrians thought the time was ripe to turn against the Christians. In July 1978, they launched massive attacks on the Christian strongholds in both East Beirut and Mt. Lebanon, slaughtering thousands of Christians and arousing violent anti-Syrian resentment. The Syrians may have calculated that their massacres of the Christians would alter the demographic balance in Lebanon irreversibly, and thus vitiate Christian claims to political dominance. Early in 1979, an attempt was made to reach a new settlement and the Lebanese government agreed to revive the Lebanese Army; the non-Syrian elements of the Arab peace-keeping force left Lebanon, leaving the Syrians supreme and unchallenged. In April 1981, after their expectations that President Sarkis would act firmly against the Christian-held enclaves were not met, the Syrians launched a fierce attack on Christian East Beirut and on the city of Zahleh in the Beqa'a (Lebanese Valley). The Syrians hoped first to induce Zahleh to surrender, and then take on the remaining Christian strongholds. The Christians fought back in defiance of the Syrian siege, but they could do little against the air assault on 9,000-foot Mt. Sinnin, which they held as a strategic link between western Lebanon and the Christian positions in the Beqa'a. When Israel intervened on behalf of the besieged Christians and shot down two Syrian helicopters, the Syrians introduced their SAM ground-to-air missiles into Lebanon in an attempt to limit Israel's freedom of action in the air.

TERROR BASE IN THE SOUTH

After Syria's takeover of Lebanon in 1976, and more so following its alignment with the PLO in 1977, the latter was able to reinforce its bases in southern Lebanon without incurring the risk of intervention on the part of the practically non-existent Lebanese Army. The south was not only beyond the reach of either the Lebanese or the Syrians, but it was also heavily populated by Palestinians on the outskirts of Tyre and Sidon. Moreover, it was conveniently located along the southern border so as to facilitate PLO operations and acts of terror against Israel. Thus, while in 1975 the PLO focused its attention on Beirut and northern Lebanon and the south was consequently quiet, the situation was reversed in 1977 when the Palestinians were defeated elsewhere in Lebanon by the Syrians and the Christians. After the fall of Tel al-Za'tar to the Christians, the PLO began transfering men and war matériel to the south rather than acceding to Syrian pressures to surrender heavy arms and other equipment positioned in its camps near Beirut and Tripoli.

The accelerated PLO build-up in southern Lebanon was aided by the group's allies in the Lebanese "left" and among groups such as the Communist Party (whose slogans can still be seen all over southern Lebanon) and the pro-Iraqi Ba'ath Party, both of which were strongly entrenched in Tyre, Sidon and the Shi'ite villages. The local Christian militias, the only possible counterweight to PLO-leftist power in southern Lebanon, were too weak and too isolated from their compatriots in the north. Sa'ad Haddad, a Lebanese army major, took command of the militias in the south, acting independently of the northern "Lebanese Front." These militias, initially organized in three separate enclaves, sought and obtained access to one another via Israeli territory through what had become known, since the summer of 1976, as the "Good Fence." The Fence, erected by Israel to protect its northern border from PLO raids, now turned into a point of contact and a channel through which Israel extended help to the people of southern Lebanon fleeing from PLO terror. Thousands of Lebanese villagers began to receive treatment in Israel's clinics at the Good Fence and to seek work in and do business with Israel, now that their ties with Beirut and other war-torn cities were all but severed. As a *de facto* state of peace grew between Israel and its Lebanese neighbours in the Haddad enclave, the Christian and Shi'ite militias asked for and obtained military assistance from Israel to defend themselves against continued PLO harassment.

In the meantime, PLO activities against Israel from southern Lebanon continued to escalate, reaching a climax, on 11 March 1978, when an Israeli civilian bus was intercepted by Palestinian terrorists and almost all its occupants murdered. The Israeli army marched across the border, on 15 March, in order to mop up the PLO bases in southern Lebanon, in what became known as "Operation Litani." The goal was to destroy the PLO's logistic and support network up to the Litani River and to prevent its future regrouping in that area. Israel subsequently withdrew under United Nations and American assurances that the UN Interim Force in Lebanon (UNIFIL) would frustrate any PLO attempt to retake its bases and launch further attacks against Israeli population centres. It quickly became evident that neither UNIFIL nor international "guarantees" would prevent renewed PLO deployment in many parts of southern Lebanon; only the Haddad-held and Israeli-backed enclave was off-limits. The PLO worked to undermine the Security Council resolutions on which the UNIFIL mandate was based. At times they simply and brutally told the "blue helmets" to leave choice strongholds and military positions (notably Beaufort Castle), and stationed their own people there instead.

To counter these moves, Israel, in 1979, adopted a policy of hitting the PLO directly within southern Lebanon and strengthening local Lebanese opposition to the terrorists. The three enclaves now acquired territorial contiguity in a 5-8 by 50 mile belt with a mixed population of Christians and Shi'ites, who for the first time cooperated through their joint militias to ward off PLO attacks. In April 1979, Haddad declared his territory to be "Free Lebanon." He professed to have no separatist aspirations; his declaration was a protest against Syrian and PLO occupation of the rest of Lebanon and a statement that genuine Lebanese sovereignty, free of any foreign yoke, existed only in the territory held by his militias.

The PLO continued to use southern Lebanon as a launching pad against Israel. It also consolidated its hold on large areas of Beirut and other coastal cities, which became logistic centres, equipment and ammunition depots, training bases for infantry and naval forces, supply ports, and launching grounds for terrorist missions against Israel or Israeli or Jewish interests abroad. In the south alone, some 6,000 PLO people were encamped in dozens of different locations, 700 of them within UNIFIL-controlled territory. They openly operated jeeps, mortars and artillery, including 130mm Russian-made guns, 155mm French-made guns, 122mm, 130mm and 240mm Katyusha rockets made in the Soviet Union and 107mm Katyushas made in North Korea. An anti-aircraft network of 14.5mm and 23mm guns together with shoulder-launched missiles afforded them a strong air defence. In view of this arms deployment, the militias in the south could not agree to surrender their arms, for fear of being slaughtered by an uncontrollable PLO.

At the beginning of 1980, the PLO sent its elite Ein-Jalut Brigade to the south, to fill the gap between the Zaharani River and the city of Damour which had been captured from its Christian population. For the first time, the organization introduced large quantities of T-34 tanks — 500 in all — to reinforce its forces and to challenge both the area under Haddad and Israeli towns and villages in the Galilee. PLO acts of terror against Israel continued unabated, including artillery and Katyusha shellings and attempts to land in Israel from the sea (November 1979 and June 1980). Israeli and Haddad forces reacted by bombing, shelling, strafing and mounting commando attacks on selected targets inside the PLO zone. Following a particularly intensive exchange of fire between the PLO and Israel, in July 1981, when the PLO military array seemed to be on the verge of collapse, a cease-fire was arranged under United States auspices.

However, from July 1981 to June 1982, under cover of the cease-fire, the PLO pursued its acts of terror against Israel, resulting in 26 deaths and 264 injured. When Israeli warnings went unheeded, air raids were mounted against the PLO on 21 April, 9 May and 4 and 5 June 1982. The PLO responded with a full range of artillery, tank and mortar fire on the Israeli population of the Galilee, forcing Israel to launch Operation Peace for Galilee on 6 June 1982.

IV. PLO IDEOLOGY AND PRACTICE [Documents 1—6]

Much has been said and written about the PLO's Palestinian National Covenant, both its original version and the amendments introduced to make it seem more palatable to Western public opinion. The controversies over what the covenant means, and the "moderate" notions occasionally injected or read into it by PLO representatives and sympathizers in Europe, have considerably blurred the issues at hand and blunted the document's explicit anti-Israel import. Every year, when the Palestinian National Council convenes, we are assured that "this time" the covenant will be amended to reflect the "new mood of moderation within the PLO." Each time these expectations prove unrealistic. At other times, "informed evaluations" by "reliable circles" have it that Arafat's Fatah group, the major component of the PLO, is in fact "moderate" and is seeking "reasonable" ways to accommodate Israel and come to terms with it. If only the Israelis were less intransigent and more reasonable, it is said, it would be possible to work out a compromise between Israel and the PLO. These "sources" "reassure" Israel that the PLO does not really mean to destroy it, and that its abandonment of the explicit rhetoric of "throwing the Jews into the sea" reflects a change of mind among the Palestinian leadership.

The following documents, all dating from 1980 or 1981 and intended for internal consumption, present the PLO, notably the Fatah group, as it actually sees itself. They reflect in no uncertain terms the real goals of the organization, as stated in Fatah's 1980 political platform:

The liberation of Palestine, a full and complete liberation; the annihilation of the Zionist entity in all of its economic, political, military and cultural manifestations. . . and the establishment of an independent democratic Palestine which would rule the entire land of Palestine.

There is no attempt at euphemism here. The destruction of Israel, even its cultural aspects, is a precondition to its replacement by a "democratic Palestine" in the entire land. In other words, no Israel in any shape or form, no co-existence with Israel and no recognition of the national liberation movement of the Jews — Zionism. Moreover, the documents present very precise ways to achieve that goal: shelling and destroying civilian settlements. We find no plans about attacking the Israeli military. This contradicts the PLO boast that it is a "national liberation" movement (how can "national liberation" be attained without defeating the enemy's military structure?), and makes the term "terrorist" seem more appropriate, for how else could one describe indiscriminate attacks against civilians?

The plans to attack Israeli towns and villages were backed up by an impressive build-up of arms and ammunition throughout southern Lebanon. It has been estimated that the personal weapons, mortars, guns and ammunition of all sorts found in hundreds of underground bunkers and caches all over the area could easily equip several infantry brigades. And yet, that massive build-up was never activated against Israel in any "liberating" move; all the fire-power, planning, ingenuity, training and political indoctrination were used to attack Israeli civilian targets or to control and terrorize the local Lebanese population.

[Document* 1]: PLO poster

The poster, showing a PLO fighter trampling on the Star of David, Israel's state symbol, features the insignia of the Fatah organization (top left) and a picture of Zuheir Muhsin, a top PLO leader murdered some time ago. The slogans on the poster vow that the struggle will go on in the path of the deceased leader.

* Each of the 124 documents in this volume will be preceded by a brief explanation (in Italics) and an English translation, where appropriate.

حركة التحرير الوطني الفلسطيني
فتح الثورة

[Document 2]: Fatah political platform

This proposed political platform, adopted by the Fourth Fatah Conference in May 1980, is part of a file entitled "the Fourth Fatah Conference" seized in the headquarters of the Kastel Brigade of the PLO near Sidon.

The Arab homeland has been subjected throughout the ages to numerous colonial raids, the last of which was the colonial Zionist raid of Palestine. This has happened due to the historical strategic importance of our country. This importance has increased in modern times, when international capitalism entered the imperialistic stage. This stage has required exploitative and expansionist activities, especially since the discovery in our region of oil, the nerve of life for the wheels of Western industry.

In order for exploitation and domination to continue, the Arab homeland had to be torn apart and fragmented into petty rival states. Consequently, the policy of partition and fragmentation became the basic norm of imperialism. For this reason the European imperialist powers have resorted to the destruction and wrecking of local forces of production, and their annexation to the international capitalist market. Their aim has been to prevent the unification of the market for the local forces of production and the establishment of a national state. They also resorted to the establishment of the Zionist entity as a base for aggression against the peoples of our Arab nation. Zionist colonialism used expulsion in order to insure the security of the aggressive base.

The emergence of the Zionist movement was accompanied on the one hand by a two-fold historical process, manifest in the collapse of European feudal systems and the consequent threat of dissolution for the Jewish ghetto, and on the other hand by the imperialist expansionist movement. Thus, the interests of European capitalism and Jewish capitalists joined, and the "Jewish State" was established in order to secure continued imperialist robbery and exploitation of our country. From the start of Jewish immigration in the late 19th century, the Palestinian people set out to defend and protect its land, especially after the Balfour Declaration and the proclamation of the British mandate over Palestine at the beginning of the 20th century.

Palestine has witnessed violent rebellions and fiery revolutions by the Palestinian masses against the British imperialists and the Zionist invaders. The Palestinian people has written, during a period of over thirty years, the most glorious chapters of heroism and sacrifice. However, the local and global balance of power, and the treacherous conspiracies on the part of Arab regimes, brought about the Palestinian misfortune of 1948. In their exile, where they had emigrated and had been expelled, our people suffered a terrible situation of destruction, fragmentation and division, and were exposed to repugnant forms of humiliation and terror. All this lasted until the historical appearance of our Fatah movement at the beginning of January 1965. This was the beginning of a new phase in the history of our people and nation.

Since our movement believes that Palestine is part of the Arab homeland, and that the Palestinian people is part of the Arab nation, and since this belief presupposes that the Zionist existence in Palestine is part of the Zionist aggressive colonialist invasion and an imperialist expansionist base, therefore the Palestinian revolution is the vanguard of the Arab nation in its struggle for the liberation of Palestine. The fight of this revolution is part of the fight of the Arab nation. The Fatah movement constitutes the revolutionary vanguard of the Palestinian people, whose struggle constitutes part of the common struggle of the peoples of the world against Zionism and world imperialism.

The Fatah movement is a national revolutionary independent movement whose goals are: the liberation of Palestine, a full and complete liberation; the annihilation of the Zionist entity in all of its economic, political, military and cultural manifestations; and the establishment of an independent democratic Palestine which would rule the entire land of Palestine, preserving the legitimate rights of all its citizens on the basis of justice and equality and without discrimination with regard to race, religion, or conviction. Its capital will be Jerusalem. The sovereign of this state will be a democratic, progressive society which secures human rights and provides for universal liberties to all its citizens. This state will be able to take an active part in the realization of the goals of the Arab nation, namely the liberation of its various regions and the construction of a progressive, united Arab society.

The struggle for the liberation of Palestine is part of the common national struggle. Therefore, the Arab nation is obliged to support it with all its material and mental powers and energies. This liberation is an Arab, religious and human obligation. Consequently, we consider all the undertakings, agreements and resolutions issued by the United Nations, the League of Nations or individual states with respect to Palestine, and which undermine the right of the Palestinian people to its entire national land, as void and unaccepted.

Our method towards the realization of our goals is the popular armed revolution, being the definite and exclusive way to the liberation of Palestine. The armed struggle is a strategy, not a tactic. The armed revolution of the

Arab Palestinian people is a decisive factor in the battle for liberation and the elimination of the Zionist entity. This struggle will be carried on without interruption until the annihilation of the Zionist entity and the liberation of Palestine are achieved. In our struggle we rely on the Arab Palestinian people as a vanguard and a basis, and on the Arab nation as our partner in our battle and destiny. Therefore, we work to meet all national forces who act on the battleground through armed action, in order to realize national unity and real cohesion between the Arab nation and the Arab Palestinian people, through the participation of the Arab masses in the battle within a united Arab front.

Our relations with the Arab countries aim at developing the positive aspects of the position taken by these states, on the condition that the security of the armed struggle will not be affected and that its escalation will continue. We do not interfere in the internal affairs of these countries, and will not allow anybody to interfere in our affairs, or to obstruct the struggle of the Palestinian people for the liberation of its homeland.

We strive to present the Palestinian identity, including its combative revolutionary elements, on the international arena. This does not contradict the common destiny of the Arab nation and the Arab Palestinian people. We also strive to establish the strongest ties with liberationist forces in the world who support our armed struggle, in order to resist Zionism and imperialism. We likewise try to convince the concerned governments in the world to stop Jewish emigration to Palestine as their contribution to solving the problem, and to oppose any political solution offered as a substitute to the annihilation of the Zionist entity which occupies Palestine, and all schemes aimed at eliminating or iternationalizing the Palestinian cause, or placing the Palestinian people under the mandate of any party whatsoever.

Believing in all this, and taking the principles, goals and methods of our movement and its internal regime as a starting point, the Fourth General Conference of the Fatah movement makes the following resolutions:

THE PALESTINIAN DOMAIN

Considering the unity of the Palestinian people, its land and its political representation, and confirming its national independent desire that the revolution should continue to victory;

And considering that the armed popular revolution is the only definite way to liberate Palestine, and that the way to its liberation is the way to unity;

And considering that democracy governs the relations within the Palestinian arena, and that democratic debate is the correct means to develop these relations;

The conference reaffirms the following:

1. The PLO is the real framework of national Palestinian unity, on the level of the revolutionary cells, the popular organizations, trade unions and all sectors of our people.

2. It is important to develop the fundamental participation of the movement in the PLO in order to secure its effectiveness, thus ensuring the crystallization of its projects and systems. This should be done in a manner which simultaneously safeguards the independence of all the organizations of the movement, and preserves the organizations, bodies, forces and foreign relations of the 'Asifa.[1].

3. To escalate the armed struggle inside the occupied territory and across all lines of confrontation with the Zionist enemy.

4. To increase the effort to organize our people wherever they live; to broaden the perimeter of action of the organizations and the popular and trade unions; to protect its temporary sojourn in the abovementioned places; to prevent its oppression, exploitation and destruction.

5. To support the defiant resistance of our people inside the occupied territory on all levels; to provide the material support necessary to continue its resistance and to escalate its struggle; to develop its national institutions in all their forms; to make an extraordinary effort to strengthen the ties with our Palestinian masses who live in the territories occupied since 1948, in order to enable them to resist the plots which aim at fragmenting their unity and blurring their Arab identity.

6. To reorganize the national Palestinian front inside the occupied territory on such foundations which will guarantee that this front can contribute to the revolution within the framework of the PLO.

7. To reaffirm the necessity of independent decision on the part of Palestinians, and to make an effort to enable the Palestinian revolutionary cells to leave the circle of Arab sponsorship.

---

1. The military arm of the Fatah group within the PLO.

The realization of the aforementioned resolutions will provide the necessary elements for opposing and foiling all those plans and plots aimed against our people and our revolution, in the form of various settlements down to the Camp David Accords, the autonomy plot, the settlement projects and the "confederation" project.

THE ARAB DOMAIN

A. On the mass level:

Since Palestine is part of the Arab homeland and the Palestinian people with its struggle is part of the Arab nation, and since the Palestinian revolution is the vanguard of the Arab nation in its battle for the liberation of Palestine [the conference resolves]:

1. The movement's bond with the Arab masses is a strategic bond which necessitates a wider participation by these masses in protecting the revolution, embarking on various forms of struggle and fighting against the imperialist Zionist base in Palestine, and against all enemies of our people and nation, and eradicating the interests of imperialism and colonialism in the region.

2. The movement must strengthen its close contacts with the Arab movements for national liberation and the Arab national progressive forces in order to embark on the joint battle for the liberation of Palestine, and the fulfilment of the goal of the Arab nation, namely the liberation of its various regions and building a progressive, united Arab society.

3. To consolidate the fighting ties with the national Lebanese forces who stand bravely in one trench with the Palestinian revolution against the enemies of both the Palestinian and Lebanese peoples and the Arab nation; to join with these forces in their battle to protect the unity and Arab character of Lebanon.

4. The solidarity of the Lebanese masses and their heroic stand, side by side with the Palestinian revolution in face of the war of elimination and extermination, must be consolidated, protected and developed so as to become a model for the ties with the masses throughout the Arab homeland at large.

5. The Jordanian area is of special importance for the revolution. It requires special consideration in order to restore it as a fundamental supporting

base of the struggle against the Zionist enemy, and to employ all the powers of the masses to achieve this goal.

6. To strengthen the solidarity of destiny with the Egyptian people who have made enormous sacrifices on the way to the liberation of Palestine; likewise to raise the capability of the national and progressive forces in Egypt in order to bring down the conspiracy of Camp David and its effects, and to return Egypt again to the Arab fold, so as to take its natural position in the leadership of the Arab struggle.

B. On the level of contacts with the Arab regimes:

Since the contacts with the Arab regimes aim at developing the positive aspects of their positions, these contacts should be based on the following principles:

1. The principles, goals and methods of the movement.

2. These contacts should not contradict the strategic contacts with the masses.

3. The attitude of each regime towards the cause of the Palestinian people and its armed revolution, and especially the commitment to the PLO in its capacity as the only legitimate representative of the Arab Palestinian people.

4. Non-intervention in our internal affairs and refraining from attempts to impose guardianship or division on our people, or attempts to oppress and exploit it; likewise refraining from any attempt to resettle our people in any territory outside its homeland, Palestine.

5. Refraining from any attempt to prevent the free activity of the revolution among the ranks of our people in its places of residence.

6. To carry out the revolution and its responsibilities for struggle on the all-Arab level, and via all Arab territories, with a view to liberating the occupied territories and mobilizing the resources of the Arab nation, both human and natural — especially oil wealth — as weapons to be used for implementing this goal.

7. To develop the Steadfastness Front so as to turn it into the main tool of action to strengthen the foundations of the PLO; to pursue the struggle against the enemy; to confront and defeat all solutions which aim at liquidating [the Palestinian issue]; and reinforcing the hands of the rest of the Arab countries in opposing any settlement, whatever its name or epithet, so that they can stand decisively against any attempt to legitimize Camp David.

THE INTERNATIONAL DOMAIN

Since the Palestinian problem has been the major issue affecting the Arab nation in its just struggle against the Zionist and imperialist enemy, and since the Middle East has a great strategic importance, the Palestinian problem has had a great international significance beyond its own inherent aspects....Our movement is part of the world liberation movement and the struggle against imperialism, Zionism, racism and their agents. We commit ourselves to alliances on the international scene in accordance with our principles and the Palestinian National Covenant.

A. In the international domain:

1. To act on behalf of the PLO so as to bring about international measures, and especially UN resolutions, which deal with the rights of our Arab Palestinian people, which will tighten the isolation of the Zionist and American enemy within this organization.

2. To act so as to turn the UN resolutions regarding Zionism as a type of racism and racial discrimination into practical measures against the Zionist imperialist colonial base in Palestine.

3. To increase our activity so as to maintain the UN resolutions which have rejected Camp David, and to strengthen positions of this sort so as to thwart any settlement at the expense of our people.

B. On the level of our friends:

1. To strengthen our strategic alliance with socialist countries, foremost of them the USSR, inasmuch as this alliance will help to frustrate effectively all American and Zionist plots against the Palestinian problem and against all issues of liberation in the world.

Document 2A-1

مشروع البرنامج السياسي

الصادر عن المؤتمر الرابع لحركة / فتح

(ايار – ١٩٨٠)

تعرض الوطن العربي على مر العصور لغزوات استعمارية متعددة كان اخرها الغزوة الصهيونية الاستيطانية لفلسطين ، وذلك نظرا للأهمية الاستراتيجية التاريخية التي تتمتع بها بلادنا . ولقد تعاظمت هذه الاهمية في العصر الحديث مع دخول الرأسمالية العالمية الى مرحلة الامبريالية وما تتطلب من عمليات توسعية واستغلالية وخاصة مع اكتشاف النفط في منطقتنا / وهو عصب الحياة لعجلة الصناعة الغربية .

ولما كان استمرار عمليات الاستغلال والسيطرة تتطلب تمزيق الوطن العربي وتفتيته الى دويلات متصارعة فأن سياسة التجزئة قد باتت هي القانون الاساسي للامبرياليه .

ولهذا فقد عمدت الامبرياليات الاوروبية الى ضرب وتخريب قوى الانتاج المحليه والحاقها بالسوق الرأسمالية العالمية لمنع توحيد سوقها المحلي واقامة دولتها القومية كما عمدت الى اقامة الكيان الصهيوني كقاعدة للعدوان على شعوب امتنا العربية ، مما ترتب عليه ان يكون الاستيطان الصهيوني اجلائيا ، ليضمن امن القاعده العدوانيه .

ولقد ترافق بروز الحركة الصهيونية الى الوجود مع عملية تاريخية مزدوجة تمثلت بانهيار الاقطاعيات الأوروبية وما تعنيه من تهديد لتذويب " الجيتو " اليهودى من جهة ، ومع حركة التوسع الاستعمارى من جهة اخرى ، وهكذا التقت مصالح الرأسماليات الأوروبية بمصالح الرأسماليين اليهود لاقامة " الدولة اليهوديه " لضمان استمرار عمليات النهب والاستغلال الاستعمارية لبلادنا ، ومنذ ان بدأت الهجرة اليهوديه في اواخر القرن التاسع عشر هب الشعب الفلسطيني للدفاع عن ارضه والذود عنها وخاصة بعد وعد بلفور واعلان صك الانتداب البريطاني على فلسطين في بدايات هذا القرن .

ولقد شهدت فلسطين انتفاضات عارمة وثورات لاهبة فجرتها جماهير شعبنا في وجه المستعمرين البريطانيين والغزاة الصهاينه وسجل الشعب الفلسطيني على امتداد اكثر من ثلاثين عاما أروع صور البطولة والتضحية غير ان موازين القوى المحلية والعالمية وفي ظل المؤامرات الخيانية للانظمة العربية قد ادت الى وقوع نكبة فلسطين عام/ ١٩٤٨ ، ولقد عانى شعبنا في منافي الهجرة والتشريد حالة رهيبة من الضياع والتمزق والشتات ، وتعرضت لابشع صور الاذلال والارهاب الى ان جاءت الانطلاقة التاريخية لحركتنا " فتح " في مطلع كانون الثاني عام/ ١٩٦٥ ليبدأ شعبنا وامتنا مرحلة تاريخية جديده ،

وايمانا من حركتنا بان فلسطين هي جزء من الوطن العربي ، والشعب الفلسطيني هو جزء من الامة العربية ، وانطلاقا من ان الكيان الصهيوني في فلسطين هو جزء من الغزوة الصهيونية العدوانية الاستيطانية وقاعدة استعمارية توسعية ، فان الثورة الفلسطينية هي طليعة الامة العربية في معركة تحرير فلسطين وكفاحها جزء من كفاحها . وتمثل حركة " فتح " الطليعة الثوريه للشعب الفلسطيني الذى يمثل كفاحه جزءا من النضال المشترك لشعوب العالم ضد الصهيونية والاستعمار والامبريالية العالميه .

Document 2A-2

"٢"

ان حركة فتح هي حركة وطنية ثورية مستقله وهدفها هو تحرير فلسطين تحريرا كـ
وتصفية الكيان الصهيوني اقتصاديا وسياسيا وعسكريا وثقافيا وفكريا ،

واقامة دولة فلسطينية ديمقراطية على كامل التراب الفلسطيني تحفظ لجميع الموا
فيها حقوقهم الشرعية على اساس العدل والمساواة دون تمييز بسبب العنصر او الديـ
او العقيدة ، وتكون القدس عاصمة لها ، ويسود في هذه الدولة المجتمع الديمقراطـ
التقدمي الذى يضمن حقوق الانسان ، ويكفل الحريات العامه لكافة المواطنين . ويتم
المشاركة الفعالة في تحقيق اهداف الامة العربية مرير اقطارها وبناء المجتمع الد
التقدمي الموحد .

ان معركة تحرير فلسطين هي جزء من النضال القومي المشترك ، ولهذا فان وا
العربية ان تدعم هذه المعركة بكافة امكانياتها وطاقاتها المادية والمعنوية والتحريـ
هو واجب عربي وديني وانساني . لهذا فأننا نعتبر انَ المشاريع والاتفاقات والقرار
صدرت او تصدر عن هيئة الامم المتحدة او مجموعة الدول او اى دولة منفردة بشان فلـ
والتي تهدر حق الشعب الفلسطيني بكامل ترابه الوطني هي باطلة ومرفوضة .

ان اسلوبنا لتحقيق اهدافنا هو الثورة الشعبية المسلحة كونها الطريق الحتمي
لتحرير فلسطين ، وان الكفاح المسلح هو استراتيجية وليس تكتيكا ، والثورة المسلحة لل
الفلسطيني عامل حاسم في معركة التحرير وتصفية الوجود الصهيوني ، ولن يتوقف هذا
الا بالقضاء على الكيان الصهيوني وتحرير فلسطين ، ونعتمد في كفاحنا على الشعب
الفلسطيني كطليعة واساس وعلى الامة العربية كشريك في المعركة والمصير . لهذا
للقاء كل القوى الوطنية العاملة على ارض المعركة من خلال العمل المسلح لتحقيق ال
الوطنية والى تحقيق التلاحم الفعلي بين الامة العربية والشعب العربي الفلسطيني .
الجماهير العربية في المعركة من خلال جبهة عربية موحدة .

اما علاقاتنا مع الدول العربية تهدف الى تطوير الجوانب الايجابية في مواقف
بشرط الا يتأثر بذلك امن الكفاح المسلح واستمرار تصاعده ، ونحن لا نتدخل في الشـ
لهذه الدول ولا نسمح لاحد بالتدخل في شؤوننا او عرقلة كفاح الشعب الفلسطيني

اننا نعمل على ابراز الشخصية الفلسطينية بمحتواها النضالي الثورى في الحقا
وهذا لا يتناقض مع الارتباط المصيرى بين الامة العربية والشعب العربي الفلسطيني ونـ
على اقامة اوثق الصلات مع القوى التحررية في العالم لمناهضة الصهيونية والامبريالية ،
كفاحنا المسلح العادل ونعمل على اقناع الدول المعنية في العالم بوقف الهجرة الـ
الى فلسطين كاسهام منها في حل المشكلة وتقاوم كل الحلول السياسية المطروحة كبدـ
تصفية الكيان الصهيوني المحتل في فلسطين وكل المشاريع الرامية الى تصفية القضية ال
او تدويلها او الوصاية على شعبها من اية جهـة .

وايمانا منا بكل ذلك وانطلاقا من مبادئ واهداف واساليب الحركة ونظامها ا
يقرر المؤتمر العام الرابع لحركة فتح مايلـــــي :

Document 2A-3

-٣-

اولا " : على الصعيد الفلسطيني

انطلاقا من وحدة الشعب الفلسطيني ووحدة ارضه وتمثيلها لسياسي ، وتثبيتا للارادة الوطنيه المستقله من اجل استمرار الثوره وانتصارها

وانطلاقا من ان الثوره الشعبيه المسلحه هي الطريق الحتمي الوحيد لتحرير فلسطين وان الطريق لتحريرها هو الطريق الى الوحده .

وانطلاقا من ان الديمقراطيه هي التي تحكم العلاقات في الساحه الفلسطينيه ، وان الحوار الديمقراطي هو الاسلوب الصحيح لتطوير هذه العلاقات يؤكد المؤتمر على مايلي :-

١- ان منظمة التحرير الفلسطينيه هي الاطار الصحيح للوحده الوطنيه الفلسطينيه على صعيد فصائل الثوره والمنظمات الشعبيه والاتحادات المهنيه وكافة قطاعات شعبنا .

٢- اهمية تطوير مشاركة الحركه بثقل اساسي في منظمة التحرير الفلسطينيه لضمان فعاليتها وبما يكفل تطوير لوائحها واجهزتها على نحو يؤمن استقلالية كافة مؤسساتها مع المحافظه على (الحركه) تنظيما ومؤسسات وقوات العاصفه وعلاقاتها الخارجيه

٣- تصعيد الكفاح المسلح داخل الارض المحتله وعبر كافة خطوط المواجهه مع العدو الصهيوني

٤- مضاعفة الاهتمام بتنظيم شعبنا في كل اماكن تواجده وتوسيع اطار عمل المنظمات والاتحادات الشعبيه والمهنيه وحماية وجوده المؤقت في هذه الاماكن ومنع اضطهاده واستغلاله او تذويبه

٥- دعم صمود شعبنا داخل الارض المحتله على كافة الاصعده وتقديم الدعم المادي اللازم لاستمرار صموده وتصعيد نضاله وتطوير مؤسساته الوطنيه بكافة اشكالها والعمل بشكل خاص على تعزيز الصلات مع جماهيرنا الفلسطينيه في الاراضي المحتله منذ عام ١٩٤٨ لتمكينها من التصدي لمخططات تمزيق وحدتها وطمس شخصيتها العربيه .

٦- اعادة تشكيل الجبهة الوطنيه الفلسطينيه داخل الارض المحتله على اسس تضمن ان تكون هذه الجبهه رافدا " من روافد الثوره وفي اطار منظمة التحرير الفلسطينيه .

٧- التأكيد على ضرورة استقلال القرار الفلسطيني والعمل على تطوير قدرة فصائل الثوره الفلسطينيه على الخروج من دائرة الوصاية العربيه .

ان تحقيق ماتقدم يشكل مقومات الضروريه لمواجهة وافشال المخططات والمؤامرات التي تستهدف شعبنا وثورتنا لتمرير التسويه باشكالها المختلفه وحلقاتها المتعدده ابتداء " بقرار مجلس الامن ٢٤٢ ومرورا " باتفاقات كامب ديفيد ومؤامرة الحكم الذاتي ومشاريع التوطين وانتهاءا " بمشروع المملكة المتحده .

..../..

Document 2A-4

-٤-

ثانيـــا ً : على الصعيد العربــــــــي •

أ ـ على المستوى الجماهيـري •

لما كانت فلسطين جزءا ً من الوطن العربي والشعب الفلسطيني جزءا ً من الامة العربيـــه وكفاحه جزء من كفاحها ولما كانت الثورة الفلسطينيه هي طليعة الامة العربيه في معركة تحرير فلسطين •

١ـ العلاقه مع الجماهير العربيه هي علاقة استراتيجيه تحتم مشاركة اوسع لهذه الجماهير في حماية الثوره وخوض كل اشكال الكفاح والنضال ضد القاعده الامبرياليه الصهيونيه في فلسطين وضد كل اعداء شعبنا وامتنا وتصفية المصالح الامبرياليه والاستعماريه في المنطقه

٢ـ لا بد من تشديد التلاحم مع حركات التحرر الوطني العربيه والقوى الوطنيه والتقدميــه العربيه لاجل خوض المعركه المشتركه لتحرير فلسطين وتحقيق اهداف الامة العربيه في تحرير اقطارها وبناء المجتمع العربي التقدمي الموحد •

٣ـ تدعيم التلاحم النضالي مع القوى الوطنيه اللبنانيه التي تقف ببساله في خندق واحد مع الثوره الفلسطينيه ضد اعداء الشعبين الفلسطيني واللبناني والامة العربيه ومشاركتهـا النضال من اجل حماية وحدة لبنان وعروبتــه •

٤ـ ان تلاحم الجماهير اللبنانيه ووقفتها البطوليه الى جانب الثورة الفلسطينيه في مواجهة حرب التصفيه والاباده يتطلب الدعم والحماية والتطويــر ليكون مثالا ً للعلاقة مع الجماهير على امتداد الوطن العربي •

٥ـ ان الساحة الاردنيه ذات اهمية خاصه للثوره تتطلب اعطائها اهتماما خاصا ً باعادتها قاعدة ارتكازيــة اساسيــه من قواعد النضال والكفاح ضد العدو الصهيوني وتوظيف طاقات الجماهير للوصول الى هذا الهدف •

٦ـ تعزيز التلاحم المصيري مع الشعب المصري الذي قدم على طريق تحرير فلسطين تضحيات جسيمه ، ورفع قدرة القوى الوطنيه والتقدميه في مصــر لاجل اسقاط مؤامرة كامب ديفيد ونتائجها واعادة مصــر ثانيــة الى الصف العربي لاخذ موقعها الطبيعي في قيادة النضال العربي •

بـ على مستوى العلاقة مع الانظمة العربيــــه •

لما كانت العلاقات مع الانظمه العربيه تهدف الى تطوير الجوانب الايجابيه في مواقفها ان هذه العلاقه يجب ان تكون محكومة بالاسس التاليـــه :ـ

Document 2A-5

ـ٥ـ

١ــ مبادئ الحركه واهدافها واساليبهــا ٠

٢ــ عدم تعارض هذه العلاقه مع العلاقه الاستراتيجيه بالجماهير ٠

٣ــ موقف كل نظام من قضية شعب فلسطين وثورته المسلحه وخصوصا الالتزام بمنظمة التحرير الفلسطينيه باعتبارها الممثل الشرعي والوحيد للشعب العربي الفلسطيني

٤ ــ عدم التدخل في شوؤننا الداخليه والتصدى لمحاولات فرض الوصايه والتبعيه على شعبنا او محاولة اضطهاده او استغلاله ، وكذلك التصدى لكل محاولة لتوطينه في اى ارض خارج وطنه فلسطين ٠

٥ــ التصدى لاية محاوله لمنع الثوره من العمل بحريه بين صفوف شعبنا في اماكن تواجده

٦ــ ممارسة الثوره لمسوؤلياتها النضاليه على المستوى القومي وعبر اية ارض عربيه في سبيل تحرير الاراضي المحتله ، والعمل على تجنيد طاقات الامه العربيه البشريه والماديه خصوصا الثروه النفطيه كسلاح لتحقيق هذا الهدف

٧ــ تطوير جبهة الصمود والتصدى لتصبح اداة فعل رئيسيه على قاعدة دعم منظمة التحرير الفلسطينيه ومواصلة الصراع مع العدو ومواجهة كافة حلول التصفيه واسقاطها وكذلك تصليب مواقف الدول العربيه الاخرى لمواجهة التسويه بكافة اشكالها ومسمياتها والوقوف بحزم امام اية محاوله لاعطاء اتفاقات كامب ديفيد غطاء" شرعيــا

ثالثــا : على الصعيد الدولــي :

لما كانت قضية فلسطين هي القضيه المركزيه للامه العربيه في صراعها العادل ضد العدو الصهيوني الامبريالي ٠

ولان منطقة الشرق الاوسط ذات اهمية دوليه استراتيجيه فقد كانت قضية فلسطين ولا تزال بالاضافه لعدالتها ونضال شعبها ذات ابعاد موثره في السياسه الدوليه وموضع صراع هي افرز بالنسبه لقضية شعبنا ونضاله معسكرا" للاعداء وآخر للاصدقاء ٠

ان حركتنــا جزء من حركة التحرر العالمي في النضال المشترك ضد الامبرياليه والصهيونيه والعنصريه وعملائها ، ونحن نقيم تحالفاتنا مع كافة الاطراف على الساحه الدوليه بما يتفق مع مبادئنا ومع الميثاق الوطني الفلسطيني ٠

أــ المنظمات الدوليــه ٠

١ــ العمل من خلال منظمة التحرير الفلسطينيه على تطوير قرارات مختلف المنظمات الدوليه وخاصه قرارات الامم المتحده المتعلقه بحقوق شعبنا العربي الفلسطيني التي تعزز عزل العدو الصهيوني والامريكي داخل هذه المنظمه ٠

Document 2A-6

—٦—

ل على ترجمة قرار الجمعيه العامه للامم المتحده الذى ادان الصهيونيه باعتبارها
ن اشكال العنصريه والتمييز العنصرى الى اجراءات وعقوبات ضد القاعده الصهيونيه
انيه الامبرياليه في فلسطين
ف العمل من اجل المحافظه على مواقف الجمعيه العامه للامم المتحده في رفضها
كامب ديفيد والعمل على تطوير هذه المواقف بما يكفل رفض كل اشكال التسويه
ب شعبنا وقضيته •

وفي مقدمتها الاتحاد السوفييتي

دقاء •

عيم التحالف الاستراتيجي مع الدول الاشتراكيه باعتبار هذا التحالف يشكل ضرورة
التصدى الجاد والفعال للمؤامرات الامريكيه والصهيونيه على قضية فلسطين ومجمل
تحرر في العالم •

زيز علاقاتنا النضاليه مع حركات التحرر في العالم التي نقف معها في خندق واحد
برياليه والصهيونيه والعنصريه والفاشيه والرجعيه •

ين العلاقات الخارجيه لحركتنا وتكثيف تحركها السياسي انطلاقا من مبادئ حركتنا
ا مع اقامة التحالفات مع القوى السياسيه الديمقراطيه والتقدميه التي تقف الى جانب
لعادل وحقوقنا المشروعه •

زيز العلاقات النضاليه مع الثوره الاسلاميه في ايران التي اطاحت باعتى قلاع
ليه في المنطقه والتي تقف معنا في نضالنا على طريق تحرير فلسطين •

عيم العلاقات مع الشعوب والدول الاسلاميه والافريقيه ودول عدم الانحياز من اجل
اقفها في تأييد القضيه الفلسطينيه ودعم نضالنا وكسب المزيد من الاعتراف بمنظمة
الفلسطينيه ممثلا " شرعيا وحيدا " للشعب الفلسطيني •

يف العمل السياسي في (المعسكر الغربي) والاستفاده من تأييد القوى السياسية
طيه والتقدميه فيها من اجل تقليص ومن ثم ايقاف الدعم للكيان الصهيوني وتحقيق عزلته
ق الاعتراف بمنظمة التحرير الفلسطينيه ممثلا " شرعيا وحيدا " للشعب الفلسطيني
الحد الاقصى من الدعم السياسي والمادى لقضيتنا ونضالنا وحقوقنا الوطنيه •
لاعداء •

ى المستوى الامريكي •

متحده الامريكيه على رأس معسكر اعداء شعبنا وامتنا كونها تنتهج سياسة معاديه
فة قوى التحرر العربيه والعالميه وتدعم الكيان الصهيوني وعملائها ولذلك لابد من تعزيز
معاديه للسياسة الاميركيه وخوض المعارك ضد هذه السياسه واسقاطها وضرب مصالحها

Document 2A-7

-٧-

ى مستوى الدول الاوروبيـــه •

لازال الكثير من الدول الاوروبيه الغربيه تنتهج سياسة لاتعترف بالحقوق الوطنيه لشعبنا وتقدم دعما على كافة المستويات للعدو الصهيوني بما في ذلك قبول (عضوية اسرائيل) في السوق الاوروبيه المشتركه وهي تتبع سياسة منسجمة مع سياسة الولايات المتحده الامريكيه ومخططاتها في المنطقـــه •

ومن ثم لابد من تكثيف الجهود لمقاومة وافشال اى مشروع او مبادره تتعارض مع حقوق شعبنا الوطنيـــه •

وختامـــا " فان المؤتمر العام لحركتنا يؤكد على ضرورة حماية وتدعيم المكتسبـــات والانجازات السياسيـــه التي تـــم تحقيقهـــا على صعيد الساحه الدوليه التي جعلت من قضية فلسطين قضية حيه تحظى باوســـع تأييد دولـــي مما جعلها طليعة حركة التحرر العالمـــي وحاملة رايتهـــا •

وثـــوره حتى النـــصـــر

[Document 3]: PLO plan to destroy Israeli towns

This document, dated 18 July 1981 and written on the stationery of the Supreme Military Council of the PLO, was found in the headquarters of the PLO in Sidon.

To: El-Haj Ismail

Greetings for the Revolution!

The Supreme Military Council has decided to concentrate on the destruction of Kiryat Shemona, Metulla, Dan, She'ar Yashuv and Nahariya and its vicinity.

Kiryat Shemona: will be distributed among all the platoons and will be shelled with improved "Grad" shells.

Metulla: will be shelled with 160mm mortars (Palestinian Liberation Front — As-Sa'iqa).

Nahariya and its vicinity will be shelled with 130mm guns — Artillery Battalion 1.

Dan and She'ar Yashuv: will be the responsibility of the eastern sector.

Revolution until victory!

Signature

18/7/81

الأخ الحاج اسماعيل

تحية الثورة وبعد

قرار المجلس العسكري الأعلى هو التركيز بتدمير كريات شمونة والمطلة والمدن ومستيريا شوف ونهاريا وجوارها

كريات شمونة: توزع على جميع الفصائل لقصفها بالجراد المعدل

المطلة : تقصف بالهاون ١٦٠ مم ار.ج.ت.ف - إصابته...

نهاريا وجوارها : تقصف بمدفع ١٣٠ مم الـ م ١٢

بالنسبة للمدن ومستيريا شوف بمستوياتها القطاع الشرقي

أكثر بالنسبة للدوريات الأرضية

وانها لثورة حتى النصر

١٨/٧/٨١

ن ١٤٠٠

عادل حبا

سري

منظمة التحرير الفلسطينية
المجلس العسكري الاعلى
العمليات المركزية
قيادة منطقة بيروت العسكرية

الأخ الحاج اسماعيل

[Document 4]: List of shellings of Israeli towns

This document, dated 15-24 July 1981, was found in PLO headquarters in Sidon. The list of targets includes 23 towns and villages, most of them in the Galilee, some of them in Major Sa'ad Haddad's area of control; it was sent by the headquarters of the Artillery of the Joint Forces in the South to the commander of the area. We have translated the first item on the list.

NAME OF SHELLED TARGET	*NO. OF SALVOS*	*UNIT IN CHARGE*
1. Kiryat Shemona	17 shells in 2 portions, each portion 120mm	Artillery of the Joint Forces in the South

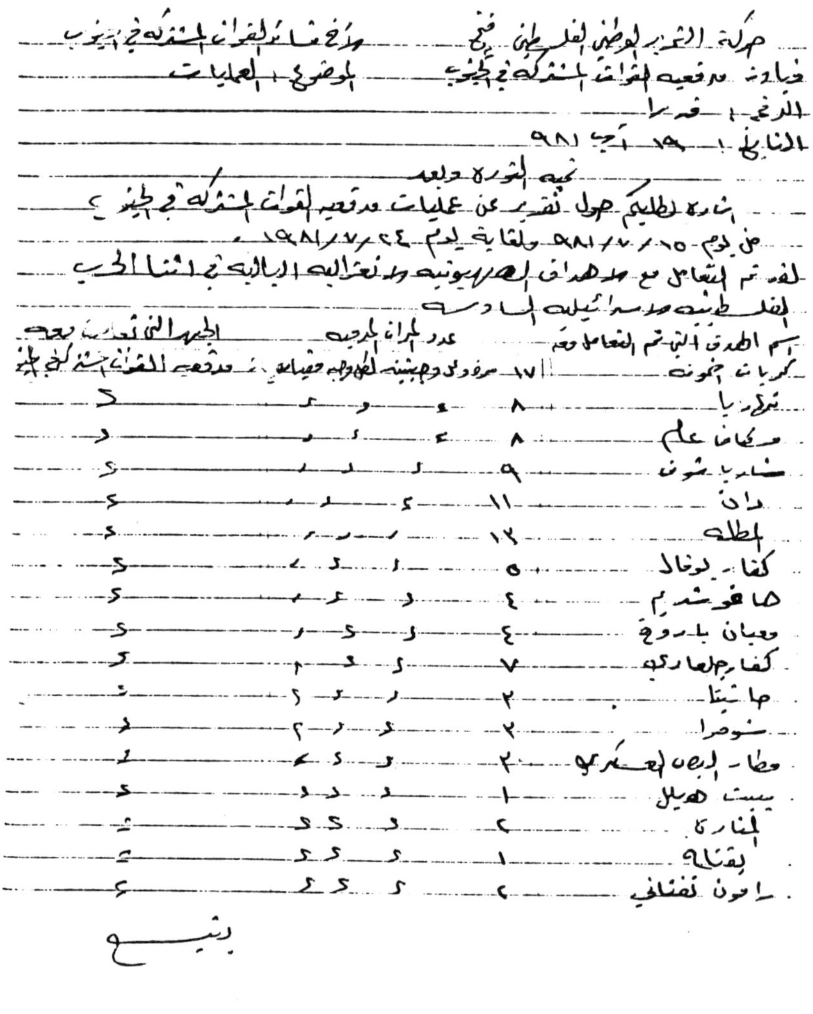
حركة التحرير الوطني الفلسطيني فتح — مدفعية القوات المشتركة في الجنوب
قيادة مدفعية القوات المشتركة في الجنوب — الموضوع: العمليات
الرقم:
التاريخ: ١٩٨١
تحية الثورة وبعد
نتشرف بإطلاعكم حول تقرير عن عمليات مدفعية القوات المشتركة في الجنوب
من يوم ١٥/٧/١٩٨١ ولغاية يوم ٢٤/٧/١٩٨١
لقد تم التعامل مع الأهداف الصهيونية والانعزالية التالية في أثناء الحرب
الفلسطينية الإسرائيلية الخامسة

اسم الهدف الذي تم التعامل معه	عدد الرمايات	الجهة التي تعاملت معه
كريات شمونة	١٧ مقذوف وعلى دفعتين كل دفعة ١٢٠ ملم	مدفعية القوات المشتركة في الجنوب
نهاريا	٨	"
مسكاف عام	٨	"
[illegible]	٩	"
دان	١١	"
المطلة	١٢	"
كفار يوفال	٥	"
هاقوشريم	٤	"
معيان باروخ	٤	"
كفار جلعادي	٧	"
حانيتا	٢	"
شوميرا	٢	"
مطار البصه العسكري	٢	"
بيت هيلل	١	"
المنارة	٢	"
[illegible]	١	"
[illegible]	٢	"

[Document 5]: Shelling Safed and other towns

The document, sent on Fatah stationery, is dated 18 July 1981.

Greetings for the Revolution!

I am strengthening your hands! Thus you will prove your worth as heroic sons of your people and your revolution! We expect Safed and Ja'un[2] to be shelled with heavy rockets tonight due to the extreme importance we attach to this.

You also have to shell the settlements in the vicinity of the border with 120mm and 160mm mortars. Proceed immediately.

You must also dispatch battle patrols, either from your troops or from the joint forces,[3] to set ambushes along the border and deep into the occupied territory.[4]

Yasser Arafat
18 July 1981

2. The Israeli town of Rosh Pina, a major crossroads in the Galilee.
3. The joint command of the PLO in southern Lebanon.
4. In the PLO lexicon, the term "occupied territory" includes Israel proper, not only the territories administered by Israel since the 1967 war.

Document 5A

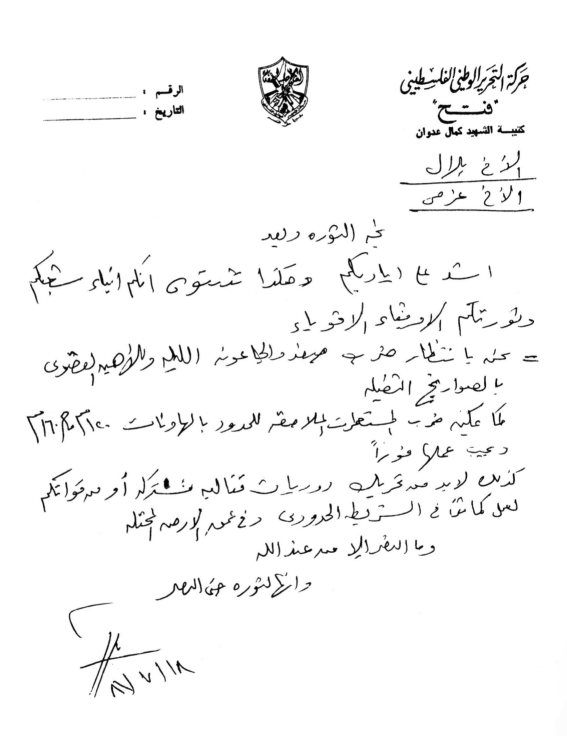

حركة التحرير الوطني الفلسطيني
"فتح"
كتيبة الشهيد كمال عدوان

الرقم : ________
التاريخ : ________

الأخ بلال

الأخ عزمي

تحية الثورة وبعد

اشد على اياديكم وهكذا تثبتون انكم ابناء شعبكم وثورتكم الاوفياء الاقوياء

= نحن بانتظار ضرب صفد والجاعونة الليلة والاهداف القصوى بالصواريخ الثقيلة

كما عليكم ضرب المستعمرات الملاصقة للحدود بالهاونات ١٢٠ مم ١٦٠ مم ويجب عملها فوراً

كذلك لابد من تحريك دوريات قتالية مشتركة أو من قواتكم للعمل كمائن في الشريط الحدودي وفي عمق الارض المحتلة

وما النصر الا من عند الله

وانها لثورة حتى النصر

١٨/٧/٨١

[Document 6]: Guidelines for attacking civilian targets in Israel

This item was found on page 10 of a document which provides guidelines for PLO terrorist activities inside Israel.

Section 6
TARGET SELECTION AND TIMING OF THE OPERATION

1. The blow must be directed at the enemy's weak point. His greatest weakness is his small population. Therefore, operations must be launched which will liquidate immigration into Israel. This can be achieved by various means: attacking absorption centres for new immigrants; creating problems for them in their new homes by sabotaging their water and electricity supply; using weapons in terrifying ways against them where they live, and using arson whenever possible.

2. Any installation which is designated as a target must meet the criterion of importance to the civilian population. Blows directed at secondary or isolated targets, whose impact passes unnoticed, are of no use.

3. Attacks can be made to multiply their impact. For instance, attacking a tourist installation during the height of the tourist season is much more useful than dealing the same blow at another time. If fuel tanks are set on fire during an energy crisis, this can be much more useful than at another time. Likewise, dealing a blow to the enemy immediately following his own attack constitutes an excellent reprisal which is beneficial to our morale.

4. Density of the population in the streets and market places of cities tends to increase on special occasions like holidays and vacations. One ought to bear this in mind in order to better select the place of action and improve the impact of the blow.

5. Attention should be given to the safety of our people. The type of action should take their safety into consideration.

Document 6A

ـ ١٠ ـ

القاعدة السادسة :

الاختيار الموفق لمكان الضربة وزمان الضربة :

١ ينبغي ان توجه الضربة الى نقاط ضعف العدو واكبر نقطة ضعف لدى العدو واستراتيجيتها هي حاجته الى السكان فيجب القيام بعمليات يكون من شأنها القضاء على الهجرة الى اسرائيل وذلك باساليب عدة منها ضرب الاماكن التي يستوعب فيها القادمون الجدد ومنها مضايقة هؤلاء في اماكن سكنهم الجديدة بصورة مركزة مدروسة بحرمانهم من الماء والكهرباء مثلا ومن هذه الاساليب (استخدام السلاح الابيض بصورة مروعة في بعض العمليات بهذه الاماكن ومنها اشعال حرائق كلما كان ذلك متيسرا ..

٢. اذا اريد ضرب مرفق من المرافق فيجب اختياره بحيث يؤثر على حياة السكان فهناك ضربات لا يكون لها تأثير كاف عندما توجه الى مرفق فرعي لا قيمة له او مرفق منعزل لا يشعر به احد .

٣. ضربات معينة تضاعف من قيمة الضربات بنسبة كبيرة جدا فضرب مرفق من مرافق السياحة في ابواب موسم السياحة اهم بكثير من نفس الضربة في وقت آخر واشعال حريق في مستودع وقود ابان ازمة الوقود هو انفع وافضل منه في وقت آخر وضرب العدو عقب توجيهه ضربة معينة يكون ردا مثارا لحميته ويعطي نتائج معنوية هامة .

للزحام في المدن والشوارع والاسواق اوقات معينة كالاعياد والعطلات ويجب معرفة ذلك بكل دقة لكي يكون اختيار مكان الضربة موفقا

٥. ينبغي مراعاة عدد الافراد والاختيار بقدر الامكان للضربات التي تحقق امن الافراد .

V. THE COMMUNIST BLOC CONNECTION [Documents 7 — 39]

The seized documents reveal a remarkable spirit of camaraderie that seems to tie the PLO very intimately to the Communist bloc. There is almost no Communist country which is not represented in one way or another in the PLO network of political and military ties. First and foremost is the Soviet Union, which seems to provide the ideological, diplomatic and military backbone of the Palestinian movement. Other Eastern bloc countries, such as Hungary and East Germany, act as surrogates for the Soviet Union and extend very substantial military training to PLO personnel. Even such "renegades" of the Communist world as China and Yugoslavia play their part, as do North Korea and Vietnam. Other Third World Communists, notably Cuba's Castro and the Sandinistas of Nicaragua, have either extended aid or served as models for PLO ideologues and military planners.

What is the unifying theme behind the support this variety of nations and cultures from different continents gives to the PLO and its component groups? In a word, "revolution." Many PLO documents begin with the salutation "Greetings for the Revolution." The frequency of the word "revolution" in PLO communications with the Communist regimes can be rivaled only by that of "imperialism," the target for the "revolution." No wonder then, that in its search for "national liberation" the PLO has chosen the path of "revolution," which implies an alliance with the "revolutionary forces" of the world against Western imperialism. No wonder that one of the recurring themes of PLO diplomacy is the attempt to damage American interests, to turn back American and Western gains and to include the Soviet Union as a full partner in Middle East negotiations.

The following documents detail the military ties between the PLO and the various Communist regimes, and also throw some light on the ideological, diplomatic and intelligence cooperation between the "Palestinian revolution" and the proponents of "world revolution." The camaraderie between the Soviets and the PLO is apparent as they discuss and coordinate worldwide diplomatic moves aimed at strengthening the Communist camp and weakening "Western imperialism." Such issues as American policy in Iran, the American-Soviet joint communiqué of October 1977, the domestic problems of Lebanon, inter-Arab rivalries and the non-aligned world are the common concern of the leaderships of the PLO and the Soviet bloc, and form the subject of their talks, in addition to the training of PLO personnel.

[Document 7]: PLO talks with Kremlin leaders

The talks were held in Moscow on 13 November 1979. The document itself was seized near Sidon in June 1982. It throws light on many international affairs such as the Teheran hostage crisis. The translator's remarks are in brackets.

SOVIET DELEGATION
Foreign Minister Gromyko
Ponomarev, Gromyko's Deputy
Grinevsky, Head of Middle East Department of Foreign Office

PLO DELEGATION
Abu 'Ammar (Yasser Arafat)
Abed al-Muhsin Abu Meizer (Member of PLO Executive Committee)
Talal Naji (Jibril Front, Member of PLO Executive Committee)
'Issam al-Qadi (Sa'iqa)
Yasser 'Abd Rabih (Democratic Front, Member of PLO Executive Committee)
Habib Kahwaji (Sa'iqa, Member of PLO Executive Committee)
Taysir Qub'a (Popular Front/Habash)
Muhamed al-Sha'er (PLO representative in the USSR)
'Abd al-Rahim Ahmed (Arab Liberation Front)

Gromyko: I welcome you on behalf of the Soviet leadership, on behalf of Brezhnev and personally upon your arrival in Moscow. The Soviet leadership appointed me and Ponomarev to discuss with you all the problems of interest to you and to us. I ask you to regard this as your point of departure, as I have no subject to raise just now.

I hope our meeting will be conducted in a spirit of friendship and affection, as were our previous meetings. I suggest, for the purpose of beginning the talks, that you tell us your opinions and at a later stage we will present ours. Afterwards, lunch will be served — today at 2 o'clock.

Abu 'Ammar: I will be brief, since one of the comrades told me that this period of time was intended for formal talks.

Gromyko: We have plenty of time . . .

Abu 'Ammar: Two hours are not enough.

Gromyko: Two and a half . . .

Abu 'Ammar: We have not talked together for a long time. Before the Baghdad Conference[5] I told you that it would be among the most important summits and its results were in fact important as I expected. This was so since the Baghdad Summit put the Arab nation as a whole against the "Camp David combination," except for two states. You undoubtedly know the decisions of the Baghdad Summit. [Therefore] I will move on to talk about the Arab foreign and economic ministers' summit.

The importance of Baghdad is that the Arabs met without Sadat, who had declared that the Arabs could not have a summit without him, and passed resolutions condemning the Camp David Accords.

The foreign and economic ministers' meeting was more important because its resolutions involved the implementation of the decisions taken at the political summit [in Baghdad] . . .

And as you know, Brzezinski carried out a visit in the region, and announced that the purpose of his visit was to prevent the implementation of the decisions of the Baghdad Conference.

Gromyko: Do you refer to his last trip?

Abu 'Ammar: The trip which preceded the meeting of the Arab foreign and economic ministers. The importance of the second Baghdad Summit[6] of Arab foreign and economic ministers — was in the coordination which found expression in a tripartite axis of Iraq, Syria and Palestine. This axis led the Steadfastness Front, and later directed the course of the entire conference.

These decisions were taken and I regard them as economic decisions — which are more important than the political decisions. And we can say that the Palestinian delegation played an important role in making these decisions.

---

5. The conference of the Rejectionist Front, which immediately followed the signing of the Camp David Accords in September 1978. This conference, in which almost all Arab countries participated, was an attempt to lure Egypt back into the Arab fold, although Egypt itself was excluded.
6. The second Baghdad Summit was held following the signing of the peace treaty between Israel and Egypt in March 1979.

Gromyko: Comrade Arafat, forgive me for interrupting you but I ask you to express your opinion about the extent to which the decisions taken at the Baghdad Conference were implemented.

Abu 'Ammar: That is precisely what I am about to talk about. Some of the Arabs wanted to provide us with a political decision and [then] manipulate the economic decisions [in their own interests]. The Palestinian delegation submitted a clear economic [working] paper, which was supported by the delegations of Syria and Iraq. A wonderful coordination was created between us so that we could stand against the bloc which was led by Saudi Arabia. This turned the whole meeting into a kind of summit conference. Then we caused the adjournment of the summit for 48 hours to enable all the delegates to return to their countries for consultations. Here I would like to repeat and stress the importance of the tripartite coordination, which played a decisive role in the success of the summit and which brought about the results you know about.
As regards the economic decisions, it is fair to say that against Egypt about 90 percent were implemented. I say 90 percent since 10 percent of the deposits have still not been withdrawn [from Egyptian banks]. Now Kamal Adham [political advisor to Saudi Arabia's King Khaled] is playing a new "game" which is an American game of rescuing Sadat from the crisis which is strangling him. Therefore he is pressing some of the rich Saudi Arabians and the like in the Persian Gulf to invest some of their money in Cairo. But all this alone will not save the Egyptian economy, it is only of small assistance.

The Egyptian economy needs $3.5 billion annually for 10 years. America has granted Egypt $192 million, and has raised this budget to $1.5 billion. America wants to bring him [Sadat] more money from Japan — a sum of $750 million — and the same applies to West Germany.

Gromyko: This amount requested from West Germany and Japan, is it to be paid annually or as a one-time grant?

Abu 'Ammar: $1.5 billion [from the United States] will be given each year. Regarding the part of Japan and West Germany, in principle is to be a one-time payment, but it is possible that the US will put pressure on them to pay one more time.

They — meaning the Americans — when they deal with the Egyptian economy, act on the assumption that it should be given "tranquilizer shots" hoping to break the ties which the Baghdad Conference created. You can see how they handle these matters, on a month-by-month and year-by-year basis.

On this matter we can say that 90 percent of the Baghdad decisions against Egypt were carried out. We demanded, in our Palestinian working paper, to punish America economically and we know it is not easy to implement this demand. But our purpose was to put this on the record, and thus stimulate a debate on the subject.

The Palestinian delegation even entered a reservation [in the protocol of the conference] after the debate [on sanctions against the United States], since the Arab punishments do not really harm the US.

What is important is that we made these resolutions and that 90 percent of them were carried out. This is a big success relative [to what is known] in the region of the Arab world. As regards the support of the Steadfastness Front from the financial point of view, all Arab states paid their dues.

Gromyko: Are you talking about a deficit caused to the PLO?

Abu 'Ammar: The deficit affected everyone [all the states which were to receive payments from the Baghdad fund, like Jordan and Syria]. The 90 percent figure referred to the sanctions against the Egyptian regime. Afterwards we went to the Islamic Conference in Fez.[7] The results of this conference are very important because they put Hassan in a situation where he was forced to stand against Sadat, when it was decided to expel the Egyptians from the Islamic group of states. The importance here is that the Egyptian people, who are religious in their belief, will undoubtedly ask: the Arabs are against us, but why is the Islamic world against us? This is extremely important and will reduce the effect of Sadat's arguments against the Arab states.

Later we went to the Organization for African Unity Congress in Monrovia. Sadat achieved a significant political victory in the congress for several reasons. One was the behaviour of the Liberian government towards the Palestinian delegation. This government denied the Palestinian delegation the right to speak and this forced the delegation to leave. The behaviour [of the Liberian government] towards the secretary-general of the Arab League, who was forced off the speaker's rostrum, compelled him, too, to leave [the conference]. Another reason for Sadat's success at the conference is that the bloc of forces that were opposed to Camp David was not represented at the

---

7 The Conference, which includes 40 Islamic states, has been convening annually since 1969. Following the signing of the Egyptian-Israeli Peacy Treaty, Egypt was expelled not only from the Arab League, whose headquarters were transferred from Cairo to Tunis, but also from the Islamic Conference, in a decision adopted in Fez, Morocco, at a meeting chaired by King Hassan II.

conference at all, or rather, was not present at all. All these factors left the arena open for Sadat, and provided him with the decisions he was interested in. I record this in order to state that when we left for the Havana Conference,[8] 49 African states were equipped with the decisions of the Monrovia Conference. Despite all this, we managed to pass [in the Havana Conference] decisions sharply condemning the Camp David Accords and we managed to change African public opinion.

Gromyko: This was a blow to the Monrovia Conference and its decisions.

Abu 'Ammar: Yes, Yugoslavia and India were against an anti-Egyptian decision. Our Cuban comrades told us when we arrived in Havana that it would be difficult to achieve an anti-Camp David stand and I suppose this was your estimate, too. Now I have no choice but to mention the fact that prior to the Havana Conference there had been a sharp disagreement between Syria and Iraq. But the Palestinian delegation played an important role in coordinating the tripartite position, as we had done at the Baghdad Conference. The two presidents, Saddam Hussein and Assad, played an important and central role in the anti-Camp David decision-making in Havana. Through this magnificent tripartite coordination and due to the role comrade Castro played — whom we shall not forget — we succeeded in constructing a massive lobby by which we achieved those well-known decisions.

Ponomarev: The Cuban comrades played an enormous role.

Abu 'Ammar: Castro's wisdom played an important role in reaching the results. One should also mention here the role of the many progressive countries that were of considerable help to us. I will proceed to talk about the Lisbon Congress, which is no less important than the Havana Congress. The latter was a congress of governments, while the former was a popular congress. It was one of those wonderful popular congresses and it was the first to be held in a European country. The Portugese Communist Party played an important role in ensuring its success and so did your solidarity committee.

Ponomarev: We sent the head of the solidarity committee and Comrade Brezhnev sent a message to the congress.

---

8. The Havana Conference was the tri-annual gathering of non-aligned states, held in the summer of 1979. The previous conference had been held in Colombo, Sri-Lanka, in 1976, and the forthcoming one is scheduled to convene in Baghdad in September 1982.

Abu 'Ammar: Right. There were many letters from kings and presidents, first and foremost that of Comrade Brezhnev. Lisbon was a turning-point in the PLO's favour in the Western world. Now, I wish to say that after our success in the first and second Baghdad Conferences, an American counterattack was launched along the following axes:

The first axis: a plot was put into action which separated Iraq from Syria, and internal problems cropped up in Syria.[9] In addition, pressure was put on King Hussein to join Camp David. Furthermore, there was the American show of strength in the [Persian] Gulf.[10]

I must admit, the show of strength in the Gulf was successful. An attempt was also made to separate the Iranian revolution from the Arabs.

The second axis: pressure [was placed] on our people in the territories to cooperate with the autonomy [plan]. One must say, they failed in this; Strauss,[11] the Israelis and the Egyptians admitted it. Now our occupied land is in turmoil with mass strikes because of Israel's decision to exile one of the mayors [Bassam Shak'a][12] because he was a PLO member and since there is a decision to get rid of them [the mayors] one by one.

We have to admit that the talks held between Burg and Mustafa Khalil[13] resulted in Khalil's agreement, according to Sadat's instructions, to the autonomy plan. So they reached some almost-final agreements except for Jerusalem, state lands and natural resources. These subjects were left for a later date.

The third axis: [the Israelis] have concentrated on us [militarily], a concentration that is close to hell in southern Lebanon. Seven months of hell created 600,000 homeless Lebanese and Palestinians, and left dozens of cities, villages and refugee camps destroyed. For this purpose Israel used all the types of arms in its possession.

---

9. During 1979-82, Syria was plagued by the "Muslim Brotherhood," rebelling in Hama and other localities against the Ba'ath regime in Damascus. The confrontation reached a climax in March 1982, when 6,000 "Brothers" were massacred and the Old City of Hama was badly damaged by Syrian tanks.
10. The dispatch of American reinforcements to the Persian Gulf following the Khomeini takeover in Teheran in February 1979 and the American hostages affair of November 1979 — January 1981.
11. Ambassador Strauss was designated by President Carter as a go-between to negotiate the Palestinian autonomy talks with Israel and Egypt.
12. Bassam Shak'a, mayor of Nablus, was one of the major inciters of unrest in the West Bank.
13. Joseph Burg and Mustafa Khalil, the respective heads of the Israeli and Egyptian delegations to the autonomy talks.

Gromyko: 600,000 Lebanese and Palestinian emigrants from the south to the north? When did the war against you start?

Abu 'Ammar: On the 9th of March 1978. I will give you an example of the violence of the war against us: Israel shelled the Rashidiye and Naher-al-Bared camps with "smart" naval torpedoes. These are guided torpedoes fired from the sea. But they do not need these weapons to attack us in the south, since their artillery is capable of reaching the targets they are interested in.

Once some of my officers asked me, 'Why do they use these weapons?' I replied, 'They gave orders to shoot with all weapons.' So the Israeli navy bombarded us with these weapons, with F-15's and F-16's, and also "Lance" missiles were used against us, which are similar to "Frog" and "Luna" missiles.

I have the testimony of Ramsey Clark.[14] After his visit to our region, Clark returned to the US and convened a press conference. He said that what happened in Lebanon was a crime. The importance of his testimony is that he is one of them. He visited the Nabatiye camp which was wiped out and only 11 [undamaged] houses were left. They bombarded it with ammunition forbidden for use according to international law such as: gas and fragmentation bombs and "cluster bombs." We fought alone, and still do so, and we do not receive any single bullet except from the Iraqi and Syrian brothers who clashed twice with the Israeli air force.

Gromyko: How do you evaluate the results of the Syrian-Israeli air combat?

Abu 'Ammar: I'm no aviation expert. What interests me are the political decisions. What matters to me is that our fighter should not feel he is alone.

Ponomarev: What is important is that they have not succeeded in breaking your steadfastness and your [ability] to endure.

Abu 'Ammar: What happened was a war. It was a miracle that we also succeeded in bearing the burden of feeding the homeless, since there was no government. We feed about 50 percent of them because the purpose of the operation by these barbaric bombardments was to consolidate the masses of southern Lebanon against us.

---

14. A former US attorney general under President Johnson, who later became an anti-Vietnam War leader. He became adversely involved with the PLO, the Iranian revolution and other sore spots of American foreign policy.

The Arab states cannot endure a war [of attrition]. Abd al-Nasser,[15] for instance, became tired of the [war of] attrition. And you remember how this fatigue was one of the reasons why he [agreed] to accept the Rogers Plan.[16]

We say: there have been seven months [of fighting] but we are ready for seventy months and more. Our children are fighting and we do not demand more. Yesterday morning a cluster bomb exploded and killed seven of our children. Until now I have not announced my military losses. We have 10-12 military casualties a day. As regards civilians, the number reached 30-35 a day. One month [Lebanese Prime Minister] Al-Hus counted 390 civilians dead and 1000 wounded who reached hospitals, though there were probably more. These are the directions of the attack. It hasn't stopped yet. Why? There is now a let-up in this hell in the south, due to an American working paper submitted by Philip Habib.[17] I will give you a copy of it so we will not waste time. The most dangerous of the statements in the paper is that they speak about convening all the parties, and they also state that this relates to Israel, Lebanon, Syria, Jordan and the PLO under the supervision of the USA. Why Jordan?

Ponomarev: Without Egypt?

Abu 'Ammar: Without Egypt. This is a new Camp David and this is the most dangerous item in the working paper. Here one can see how serious the next summit is. The seriousness results from the fact that a few Arab parties agreed to it and worked to bring all the parties together with or without their knowledge. The Lebanese are about to submit a working paper which will blow up the whole conference. The essence of this paper is: the evacuation of the Palestinians from the south. The seriousness of this paper is not because of the expulsion of the Palestinians from the south, but because of two points:

1. This is a mine which will explode in the summit. Therefore the summit will end in failure. A few Arab states will free themselves of the commitments they undertook in Baghdad.

2. If the Lebanese do not obtain their goals at the conference, they will turn to internationalization [of the Lebanese problem].

---

15. President of Egypt, 1955-1969.
16. William Rogers, American Secretary of State under President Nixon, promulgated a plan, in 1970, calling for Israeli withdrawal from the administered territories in return for Arab recognition and some minor territorial rectifications.
17. Habib, then a senior State Department official, had been assigned trouble-shooting duties under the Carter administration. President Reagan recalled him from retirement in the summer of 1981 as a negotiator in the Lebanese crisis.

We have been successful regarding the stages of the next summit. During my last visit to Baghdad I reached an agreement with President Saddam Hussein on tripartite coordination, at the last conference; this can be considered a success. Saddam told me that the Palestinians have priority in everything.

On my return I met with President Assad and I told him about this. He was pleased and agreed to this tripartite coordination. This is very important since it will limit the freedom of manœuvre of the hostile forces at the conference and this is what we agreed on in the Steadfastness Front summit during our single meeting in Algeria.

I have to add a fourth axis of the American counterattack: the deployment of two Egyptian divisions along the Libyan border in order to put American-Egyptian military pressure on Mu'ammar.[18] They say that they do not need to conquer Libya, but only to reach Tobruk. This means taking control of the oil wells and the establishment of a Libyan government based on the opposition forces that have begun to organize in Egypt. We must not underestimate it, despite the big parade Qaddafi staged on 1 September.[19] I must say that this pressure influenced the Libyan political position slightly and this is the reason for the visit to Libya of Newsome, American State Department Director for African Affairs.

The fifth axis of the American counterattack is to encourage the Egyptian regime to supply arms and ammunition — and possibly forces too — to the King of Morocco. This means the return of the king to the Camp David group by exploiting the defeats he suffered in the desert.[20] Therefore we went about a month ago to Morocco and Algeria and achieved good results. We received from King Hassan, after a three-and-a-half-hour meeting, his consent for a referendum. This is an important political achievement that we gained in North Africa. I returned later to Algeria, and informed President Chadli about the matter. A few days ago I informed the Polisario leaders about it and we await their reply.

Ponomarev: What do you mean by a referendum? A disengagement of forces?

Abu 'Ammar: Self-determination for the inhabitants of the desert.

---

18. Mu'ammar Qaddafi, President of Libya.
19. 1 September 1979 was the tenth anniversary of the Libyan Revolution. The event was commemorated with a military parade in Tripoli.
20. This refers to Morocco's protracted war in the Sahara against the Algerian-supported Polisario.

Gromyko: Do both sides agree to a referendum?

Abu 'Ammar: The King of Morocco agreed and I await the reply of the Algerians and of the Polisario leaders. Regarding the counterattack, a very dangerous conference was held. This conference of the foreign ministers of the Gulf States and Saudi Arabia discussed the security of the Gulf. Iraq is located in the Gulf and the question is: Why was it not invited to the conference? The main subject on the agenda, according to them, was the Palestinian-Iranian alliance and the danger it presents to them. They made plans to cope with this subject, which exists only in their imagination.

We succeeded in escalating military activities in the occupied territories. It is enough to point to the report of the defence committee of the Knesset. It says there that there are 111,000 police and security men mobilized to guard the security in Israel apart from the army. Our steadfast stand in the south is today powerless in the full sense of the word. I can tell you in detail what it consists of: the range of our 23mm machine guns is 3.5 kilometres. The Israeli aircraft fly above this range and strike our machine guns, one by one, without running into any response. Isn't this an injustice, comrade, that I should stand facing the most advanced American weaponry with primitive weapons, whereas the Polisario has the most advanced weapons and missiles against the simple Moroccan weapons? What does all this mean?[21] Must I fight with my body and the bodies of our children and women? This is the weakness of the Palestinians.

Parallel to this military steadfastness, we have made major political moves, for example: our missions to Asia, Africa and Latin America are still intact. When Nyerere decided to turn the PLO office into an embassy,[22] he said he discovered the organization at Havana. We received 189 delegations during six months from all over the world.

Gromyko: Most of whom were representatives of popular organizations?

Abu 'Ammar: Yes, all. I am not speaking about the official delegations. We maintain coordination with the Afro-Asian Solidarity Committee, with the World Peace Council and other international institutions, such as the Democratic Lawyers Association, which some time ago held a symposium in Paris

21. The detailed descriptions of Israeli strikes against PLO positions and camps in southern Lebanon, and the analogy of the PLO with the Polisario, are obviously calculated to get the Soviet Union to provide the Palestinians with more sophisticated weaponry in order to close the gap of Israel's superiority.
22. President Nyerere of Tanzania, who befriended the PLO delegations at the Non-aligned Conference in Havana, raised the PLO office in Dar-al-Salam to the rank of embassy.

and condemned Camp David from the judicial point of view. We made diplomatic moves in the countries we visited: Vienna, Ankara, Madrid, Lisbon and lately the meeting I had with Marchais[23] in order to obtain an invitation for a visit to France. All this in addition to other activities which we conduct, aware as we are of the fact that such activities have an influence only up to a certain limit. We have no illusions about them.

We have rejected the old idea of avoiding places where the Israelis appear. We have to challenge them at conferences, as was the case at the conference of the Association of Political Science Lecturers,[24] where Comrade Ponomarev participated, since our case is stronger. That happened in the Rome symposium too.

Now let us talk about an urgent subject. We are afraid of what might happen in Iran. The Americans contacted us through some Arab states and others and our answer was clear: we are not intermediaries, we stand by the Iranian revolution.[25]

Gromyko: Did the Americans contact you on their own initiative?

Abu 'Ammar: Not us [directly but through] Ramsey Clark, who is one of our sympathizers. We do not mediate, we support the Iranian revolution in its joy and in its sorrow. Khomeini's position is good and he shows understanding towards this position of ours. We sent the director of military operations to Iran, since the military option is possible, although it is not likely. But in order to be sure, I would like to ask my comrades for their estimate, since their estimate is more accurate than ours. Prior to my arrival here, Khomeini contacted me and asked for an assessment of the situation, because we observe the picture from the outside, while they see it from the inside. We think something might happen from the direction of Amman. I tried to be as brief as possible, but we must expect an escalation in Lebanon during or after the summit, in order to assist Sarkis[26] to present his view. Pressure is being put on our people in the occupied land to agree to autonomy between now and May 1980, when the municipal elections take place.[27] We intend to discuss our problem in the UN, and would like to have your support for the success of the Havana resolution. This is a very important point.

---

23. Georges Marchais, the leader of the French Communist Party.
24. The International Conference of Political Scientists held in Moscow in the summer of 1979, to which an Israeli delegation was accepted after many delays on the part of the Soviets.
25. Commitment to the revolution, any "people's revolution," seems to be the PLO's guideline.
26. President of Lebanon, 1976-1982.
27. Municipal elections were to be held in the West Bank. Arafat is alluding to the autonomy talks which had started between Israel, Egypt and the US, with Israel attempting to lure West Bank leaders to lean towards the autonomy solution.

There are rumours among Israeli circles about inflicting a fatal preventive attack on Syria. We say this because in Israel there are political and economic problems which the Israelis may try to escape by exporting them. The starting point for this attack will be Lebanon, since it is considered a weak point. They will attack us and the [Lebanese leftist] National Movement and later hit Syria. It would be easy to inflict a blow on the Syrian forces in Lebanon, since they are fulfilling a security mission and not a military one.[28]

Ponomarev: There are two questions: Comrade Arafat, with the unprecedented relationship with Austria, did you present your assessment of these achievements in your meetings with Kreisky and Brandt?

The second question concerns the Syrian troops present on Lebanese territory: do they supply you with arms? Do they participate with you in stopping the aggression?

Abu 'Ammar: I will begin with the answer to the second question: The Syrian troops are at latitude 37.10 and the fighting, until now, takes place south of this line. They are not present in the area of the fighting between us and the Israelis. Nevertheless there were two air clashes between Israel and Syria. The Syrians also decided to send some air defence units in order to protect the [refugee] camps in their areas from Israeli air raids. This, especially after Israel announced it will strike at these camps, because the fighters start off from them. We should not overlook the fact that both Dayan and Weizman[29] announced that this will be done in coordination with America, which makes it important for Syria to make a political decision to counteract.

As regards your first question, about the horizons of political activity, what is important to us in this context is to explain our problem to world public opinion, as, for example, to the non-aligned states.

I recall participating in a conference in Algeria in 1973 and, despite the fact that the conference took place in Algeria, we did not achieve there what we tried to achieve. But during the past six years our activities among the non-aligned states produced results at Havana. Our activity in Europe is based on Europe's need for Arab oil.[30] Oil has not yet been introduced as a

28. Refers to the Syrian-dominated "Arab Deterrent Force," which was supposed to keep order in Lebanon under the Arab League mandate.
29. Moshe Dayan and Ezer Weizman, respectively foreign minister and defence minister of Israel at that time.
30. This is the first admission by an Arab leader that the Europeans can be, and in fact are, squeezed into adopting a pro-PLO line due to their dependence on Arab oil.

factor in the battle, but there is apprehension of that there. Some of the Arab states help us in this respect.

Ponomarev: Kreisky became a friend of the Arabs?

Abu 'Ammar: Nobody says so. But we have to profit from it.

Ponomarev: It was an achievement, at least, that after your meeting with him cracks appeared within the Zionist camp. This is because he was previously among Israel's advocates.

Gromyko: Good. Thank you for the news you brought about some of the international problems and the assessment of the present situation.

First of all I will speak of the main problems of international politics, and about our position concerning these problems, although this position is known and I can discuss it in brief.

The USSR continues its principled policy regarding the Middle East as it did in the past. We are in favour of Israel's withdrawal from the occupied territories and in favour of granting the Palestinians their legitimate rights and the establishment of their independent state, together with the right of all states in the region to be sovereign. This is the essence of our position regarding problems of the Middle East.

We favour a comprehensive settlement, on condition that it be a just one. Leaders in the Arab world concentrate on a just solution and we share this view.

Sadat and the Americans speak of a just solution but their solution is unjust. Now too, as in the past, we sharply condemn separate agreements with the aggressors including the Camp David Accords.

The external form which is used to present these accords is irrelevant. Their essence did not change. They are accords of treason for the Arabs and their interests.[31] The whole world knows our position and our view regarding the Camp David Accords. In our talks with the Americans we do not use gentle language. In our meeting with Carter in Vienna, Comrade Brezhnev presented

31. This is an attempt by the Soviet foreign minister to assume a role in the Middle East peace process by dismissing the Camp David Accords as an "American-Egyptian treason" of the Arab camp. He does not hide his hostility toward Sadat and toward American Middle East policy.

the steady Soviet position regarding the various problems. We want our Arab friends to know about this steady principled position of ours.

We attach special importance to the problem of unity in the Arab world. The more the Arab world is united, the more Egypt's situation and the situation of its leadership deteriorate. We identify with your views regarding the two Baghdad conferences. We observed the unity of the Arab peoples expressed in these two conferences where it was decided to take a correct posture towards the policy of imperialism, Israel and the Egyptian leadership. We were very satisfied with the success of the two conferences and the unity of the Arab peoples achieved there. We sincerely appreciate — and this is the clear-cut opinion of the Soviet leadership — the role of the PLO leadership and the role you, Comrade Arafat, played personally in these two conferences.

Some of the participants of the conferences would have been ready to "bend" to the aggressor were it not for the role you played. There were differences of opinion in the conference, but the result was favourable and it was expressed in the successful resolutions.

The Soviet leadership is interested that there be no retreat from these successes and achievements. They must be the basis for the next action. You can play a role in this matter. Your role will be of great importance in the future.

We attached importance to my conversation with King Hussein, the substance of which was to adhere to the need to establish an independent state, if the Palestinians so wish. We notified Khaddam[32] about this Jordanian position and he said, "I respect this declaration but I have my doubts regarding the king's sincerity and the seriousness of his declaration." It serves our common interests that the king should not retreat from his declaration. You emphasized the importance of cooperative action between you, Syria and Iraq in the struggle against Camp David. We attribute great importance to this. You can play a positive role in overcoming the differences between Syria and Iraq. You have not exhausted your possibilities in this regard yet.

There is another matter which you did not mention because of lack of time, which is the Saudi Arabian position in the last conferences — a position which was much more positive than we expected. Possibly it was influenced by the atmosphere prevailing at these conferences. The Syrians believe that there are several weak points in Saudi Arabian policy, expressed in the

32. 'Abd-al-Halim Khaddam, Foreign Minister of Syria.

feelings of some members of the royal family who think that their defence and support can come only from the Americans.

It seems that the Steadfastness Front states have already gained some experience in handling Saudi Arabia and in applying pressure on it.

Abu 'Ammar: Not all of them. Democratic Yemen [South Yemen] is different in this regard, especially after the treaty it signed with you.

Gromyko: Not decisively. The idea is the influence of the PLO and of other Arab elements. We think you should exploit this experience, because of the importance of Saudi Arabia's role in the Middle East problem. As for Democratic Yemen, its situation is delicate and difficult. But it goes along with the general policy stream of the Steadfastness Front. Saudi apprehensions about our friendship treaty with South Yemen have no basis; we do not interfere in the internal affairs of any country. The position of the Moroccan king is not based on principle; we should prevent these differences of opinion from removing King Hassan II from the Arab consensus.

Your evaluation of the Israeli-Egyptian-American steps concerning the West Bank was correct. We are witnessing an imperialist-Israeli-Sadat conspiracy. We could make some sharp statements on this matter, but the important thing is that we agree with your evaluation. You mentioned the American counterattack. The Arabs are capable of responding to it if they unite in a struggle against it.

What is happening in southern Lebanon is part of the conspiracy and the spearhead of this conspiracy, and is directed against the Palestinian resistance, against Syria, and against Lebanon as a sovereign state. When we analyze this situation, we discover that the alliance between Syria and the Palestinian resistance in southern Lebanon plays a decisive role in the struggle against the American offensive. You mentioned the difficulties facing you in southern Lebanon. Despite the physical distance between us, we appreciate the extent of these difficulties and the efforts of the Palestinian resistance and Syria to thwart the American attack.

As for the Tunis Conference, there are differences of opinion regarding the success or failure of this conference. There are reports that Saudi Arabia will not play an honourable role concerning southern Lebanon. But the five Steadfastness Front states can play a role in blocking the imperialist assault, bearing in mind that such a role is the core for national action, the purpose of which is to bring about the success of the summit.

The way you described Philip Habib's proposals was to the point and accurate. These are imperialistic proposals and are hostile to the Arabs. We hope the evaluation of the Arab states with regard to these proposals will be similar.

We also agree with you as far as the internationalization of the Lebanese crisis is concerned. If this dangerous conspiracy succeeds, then it will pave the way for America to influence her friends in Europe to cause the internationalization of the Lebanese crisis. It will have a negative impact on Arab interests and, consequently, it will improve the ability of Sadat and Israel to extend their influence. I wish to emphasize that the Soviet position regarding these conspiracies — like the autonomy conspiracy and the conspiracy to internationalize the Lebanese crisis which Philip Habib brought — is no different than the position of the Arabs who adhere to their principles. Furthermore, we know that our socialist comrades share the same view.

We heard with satisfaction your statement that 90 percent of the Baghdad resolutions were implemented. This is a success for the Arabs. It is the first time I have heard such a clear and accurate assessment.

Now I wish to move on to some international problems.

Iran: I refer to the recent events concerning the occupation of the American embassy in Teheran and the American activity connected with it.

The Americans contacted us a few days ago requesting that we play a role in the affair through the senior foreign diplomat in Teheran, the Czech ambassador, for the purpose of freeing the American diplomats.

We informed the Americans that we adhere to international agreements and that our position results from the contents of these agreements [relating to diplomatic immunity].

If we look at this problem from the point of view of international agreements, then we must show understanding to the Americans and there is no justification for Iran to criticize us.

If we don't consider it within this framework, but rather from the point of view of American-Iranian relations, then we do not wish to protect American interests, despite their request that we do so. Therefore, we will not get involved in a complicated discussion on the subject and in no way are we going to protect the Americans in this matter. We think there are no differences of opinion between us in this matter, despite the difference in status between us — we as a state and you as a national liberation movement. This is quite satisfactory.

So far we have not received the American reaction to our response.

Abu 'Ammar: The Iranians understood from your delegate that he accepted the American request.

Gromyko: Our representative did not object to the announcement of the Security Council chairman, since this is a brief declaration concerning international agreements regarding the diplomatic corps.

Abu 'Ammar: Let us not forget that the declaration includes some threats of the use of force.

Gromyko: We read this declaration and found in it no more than the formulation of international agreements regarding diplomatic representation, and this formulation is balanced. There was a sharp dispute on the subject relating to hints about using force. Our position, which rejects and condemns such actions, is clear.
When the Iranian revolution broke out, there were talks then about the use of force. We opposed this logic and our position remains as it was.

We are now just prior to the presentation of the Palestinian issue in the UN. This matter is very important to us and to yourselves. The question is: what do you expect from the discussion? What is your minimum demand of this discussion? Did you think carefully about the form in which the subject will be presented and how it can be achieved? I ask you to answer this after I finish my words in a short while.

We will no doubt support and assist the Palestinian and Arab position, and we will back every proposal and every plan which you submit to the UN. This support also applies to our socialist comrades.[33] The last question is, and it is only a question: it is known that America — when it talks with us about the Palestinian problem — its delegates tell us: How is it possible for us to recognize the PLO and the establishment of an independent Palestinian state when the PLO does not recognize Israel and the well-known UN resolutions? We heard the very convincing argument from your side regarding the motives

33. A blank cheque commitment on behalf of the entire Soviet bloc to support automatically any PLO or Arab position, regardless of its merit.

for your refusal to accept those resolutions, since they deal with refugees and make no mention of the "Palestinian people." These reasons are known. But in our talks with the Americans, we always confront this obstacle and this limitation which cannot be overcome.

Here I wish to ask you a question: Are you considering certain tactical[34] concessions in return for getting recognition from the hostile camp? Are you considering recognizing these international resolutions? And are you also considering recognizing Israel's right to exist as an independent sovereign state? I remember my conversation with Yigal Allon[35] who asked me, "How can we talk with the PLO when they do not recognize Israel's right to exist as an independent state, and when the PLO does not even recognize the UN resolutions?" He also told me that if the PLO recognized Israel and the UN resolutions, the situation would be different, and in that case we [Israel] would have dealt with it in a different manner.

My question to Allon was: Which side will make the first step, the PLO or Israel? Allon replied, "If Israel would have initiated a declaration in that direction, the PLO would not have agreed to issue a similar declaration on its behalf, based on the recognition of Israel and the UN resolutions." Now the government [in Israel] has changed,[36] and I do not know what your [PLO] position is now.

I would also like to ask you, is your position to reject all concessions on this problem, even those not involving principles? What matters to you is the establishment of a Palestinian state, and, notwithstanding the differences that may exist [among yourselves], the establishment of a Palestinian state is the foundation and contains all the other things.

During the discussions with the Americans we felt we were at a dead end. Here I would like to know what your opinion is and please regard it as a question only. . .

Ponomarev: You spoke alone, whereas both of us spoke: Gromyko presented to you in detail the general direction of the Soviet leadership towards

34. Very significantly, Gromyko does not ask the PLO to make any substantive concessions with regard to recognizing Israel, but only to make tactical changes in its rhetoric, in order to lure the "hostile" West into recognizing the PLO.
35. A former Israeli foreign minister. He met with his Soviet counterpart in 1975 during the UN General Assembly session in New York.
36. In May 1977, the Labour Party, of which Allon was a leader, lost the elections and the Likud government took power.

the Middle East and the Palestinian problem. We know, from reports we have received and from reports you have, that the PLO marches onward, and you have outgrown the framework of an Arab liberation movement. The facts are known to us and the recognition by many states is known. We are very satisfied.

We have assisted and will continue to assist in the future [concerning recognition].

We think that the greetings Comrade Brezhnev conveyed to you congratulating you on your birthday help in this matter, as did the message Comrade Brezhnev sent to Barcelona. This will help you from the Arab and international points of view, to enable the world and the Arabs to understand the principles of Soviet policy towards you.

You now face two major events:

1. The Tunis Conference.

2. The UN debate on the [Palestinian] problem.

You raised the subject of consultations on this matter [of the UN debate]. We always asked you to consult us on this subject. It is very important that we know in advance the steps of the adversaries in the UN so that we can exploit the UN stage by exposing aggressive actions which Israel conducts in southern Lebanon. It cannot be condemned inside Israel,[37] but Israel has friends in the US and it is useful to campaign to expose Israel's actions against elderly people and children, using all propaganda means.

As regards the Tunis Conference, you know more than we do. We agree with your opinion that it is not worth devoting the whole conference to discussing the subject of southern Lebanon and to avoid a debate on the overall problem, the Middle East problem. It is very important that you mobilize all your resources for this purpose and that your Arab friends are active so that the conference will make the right decisions.

It is important that we devote special attention to Algeria. Lately we have had strong ties with Algeria. We received a party delegation [from Algeria] and sent a comrade, Brezhnev's deputy, to participate in the ceremonies in

37. This refers to Israel's peace movement, which criticized the government for its preventive raids against PLO positions in Lebanon.

Algeria. They told us that President Ali Chadli Ben Jedid and Party Leader Salah Yachiawi are determined to continue Boumedienne's policy. The Algerians said the same things to our delegation chief who attended their ceremonies. Algeria's word has considerable weight now.

Lately we had contacts with the National Movement in Lebanon, especially with the Communists and Jumblatt. All of them stressed that their relations with the Palestinians are good and that they are participating in the fight against the Israelis and against the reactionary leadership in the country [Lebanon].[38]

Abu 'Ammar: There is a joint command which I head.

Ponomarev: For this reason it is very important that the relationships be good, not only with the anti-imperialist organizations in Lebanon, but also with the other forces, like Franjieh[39] for instance. We must have influence with the leadership of the Lebanese state. It is necessary that the Syrians play a role in the contacts with Lebanon. Of course, you, because of your presence in Lebanon, must take care that your relations with the Lebanese state should not worsen because then your situation would be difficult.

Abu 'Ammar: Our relations with Al-Hus [Lebanon's prime minister] are good, with President Sarkis — not bad. The relations with the Islamic Council, with the National Front and with President Franjieh — good. This year we spent 19 million Lebanese pounds on reparations for the south and nine million pounds on treating civilians.

Ponomarev: This is your message and it is good. You have to present it in the UN and in Tunis. To conclude I would like to stress that in all our talks with the Arabs, especially with President Assad, we stressed a just and comprehensive solution to the Palestinian problem. We declared this position in formal talks, through the party and the various popular organizations.

Lately we established a committee for friendship and solidarity with the Palestinian people. When the Vietnamese people struggled with the USA, we established a similar solidarity committee. Vietnam, as we know, later won and we hope that this time victory will be achieved too. The committee has been established and we wish you every success.

---

38. This attests to Soviet collusion with the pro-PLO forces in Lebanon (Jumblatt's Socialists) and its subversion of the pro-Western ("reactionary") forces there.
39. Suleiman Franjieh was president of Lebanon from 1970 to 1976. He comes from the northern township of Zagharta and leads a pro-Syrian group among the Maronite Christians of Lebanon.

Abu 'Ammar: For our part we set up a committee for solidarity with you. As for Comrade Gromyko's question, we are ready to reply to it, if it will lead to any results, since it indeed deserves an effort on our part.

Knowing that we are the victim, we raised many possible solutions, while none of our enemies presented any. We said: A democratic state where Jews and Arabs will live.[40] They said: This means the destruction of Israel.

In 1974, we said we will establish the Palestinian state on every part of land which Israel withdraws from, or which will be liberated, and this is our right. Article 1 in the partition plan which was imposed on our people says: a Palestinian state and Israel. The reconciliation Committee in Lausanne admitted the existence of two problems: the return of the refugees and recognition of a Palestinian state. They [the Israelis] said: this [will become] a Communist state which will strive to destroy Israel. When the US-Soviet joint communiqué was published [the Vance-Gromyko statement in New York on 1-2 October 1977] we announced that we agreed to it. What did the others offer? I can stand in front of the UN and ask: What did the others propose? They suggested that the PLO was through; a military attack [on us] in 1978; hell directed at us from the south; the despicable crime called "Camp David."

We have proposed all these things and they have offered nothing. I say that I agree to the Soviet-American communiqué, and accept what you agreed upon with the Americans.

Gromyko: The Soviet-American communiqué mentions the Geneva Convention and Palestinian rights. This communiqué, which you asked about, did not have results in the field. If it were implemented, the circumstances would have been more favourable. I do not wish to put pressure on you to reply on this subject.

If there is a change in your position, I ask you to notify us, since one cannot escape this issue. In every statement, the Americans say: How can we recognize an organization while they are not ready to recognize anything? This is demagoguery, but we have to know how to deal with it. I ask you to think about it and to make your comments.

Abu 'Ammar: The USA itself cancelled the Soviet-American communiqué; it pushed Sadat to go to Jerusalem. We were told: if you recognize 242 after

40. This refers to the formula adopted by the PLO that calls for a "free, democratic Palestine" but provides that such a country have an Arab character.

you add your reservations — we will recognize you, open the dialogue with you and take the commitment to establish a state. This was in 1977.

Later the USA withdrew from this. Through Rashad Faron they told us, "The train of settlement is moving along. If you want, join it — if not, you may do whatever you wish." Later they offered us a formula relating to 242 — that we should announce our consent to it — and this was for the sole purpose of starting the dialogue with us.

Ponomarev: They conspired with the Egyptians and fortified their positions.

Abu 'Ammar: This strengthens our and your view. They manœuvre to avoid the issue. Part of the American plan still suggests that Jordan be the alternative to the PLO, and this is what the Israeli Labour Party officially declares. Nevertheless, our relations with Jordan are good and we try to overcome all differences of opinion. We published together with the Jordanians two joint statements in which [Jordan] emphasized our right to return and to establish a state. We have a joint committee and we try to cultivate these relations despite all the efforts to put obstacles in the way.

Referring to Iran, we are not mediators. We are on the Iranian side, and agree to what Khomeini agrees to and not to what Bazargan or Shariat Madari agree to.[41]

Gromyko: I thank you for the useful discussion. We think that we march with you on the same path concerning the Middle East problem. The Soviet Union is a friend of the Arabs and does not tend to change its friends. We hope that the Arabs and the PLO feel the same way.

Abu 'Ammar: The PLO has no doubts.

Gromyko: If there is any point in publishing a joint communiqué, we have a draft we ask you to look at.

---

41. Mehdi Bazargan, the first prime minister of the Islamic revolutionary regime, and Ayatollah Shariat Madari were two of the more moderate elements in Khomeini's entourage. Both were later stripped of power.

Document 7A-2

• ٢ •

غروميكـــو : أتقصد الجوله الاخيره له •

أبــوعمــار : الجوله التي سبقت اجتماع وزراء الخارجيه والمال العرب ، أهمية مؤتمر بغداد الثاني (وزراء الخارجيه والمال العرب) هو هذا التنسيق الذى ظهر على شكل محور ثلاثي العراق ــ سوريا ــ فلسطين • هذا المحور قاد الصمود والتصدى ثم قاد المؤتمر ككل • خرجت هذه القرارات والتي اعتبرها كقرارات اقتصاديه اهم واخطر مـــن القرارات السياسيه • ونستطيع أن نقول أن الوفد الفلسطيني كان له دور هام في صنع هذه القرارات •

غروميكـــو : رفيق عرفات آسف لقطع حديثكم و ولكن أريد أن تدلوا برأيكم في تنفيذ هذه القرارات التي اتخذت في قمة بغداد •

أبــوعمــار : هذا ما سأتحدث عنه ، لقد أراد بعض العرب أن يعطونا القرار السياسي ويتلاعبوا هم بالقرار الاقتصادى ، الوفد الفلسطيني قدم ورقة اقتصاديه واضحه أيده فيها الوفدان العراقي والسورى ، وكان هناك تنسيقا رائعا بيننا ، بحيث تمكنا من الوقوف في وجه التكتل الذى تقوده السعوديه مما جعل المؤتمر المذكور يتحول الى مؤتمر قمه • نقد أوقفنـــا المؤتمر لمدة ٤٨ ساعه كي يذهب المندوبون الى دولهم ويتشاوروا معها ، وهنا أعيـــد التأكيد على أهمية التنسيق الثلاثي الذى كان دوره حاسما في انجاح المؤتمر ، وأدى الى النتيجه التي تعرفونها •

القرارات الاقتصاديه التي اتخذت نستطيع أن نقول نفذ منها ٩٠٪ ضد مصر • أقول ٩٠٪ لان ١٠٪ من الودائع لـم تسحب كاملا بعد • والآن كمال أدهم يلعب لعبـــــه جديده ، هي لعبه أمريكيه لاخراج السادات من أزمته الخانقه ، اذ يقوم بدفع بعـــض الاثرياء السعوديين والخليجيين لتوظيف بعض أموالهم في القاهره • ولكن هذه لن تنقذ الاقتصاد المصرى فقط تساعده قليلا • فالاقتصاد المصرى بحاجة الى ٣ر٥ بليون دولار سنويا ولمدة عشر سنوات • أمريكا أعطته ١ر٢ مليار دولار رفعتها الى ١ر٥ مليار ، وتريد أمريكا أن تجلب له من اليابان ٧٥٠ مليون دولار ومثلها من ألمانيا الغربيه •

غروميكـــو : هذا المبلغ المطلوب من ألمانيا واليابان دفعات سنويه أم لمره واحده •

أبــوعمــار : ١ر٥ مليون دولار دفعه سنويه أما حصة ألمانيا واليابان فهي مبدئيا دفعة لمرة واحده يمكن أن تضغط أمريكا لتدفع مره أخرى •

انهم أى الامريكان ينطلقون في معالجتهم للاقتصاد المصرى الى اعطائه المسكنـــات بانتظار فرط عقد قمة بغداد ، لذلك تراهم يعالجون الأمور شهرا وراء شهر وسنة وراء اخـــرى •

Document 7A-1

محضـر المحـادثـات بيـن

الوفديـن الفلسطينـي والسوفيـتي

....

الوفـد السوفيـتي :

غروميكـو ، بوناماريوف ، نائب غروميكو ، رئيس دائرة الشرق الأوسط في الخارجيـه السوفيتيـه ، غـرونونسكـي .

الوفد الفلسطينـي : أبوعمار ، عبد المحسن أبو ميزر ، طلال ناجي ، عصام القاضي ، ياسر عبد ربه حبيب قهوجي ، تيسيـر قبعه ، محمد الشاعـر ، عبد الرحيم أحمـد .

بدأ الاجتماع في الساعه الثانية عشره من يوم ١٣/ ١١/ ١٩٧٩ في الكرملين .

غروميكـو : أرحب بكم باسم القياده السوفيتيه وباسم بريجنييف شخصيا بمناسبة وصولكم موسكو . لقد كلفتني القياده السوفيتيه أنا وبوناماريوف في الحديث معكم في كل القضايا التي تهمنا وتهمكم . فأرجو أن تنطلقوا من هذا الوضع وليس لدى أى شيء . وأتأمـل أن يتميز لقاءنا بالود والمحبه كما كانت لقاءاتنا في الماضي . اقترح لبدء الحديـث أن تقولوا لنا وجهة نظركم ، ثم ندلي بوجهة نظرنا ، بعد هذه المقابله هناك حفلـة غداء اليوم في الساعه الثانيه .

أبوعمار : سأختصر لان أحد الرفاق أخبرني بان هذه الفتره مخصصه للمحادثات الرسميـه .

غروميكـو : هناك وقت طويل .

أبوعمار : ساعتين لا تكفي .

غروميكـو : ساعتين ونصـف .

أبوعمار : نحن لم نتحدث مع بعض منذ فترة طويله . قبل مؤتمر بغداد قلت لكم أنه من أهم المؤتمرات ، وجاءت نتائجه كما توقعت مهمه . وذلك لان مؤتمر قمة بغداد قد وضع الأمة العربيه كلها ضد مثلث كمب ديفيد باستثناء دولتين أنتم تعرفون قرارات قمـة بغداد . سأقفز لاتحدث عن مؤتمر وزراء الخارجيه والمال العرب .

أهمية بغداد أن العرب اجتمعوا بدون السادات الذى كان يقول أن العرب لا يجتمعون بدوني . وأخذوا قرارات تدين اتفاقيات كمب ديفيد .

اجتماع وزراء الخارجيه والمال كان أخطر لان قراراته كانت تنفيذيه لقرارات القمـه السياسيه . وانتم تعلمون أن بريجنسكي قام بجولة في المنطقه وأعلن أن هدف جولته هو منع تنفيذ قرارات بغداد .

Document 7A-4

-٤-

القرار الذى صدر في هافانا ضد كمب ديفيد • فبواسطه هذا التنسيق الثلاثي الرائع ودور الرفيق كاسترو الذى لن ننساه له استطعنا أن نشكل لوبي ضخم انتزعنا بواسطته تلك القرارات المعروفه •

بوناماريوف : كان للاصدقاء الكوبيين دورا ضخما •

أبوعمار : كان لحكمة كاسترو دورا مهما في النتائج ، ولا بد هنا من ذكر دور العديد من الدول التقدميه التي ساعدتنا مساعده كبيره •

أنتقل للحديث عن موءتمر لشبونه الذى لا يقل أهميته عن موءتمر هافانا فالأول شعبي والثاني حكومي ، وهو من الموءتمرات الشعبيه الرائعه وهو أول موءتمر يعقد بهذه الضخامه في بلد أوروبي ، وقد لعب الحزب الشيوعي البرتغالي دورا مهما في انجاحه وكذلك لجنة التضامن عندكم •

بوناماريوف : نحن أرسلنا رئيس لجنة التضامن ، وكذلك ارسل الرفيق بريجينيف رساله الى الموءتمر •

ابوعمار : نعم كانت هناك كميه ضخمه من الرسائل أرسلها الملوك والروءساء وفي مقدمتهم الرفيق بريجنييف •

برشلونه نقطة انعطاف في العالم الغربي •

والآن أريد أن أقول شيئا بعد نجاحنا في موءتمر بغداد الأول والثاني حدث هجوم أمريكي معاكس واتخذ المحاور التاليه :

المحور الأول : حدثت الموءامره التي فصلت العراق عن سوريا • اثارة المشاكل داخل سوريا ، الضغط على الملك حسين للحاق بكمب ديفيد ، استعراض القوه الذى مارسته امريكا في الخليج ، ولا بد من القول أن عملية استعراض القوه في الخليج قد لاقت نجاحا • محاولة خلق تناقض بين الثورة الايرانيه والعرب •

المحور الثاني : الضغط على أهلنا في الداخل للتعامل مع الحكم الذاتي • ولا بد من القول أنهم قد فشلوا في ذلك باعتراف شتراوس والاسرائيليين والمصريين والآن أرضنا المحتله تغلي اضرابات ضخمه بسبب قرار اسرائيل القاضي بطرد أحد روءساء البلديات ، وذلك لكونه أحد رجالات منظمة التحرير اذ أن هناك قرارا بالتخلص منهم واحدا تلو الآخر •

لا نم نعترف أن المحادثات التي جرت بين بورغ ومصطفى خليل توصلت الى موافقة الثاني بأمر من السادات على الحكم الذاتي ، اذ توصلوا الى بعض الاتفاقات شبه النهائيه ، ما عدا موضوع القدس والأراضي الأميريه والمرافق العامه فقد تركت لما بعد

Document 7A-3

٠٣٠

رغم ذلك نستطيع أن نقول أن ٩٠٪ من قرارات بغداد قد نفذت ضد مصر ٠ نحن في ورقة العمل الاقتصاديه الفلسطينيه طالبنا أن تعاقب أمريكا اقتصاديا ونحن نعرف حينما طالبنا بذلك بانه ليس سهلا ، ولكن هدفنا أن نسجل ذلك ونثير نقاشا حولـــه والوفد الفلسطيني سجل بعد النقاش تحفظا لان أمريكا لم تطالها عقوباتنا العربيه ٠ المهم أننا أخذنا القرارات ونفذ منها ٩٠٪ وهذه نسبة نجاح كبيره بالنسبة للمنطقــه العربيـــه ٠ ماليا بالنسبه لدعم الصمود ، كل الدول العربيه دفعت ما عدا الجزائـــر وليبيا وهذا خلق نقصا في حدود ٢٥٪

غروميكـــــو : النقص لمنظمة التحرير٠

أبـــوعمـــار : النقص للجميع ٠ أنا أتكلم ٩٠٪ بالنسبة للعقوبات ضد النظام المصـــرى ٠
بعد ذلك ذهبنا الى المؤتمر الاسلامي في فاس، والذى اكتسبت نتائجه أهميتها لانهـــا وضعت الحسن الثاني في موقف كان فيه مضطرا للوقوف ضد السادات ،حينما أخذ قرار طرد مصر من المجموعه الاسلاميه وأهمية ذلك أن الشعب المصرى المتدين سوف يسأل اذا كـــان العرب ضدنا فلماذا العالم الاسلامي ضدنا أيضا ؟ هذا شيء مهم ويقلل من حجـــج السادات ضد العرب ٠

جئنا بعدها الى مؤتمر منظمة الوحده الافريقيه في مونروفيا ، والذى حقق فيه السادات انتصارا علينا ، ولهذا عدة أسباب منها تصـــرف حكومة ليبيريا مع الوفد الفلسطيني ، فقـــد منعته من أن يلقي كلمته مما اضطره للمغادره ، وكذلك تصرفها مع أمين عام جامعة الدول العرب الذى أنزل من على المنصه الرئيسيه مما اضطره أيضا للمغادره ، ومنها أيضا وهذا مهم جـــدا فان التكتل القوى الذى يقف ضد كامب ديفيد لم يكن ممثلا في المؤتمر أو بالاحرى لم يكـــــن موجودا ٠ كل هذا أفرغ الميدان للسادات واعطاه القرار الذى يريده ٠

أذكر ذلك لاقول أنه عند ذهابنا الى هافانا كانت الدول الافريقيه الـ٤٩ متسلحة بقرار مونروفيا ، رغم ذلك فقد استطعنا انتزاع قرار ادانه شديد لكمب ديفيد وأن نغير الرأى العام الافريقي ٠

غروميكـــــو : هذا ضرب لمنروفيا وقراراتهـــا ٠

أبـــوعمـــار : نعم ٠ وكان موقف اليوغوسلاف والهنود ضد اتخاذ أى قـــرار ضد مصـــر وأصدقاؤنا الكوبيون قالوا لنا حينما ذهبنا الى هافانا أنه من الصعب أخذ موقف ضد كمب ديفيد ، وأعتقد أن ذلك كان تقديركم أيضا ٠هنا لا بد لي أن أشير أنه قبل هافانا كان هناك خلافا شديدا بين سوريا والعراق ، ولكن الوفد الفلسطيني لعب دورا هاما في تنسيق الموقـــف الثلاثي كما كنا في بغداد ٠ ولعب الرئيسين صدام والاسد دورا مهما ورئيسيا في اتخاذ

Document 7A-6

-٦٠-

عسكريه ، أما المدنيين فوصلوا من ٣٠ ــ ٣٥ اصابه يوميا . في شهر واحد سجل الرئيس الحص ٣٩٠ قتيلا وألف جريح مدني هؤلاء من الذين مروا على المستشفيات بالتأكيد هناك غيرهم

هذه هي اتجاهات الهجوم وهو لم يتوقف بعد لماذا ؟ هناك الآن تخفيف للجحيم في الجنوب سببه ورقة العمل الامريكيه المقدمه من فيليب حبيب وسأعطيكم نسخه عنها حتى لا نضيع الوقت . أخطر ما فيها أنهم يقولون باجتماع جميع الاطراف وقالوا ان ذلك يعني اسرائيل ولبنان وسوريا والاردن ومنظمة التحرير باشراف امريكا .

لماذا الاردن ؟ .

بوناماريوف : بدون مصر

أبوعمار : بدون مصر ، هذا كمب ديفيد جديد ، وهذا أخطر ما في الورقه هنا تأتي خطورة مؤتمر القمه القادم ، وخطورته أن بعض الاطراف العربيه قد وافقت عليه وعملت على عقد ، سواء أكان ذلك بقصد أم بغير قصد . اللبنانيين سيقدموا ورقة عمل سوف تفجر المؤتمر ، مفادها الانسحاب الفلسطيني من الجنوب ، خطورة هذه الورقه ليست ازالة الفلسطينيين من الجنوب ولكن مسألتين :

١) لغم ينفجر داخل مؤتمر القمه . وبالتالي يخرج المؤتمر فاشلا ، وتتحلل بعض الدول العربيه من التزاماتها التي وافقت عليها في بغداد .

٢) اذا لم يأخذ اللبنانيون ما يريدوه من المؤتمر فانهم سيلجأون للتدويل

لقد حققنا نجاحا بالنسبة لمجريات مؤتمر القمة القادم ، في زيارتي الاخيره لبغداد توصلت الى اتفاق مع الرئيس صدام على التنسيق الثلاثي كما حدث في المؤتمر السابق ، وهذا يعتبر نجاحا . والرئيس صدام أبلغني قوله ان لفلسطين الاولويه في كل شيء . لقد قابلت بعد عودتي الرئيس الاسد وأبلغته ذلك فأبدى ترحيبا وموافقه على هذا التنسيق الثلاثي ، هذا مهم جدا لانه يقلل من حرية الحركه للقوى المعاديه داخل المؤتمر ، وهذا ما اتفقنا عليه في قمة الصمود حيث عقدنا جلسه واحده في الجزائر .

لا بد أن أضيف محورا رابعا للهجوم الامريكي المعاكس وهو وجود فرقتين مصريتين على الحدود الليبيه ، لتشكيل ضغط عسكرى أمريكي مصرى على معمر ، اذ يقولون انهم ليسوا محتاجين الى احتلال ليبيا فقط الوصول الى طبرق ومعنى ذلك احتلال منابع النفط وتشكيل حكومه ليبيه من المعارضه التي بدأت تتجمع في مصر . ولا بد من عدم الاستهتار

Document 7A-5

- ٥ -

المحور الثالث : ركزوا علينا تركيزا جهنميا في جنوب لبنان ، سبعة أشهـــر
--------- من الجحيم ، نتيجتها ستمائة ألف مهجر لبناني وفلسطينـــي
عشرات المدن والقرى والمخيمات دمرت ، واستخدمت اسرائيـــل
في ذلك كل أنواع الأسلحة التي بحوزتها .

غروميكــو : ستمائة ألف مهجر لبناني وفلسطيني من الجنوب الى الشمال ، ومنذ أى وقد بدأ الحرب عليكم .

أبوعمــار : ٩/آذار/٩٧٨ . سأعطيك مثالا على عنف الهجوم الذى نتعرض له ، نقد قصفت اسرائيل مخيم الرشيديه ونهر البارد بطوربيدات بحريه اسمها سمارت وهي طوربيدات موجهه ، ضربوها من البحر ، انهم لا يحتاجوا هذه الاسلحه لضربنا في الجنوب لان مدفعيتهـــم تستطيع أن تصل الى الاهداف التي يريدوها . لقد سألني بعض ضباطنا عن سبب استعمال هذا السلاح، قلت لهم صدرت الأوامر لكل الأسلحه أن تضرب . فضربتنا البحريـــــــه بهذا السلاح . ف ١٥ ، ف ١٦ تستخدم ضدنا وكذلك اللانس روكيت وهو مثل صاروخ الفروغ واللونا تستخدم ضدنا ، عندى شهاده رمزى كلارك الذى بعد زيارته للمنطقـــه عاد وعقد مؤتمرا صحفيا وقال ان ما يحدث جريمه ، وأهمية شهادته أنه [illegible] . زار مخيم النبطيه الذى مسح ولم يبقى منه سوى ١١ بيتا ، لقد ضربونا بالأسلحه المحرمه دوليـــا الغاز بومب ، والفريجمنتيشن بومب والكلاستر شيل . لقد قاتلنا ولا زلنا نقاتل منفرديـــن لم يصلنا طلقة واحده ، الا من الأخوة العراقيين ، وكذلك السوريين ، اشتبكوا مرتين مـــع الطيران الاسرائيلي .

غروميكــو : كيف تقيموا نتائج الاشتباكات الجويه السوريه الاسرائيليه .

أبوعمــار : لست خبير طيران . يهمني القرار السياسي ، يهمني أن يشعر مقاتلنا أنه ليس وحيدا .

بوناماريوف : المهم أنهم لم يستطيعوا أن يكسروا صمودكم وصبركم .

أبوعمــار : ما حدث ملحمه ، معجزه ، لقد تحملنا حتى اطعام المهجرين ، اذ ليس هناك حكومه نحن نطعم في حدود ٥٠٪ منهم ، لان هدف العمليه من هذا الضرب الوحشي هو تأليب الجماهير الجنوبيه ضدنا ، ان دولاعربيه لم تستطع أن تتحمل الاستنزاف فعبد الناصر تعب من الاستنزاف وتذكروا أن هذا من أسباب قبوله بمشروع روجـــرز ، نحن نقول لهم سبعة شهور مستعدين لسبعين شهر وأكثر ، أطفالنا يقاتلون لســـت مطالبنا بأكثر من هذا ، أمس صباحا انفجرت قنبلة كلاستر بومب قتلت سبعة أطفالا . أنا لحد الآن لم أعلن خسائرى العسكريه ، نحن لدينا يوميا من ١٠ ــ ١٢ اصابـــه

Document 7A-8

•٨•

اكتشف المنظمه في هافانا • لقد استقبلنا ١٨٩ وفدا خلال ستة أشهر من جميع المناطق في العالم •

غروميكو : أغلبهم ممثلين منظمات شعبيه •

أبو عمار : نعم جميعهم • أنا لا أتحدث عن الوفود الرسميه •

نحن ننسق مع لجنة التضامن الآسيوي الافريقي ومجلس السلم العالمي وغيرها من المؤسسات العالميه كجمعية الحقوقيين الديموقراطيين التي أقامت قبل فترة ندوة في باريس وادانة كمب ديفيد من الوجهة القانونيه •

تحركنا الدبلوماسي على الدول التي زرتها فيينا – انقره – مدريد – لشبونه وأخيرا اللقاء الذى تم بيني وبين مارشيه من أجل الحصول على دعوة لزيارة فرنسا وغيرها من النشاطات التي نقوم بها • مع معرفتنا أن لهذه التحركات سقف محدود لا نبني عليها أوهاما •

نحن رفضنا الفكره القديمه القائله بعدم حضور المكان الذى يحضره الاسرائيليون يجب أن نكون قبلهم في المؤتمرات ، كالمؤتمر الذى عقدته جمعية أساتذة العلوم السياسيه والذى حضره الرفيق بوناماريوف ذ أي حضرنا أتون • وكما حدث في ندوة روما •

نأتي على موضوع سريع نحن متخوفين لما يمكن أن يحدث في ايران ، اتصل بنا الامريكيين عن طريق عدد من الدول العربيه وغيرها ، كان جوابنا واضح نحن لسنا وسطاء نحن مع الثورة الايرانيـــــه •

غروميكو : اتصل الامريكيون بكم بناء على مبادره ذاتيه •

أبو عمار : ليس بنا ، اتصل رمزى كلارك وهو أحد المتعاطفين معنا نحن لسنا وسطاء ، نحن مع الثورة الايرانيه في السراء والضراء • موقف الخميني جيد ومتفهم لموقفنا هذا ، نحن أرسلنا مدير غرفة العمليات العسكريه ، لان الاحتمال العسكرى وارد رغم كونه احتمالا ضعيفا ولكنه قد يقع ، أريد أن أسأل أصدقائي عن تقديراتهم حتى نطمئن لان تقديراتهم أدق من تقديراتنا ، قبل قدومي الى هنا اتصل بي الامام الخميني طالبا تقدير موقف لاننا نرى الثوره من الخارج وهم يروها من الداخل • نحن نعتقد أنه من عمان يمكن أن يحدث شيء •

حاولت أن أختصر قدر الامكان ولكن يجب أن نتوقع تصعيد في لبنان بعد القمه أو أثنائها حتى يساعدوا سركيس في طرح نظريته • هناك تركيز على لعلنا في الجنوب المحتل من أجل الموافقه على الحكم الذاتي من الآن وحتى أيار ١٩٨٠ حيث ستكون الانتخابات البلديه • معركتنا في الامم المتحده نريد مساعدتكم لانجاح القرار لتقسيم

Document 7A-7

•٧•

بذلك رغم الاستعراض الكبير الذى أقامه القذافي في الفاتح من سبتمبر • لا بد لي من الاشاره الى أن هذا الضغط قد أثر قليلا في الموقف السياسي الليبي وهذا سبب زيارة بنوسم وكيل وزارة الخارجيه الأمريكيه لشؤون افريقيا الى ليبيا •

المحور الخامس : للهجوم الأمريكي المعاكس هو دفع النظام المصرى الى اعطاء اسلحه وذخائر ومحتمل قوات الى ملك المغرب • وهذا يعني عودة الحسن الثاني الى حظيرة كمب ديفيد مستغلين الهزائم التي لحقت به في الصحراء ، لهذا تحركنا الى المغرب والجزائر قبل حوالي شهر ووصلنا الى نتائج جيده ، لقد حصلنا من الملك الحسن بعد جلسة استمرت ثلاث ساعات ونصف على موافقته على الاستفتاء ، وهذا انجاز سياسي مهم حصلنا عليه في شمال أفريقيا • عدت بعدها وبلغت الرئيس الشاذلي بذلك وبلغت قبل أيام مسؤولي البوليساريو ونحن ننتظر جوابهم •

بوناماريوف : ما هو المقصود بالاستفتاء ؟ هل فصل بين القوات •

أبوعمار : حق تقرير المصير لاهل الصحراء •

غروميكو : هل كلا الجهتين موافقين على الاستفتاء ؟

أبوعمار : وافق الحسن وانتظر جواب الجزائريين والصحراويين •

في اتجاه الهجوم المعاكس حصل اجتماع من أخطر الاجتماعات ، هو اجتماع وزراء الخارجيه لدول الخليج والسعوديه ولبحث أمن الخليج • العراق موجود في الخليج لماذا لم يدعى للاجتماع ؟ الموضوع الرئيسي الذى بحث على حد زعمهم هو التحالف الفلسطيني الايراني وخطره عليهم ووضعوا خططا لمواجهة هذا الموضوع الموجود فقط في مخيلاتهم •

لقد نجحنا في تصعيد عملياتنا العسكريه داخل الأراضي المحتله ـ ويكفي أن نذكر تقرير لجنة الأمن في الكنيست التي قالت فين أن هناك ١١١ ألف رجل شرطي ورجل أمن مجندين للحفاظ على الأمن في اسرائيل ما عدا الجيش مضافا الى ذلك معجزة الصمود العسكرى في الجنوب فهي بقدر ما هي معجزه سأقول لكم كم هي محزنه ، رشاشاتنا ٢٣) مداها ٥ر٣ كم ، الطيارات ترتفع فوق هذا المستوى وتضرب رشاشاتنا واحدا تلو الآخر اذ ليس هناك تكافىء • أليس هذا ظلما يا رفيق ؟ أن أقاوم أحدث الأسلحه الأمريكيه باسلحة بسيطه ؟ في الوقت ألذى تمتلك فيه البوليساريو أحدث الأسلحه والصواريخ أمام السلاح المغربي البسيط ، ماذا يعني ذلك ؟ انه يعني أنني أقاتل بلحمي وبلحم أطفالنا ونساؤنا ، هذه هي المعجزه الفلسطينيه •

بجانب هذا الصمود العسكرى تحركنا سياسيا بشكل واسع فعلى سبيل المثال فان وفودنا الى آسيا وافريقيا وامريكا اللاتينيه لا تنقطع نيريرى قال كلمه حينما حول مكتب منظمة التحرير الى سفاره ، بانه

Document 7A-10

-١٠-

بوناماريوف : س١ هناك سؤالين لقد عرضت يا رفيق عرفات بعض اتصالاتكم التي لم يسبق لها مثيل في الماضي مثل النمسا واجتماعكم مع كرايسكي وبرانت ، ما هو تقييمكم لمثل هذه الاتصالات

س٢ : حول القوات السوريه المرابطه في الأراضي اللبنانيه ، هل تقدم لكم السلاح ؟ ، وهل تشاركم في التصدى للعدوان ؟

أبوعمار : سأبدأ بالاجابه عن السؤال الثاني ، القوات السوريه موجوده على خط عرض ١٠ر٣٧ والقتال يحدث جنوب هذا الخط حتى الآن ، لذلك هي غير موجوده في منطقة العمليات بيننا وبين الاسرائيليين ، ومع ذلك حدث الاشتباكين الجويين بين اسرائيل وسوريا ، السوريون أخذوا أيضا قرارا بارسال بعض الوحدات من قوى الدفاع الجوى لحماية المخيمات الواقعه ضمن مناطق تواجدهم من الغارات الاسرائيليه ، وخاصة بعدما أعلنت اسرائيل أنها ستضرب هذه المخيمات ، لان المقاتلين يخرجون من هذه المخيمات ، ولا ننسى أن دايان وايزمن أعلنا أن ذلك يتم بالتنسيق مع أمريكا ، وهنا أهمية القرار السياسي الذى اتخذته سوريا بالتصدى .

أما بالنسبة لآفاق الحركة السياسيه (سؤالك الأول) فان ما يهمنا هو انفهام الرأى العام العالمي قضيتنا ، مثلا في دول عدم الانحياز أذكر أنني حضرت المؤتمر الذى عقد عام ٧٣ في الجزائر ، والذى رغم انعقاده على أرض الجزائر فاننا لم نستطع أخذ ما نريد من المؤتمر ، ولكن حركتنا داخل دول عدم الانحياز طيلة السنوات الست الماضيه أعطت هذه النتائج التي أظهرت في هافانا ، حركتنا في اوروبا منطلقه من حاجة اوروبا الى البترول ، البترول لم يدخل المعركه وهناك تخوف من ذلك . بعض الدول العربيه تساعدنا في هذا المجال .

بوناماريوف : كرايسكي اصبح صديقا للعرب

أبوعمار : لا أحد يقول ذلك . ولكن يجب أن نستفيد من ذلك .

بوناماريوف : على الأقل أظهرت بعض الشروخ في المعسكر الصهيوني بعد لقائكم معه . لانه في السابق كان من المدافعين عن اسرائيل .

غروميكو : جيد . شكرا على هذه المعلومات التي قدمتموها عن عدد من المسائل الدوليه وتقييمكم للوضع الراهن .

بادىء ذى بدء سأتطرق الى المسائل الجوهريه في السياسه الدوليه وسأتحدث عن موقفنا من هذه القضايا ، رغم أنه موقف معروف وهذا يساعد على الاختصار .

الاتحاد السوفيتي كما كان في الماضي يواصل سياسته المبدئيه تجاه الشرق الأوسط فنحن مع انسحاب اسرائيل من الأراضي المحتله ومع تحقيق الحقوق الشرعيه للفلسطينيين

Document 7A-9

" ٩ "

اتخذت في هافانا نقطة مهمه جدا ، هناك حديث في الاوساط الاسرائيليه عن ضربـــه
وقائيه اجهاضيه ضد سوريا ، نحن نقول هذا الكلام لان اسرائيل فيها متاعب سياســيه
واقتصاديه . محتمل أن يهربوا من هذه المتاعب بتصديرها للخارج . نقطة انطلاق
الهجوم من لبنان باعتبارها نقطة الضعف ، يضربوننا ثم يضربون الحركه الوطنيه ، ثــم
يضربوا سوريا ، فضرب القوات السوريه في لبنان سهلا فهي تقوم بدور أمني وليس دورا
عسكريـــا .

وشكـــرا .

Document 7A-12

-١٢-

في المؤتمرات الاخيره ، اكثر مما كنا نتوقع ، ولعلها تأثرت بالجو العربي الذى ساد في كل المؤتمرات . وهذا رأى السوريين ، الذين قالوا أن هناك بعض نقاط الضعف في السياسه السعوديه ، متمثلة بشعور بعض أطراف العائلة المالكه أن حمايتهم ومساندتهم موجوده فقط عند الامريكيين . ويبدو أن الاطراف المشتركه في الصمود والتصدى قد اكتسبوا خبره في التعامل مع السعوديه وممارسة النفوذ عليها .

أبوعمار : ليسوا كلهم ، فاليمن الديمقراطي غير ذلك ، خصوصا بعد المعاهده معكم .

غروميكو : ليس بشكل حاسم وانما المقصود تأثير المنظمه والجهات العربيه الاخرى ونرى من المفيد أن تستغلوا هذه التجربه ، لان دور السعوديه مهم في قضية الشرق الاوسط . فيما يتعلق باليمن الديموقراطي موقفها حساس وصعب ، ولكنها مع التيار العام في الصمود والتصدى ان مخاوف السعوديه من معاهدة الصداقه مع اليمن الجنوبي ليس له أساس فنحن لا نتدخل في الشؤون الداخليه لاى قطر .

موقف ملك المغرب ليس مبدئيا وليس سهلا ، يجب أن نمنع هذا الخلاف من أن يبعد الحسن الثاني عن الاجماع العربي .

كان تقييمكم صحيحا بالنسبة للمخطوات الاسرائيليه المصريه الامريكيه تجاه الضفة الغربيه اذ أننا نشاهد تنفيذ المخطط الامبريالي الاسرائيلي الساداتي ، نستطيع أن نستعمل عدد من الالفاظ القاسيه ، ولكن نحن مع تقييمكم لها ، تحدثتم عن الهجوم الامريكي المضاد بامكان العرب الرد عليه اذا كانوا موحدين في مواجهته .

ان ما يحدث في جنوب لبنان هو جزء من المخطط ورأس الحربه فيه موجه ضد المقاومه وسوريا ولبنان كدوله ذات سياده ، لو أعطنا تقييم لهذا الموقف لوجدنا دور حاسم للتحالف بين سوريا والمقاومه في جنوب لبنان في مواجهة الهجوم الامريكي . تحدثتم عن المصاعب التي تواجهونها في جنوب لبنان ونحن رغم المسافة نقدر هذه المتاعب ، ونحن نقدر هذه الجهود للمقاومه وسوريا لاحباط الهجوم الامريكي .

بالنسبة لمؤتمر تونس هناك تقديرات مختلفه حول نجاحه أو عدمه ، هناك معلومات مفادها أنه قد يكون للسعوديه دور غير شريف تجاه جنوب لبنان ، ولكن يمكن أن تلعب دول الصمود الخمس دورا في التصدى للهجمة الامبرياليه باعتبارها نواة للعمل الوطني ، من أجل انجاح القمه .

كان وصفك لاقتراحات فيليب حبيب وصف موضوعي وصحيح . انها مقترحات امبرياليه معاديه للعرب ، ولدينا أمل أن تقيم الدول العربيه هذه المقترحات بهذا الشكل ، كما أننا نشاركم الرأى في موضوع تدويل الازمة اللبنانيه لو نجح هذا المخطط الخطير سيمهد

Document 7A-11

• ١١ •

واقامة دولتهم المستقله ، ومع حق جميع دول المنطقه أن تكون دول ذات سياده ، • هذا
لب موقفنا من قضايا الشرق الأوسط •

نحن ندعو ونقف الى جانب التسويه الشامله ، ولكن شرط أن تكون عادله ، مسؤولي
الدول العربيه يركزون على عدالة التسويه ونحن نشاركهم ذلك • السادات والامريكان
يقولون عن تسويه عادله ، ولكن تسويتهم ليست عادله ، وكما في الماضي لا زلنا ندين بشده ،
الاتفاقيات المنفرده مع المعتدين ، وكذلك اتفاقيات كمب ديفيد المعقوده معه • ومهما
كانت واجهة هذه الاتفاقيات قديمه أم جديده فان جوهرها واحد لا يتغير • انها
اتفاقيات خيانيه ضد العرب ومصالحهم ، ان العالم بأسره يعرف موقفنا ووجهة نظرنا من
اتفاقيتي كمب ديفيد ، ونحن لا نلطف عباراتنا عن حديثنا مع الأمريكيين ، والرفيق بريجنييف
عند لقاءه مع كارتر في فيينا عرض الموقف السوفيتي المبدئي والثابت حول مختلف القضايا
ونريد من أصدقائنا العرب أن يعرفوا هذا الموقف المبدئي والثابت لنا •
اننا نعير اهميه خاصة لقضية الوحده في العالم العربي ، فكما ازداد تلاحم العرب كلما تدهور
وضع مصر وازداد وضع قيادتها سوء ، نحن نشاركم وجهات نظركم حول مؤتمري بغداد •
ونحن نرى أن وحدة الشعوب العربيه تجلت في هذين المؤتمرين واتخذت موقفا جيدا من
سياسة الامبرياليه واسرائيل والقياده المصريه ، ونحن كنا سعداء جدا لنجاح المؤتمرين
وكنا سعداء لوحدة الشعوب العربيه التي تحققت بينهما • ونحن نقدر حق التقدير
وهذا رأى راسخ للقياده السوفيتيه دور قيادة المنظمه ودوركم الشخصي يا رفيق عرفات
الذي لعبته داخل المؤتمرين • لقد كانت بعض الاطراف مستعده للانحناء أمام المعتدى
لولا دوركم ، كان هناك خلافات ولكن النتيجه كانت جيده ، وتمثلت في قرارات ناجحه • ان
القياده السوفيتيه يهمها أن لا يكون هناك تراجع عن هذه النجاحات والانجازات ، بل
يجب أن ينظر اليها كأساس في المضي في العمل المقبل • وانتم تستطيعون أن تلعبوا
دورا بذلك • ودوركم سيكون كبيرا في المستقبل ، لقد اهتممنا بحديث ملك الاردن معي
والذى مفاده تمسكه بوجوب قيام دولة مستقله ، اذا رغب الفلسطينيون بذلك ، وقد أخبرنا
وكما اقدر هذا التصريح ولكنه لدي بعض الشكوك حول جدية الملك
خدام بهذا الموقف الاردني وجدية هذا التصريح • ان ما يخدم مصالحنا المشتركه
هو عدم تراجع الملك عن تصريحه هذا • ركزتم على أهمية العمل بين الجهات الثلاثه
سوريا والعراق وأنتم وذلك في نضالكم ضد كمب ديفيد • نحن نعير أهمية كبرى له ، بعض
التعقيدات القائمه بين سوريا والعراق تستطيعون أن تلعبوا دورا ايجابيا في صدد التغلب
عليها ، لكم دور وامكانياتكم لم تستنفذ بعد • هناك موضوع آخر مرتبط بوحدة العالم العربي
لم تتطرقوا اليه نظرا لضيق الوقت هو موقف العربيه السعوديه ، الذى كان لها موقفا ايجابيا

Document 7A-14

•١٣•

الامريكان الفرصه لاصدقائهم في أوروبا لتدويل الازمة اللبنانيه ، وهذا سينعكس سلبيا على مصالح العرب ، وبالتالي تزداد امكانية السادات واسرائيل في بسط نفوذهم ، أريد أن أؤكد أن المقصود بهذه المخططات مثل الحكم الذاتي ومخطط التدويل الذى أحضره فيليب حبيب ، فان الموقف السوفيتي منها لا يختلف عن موقف العرب المتمسكين بمبادئهم ، ونعرف أيضا أن لاصدقائنا الاشتراكيين نفس الموقف استمعنا ببالغ الارتياح لتصريحكم بتطبيق ٩٠٪ من مقررات بغداد ، وهذا نجاح للعرب وهذه أول مره اسمع تقييما بهذا الشكل الواضح والدقيق ٠

الآن أريد أن أنتقل الى بعض القضايا الدوليه

ايـــران : المقصود الاحداث الاخيره المتعلقه باحتلال السفاره الامريكيه في طهران ، والنشاط الامريكي المختص بالموضوع ٠

الامريكيون توجهوا الينا منذ أيام لنقوم بدور عن طريق عميد السلك الدبلوماسي هناك وهو السفير التشيكوسلوفاكي لتسهيل تحرك الدبلوماسيين الامريكان ، نحن أعلنا للامريكان أننا متمسكون بنصوص الاتفاقات الدوليه وموقفنا نابع من ذلك (الاتفاقات المتعلقه بحصانة الدبلوماسيين) ٠

لو نظرنا الى الموضوع في اطار الاتفاقات الدوليه ، فلا بد لنا من التجاوب مع الامريكيين ، حيث لا مبرر لايران في توجيه النقد ، ولكن لو خرجنا من هذا الاطار للنظر في العلاقات الامريكيه الايرانيه ، فنحن لسنا راغبين في حماية المصالح الامريكيه رغم طلبهم منا ذلك ، لذا فلن نتورط في الحديث في هذا الموضوع ولن نحمي الامريكان لهذا الخصوص ، في رأينا ليس هناك خلاف بيننا وبينكم حول هذا الموضوع ، مع الاختلاف في أوضاعنا كدوله وأوضاعكم كحركة تحرر وطني وهذا يثير الارتياح ، نحن لحد الآن لم نحصل على رد فعل أمريكا على جوابنا ٠

أبـــوعمـــار : فهم الايرانيون من منذ ويكم أنه موافق على الطلب الامريكي ٠

غروميكو : منذ وينا لم يعارض التصريح الذى أدلى به رئيس مجلس الامن ، لانه تصريح مختصر ومتعلق بالاتفاقيات الدوليه حول السلك الدبلوماسي ٠

أبوعمـــار : لا ننسى أن البيان يحتوى على بعض التهديدات واستعمال القوه ٠

غروميكـــو : اطلعنا على هذا التصريح وليس فيه أبعد من نصوص الاتفاقات الدوليه حول التمثيل الدبلوماسي والصياغه متزنه ، وكان هناك نقاش حاد حول ذلك ، فيما يتعلق بتلميحات حول استخدام القوه فان موقفنا واضح من حيث الرفض والادانه لمثل هذه الاعمال ٠ كان الكلام يدور حول استخدام القوه عند انفجار الثورة الايرانيه ، وقفنا ضد هذا المنطق ولا زال موقفنا على حاله ٠

Document 7A-13

- ١٤ -

نحن على وشك طرح الموضوع الفلسطيني على الأمم المتحده ، وهذا مهم لنا ولكـــم هناك سؤال : ماذا تتوقعون من هذا البحث؟ ما هو الحد الأدنى الذى تطلبونـــه من هذا البحث ؟ هل فكرتم جيدا بكيفية طرح الموضوع ، وكيف يمكن تحقيق ذلك ، أرجـــو أن تجيبوا عليه بعد أن أنهي بعد قليل .

نحن بلاشك سندعم ونؤيد الموقف الفلسطيني والعربي ، ونؤيد كــل مقتـــرح وكل مشروع تقدمونه للأمم المتحده ، وهذا ينطبق على أصدقائنا الاشتراكيين ، السؤال الاخير مجرد سؤال .

المعروف أن أمريكا وقت الحديث عن قضية فلسطين يقول ممثليها في خطبهم كيف يمكـــن لنا الاعتراف بالمنظمه وقيام دولة مستقله ، والمنظمه لا تعترف باسرائيل وبقرارات الأمم المتحده المعروضه . لقد سمعنا الشرح المقنع جدا من طرفكم الخاص باسباب رفضكم لهذه القرارات لكونها تنص على اللاجئين ولا تقول شيئا عن الشعب الفلسطيني . هذه أسباب معروفه . ولكن في حديثنا مع الامريكيين نصطدم بجدار وعقبه لا يمكن تجاوزها هنا أريد أن أسألكم ، ألا تفكرون ببعض التنازلات التكتيكيه مقابل الاعتراف بالمنظمه من قبل المعسكر المعادى ؟ وهل تفكرون بموضوع الاعتراف بهذه القرارات الدوليه ؟ وفي الاعتراف بحق اسرائيل في الوجود كدولـــه ذات سياده ؟ أنا أذكر أنني تحدثت مع ييغال آلون وقد قـــال لـــــي كيف يمكن لنا الحديث عن منظمة التحرير وهي لا تعترف بحق اسرائيل في الوجود كدولـــه مستقله ولا تعترف أيضا بقرارات الأمم المتحده ، وقال لو اعترفت المنظمه بنا وبالقرارات الدوليه لكان الوضع مختلف ، في هذه الحاله نعالج الوضع بصوة اخرى .

السؤال من هو الذى يقوم بالخطوه الأولى المنظمة أم اسرائيل . قال آلون لو عملـــت اسرائيل تصريحا بهذا الخصوص فان المنظمه لا توافق على اصدار تصريح مماثل من جهتها قائم على الاعتراف باسرائيل وبالقرارات الدوليه . الآن تبدلت الحكومه ولا أدرى ما هـــو موقفهم الآن .

أسألكم هل موقفكم رافض لكل التنازلات الغير مبدئيه في هذه القضيه . المهم بالنسبة اليكـم اقامة الدولة الفلسطينيه ، مهما اختلفت الآراء فقيام الدوله هو الأساس ، وهو يشمل كل شيء .

في حديثنا مع الامريكيين كنا نشعر بمأزق وهنا أريد أن أعرف رأيكم وهذا مجرد سؤال .

بوناماريوف : أنتم تكلمتم لوحدكم أما نحن فتكلمنا اثنين .

لقد عرض غروميكو بالتفصيل الاتجاه العام للقياده السوفيتيه تجاه الشرق الأوسط وقضيـــة فلسطين ، نحن نعرف من المعلومات المتوفره لدينا ومن معلوماتكم أن منظمة التحرير تتقدم وقد خرجتم من نطاق كونكم حركة تحرر عربي ، فالوقائع معروفه بالنسبة لنا ، فاعتراف عديـــد من الدول بكم نحن مرتاحون اليه وسعداء جدا به ، نحن ساعدنا وسنساعد على ذلـــك

Document 7A-16

"١٦"

أبـو عمـار : علاقتنا بالحص جيده ، مع الرئيس سركيس لا بأس بها ، مع المجلس الاسلامي مع الجبهة القوميه مع الرئيس فرنجيه كلها جيده ، نحن في هذا العام صرفنـــــا ١٩ مليون ليره لبنانيه كتعويضات في الجنوب ، وصرفنا ٩ ملايين ليره لعـــــلاج المدنيين .

بوناماريوف : هذه رسالتكم وهي جيده ، يجب أن تظهروها في الأمم المتحده ، وتونس وختامـا أريد أن أؤكد لكم أننا في جميع محادثاتنا مع العرب وخاصة مع الرئيس الأسد كنا نصر على الحل العادل والشامل للقضيه الفلسطينيه ، هذا موقفنا أعلنـــاه في المباحثات الرسميه وعن طريق الحزب والمنظمات الشعبيه المختلفه . وفي الفتره الأخيره أنشأنا عندنا لجنه للصداقه والتضامن مع الشعب الفلسطيني . حينما كان الشعب الفيتنامي يناضل ضد أمريكا شكلنا مثل هذه اللجنه للتضامن معـــــه ومعروف أن فيتنام انتصرت بعدها ونأمل أن يتكرر النصر ، فاللجنه شكلت ونتمنـــى لكم كل النجاح .

أبـو عمـار : نحن شكلنا من جهتنا لجنـة للتضامن معكم .

بالنسبة لسؤال الرفيق غروميكو ، اذا كان وراءه نتائج فنحن على استعداد للاجابه لانه يستحق أن نبذل مجهودا ، نحن طرحنا حلول كثيره مع العلم باننا الضحيـــه في الوقت الذى لم يقدم فيه أى من أعدائنا أى حل ، نحن قلنا الدولة الديموقراطيه التي يعيش فيها العرب واليهود ، قالوا هذا تدمير لاسرائيل في سنة ١٩٧٤م قلنا نقيم الدوله الفلسطينيه على أى جزء تنسحب منه اسرائيل أو يتم تحريره ، وهذا حقنا ، قرار التقسيم الذى فرض على شعبنا يقول بند رقم واحد فيه دولة فلسطينيـه واسرائيل في اجتماع لجنة التوفيق في لوزان لم تدخل في الأمم المتحده ، قبل أن اعترفت بمسألتين : عودة اللاجئين والاعتراف بالدوله الفلسطينيه ، قالوا هذه الدوله شيوعيه وتريد أن تدمر اسرائيل ، نحن أعلنا حينما صدر البيان السوفيتي الأمريكـي أننا نقبل به ، ومع ذلك ماذا قدم الآخرون أستطيع أن أقف أمام الأمم المتحده ، وأقول ماذا قدم الآخرون ، قدموا "وداعا لمنظمة التحرير" حمله عسكريه سنة ٩٧٨ ، قدموا لنا جهنم التي فتحت علينا في الجنوب ، قدموا هذه الجريمة البشعه التـــي اسمها كامب ديفيد .

قدمنا كل هذه الأشياء ولم يقدموا شيئا ، أنا أقول أنني موافـق على البيان السوفيتي الأمريكي ، أقول أنا موافق على ما اتفقت أنت والامريكان عليه .

Document 7A-15

٠ ١٥ ٠

نحن نرى التحيه التي بعث بها الرفيق بريجنييف اليكم بمناسبة عيد ميلادكم قد ساعد على ذلك ، شأنه شأن الرساله التي بعث بها الرفيق بريجنييف الى برشلونه هذا الأمر يساعدكم عربيا ودوليا في افهام العالم والعرب جوهر السياسه السوفيتيه تجاهكم

أنتم أمام حدثين بارزين :

- مؤتمر تونس
- بحث القضيه في الأمم المتحده

لقد طرحتم موضوع مشاورات بهذا الصدد ، كنا نطلب منكم دائما أن نتشاور بهذا الصدد ، المهم جدا بهذا الشأن أن نعرف مسبقا خطوات الخصم في الأمم المتحده وأن نعرف كيف نستغل بشكل نموذجي منبر الأمم المتحده لكشف الأعمال الهجوميه التي تقوم اسرائيل في جنوب لبنان ، من المستحيل القيام بعمليه الفضح هذه داخل اسرائيل نفسها ولكن في امريكا هناك أصدقاء لاسرائيل فمن المفيد أن نقوم بالحمله لاظهار ما تقوم به اسرائيل تجاه الشيوخ والأطفال ، مستغلين بذلك كل وسائل الاعلام .

فيما يتعلق بمؤتمر تونس فأنتم تعرفون أكثر منا ، نحن موافقين على رأيكم بانه لا يجوز تحويل هذا المؤتمر كليا لبحث جنوب لبنان وابعاد بحث القضيه الكليه قضية الشرق الأوسط ، من المهم جدا أن تجندوا كل طاقاتكم من أجل هذا الهدف ، ويكون رفاقكم العرب نشطاء كي يتوج المؤتمر بقرارات سليمه ، من المهم أن نعير اهتمام خاص بالجزائر في الآونه الأخيره كان لنا صلات وثيقه مع الجزائر ، نحن استقبلنا وفد حزبي أرسلنا الرفيق نائب بريجنييف لحضور احتفالات الجزائر ، لقد قالوا لنا بان الرئيس الشاذلي بن جديد والرئيس الحزبي صالح يحياوى بانهما مصممان على السير في طريق بومدين ، نفس الكلام قالوه لرئيس وفدنا الى احتفالاتهم و وزن الجزائر حاليا كبير .

في الآونه الأخيره أجرينا اتصالات مع الحركة الوطنيه في لبنان ، بشكل خاص مع الشيوعيين ومع جنبلاط ، كلهم أكدوا لنا أن علاقاتهم مع الفلسطينيين جيده ، ويناضلوا كتفا الى كتف ضد الاسرائيليين والقياده الرجعيه في البلاد .

أبو عمار : هناك قياده مشتركه وأنا قائدها .

بوناماريوف : لهذا السبب من المهم جدا أن تكون العلاقات جيده ، ليست مع هذه المنظمات المعاديه للامبرياليه في لبنان وانما مع القوى الأخرى مثل فرنجيه مثلا . يجب أن نؤثر على قيادة لبنان كدوله ، للسوريين يجب أن يكون دور في التعامل مع لبنان ، طبعا بوجودكم في لبنان يجب أن لا تكون علاقتكم سيئه مع لبنان الدوله لان وضعكم يصبح صعبا .

Document 7A-18

"١٨"

ملاحظات حول الزيارة :

----

١) انها زيارة مؤجلة منذ أكثر من أربعة أشهر وبالتحديد منذ اتفاقية سالة ٢ ، والسوفييت هم المسؤولين عن التأجيل ، لعدم تحديدهم موعدها .

٢) وضح من تشكيل الوفد بهذا الشكل الموسع انها زيارة روتينية هدفها اعلامي لا أكثر ولا أقل .

٣) ظهر من خلال المحادثات عدم ارتياح السوفييت لتحرك المنظمة الدولي ، وتحديداً تجاه لقاء أبو عمار مع كرايسكي ، وعبروا عن ذلك بصيغ مختلفة ، كقول بوناماريوف وبشكل تشكيكي هل أصبح كرايسكي صديقا للعرب ؟ رغم تراجعه عن اسلوبه التشكيكي هذا بعد رد أبو عمار عليه .

وعبر غروميكو عن ذلك بقوله " ان الاتحاد السوفيتي لا يغير اصدقاءه ، ونأمل من أصدقائنا العرب والفلسطينيين أن يكونوا كذلك .

حاول أبو عمار نفي تهمة الشك بموقف المنظمة ، ولكن غروميكو لم يعر هذا النفي انتباهاً .

كان واضحا أن السوفييت مستائين جدا من تصرف المنظمة ، لانه على ما يبدو مقدمة لهم معلومات من بعض فصائل المقاومة مفادها أن هناك تحولا في موقف المنظمة تجاه أمريكا ، عبر عن ذلك الوفد الأرمني الذي استقبلنا في مطار ريفيان عاصمة أرمينيا حينما قال لنا ونحن معه في السيارة جيد انكم حضرتم الى موسكو لان هناك معلومات عديدة ، هنا تتهمكم بالتحول نحو أمريكا (لم يكن أبو عمار معنا في نفس السيارة) .

٤) الزيارة كان مقررا لها ثلاثة أيام ولكنها اختصرت ليوم واحد . لقد حاول أبو عمار مقابلة وزير الدفاع السوفيتي ، الا أنهم اعتذروا على ما يبدوا عن ذلك ، اضافة الى تبليغهم أبو عمار سلفا أنه لن يقابل أى من بريجنييف وكوسيغين . الأمر الذى جعله يسرع في العودة ، لانه لم يبقى مبررا للبقاء .

٥) أبدى السوفييت اهتماما خاصا بالسعودية ، وقالوا لابي عمار تستطيع أن تنقل على لساننا أن المعاهدة مع اليمن الديموقراطيه لن يكون لها انعكاس سلبي على الأوضاع في المنطقة ، ونحن لن نتدخل في شؤون أحد الداخليه ، وتستطيع أن تعطيهم كل التطمينات اللازمه .

وثورة حتى التحرير

أمين سر الجبهه

عبد الرحيم أحمد

Document 7A-17

- ١٧ -

غروميكو : هناك في البيان السوفيتي الامريكي حول عقد جنيف والحقوق الفلسطينيه ، هذا البيان الذى سألت عنه لم ينعكس فيما بعد ، طبعا لو نفذ هذا البيان لكانت الظروف أكثر ملائمة ، لا أريد على الاطلاق الالحاح على الجواب في هذا الموضوع ، اذا كان هناك تعديل في موقفكم أرجو أن تبلغونا ، لان هذا الموضوع لا يمكن الهرب منه الامريكان في كل تصريح يقولون كيف نعترف بالمنظمه وهم لا يعترفون بشيء ، هذه ديماغوجيه ولكن يجب أن نعرف كيف نواجه ذلك ، أرجو أن تفكروا به وتبدوا ملاحظات

أبو عمار : البيان السوفيتي الأمريكي الذى عطله هو أمريكا ، وهي دفعت السادات للذهاب الى القدس لقد قالوا لنا اذا تعترفوا في ٢٤٢ مع تحفظات تضعونها فاننا نعترف بكم ونفتح معكم حوار ، ونتعهد بدولة كان ذلك في عام ٩٧٧ تراجعت أمريكا بعد ذلك عن هذا الموضوع أخبرونا على لسان رشاد فرعون بان قطار التسويه سائر اذا أردتم اللحاق به والا فانتم احرار ، ثم قدموا صيغة لنعلن موافقتنا عليها بالنسبة ٢٤٢ ، وذلك من أجل شيء محدد فقط هو الحوار معنا ·

بوناماريوف : تواطئوا مع مصر ومواقفهم تعززت ·

أبو عمار : هذا يؤكد وجهة نظرنا ونظركم ، وانهم يراوغون ، لا زال جزء من الخطه الأمريكيه أن يكون الاردن هو البديل عن المنظمه ، وهذا ما يصرح به حزب العمل رسميا ، ومع هذا فان علاقتنا مع الاردن علاقه جيده ، ونحاول أن نتجاوز كل الخلافات ، عملنا معه بيانين مشتركين اكد فيها حقنا في العوده والدوله ، بيننا لجنه مشتركه ، نحاول أن ننمي هذه العلاقات رغم كل المحاولات التي تضع العراقيل في وجهها ·

بالنسبة لايران نحن لسنا وسطاء ، نحن مع ايران ومع ما يوافق عليه الخميني وليست بازركان أو شريعتمداری ·

غروميكو : اشكركم على هذا الحديث المجدى ، نحن نرى اننا نسير معكم في طريق واحد بالنسبة لقضية الشرق الأوسط ، الاتحاد السوفيتي صديق للعرب ولم يعتد تغيير اصدقائه ، ونأمل أن يبادلنا العرب والمنظمه نفس الاحساس ·

أبو عمار : المنظمه ليس بها شك ·

غروميكو : اذا كان من المفيد أن ننشر بيانا مشتركا ، عندنا مشروع أرجو أن تطلعوا عليه ·

انتهى

[Documents 8 – 15]: Graduation diplomas of PLO personnel in Communist countries

[Document 8]: Soviet diploma

Awarded by Soviet Ministry of Defence to Zyad Ibrahim Sharkas, who completed a course for infantry platoon commanders in July 1981.

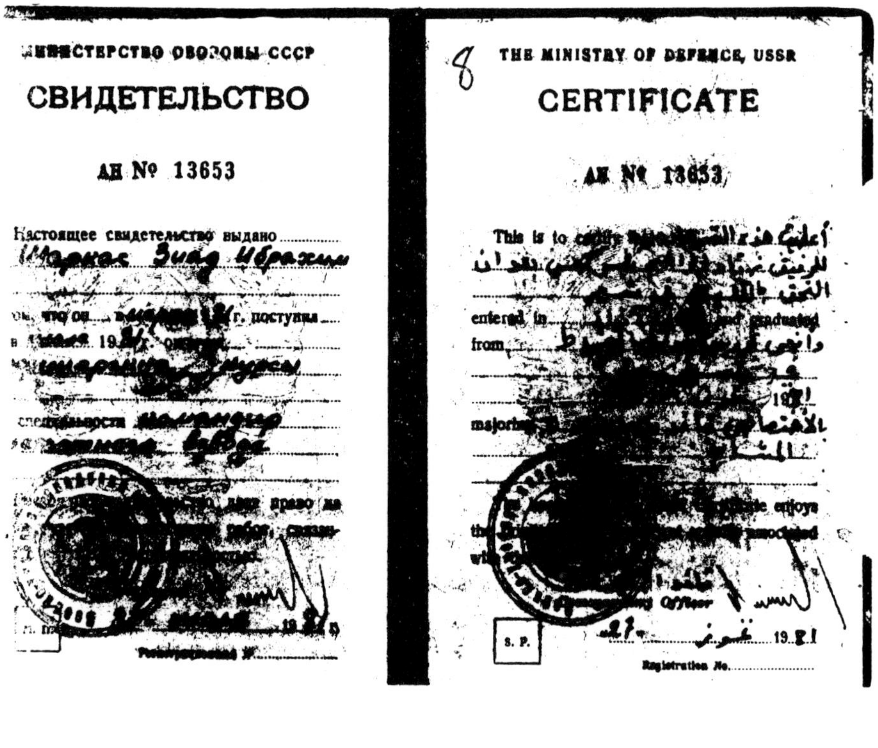

МИНИСТЕРСТВО ОБОРОНЫ СССР

СВИДЕТЕЛЬСТВО

АН № 13653

Настоящее свидетельство выдано

THE MINISTRY OF DEFENCE, USSR

CERTIFICATE

AH № 13653

This is to

entered in ... graduated

from

majoring

enjoys

Officer

S. P.

19.81

Registration No.

[Document 9]: Soviet diploma

Awarded by Soviet Ministry of Defence to Rafat 'Abd-al-Rahman Ahmad Silmi, who completed a course for platoon commanders (reconnaissance) in January 1981.

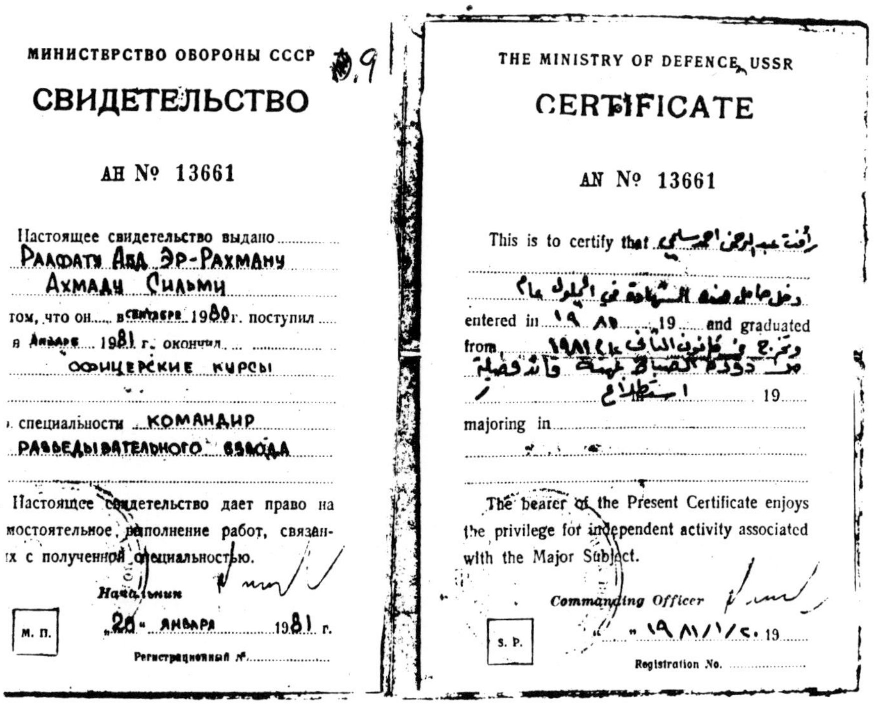

9

МИНИСТЕРСТВО ОБОРОНЫ СССР

СВИДЕТЕЛЬСТВО

АН № 13661

Настоящее свидетельство выдано Раафату Абд Эр-Рахману Ахмаду Сильми

том, что он в сентябре 1980 г. поступил в январе 1981 г. окончил офицерские курсы

по специальности командир разведывательного взвода

Настоящее свидетельство дает право на самостоятельное выполнение работ, связанных с полученной специальностью.

Начальник

М. П. „20" января 1981 г.

Регистрационный №

THE MINISTRY OF DEFENCE USSR

CERTIFICATE

AN № 13661

This is to certify that رأفت عبد الرحمن احمد سلمي

دخل حامل هذه الشهادة في الكلية عام

entered in ١٩٨٠ 19 and graduated

from وتخرج في كانون الثاني عام ١٩٨١ من دورة الضباط جهة قائد فصيلة استطلاع 19

majoring in

The bearer of the Present Certificate enjoys the privilege for independent activity associated with the Major Subject.

Commanding Officer

S. P. " ١٩٨١/١/٢٠ 19

Registration No.

[Document 10]: Soviet diploma

Awarded to Captain 'Abd-al-'Aziz Mahmud Abu Fedda in March 1976, upon completion of a course for infantry battalion commanders.

МИНИСТЕРСТВО ОБОРОНЫ СССР 10

СВИДЕТЕЛЬСТВО

АН № 13765

Настоящее свидетельство выдано капитану Абдул-Азизу Махмуду Абу-Феддаху в том, что он в окт. 1975 г. поступил и в марте 1976 г. окончил I Высшие Офицерские курсы „Выстрел"

по специальности: командир пехотного батальона.

Настоящее свидетельство дает право на самостоятельное выполнение работ, связанных с полученной специальностью.

Начальник I курсов „Выстрел"

М. П.

26 „ марта 1976 г.

Регистрационный № 3012/146

THE MINISTRY OF DEFENCE, USSR

CERTIFICATE

AN № 13765

This is to certify that Captain Abdul-Aziz Mahmood Abu-Fedda entered in October 1975 and graduated from the Vystrel Academy in March 1976 majoring in the course of Infantry Battalion Commander.

The bearer of the Present Certificate enjoys the privilege for independent activity associated with the Major Subject.

Commanding Officer, Vystrel Academy

S. P.

26 " March 1976

Registration No. 3012/146

[Document 11]: Soviet diploma

Awarded by the Ministry of Defence to Muhammad Mabry Hussain upon completing a course for electrical technicians at the Odessa Military School in June 1980.

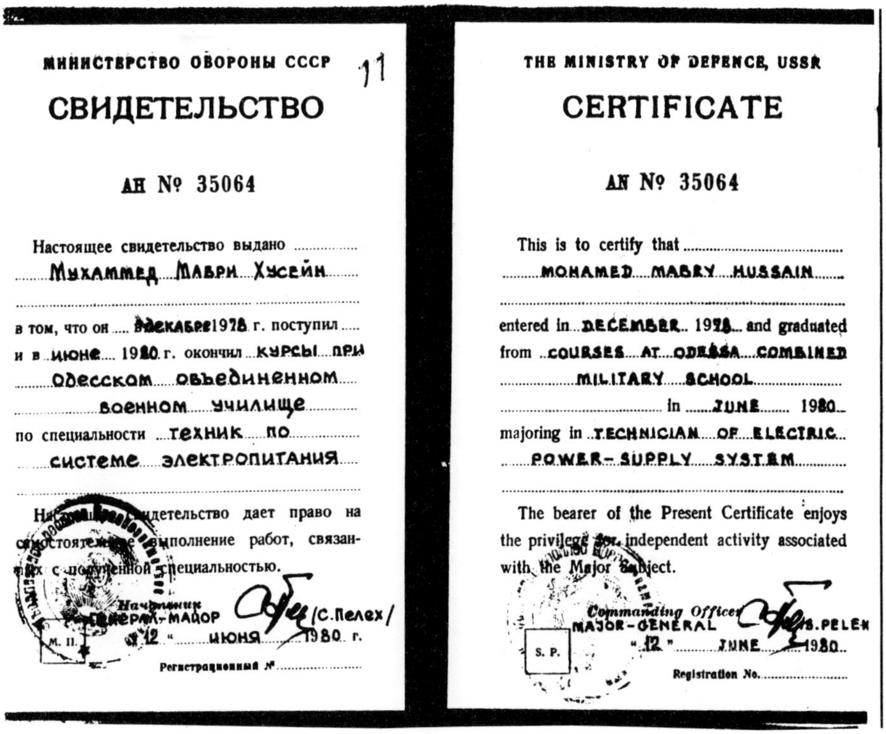

МИНИСТЕРСТВО ОБОРОНЫ СССР

11

СВИДЕТЕЛЬСТВО

АН № 35064

Настоящее свидетельство выдано Мухаммед Мабри Хусейн

в том, что он в декабре 1978 г. поступил и в июне 1980 г. окончил курсы при Одесском объединенном военном училище

по специальности техник по системе электропитания

Настоящее свидетельство дает право на самостоятельное выполнение работ, связанных с полученной специальностью.

Начальник генерал-майор /С. Пелех/

« 12 » июня 1980 г.

М. П.

Регистрационный №

THE MINISTRY OF DEFENCE, USSR

CERTIFICATE

AN № 35064

This is to certify that MOHAMED MABRY HUSSAIN

entered in DECEMBER 1978 and graduated from COURSES AT ODESSA COMBINED MILITARY SCHOOL in JUNE 1980

majoring in TECHNICIAN OF ELECTRIC POWER-SUPPLY SYSTEM

The bearer of the Present Certificate enjoys the privilege for independent activity associated with the Major Subject.

Commanding Officer MAJOR-GENERAL S. PELEH

« 12 » JUNE 1980

S. P.

Registration No.

[Document 12]: Hungarian diploma

Awarded to Muhammad Farlin Kador by the Hungarian Military Academy upon completion of a course for T-34 tank drivers, in February 1981.

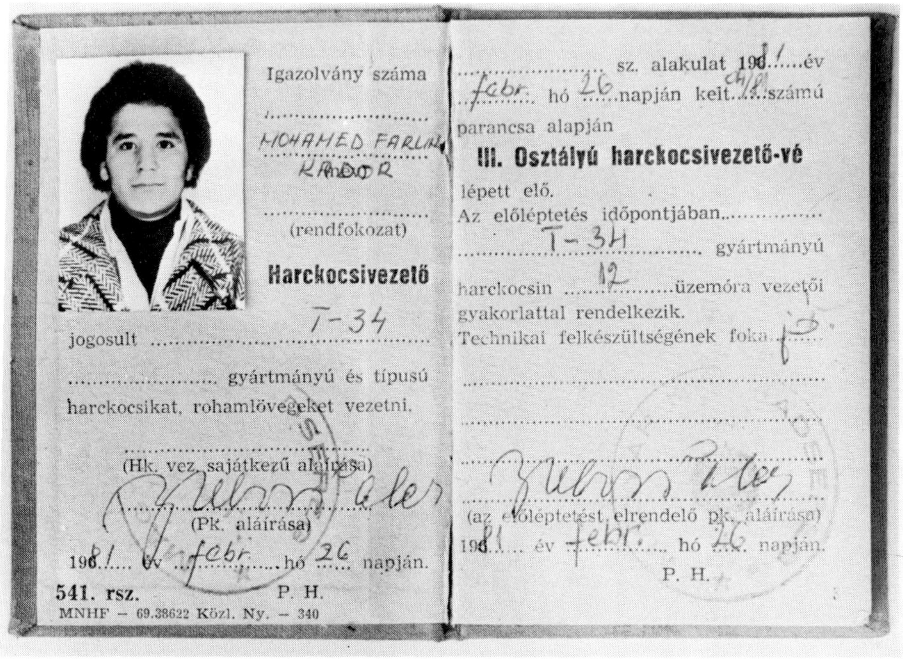

Igazolvány száma

MOHAMED FARLIN KADOR

(rendfokozat)

Harckocsivezető

jogosult T-34

gyártmányú és típusú harckocsikat, rohamlövegeket vezetni.

(Hk. vez. sajátkezű aláírása)

(Pk. aláírása)

1981 év febr. hó 26 napján.

541. rsz. P. H.

MNHF – 69.38622 Közl. Ny. – 340

sz. alakulat 1981 év febr. hó 26 napján kelt 4/81 számú parancsa alapján

III. Osztályú harckocsivezető-vé

lépett elő.

Az előléptetés időpontjában T-34 gyártmányú harckocsin 12 üzemóra vezetői gyakorlattal rendelkezik.

Technikai felkészültségének foka jó

(az előléptetést elrendelő pk. aláírása)

1981 év febr. hó 26 napján.

P. H.

[Document 13]: Yugoslav permit

Issued to the officer 'Awad Esead Ziad.

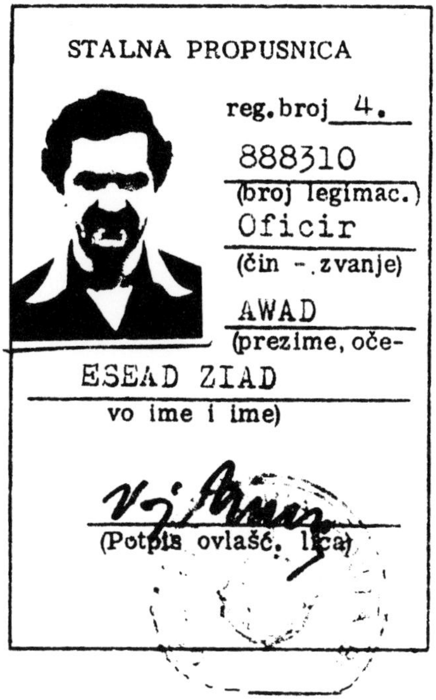

STALNA PROPUSNICA

reg.broj 4.

888310
(broj legimac.)

Oficir
(čin - zvanje)

AWAD
(prezime, oče-

ESEAD ZIAD
vo ime i ime)

(Potpis ovlašć. lica)

[Document 14]: Vietnamese diploma

Awarded to Mahmud 'Abdul-Fattan Zeidan in May 1980, upon completion of a course in Vietnam.

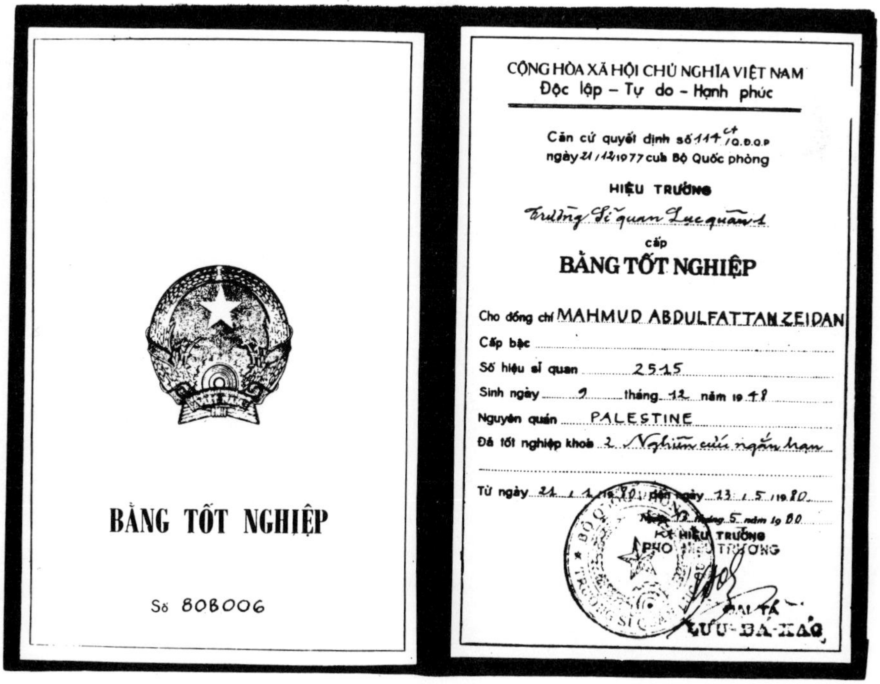

BẰNG TỐT NGHIỆP

Số 808006

CỘNG HÒA XÃ HỘI CHỦ NGHĨA VIỆT NAM
Độc lập – Tự do – Hạnh phúc

Căn cứ quyết định số 114 ct/Q.Đ.Q.P
ngày 21/12/1977 của Bộ Quốc phòng

HIỆU TRƯỞNG

Trường Sĩ quan Lục quân 1

cấp

BẰNG TỐT NGHIỆP

Cho đồng chí MAHMUD ABDULFATTAN ZEIDAN
Cấp bậc
Số hiệu sĩ quan 2515
Sinh ngày 9 tháng 12 năm 1948
Nguyên quán PALESTINE
Đã tốt nghiệp khoá 2 Nghiên cứu ngắn hạn

Từ ngày 21/1/1980 đến ngày 13/5/1980

Ngày 13 tháng 5 năm 1980
KT HIỆU TRƯỞNG
PHÓ [illegible] TRƯỞNG

[Document 15]: Soviet diploma

Awarded to Colonel Rashad Ahmad 'Abd-al-'Aziz al-Nebris by the Soviet Ministry of Defence, upon completion of a course for armoured battalion commanders in January 1981.

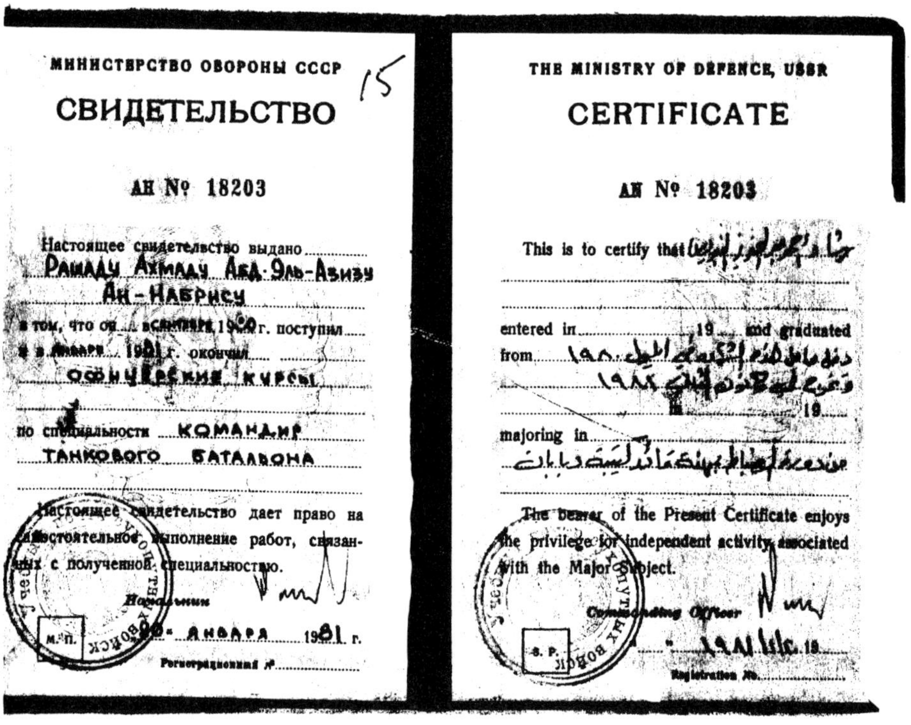

МИНИСТЕРСТВО ОБОРОНЫ СССР

15

СВИДЕТЕЛЬСТВО

АН № 18203

Настоящее свидетельство выдано Рашаду Ахмаду Абд-Эль-Азизу Ан-Набрису

в том, что он в сентябре 1980 г. поступил и в январе 1981 г. окончил офицерские курсы

по специальности командир танкового батальона

Настоящее свидетельство дает право на самостоятельное выполнение работ, связанных с полученной специальностью.

Начальник

января 1981 г.

Регистрационный №

THE MINISTRY OF DEFENCE, USSR

CERTIFICATE

АН № 18203

This is to certify that

entered in ... 19... and graduated from ... 19...

majoring in

The bearer of the Present Certificate enjoys the privilege for independent activity associated with the Major Subject.

Commanding Officer

19

Registration No.

[Document 16]: Armour course in Hungary

The document lists 3 officers and 8 NCO's.

حركة التحرير الوطني الفلسطيني
فتـــح
القيادة : العامه لقوات العاصفــه
قيادة : قوات الكرامـــه

الرقــم : ـــع ٣ / ٥ / ١٢٨٦
التاريخ / / ايلول ٨١

الاخوه / مديرية التدريب في قوات العاصفه
الموضوع / الـــــدورات

تحية الثوره وبعد ،

كتــاب العمليات رقم المجر / ١٥٨ تاريخ ٨١/٨/٢٢

١ــ ارسل اليكم الاخوه المذكورين تاليا من مرتبنا / القوه المحمولـــــــــه منسبينا لدورة الدروع التى ستعقد في المجر وهم :ــ

٣٢١٣٦	ملازم اول سليمان عبد العزيز
١١٦٤٤	ملازم حسني حسين احمد
٣١٤٩١	ملازم اسماعيل محمود ابراهيم
٣٢٦٥٢	ساعد نظمي سعيد محمد
٣٢٢٧٣	رقيب اول سلامه سالم ابو حويمان
٤١٠٥٢	= عبد الحميد محمد عبد الحميد
٨٠٣٧٢	= احمد خليل زيـــد
٨٧٢٤٥	سهيل توفيق ابو الجديان
٩٠٨٠٩	عزمي حسني صـــلاح
٩١٥٧٠	صبحي محمود مصطفى
٩٢٨٧٥	محمد سويلم غواشمه
	جمال نصر الخطيب

٢ــ يرجى اجرائكم واعـــــلامنا التحاقهـــم ،

وثوره حتى النصـــــــر ،

العقيد الركن
قائد قوات الكرامـــه
ابو هـــاجم

نسخه الى :ــ
العمليات المركزيه اشاره لاعداد للعلم
القوه المحموله لارسالهم لمعسكر التدريب
الحفـــــــظ

[Document 17]: Air defence course in Vietnam

A PLO order asking area and unit commanders to appoint candidates for an air defence course in Vietnam to begin on 20 December 1981.

حركة التحرير الوطني الفلسطيني
"فتح"
القيادة العامة لقوات العاصفة

الرقم سام / ٢٤٥
التاريخ ١٣/ ١٢/ ١٩٨١

قائد قوات اليرموك (١)
قائد قوات الكرامه (١)
قائد قوات ألقسطل (١)
قائد قوات اجنادين (١)
قائد قوات المليشيا (١)
قائد قوة الـ١٧ (١)
وحدة الدفاع الجوى (١)
جيش التحرير الفلسطيني (١)
الكفاح المسلح (١)

تحية الثوره وبعد

١ . تقرر ايفاد عدد من الضباط الى جمهورية فيتنام الاشتراكيه وذلك للاطلاع على نظام الدفاع الجوى في فيتنام ولمدة خمسة واربعون يوما .

٢ . يرجى ارسال منسبيكم الينا مع جوازات سفرهم حيث من المفروض ان يكون الوفد في فيتنام يوم ٢٠/ ١٢/ ١٩٨١ .

وثوره حتى النصر .....

القياده العامه لقوات العاصفه
" ابو الوليد "

[Document 18]: Armour courses in Hungary

A list of 32 PLO trainees to be dispatched to various armour courses in Hungary in December 1981.

حركة التحرير الوطني الفلسطيني
«فتح»
القيادة العامة لقوات العاصفة
العمليات المركزية

الرقم ....
التاريخ ....

الإخوة القيادة العامة لقوات العاصفة

الموضوع: انتخاب دورة الكلية العسكرية في ألمانيا الديمقراطية

تحية الثورة وبعد

إشارة لكتابكم رقم ألمانيا الديمقراطية ٢٦/١ وتاريخ ١٩٨١/١٢/٢

١- اجتمعت اللجنة بكامل أعضائها وتم اختيار الإخوة المذكورين في الكشف المرفق وعددهم (٣٢) طالبا تتوفر فيهم الشروط المطلوبة حسب كتابكم أعلاه

٢- لم يتم فحصهم طبيا لهم جميعا من قبل اللجنة، لذا يرجى إجراء ذلك عن طريقكم

٣- توصي اللجنة المباشرة بتجميعهم فوراً في الكلية العسكرية وتحت إشراف كادر جيد ومناسب للعسكرية لإعدادهم للالتحاق بالدورة في الوقت المحدد

وثورة حتى النصر

رئيس اللجنة
العقيد
ابو هاجم

عضو [signature] ١٢/٢٩

عضو غسان

عضو ابو لؤي [signature]

Document 18A-2

حركة التحرير الوطني الفلسطيني
« فتح »
القيادة العامة لقوات العاصفة
العمليات المركزية

الرقم ....
التاريخ ....

مسلسل	الأسم	مسلسل	الأسم
١-	عصام عبدالرزاق الموتي	١٩-	زياد خالد محمود أبوالرب
٢-	فايز رفيق حمدان	٢٠-	يوسف دخل الله عبدالله سلامه
٣-	منصور محمد منصور	٢١-	رضوان أبراهيم فرد حامد
٤-	جمال حمدي عطور	٢٢-	جمال محمد حسن درباس
٥-	أبراهيم خالد محمد خالد	٢٣-	هشام حسن فريجه
٦-	مصطفى موسى مصطفى	٢٤-	أبراهيم مصبح البلوي
٧-	فاخر فخر الأسعد	٢٥-	خالد حسن اليازجي
٨-	محمد أحمد على الثقافي	٢٦-	محمد شحادة رشيد
٩-	جعفر ابراهيم أحمد رشيد	٢٧-	عائذ محمد أبو بكر
١٠-	سليمان محمد محمود قنديل	٢٨-	حسام عبدالعزيز حسن عودة
١١-	عماد الدين قاسم أحمد	٢٩-	نضال صلاح صفوان
١٢-	ماهر سليمان محمد شحاده	٣٠-	على خلف حسن شتيوي
١٣-	يوسف دياب أحمد	٣١-	سليمان صالح سليمان
١٤-	هشام عبدالعزيز مطيط	٣٢-	هاني خالد التميمي
١٥-	عوض صالح حامد		
١٦-	هشام صالح يوسف سليمان		
١٧-	عبدالكريم محمد ناجي		
١٨-	سليمان محمد حسين ابو بكره		

٢٩/١٢

ابو لؤي

[Document 19]: Company commander course in Bulgaria

A report on misbehaviour of a PLO participant in a course for company commanders in Bulgaria, 29 August 1980. Lt. Mahmoud Muhammad al-Rawai', who signed the report to the PLO operations staff, begs that he be allowed to complete his course. The names of another nine PLO participants appear in the report.

السيد مدير العمليات المركزية

الموضوع: تقرير حول دورة بلغاريا العسكرية

تحية وبعد

لقد وصلنا الى صوفيا يوم ٢٩/٨/١٩٨٠، حيث نقلنا الى مكان انعقاد الدورة في مدينة «فراتسا»، وحيث وجدنا أن الأصدقاء البلغار كانوا قد وفروا لنا كل الحاجات والامكانيات اللازمة والتي تفي وتفوق كل ما نحتاج. أما من ناحية التدريب فقد توفرت كذلك كل متطلباته بصورة منظمة، ما عدا مسألة المترجمين الى اللغة مباشرة، حيث كانت تتم الترجمة من اللغة البلغارية الى اللغة الانجليزية، ثم الى اللغة العربية. هذا وقد سار التدريب - بالرغم من ذلك - بشكل طبيعي، مع العلم بأننا جميعًا وحتى الاصدقاء البلغار متفقون بأنه لو كانت الترجمة من اللغة البلغارية الى اللغة العربية مباشرة لكان أفضل بكثير، ويبدو أن مسألة الترجمة الى اللغة العربية مباشرة تشكل مشكلة بالنسبة لوزارة الدفاع البلغارية لكون هذه الدورة - على ما يبدو - هي الأولى من نوعها. ومنذ الأيام الأولى بدأت بعض الاصوات تشتم وتسب على البلغار وتنعتهم بالتقصير، وتطالب البلغار بتنفيذ مطالب لا تليق بمثل شعبنا، ولا تعطي صورة صحيحة عن تقاليدنا النضالية، وهي مطالب استفزازية مثل:

- طالب الاخوة قادة الكتائب أن تكون لهم "امتيازات" مختلفة عن السرايا، ومخالفة للترتيبات المقررة من قبل قيادة الكلية، والمتمثلة في أن يكون لهم قاعة خاصة بهم للطعام دون غيرهم من الرتب الأخرى
- أن تكون من حقهم "النزول" لفراتسا بعد الدوام وبشكل دائم.
- فرض الأخ (الرائد رضوان أبو الغصان والرائد سميح الناطور والنقيب محمد أبو غربية) أنفسهم كقيادة لكل المجموعات من كتائب وسرايا وفصائل مخالفين بذلك قرارات مديرية التدريب ودون مشورة أحد في الدورة.
- طالبوا من البلغار أن يدمجوا الفصائل مع السرايا مخالفين بذلك أيضًا ترتيبات مديرية التدريب، ودون الرجوع الى أحد في الدورة، مع العلم بأن البلغار كانوا قد جهزوا للفصائل مكانًا خاصًا يتناسب مع مستواهم التدريبي.
- لقد طالبوا كذلك أن يكون لهم لباس خاص كما هو لباس الضباط البلغار مثيرين ضجة حول ذلك، وعكسوا هذا الموقف على السرايا والفصائل.

ورغم استجابة الاصدقاء البلغار لمعظم هذه المطالب، إلا أن

Document 19A-2,3

(٢)

الرائد رضوان والرائد سميح مع آخرين ، قد زادوا من حدة مواقفهم ، وهم رفضوا على
إعلان الإضراب احتجاجاً على عدم وجود مترجمين من اللغة البلغارية إلى اللغة العربية
مباشرة ، وحددوا يوماً للإضراب عن التعليم نهائياً حتى يُستجاب لمطلبهم ، وكان
ذلك دون الرجوع إلى المشتركين في الدورة والتي تشمل عديداً من الإخوة والرفاق
من كافة المنظمات الفلسطينية ، فقمت مع مجموعة من الزملاء بالاتصال بقيادة
الدورة (وخاصة بالأخ الرائد رضوان) وبينت بأن هذا الموقف يتعارض مع سياسة
منظمة التحرير ويضر بالصداقة الفلسطينية البلغارية ، كما يستدعي هذا الأمر أخذ
موافقة العمليات المركزية ، ولا يحل مشكلة المترجمين ، وكان رأينا الذي اقترحناه
على الأخ الرائد رضوان أن يتصل هو والمقدم علي قاسم بمكتب منظمة التحرير في
صوفيا لإجراء الاتصالات المناسبة … الرسمي … سواء … قيادتنا
في بيروت … مع وزارة الدفاع البلغارية ، على أن تبقى الدراسة تسير
بشكل طبيعي حرصاً على سمعة الدورة وعلى حسن العلاقة مع بلغاريا .
فتظاهر بالموافقة ، ثم فوجئنا في اليوم الصباحي بأن الرائد سميح وكذلك
الرائد رضوان والنقيب وجيه يطلبون منا دخول قاعات الدروس ، وطلبوا
من المترجمين الطلاب أن يمتنعوا عن الترجمة ، وكادت أن تنشب … بينهم إلى
… نتيجة لهذا الموقف ، إلا أنني وبعض الإخوة والرفاق … نجحنا
… في … خوفاً من تفاقم الأمور ، ورغم ذلك … تعطل
التعليم مدة يومين أو أكثر نتيجة لهذا الموقف ، وعكس استياءً … بدا لدى
مدربينا البلغار ، مما استدعى حضور نائب المنطقة العسكرية الذي …
باستياء ، والذي تحدث عن قضية الترجمة وبأنها تشكل مشكلة لديهم ،
ويمكن بالصبر والاتصال بالمسؤولين والاستمرار في تلقي الدروس … أن تحل
هذه المشكلة ، ورغم ما أبداه المسؤول من البلغار من استعداد لحل هذه
المشكلة إلا أن نفراً من الزملاء على رأسهم (الرائد سميح الناطور) والأخ
علي من دورة السرايا وهو لبناني الأصل وهو معادي للشيوعية والعلاقات
الفلسطينية البلغارية ، وليس ليهمه إلا الدورة وتخريبها وتحميل البلغار
مسؤولية ذلك) ، هذا وقد علمنا بأن الإخوة في صوفيا قد أضربوا عن
التعليم ، وفي اليوم التالي للإضراب حضر الأخ المقدم علي قاسم والأخ لؤي
وحدثنا حول موضوع الإضراب في اجتماع لكل الدورة ، حيث قال : نحن قد
أخطأنا سياسياً في هذا الموقف ، وكان من المفروض ألا يحدث ذلك ، كما
تحدث عن الموقف المبدئي لبلغاريا مع الشعب الفلسطيني وقضاياه العادلة
شعبنا ، ولم يكن الأخ رضوان أو سميح في هذا الاجتماع ، وقد حدثت بعض
التصرفات التي أشرنا إليها سابقاً وغير المقتنعة بحديث لؤي وعلي قاسم

وعند عودة الإخوة (رضوان وسميح) من صوفيا حيث كانا قد ذهبا لإحضار
المقدم علي قاسم ومناقشة الأمور معه ، في الوقت الذي وصل فيه إلى "فراتسا"
دون أن يلتقوا ، حاولا (رضوان وسميح) تبرير الإضراب ، ورفضا الاعتراف
بأن هذه الدعوة خاطئة ، مؤكدا أنهما مصران على المطالبة بالمترجمين بالصورة
التي يريانها مناسبة .

وبعد أن حلت جزئياً قضية المترجمين في "فراتسا" حيث حضر طالبان
فلسطينيان للترجمة ، استمر موقف هذه الزمرة في عرقلة التعليم والتدريب ،
مما تأكد بأن هنالك اتجاهاً يعمل لإفشال الدورة ، حيث تمت مجموعة
من الممارسات غير صحيحة مثل :

– المطالبة بأن تقوم سرية من القوات البلغارية بتنفيذ المشروع العملي بدلاً
منهم ، وأن يكتفوا هم فقط بالمراقبة ووضع الملاحظات ، وقد أثار
هذا الموقف انزعاجاً لدى البلغار .

– رفض الإخوة في قادة الكتائب أن يحملوا تجهيزات الميدان ، ورفضوا
أوامر المدرب والذي أبلغ بدوره ذلك إلى قائد الكلية ، ولكي يتفادى
البلغار حصول مشكلة ، أحضروا أفراداً منهم لحمل التجهيزات في الباص ،
وحمل الجميع ونقلهم إلى ميدان التطبيق .

– اعتراضهم على بعض المواد المقررة في المنهج مثل (صيانة الآليات)
مثلاً وادعائهم بأنهم يعرفون أكثر من مدربيهم ، وتعرضهم لهم أثناء
إلقاء الدروس ومحاولة تخطيئهم والتقليل من شأنهم ، ومثالاً على ذلك
… في قسم الكتائب قد حضر إلى ميدان التطبيق التكتيكي
في درس خاصة بقيادة السرايا تاركاً دروسه ، وتدخل مباشرة في الدرس
دون إذن من النقيب البلغاري ، وادعى أن هنالك خطأ في التعليم مما
استدعى النقيب البلغاري لأن يطلب منه بكل أدب عدم التدخل في درسه
والعودة إلى درسه .

– وفي إحدى دروس التطبيق (ترتيب ما قبل القتال) للسرايا ، وعندما طلب
منا المعلم البلغاري تنفيذ ذلك بالسير ثمانية كيلومترات كما المفروض اعتبره
هؤلاء "انتقاماً" وبدأوا يحرضون على عدم تنفيذ هذا الأمر ، وطلبوا
أن تنفذه وحدات بلغارية أمامهم وبدلاً منهم . وفي ضوء ذلك بدأت
مناقشات حادة كادت أن تفشل الدرس ، وقام مجموعة من الإخوة وكنت
أحدهم بإقناع المتنقصين ، بأن هذا تدريب مطلوب ولا حاجة من أجله ، ويجب
أن يكون قائد السرية قادراً على السير ثمانية كيلومترات كما يستوجب موضوع
(ترتيب ما قبل القتال) وكما هو معروف .

Document 19A-4,5

(٤)

واستمرت محاولات تخريب الدورة، وفي نفس اليوم وأمام الطابور، وكنا في اجتماع عام للذهاب إلى تناول الغداء ولم يكن يوجد أحد من البلغار، تحدث الأخ الرائد صبحي بأن بعض الزملاء قد تحدث إليه مستاءين من أسلوب التعليم، ومشككاً في جدواه أو فائدته، وطالبوا بتبليغ ذلك إلى آمر الكلية واستعداد الرائد صبحي لتبليغ ذلك إلى آمر الكلية والجنرال الذي سيحضر من صوفيا إلى ثلاثتنا للمشاركة في عيد الجيش، وبدأ التوتر في صفوف المجتمعين وأصبحت شبيهة بالفترة السابقة التي حدثت في قضية الاضراب الخاص بالترجمة،

وقد استأذنت موجهاً حديثي إلى الأخ الرائد صبحي وحذرته من تنفيذ ذلك، وطلبت أن يكون حديثي متكاملاً في الاجتماع المسائي للدورة كالعادة. وفوجئت بمقاطعة من الأخ "وجيه" الذي طلب مني أن أتحدث في تلك اللحظة فوراً وليس أمام الاجتماع المسائي، فقلت له إن الوقت غير مناسب فنحن متوجهون الى تناول طعام الغداء، وسيكون المجال أفضل عند اجتماع المساء، فرد علي باستفزاز وصراخ وبطريقة غير لائقة أمام كل المجتمعين، مما اضطرني أن أرد عليه بطريقة تليق بحديثه ولم تحدث أية مضاعفات، إلا أنني فوجئت بأن الاجتماع لم ينعقد كالعادة، وسمعت بأن الأخ رضوان ووجيه قد أرسلا تقريراً، ودون إشعاري أو مناقشتي حتى ليوم عودتي إلى بيروت.

ولقد حصلت عدة مشاكل ومشادات عنيفة وداخلية وإساءات كثيرة دون أن يبلغ فيها أو تكتب فيها التقارير مثل:

— إن الكثير كان يخرج "فسحة" ويعود بعد الوقت المحدد من قبل المدرسة [illegible] من قبل دورة الكلية لقادة لدورة الفلسطينيين وأمام الاجتماع العام في الطابور، كالمشادة العنيفة التي حصلت بين "أسد بغداد" و"سميح" وذلك لمرتين وإحداهما أمام البلغار داخل المطعم.

— كذلك مشادة بين اثنين من قادة السرايا في الطابور "طابور الهندسة" وأمام البلغار وهما (جبار وجواد)

— كذلك مشادة كلامية تطورت إلى ضرب بالكراسي واستخدام الأكواب الزجاجية في المهجع، مما أدى إلى حدوث جراح بين الأخوين وهما (فتحي ونوح) وجرى معالجتهما من قبل الأصدقاء البلغار، وكان أقصى إجراء اتخذ ضدهما هو توجيه إنذار من قيادة الدورة الفلسطينية في فرانسا.

— وكذلك عدة قضايا أخلاقية في (فرانسا) لا تليق بدورتنا وبمهمتنا، لدرجة أن هناك أشخاصاً تعرفهم رضوان حسب قوله، أقاموا علاقات جنسية مع فتيات متحللين أسمر، وقد حضرت إحدى الفتيات إلى البوابة وطلبت إرضواء للزواج معها، مع اعتراض البلغار على ذلك والنصيحة بعدم الاقتراب من أمثال هذه الفتاة.

— وكذلك المحاولات الدائمة لاستفزاز البلغار في المحاضرات السياسية مثل: ما الذي قدمه المعسكر الاشتراكي للثورة، وذلك في معرض الاستهزاء والتقليل من المساعدات الاشتراكية، وطالبوا بأحاديثهم الاتحاد السوفياتي. وكذلك الإساءة إلى المنظمات الفلسطينية كالديموقراطية والجبهة الشعبية والمنظمات الفلسطينية الأخرى. وبهدف خلق تكتلات في الدورة وتنافس بين (الرائد رضوان وصبحي) على قيادة الدورة.

ولقد كنت أحاول أن أبين خطورة هذه الممارسات، وكنت أجد تجاوباً من معظم زملاء الدورة، وبروح أخوية لنا نعمل على وقف مثل هذه الممارسات السيئة، على قاعدة الحرص على العلاقة والصداقة بالأصدقاء البلغار، والتي كانت من إحدى توجيهات وتوصيات الأخ القائد العام للثورة الفلسطينية، وكذلك بروح الحرص على استمرار الدورة وتماسكها والاستفادة منها، ولتكون صورة مشرقة لنضال شعبنا وثورته.

والظاهر أن هنالك أفراداً موتورين كانوا أداة هدم للدورة، وللإساءة ليس لأنفسهم فقط، وإنما للروح الانضباطية الثورية لمناضلي شعبنا، وأعطوا صورة سيئة عن المناضل الفلسطيني وأساءوا بشكل فظ ومسيء للمدرسين البلغار وإلى علاقة الصداقة المتينة التي تربط بين [illegible] الشعبين الفلسطيني والبلغاري.

وكمحاولة لخروج هؤلاء من مأزقهم ومن التبعات التي قد تصيبهم نتيجة لكل هذه الممارسات السيئة، والعقاب الذي سينزل بهم، وجهوا تهمتهم إلى أكثر الناس انضباطاً، وتشبثاً بمسلكياتهم، وأكثر الناس حرصاً على استمرار الدورة ووحدتها وتماسكها، وأكثر الناس دعوة إلى تنمية العلاقات بين الأصدقاء في البلدان الاشتراكية ومنهم الأصدقاء البلغار، وكان لا بد من كبش فداء"، فكان في شخصي.

لست في معرض دفاع عن نفسي، فهذا ما لا يمكن أن يخطر على بالي ولا على بال المناضلين الوطنيين الشرفاء وكل التقدميين الذين عرفوا وتعرفوا إلى فكري ونضالي وممارستي التي لا يمكن أن تكون موضوع مناقشة. ولكنني أشير إلى أنه أكثر من نصف الدورة قد تضامنوا معي، وأعلنوا عن استعدادهم لمرافقتي والسفر معي وإلغاء هذه الدورة بالنسبة إليهم، احتجاجاً على سلوك تلك الفئة، وتضامناً معي لموقفي الصحيح ...

Document 19A-6

(٦)

ولكنني رفضت إلغاءهم لدورتهم، وأكدت عليهم أن يبقوا في الدورة، وأن
يتابعوا عملهم، وأن يحاولوا التخفيف ما أمكن من مسلكية هؤلاء المشينة،
وأن تستمر الدورة موحدة، وأن تستفيد منها، وأن يحافظوا على علاقة
طيبة بين المدربين البلغار، وإعطاء صورة مشرقة عن شعبنا ونضاله وحبه
للعلم والنظام، وأن يحاولوا باستمرار أن يحلوا المشاكل الطارئة بالحوار
الموضوعي والديموقراطي.

لقد فوجئت باستدعائي من قبلكم، وقطع الدورة فوراً،
لمهمة عسكرية في لبنان. ولا أتكلم أن اتجاهي السياسي، وعلاقتي الطيبة مع
معظم أفراد الدورة، ودفاعي عن الانضباط، وعن استمرار الدورة بصورة صحية
وشجبي لكل ما يسيء إلى سمعة شعبنا، والعلاقات الطيبة بين شعبنا
بقيادة منظمة التحرير الفلسطينية، وبين الشعب البلغاري، كل هذه الأشياء كانت
الأسباب الخفية لاستدعائي الفوري إلى بيروت وقطع الدورة،
ولهذا فإنني أتوجه إليكم بصدقة أن تأمروا بعودتي الفورية للالتحاق
بالدورة، ومحاسبة المسؤولين - كل المسؤولين - عن تلك الممارسات
السيئة التي أشرت إليها في تقريري هذا.

وإنها لثورة حتى النصر

مقدمه
الملازم: محمود محمد الرواغ
مرتبات جيش التحرير الفلسطيني
التوقيع:

تاريخ
صورة إلى: -
١- مستر أمر جيش التحرير الفلسطيني في لبنان.
٢- مديرية التدريب العسكري.

[Document 20]: Company commander course in China

Four units of the PLO are urged to dispatch three officers each, for a course for company commanders in China.

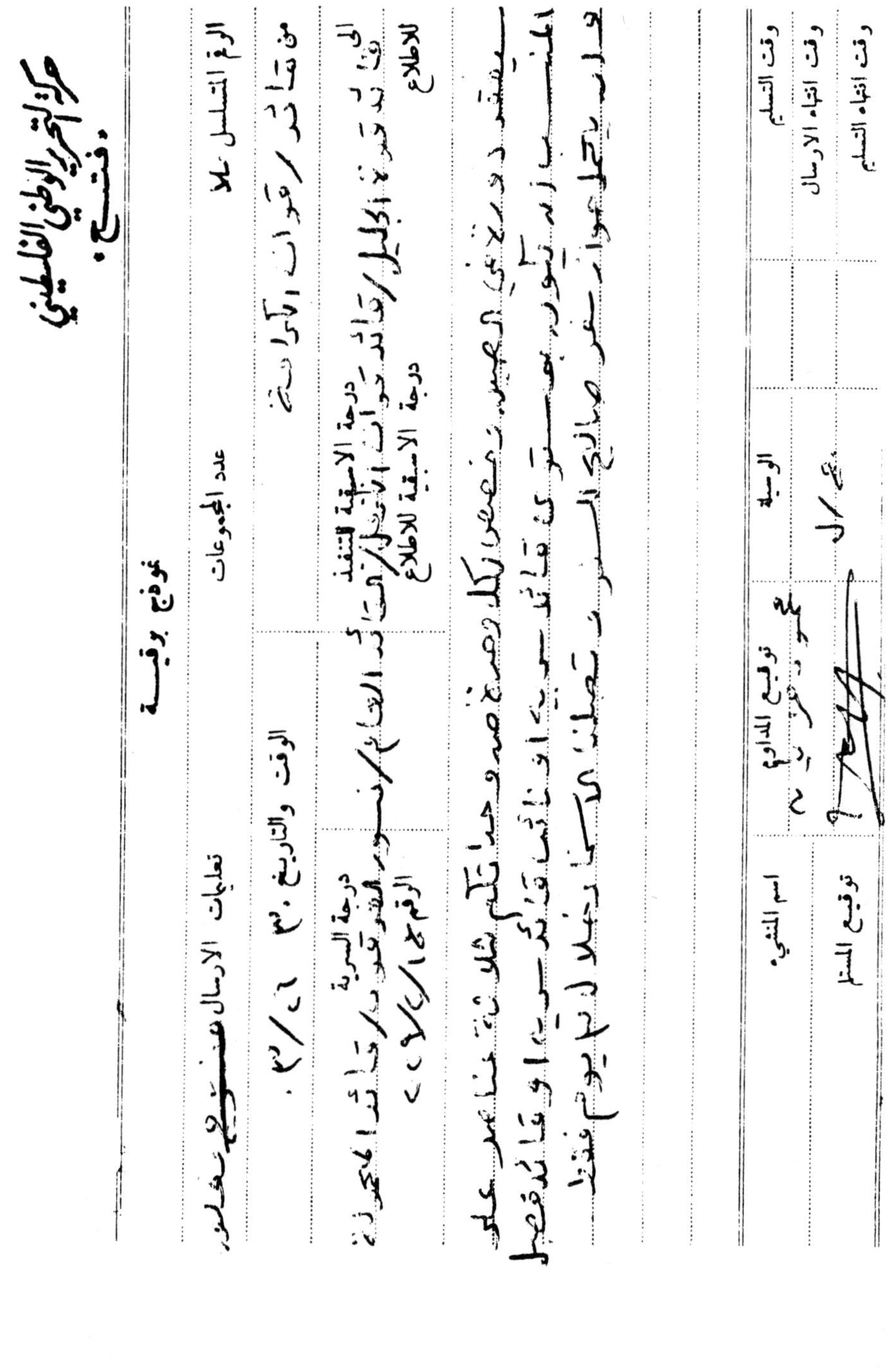

[Document 21]: Course in Yugoslavia

Major 'Awd-allah Ahmed 'Umar abu-Leil, the commander of the Galilee Battalion in Fatah, is sent off for a course in Yugoslavia, 28 August 1981.

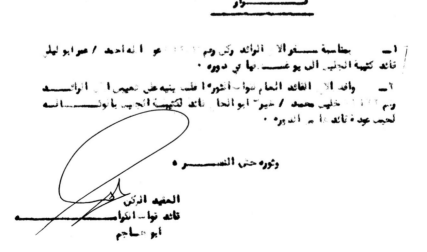

حركة التحرير الوطني الفلسطيني
فتح
القيادة العامة لقوات العاصفة
قيادة قوات الكرامة

الرقم :- أ/٩/١/
التاريخ / /آب ١٩٨١

قرار

١- بمناسبة سفر الأخ الرائد ركن رقم عوض الله احمد / عمر ابو ليل قائد كتيبة الجليل الى يوغسلافيا في دورة .

٢- وافق الأخ القائد العام لقوات الثورة على تعيين الأخ الرائد رقم خليل محمد / خير ابو النجا قائد لكتيبة الجليل بالوكالة لحين عودة قائدها من الدورة .

وثورة حتى النصر .

العميد الركن
قائد قوات الكرامة
ابو هاجم

[Document 22]: Army engineers course in East Germany

On 11 January 1982, a cable from Fatah headquarters asks all units to send their candidates for a three-year course for army engineers in East Germany, at the end of which the rank of second lieutenant would be awarded.

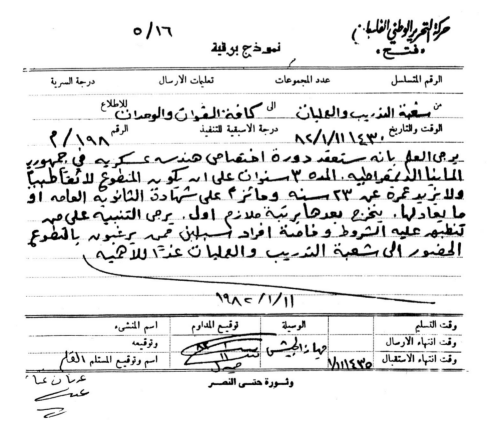

حركة التحرير الوطني الفلسطيني
«فتح»

٥/١٦

نموذج برقية

الرقم المتسلسل — عدد المجموعات — تعليمات الارسال — درجة السرية

من شعبة التدريب والعمليات — الى كافة القوات والوحدات — للاطلاع

الوقت والتاريخ ١٤٣٠ ٨٢/١/١١ — درجة الاسبقية للتنفيذ — الرقم ١٩٨/م

يرجى العلم بانه ستعقد دورة اختصاص هندسة عسكرية في جمهورية
المانيا الديمقراطية. المدة ٣ سنوات على ان يكون المتطوع للانتقاء طبعاً
ولا يزيد عمره عن ٢٣ سنة وحائز على شهادة الثانوية العامة او
ما يعادلها. يتخرج بعدها برتبة ملازم اول. يرجى التنبيه على من
تنطبق عليه الشروط وخاصة افراد اشبال ممن يرغبون بالتطوع
الحضور الى شعبة التدريب والعمليات عند ١٠ للاهمية

١٩٨٢/١/١١

وقت التسليم		الوسيلة	توقيع المداوم	اسم المنشىء
وقت انتهاء الارسال		جهاز الجيش		وتوقيعه
وقت انتهاء الاستقبال	١٤٣٥/١/١١			اسم وتوقيع المستلم القلم

عدنان عمار

وثورة حتى النصر

[Document 23]: Air defence course in North Korea

A Fatah report of 21 January 1980 certifies that the 21 NCO's listed here have successfully completed an air defence course in North Korea that was given from 1 April to 10 October 1979.

حركة التحرير الوطني الفلسطيني
"فتح"
القيادة العامة لقوات العاصفة
العمليات المركزية

الرقم ....
التاريخ ....

الملحق (أ) كتاب العمليات المركزية رقم [illegible] تاريخ [illegible]

تسلسل	الاسم	الوحده
٠١	محمد خلف عبد الهادي الطوباسي	التسليح
٠٢	عوني حسين محمد ... ار (طلال محمود)	الدفاع الجوي
٠٣	كمال عبد العزيز ناجي	القطاع الغربي
٠٤	احمد محمود كايد	القسطال
٠٥	شريف محمد بدر نمايره	القسطال
٠٦	صايل حسن علي	الامن العسكري
٠٧	يحيى احمد خليل مدار	الامن العسكري
٠٨	فوزي محمد اسماعيل	مديرية التدريب
٠٩	صالح نصر احمد الحاج	الكرامـــه
١٠	فرج محمد سليمان العابدي	اجنادين
١١	حلمي محمد عبد الحليم	اجنادين
١٢	محمود محمد مصطفى	المليشيا
١٣	جاسر احمد عبد الحافظ	المليشيا
١٤	عدنان محمد ملسم	حرس القائد العام
١٥	عيسى صالح شحاده	الادارة العسكريه
١٦	احمد محمد عبد ربه	اليرموك
١٧	عبد الله سعد احمد جابر	اليرموك
١٨	محمد قاسم ابو خضرا	القطاع الغربي
١٩	حميد حسين محمد البواب	الامن الغربي
٢٠	عبد الصافي صالح الشريف	القطاع الغربي
٢١	لطفي محمد حسان	الكرامـــه

Document 23A-2

حركة التحرير الوطني الفلسطيني
"فتح"
القيادة العامة لقوات العاصفة
العمليات المركزية

الرقم ع١/٨/ ٢٠
التاريخ ١٩٨٠/١/٢١

الى ....الأخوة/ الرفاق الجوي.............

الموضوع : دورة كوريا

تحية الثوره وبعد ٠

– انهى المذكورون في الملحق (أ) المرفق دورة قادة سرايا التي عقدت في كوريا من ١٩٧٩/٤/١ ولغاية ١٩٧٩/١٠/١٠ واجتازوا الدوره بنجاح ٠

يرجى العلم واجراءاتكم

وثورة حتى النصر ٠٠٠

العميد الركن
مدير العمليات المركزيه
ابو الوليد

نسخه الى :

– الاداره العسكريه ٠
– الماليه المركزيه ٠
مع نسخه من الملحق (أ) ٠

[Document 24]: East German Military Academy course

All Fatah units are urged to send candidates to an expanded course in the East German Military Academy. The candidates are to report for interview on 22 February 1982.

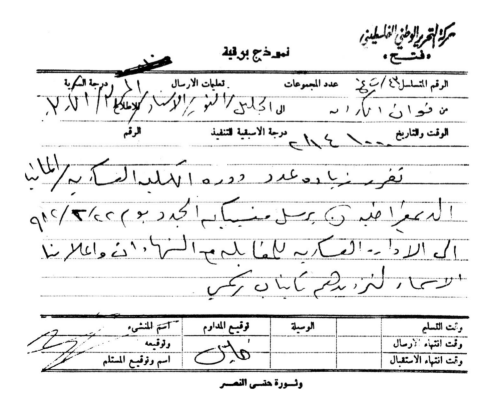

حركة التحرير الوطني الفلسطيني
«فتح»

نموذج برقية

[redacted]

الرقم المتسلسل ٤٤/ت ع — عدد المجموعات — تعليمات الارسال — درجة السرية

من قوات الكرامة — الى الجميع / التوجيه / الاسناد / للاطلاع

الوقت والتاريخ ١٤١٠٠١ — درجة الاسبقية للتنفيذ — الرقم

تقرر زيادة عدد دورة الكلية العسكرية / المانيا الديمقراطية يرسل منتسبيها الجدد يوم ٢٢/٢/٩٨٢ الى الادارة العسكرية لمقابلتهم الساعة ٠٩٠٠ واعلامنا بالاسماء لتزويدهم بكتاب رسمي.

وقت التسليم		الوسيلة	توقيع المداوم	اسم المنشيء
وقت انتهاء الارسال				وتوقيعه
وقت انتهاء الاستقبال				اسم وتوقيع المستلم

وثورة حتى النصر

[Document 25]: Staff college in Yugoslavia

A cable-order from Fatah headquarters to its units to send candidates to a staff college in Yugoslavia.

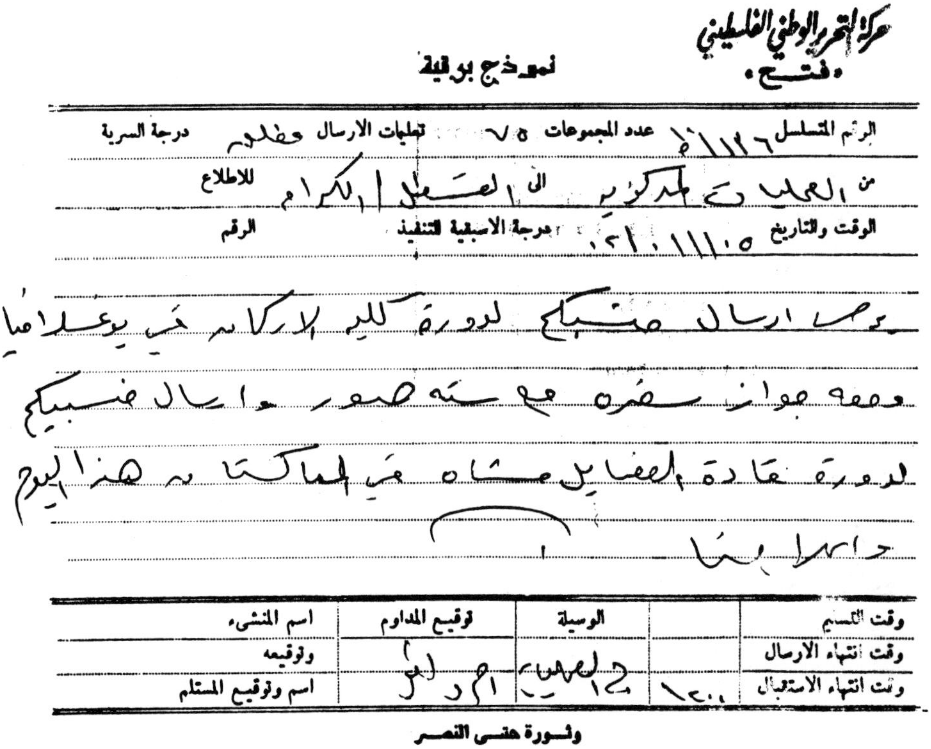
حركة التحرير الوطني الفلسطيني
«فتح»

نموذج برقية

الرقم المتسلسل	عدد المجموعات ٧٥	تعليمات الارسال عاجل	درجة السرية
من العمليات المركزية	الى القطاعات الكرام		للاطلاع
الوقت والتاريخ		درجة الاسبقية للتنفيذ	الرقم

وقت التسليم		الوسيلة	توقيع المداوم	اسم المنشىء
وقت انتهاء الارسال				وتوقيعه
وقت انتهاء الاستقبال				اسم وتوقيع المستلم

وثورة حتى النصر

[Document 26]: Courses in Eastern bloc countries

A list of courses taken by officers and NCO's of the September Martyrs Battalion/Kastel Brigade/Fatah in Eastern bloc countries. The handwritten document was captured in Sidon.

No.	Military ID. No.	Rank	Name	Date Rank Received	Course	Place	Date
1.	31487	Major, staff officer	Faisal Muhammad al-Sheikh Yussuf	—	1. Sa'iqa	Syria	1968
					2. Cadre	"	"
					3. Military Academy	China	—
					4. Battalion Commander	Moscow	
					5. Staff Officers	Pakistan	1979
2.	44552	Captain	Jamal Ya'kub Zaidan	1 February 1976	1. Basic	Jordan	1968
					2. Frogmen	Syria	1969
					3. Fedayin Commanders	Moscow	1972
					4. Armour	Syria	1978
					5. Armour	Hungary	1980
3.	41054	First Lieutenant	Fadl Muhammad 'Uthman	1975	1. Sa'iqa	Baghdad	1968
					2. Platoon Commanders	Moscow	1975-76
					3. Company Commanders	Vietnam	1977-78
4.	44818	First Lieutenant	Muhammad 'Abd-Allah Salamah	1 January 1976	1. Sa'iqa Instructor		1967
					2. Platoon Commanders	Baghdad	
					3. Company Commanders	China	1977
					4. Armour	Syria	1978
					5. Armour	Lebanon	
					6. Armour Company Commananders		
5.	32242	Captain	Jawad Ahmad 'Abd al-Ghani	1 January 1976	1. Military College	Algeria	1969
					2. Mortar		1970
					3. Armour	Syria	1978
					4. Political Cadres	China	1978-79
					5. Political Cadres	Bulgaria	1979-80

No.	Military ID. No.	Rank	Name	Date Rank Received	Course	Place	Date
6.	22145	Captain	Faruq Muhammad Musa al-Yussuf	Again on 15 Nov. 1979	1. Service in PLA (Palestine Liberation Army)		
					2. Weaponry		1968
7.	31492	Second Lieutenant	Ratib Musa Mahmud Abu-Samarah	1975	1. Sa'iqa	Baghdad	1968
					2. Explosive Engineering	Baghdad	1968
					3. Cadre	Syria	1969
					4. Military Academy of the Fatah		1974-75
					5. Infantry Company Commanders	Moscow	1977
					6. Armour	Syria	1978
					7. Armour	Hungary	1979
8.	71281	Second Lieutenant	Yasin Khadr Muhammad	1 September 1976	1. Fighter	Syria	1968
					2. Fighter	Syria	1974
					3. Military Academy, Fatah		1976
					4. Armour	Syria	1978
					5. Armour	Hungary	1980
					6. Armour Company Commanders	Moscow	
9.	13644	Second Lieutenant	Ahmad Mustafa Hamden Ghana'im	1 June 1977	1. Jordan Valley		1965
					2. Jordan		1966-67 (for twelve months)
					3. NCO		1969
					4. Sa'iqa	Syria	1970

					5. Sa'iqa	Syria	1971
					6. Commando	Algeria	1972
					7. Military College		
					8. Armour	Syria	1978
					9. Tank Company Commander	Pakistan	1978
					10. Administration and Control at the Planning Centre	Beirut	1979
10.	51009	Second Lieutenant	Ibrahim Shahadeh 'Amr	1 June 1977	1. Fighter	Jordan	1968
					2. Military Academy	Algeria	1975-76
					3. Armour Company Commanders	Pakistan	1978
					4. Armour Communications	Pakistan	
11.	74709	Second Lieutenant	Sa'id Ibrahim al-Ghazzi	1 June 1977	1. Military Academy	Algeria	1975-6
					2. Armour Company Commanders	Pakistan	1978
					3. Armour	Hungary	1979
12.	46897	Second Lieutenant	Khaled 'Isa 'Abd Hassan	1 June 1977	1. Military Academy	Algeria	1975-76
					2. Political Education	Beirut	1978
					3. Basic Course in Armour	Pakistan	1979
					4. Armour	Hungary	1980
					5. Armour Company Commanders		
13.	22563	Second Lieutenant	Muhammed Bashir al-Durzi	1 June 1977	1. Service in the Syrian Army		
					2. Political Education		1979

No.	Military ID. No.	Rank	Name	Date Rank Received	Course	Place	Date
14.	31590	Second Lieutenant	Yussuf Mahmud al-Sheikh Musa	1 June 1977			
15.	13041	Second Lieutenant	Ibrahim Suleiman al-Shuruf	27 April 1978	1. Weaponry 2. Military College, Fatah 3. Armour	Jordan Syria	 1978
16.	52524	Second Lieutenant	Husayn Muhammed Ahmad Sa'id	27 April 1978	1. Fighter 2. Military College, Fatah 3. Armour	Syria Hungary	1969 1978 1979
17.	13463	Second Lieutenant	Ribhy Muhammad Ibrahim al-Sheikh	27 April 1978	1. Military College, Fatah 2. Political Education 3. Armour	 Hungary	1978 1979 1979
18.	15361	Second Lieutenant	Mustafa Hasan Mustafa Qindil	27 April 1978	1. Military College, Fatah 2. Armour 3. Political Education 4. Social Sciences 5. Armour	 Syria Bulgaria Hungary	1978 1978 1979 1979 1980
19.	31708	Second Lieutenant	Ahmad Hasan Ahmad Jaber	27 April 1978	1. Navy 2. Fighter 3. Military College, Fatah 4. Political Education 5. Summer 6. Armour	Syria Syria Hungary	1969 1972 1978 1978

20.	13952	Second Lieutenant	Muhammad Mustafa 'Abd-al-Rahman	27 April 1978	1. Sa'iqa		1970
					2. Sa'iqa		1972
					3. Military Academy, Fatah		1978
					4. Armour	Syria	1978
					5. Armour	Lebanon	
21.	15372	Second Lieutenant	Ibrahim Raja Salih al-Hamzat	27 April 1978	1. Military Academy, Fatah		1978
					2. Reconnaissance		1979
					3. Political Education		1979
					4. Armour	Hungary	
22.	73937	Second Lieutenant	Ahmad Muhammed Ahmad Mar'i al-Sharqawi	27 April 1978	1. Military Academy, Fatah		1978
					2.	Egypt	
					3. Anti-aircraft Company Commanders	Moscow	
23.	46379	Second Lieutenant	Daoud Salameh Muhammad Jum'a	27 April 1978	1. Military Academy, Fatah		1978
					2. Engineering	Syria	1971
					3. Armour	Syria	1978
					4. Political Education		1979
24.	22029	Second Lieutenant	Ahmad Fadl Muhammad Abu Khalil	27 April 1978	1. Military Academy, Fatah		1978
					2. Armour	Syria	1978
					3. Political Education		
					4. Armour	Hungary	
1.	21008	Seargent-Major	Sha'ir Mustafa Ibrahim Mustafa	1 Feb. 1977	1. Political Cadres	Syria	1972
					2. Platoon Commanders	Zahrani	1977
					3. Armour Platoon	Pakistan	1978
					4. Armour Company Commanders		1979
					5. Armour Mechanic	Hungary	1980

No.	Military ID. No.	Rank	Name	Date Rank Received	Course	Place	Date
2.	53477	Seargent-Major	Abd al-Rahman Ahmad Hussein a-Sharif	6 April 1977	1. Light Weaponry 2. Communications 3. Armour 4. Military Academy (did not graduate, stayed for six months)	 Hungary Cuba	 1980 1979
3.	24767	Seargent-Major	Sabir Abid Hadid	1 April 1977	1. Fighter 2. Armour 3. Armour 4. Driver	 Syria Hungary	1975 1978 1979
4.	13149	Seargent-Major	‘Abd al-Hadi Dawud Yussuf		1. Sa‘iqa 2. Communications 3. 4. 5. 6. Transporting Officer 7. Political Education 8. Armour	 Hungary	
5.	23151	Seargent-Major	Hasan Salim Saqqar	1 April 1977	1. Fighter 2. Political Cadres, Fatah	Baghdad Syria	
6.	21379	Seargent-Major	Ali'Abd Hamidi	1 April 1977			

Document 26A-1,2

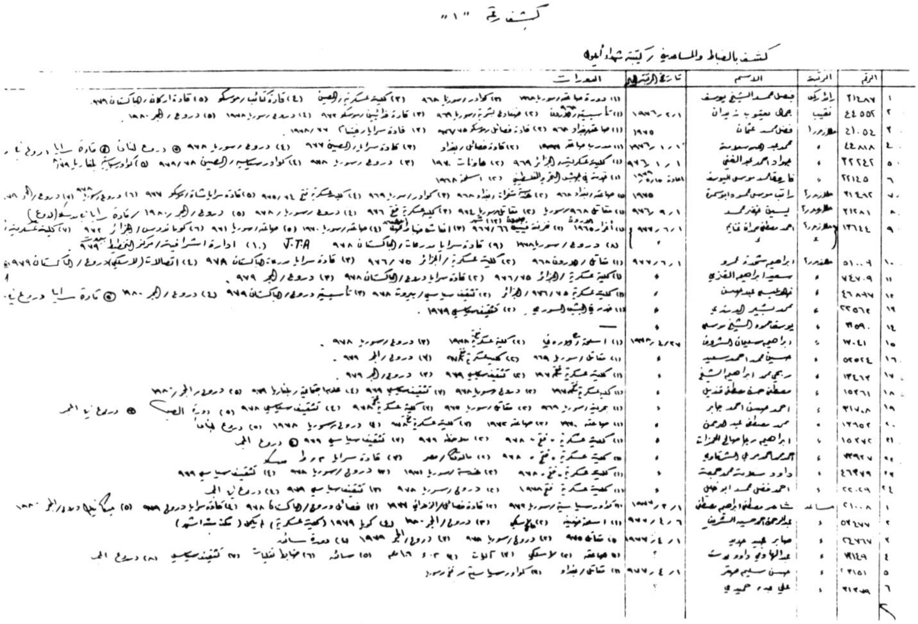

كشف رقم "١"

كشف بالضباط والمساعدين / كتيبة شهداء أيلول

	الرقم	الرتبة	الاسم	تاريخ الرتبة	الدورات
١	٢١٤٨٧	رائد ركن	فيصل محمد الشيخ يوسف		[illegible]
٢	٤٤٥٥٢	نقيب	جمال يعقوب زيدان	١/٢/١٩٧٦	[illegible]
٣	٤١٠٥٤	ملازم أول	فضل محمد عثمان	١٩٧٥	[illegible]
٤	٤٤٨١٨	"	[illegible]	[illegible]	[illegible]
٥	٢٢٢٤٢	"	جواد احمد عبد الغني	١/١/٩٧٦	[illegible]
٦	٢٢١٤٥	"	[illegible]	[illegible]	[illegible]

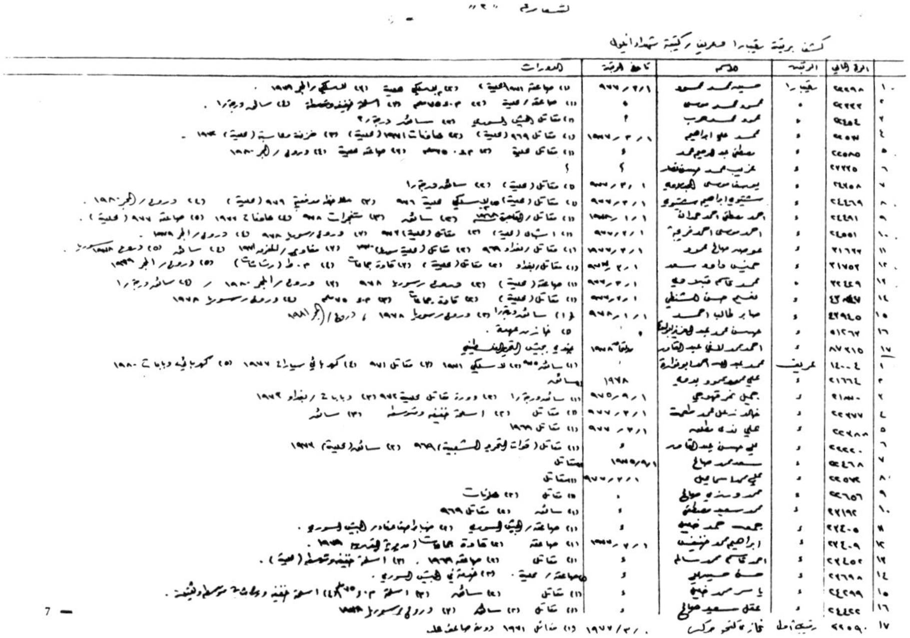

كشف رقم "٢"

كشف برتبة مساعد / كتيبة شهداء أيلول

	الرقم العالي	الرتبة	الاسم	تاريخ الرتبة	الدورات
١	[illegible]	مساعد	[illegible]	١/٢/٩٧٦	[illegible]
٢	[illegible]	"	[illegible]	"	[illegible]
٣	[illegible]	"	[illegible]	؟	[illegible]
٤	[illegible]	"	محمد علي ابراهيم	١/٣/١٩٧٧	[illegible]

7 —

[Document 27]: Report on PLO mission in USSR

This report, addressed to Arafat, contains details of a PLO military training mission to the Soviet Union.

The brother, head of the PLO Executive Committee, the General Commander of the Palestinian Revolutionary Forces, the brother Yasser Arafat, may Allah protect him!

Subject: Report on the Palestinian delegation to the Soviet Union
Date of Report: 22 January 1981

On 1 September 1980 the delegation arrived in Simferopol in the Soviet Union, where it had been decided to hold the courses. The delegation numbered 194 officers and NCO's. Courses were given for the following posts:

1. Tank battalion commander
2. Tank company commander
3. Infantry company commander
4. Reconnaissance company commander
5. Infantry platoon commander
7. Anti-tank platoon commander
8. Sagger missile platoon commander
9. Anti-aircraft platoon commander

Factions of the Resistance (movement) as follows:

1. The Palestinian National Liberation Movement — Fatah
2. The Palestine Liberation Army
3. The Armed Struggle
4. The Popular Front
5. The Democratic Front
6. The General Command
7. Sa'iqa
8. The Arab Front
9. The Popular Struggle Front
10. The Palestine Liberation Front

Studies began in all the courses in a regular fashion, according to the programme which had been prepared. The delegation command studied the programme for each course and made comments, which were taken into account by the heads of the college and implemented in the study programme as far as possible, especially in connection with theoretical issues which suit our conditions and combat procedures in towns, mountains, and coastal plain defence.

After classroom studies were completed in the various courses attended by the delegation, the time arrived for final manœuvres, in which all members of the delegation participated. The exercise included:

1. Command and staff exercise (work on maps).
2. Tactical exercise.

When discussing the exercise, the delegation command proposed that the command and staff exercise involve the entire delegation, in accordance with the specialization in each course and its role in the battle; the tactical exercise would then follow. However, the college commanders pointed out that the method which the delegation command wanted to use was not feasible, due to its heavy demand on resources which the college was unable to provide under the circumstances. In the end, the delegation command accepted the college's opinion, and the exercise was carried out in the following way:

1. Command and staff exercise at brigade level:

   The battalion commander students comprised the brigade command in the exercise. The brigade staff was made up of students from other courses. Altogether 17 officers participated. Work on the map lasted for three consecutive days. The result was excellent according to the officers who supervised on behalf of the college. The work was done under the daily and personal supervision of the college commander. The command and staff exercise included the following stages:

   a) Advance when expecting an encounter battle; carrying out an encounter battle
   b) Attack in direct contact
   c) Defence

2. On the fourth day of manœuvres, the tactical exercise was begun by members of the delegation — an infantry company reinforced by a tank company in a direct contact attack. All types of organic and

attached weapons were used in the exercise imitating a real battle. The exercise was carried out in earnest by the Palestinian combatant, despite the difficult weather conditions. The exercise was a success; it earned the praise of teachers, observers, and other delegations at the college.

Achievements of the delegation:

1. In instruction

a) The subject matter was picked up very well. The teachers saw that the Palestinian delegation was the best in rapid learning, compared with the other delegations.

b) The anti-tank course teachers noticed that trainees prepared their guns and took up firing positions in less than the required time.

c) Teachers who accompanied anti-aircraft course trainees on their trip to the firing range reported that they performed very well.

d) The delegation did well in discussions on political topics in the framework of the political lessons; the Soviet comrades deem such lessons very important and concentrate on them.

2. Ties [between nationalities at the school]

a) Creation of good ties with instructors and workers at the college.

b) Familiarization with the customs and traditions of the peoples of the host country.

c) Explanation of the Palestinian cause, the role of the PLO as the only legitimate representative of the Palestinian people, and the Palestinian revolution until the realization of victory and the establishment of an independent state.

d) Getting to know the other delegations and liberation movements, and establishing good ties while explaining our case, whether during personal meetings or in the framework of official meetings.

The commander of the delegation from South Africa showed full understanding for our revolution and cause, so much so, that during the closing ceremony for his delegation, he spoke in front of all the delegations and the Soviet comrades about the Palestinian revolution and Yasser Arafat more than about himself and the host country.

Negative aspects of the mission:

1. From the point of view of the college

a) Shortage of Arabic interpreters. At first the delegation command had many difficulties concerning this matter. Because of the constant request, the college was compelled to supply interpreters, but they did not succeed in rendering exact military translations. In the end, in cooperation with trainees of the other courses and with the new interpreters, they overcame the problem, but not without great difficulty.

b) Shortage of audio-visual material.

c) The training period for the anti-tank, missile and anti-aircraft courses ended 15 days before the departure date, forcing the college to repeat many of the lessons and subjects.

d) Due to the size of the Palestinian delegation and the presence of other delegations, a third of the members of the delegation had to sleep ten to a room. This caused difficulties, which were only overcome by a joint effort.

2. From the point of view of the delegation

a) The participants in the courses did not correctly understand the political aspects of sending military delegations abroad. As a result, the upper echelon of the delegation, namely the participants in the battalion officer course, refused to study and asked to return, using all sorts of illogical excuses. If this is considered according to the correct military criterion, and despite the possibility of overcoming these difficulties very simply — if each one of them had remembered the orders he received during his meeting with the commander of the struggle before the trip, the situation would have been entirely different. This was noted by the delegation command in the report which was sent to Your Excellency through the representative of the organization in Moscow, Colonel al-Sha'ar, on 22 September 1980.

b) Those responsible in most of the organizations were not careful in choosing candidates for the course and the delegation command was forced to send a few of them home. Following are the names of the people sent home, and the reasons for their return:

First Batch:

(1) Ra'ad Ahmed Razaq al-Madani — from the PLA — was sent on a reconnaissance company commander course. He asked to be transferred to the course for tank battalion commanders. When the delegation command and PLO representative objected, he asked to return on the grounds that there was no point in keeping him there.

(2) Haydar Jawad Safa — from the Democratic Front — tried to create an organizational problem between the Democratic Front and the Popular Struggle Front, together with comrade 'Afif al-Masri of the Popular Struggle Front.

(3) Hassan Radha Bakr — from Sa'iqa — asked to return on the grounds that his state of health did not allow him to continue his studies. This was agreed upon in the presence of the delegation command and a representative of the organization.

(4) Muhammad Radha Mahrar — from Sa'iqa — asked to return because his state of health did not allow him to continue his studies. This was agreed upon in the presence of the delegation command, a representative of the organization, and the trainees' escort.

(5) Sahil al-Bitr — from the PLA — asked to return because his state of health did not allow him to continue his studies. This was agreed upon in the presence of the delegation command and a representative of the organization.

(6) Lieutenant Ibrahim al-Mahdun — from the PLA — asked to return because his state of health did not allow him to continue his studies. When the Bulgarian "brother" came there together with Ra'ad Tamarzi, the commander of his unit, he tried to persuade him [to stay] but to no avail.

Second Batch:

(1) Ali Ahsan al-Najar — Palestine Liberation Front — failed in commanding the missile course, and was a bad example in military discipline because he used to jump from the college wall, in contravention of orders. The delegation command also found out that he was connected with the smuggling of counterfeit dollars.

(2) ‘Afif Muhammad al-Masri — Struggle Front — did not behave himself outside the college. He spent his time with one of the girls of doubtful character and accompanied her home. His clothes were later taken by a man who claimed to be the girl's brother. He left her home without his clothes and reported the incident to the militia, which returned his clothes.

(3) Fawzi al-Asadi — Struggle Front — spoke with the representative of the organization, Colonel al-Sha‘ar, in an unbecoming manner. Al-Sha‘ar asked that he be returned. He was given another chance and therefore was not sent back in the first batch.

When Colonel Abu Majdi came, the abovementioned asked to immediately meet with him; following the meeting (I do not know what went on there) Abu Majdi met with the delegation command and the course commander, and mentioned his name as one of those destined for return. When I asked him why, he answered me that the above was a bad man and had to be returned. The comrade commander of the college also informed me that he was one of those who violated discipline by jumping from the wall of the college.

(4) Darwish Dhib Sa‘ad — Arab Liberation Front — is indecent and a pervert. He got mixed up with a girl of doubtful character. He claimed that she took his money together with a report for the delegation command. The commander of the delegation himself brought him from the city, drunk as a lord.

(5) Ahmad al-Sharqi — Sa‘iqa — testified to the Simferopol inspector-general during the investigation of a claim made by one of the members of the delegation, Hassan Qassem Hussein, that the militia and unidentified people had beaten him and taken his money. In the course of this evidence, al-Sharqi

attacked the commander of the college, and threatened the college in the name of the members of the delegation that if his friend's money was not returned, "something would happen." Later on he said to the inspector that when the Golan was captured, Israel carried out body searches on the people but did not take their money, while you — i.e. the Russians — steal the people's money. This behaviour brought on a serious response by the commander of the college and he demanded that the man be returned, if possible.

(6) Salim Samir Asbar — PLA — irregularities in training and malingering despite the warnings given him.

(7) Mahmud Nimr Shaqiqat — Fatah — returned on his own request. He incorrectly claimed that he had problems with the Soviet comrades. We talked with him in order to prevent his return, but he stuck to his position. It was decided to grant his request in the presence of the "brother" Abu Majdi, and his report to the delegation command is attached herewith.

c) The problem of counterfeit dollars

I have already given Your Excellency the report on this problem through the organization's representative in Moscow, Colonel al-Sha'ar, on 8 October 1980.

To His Honour the General Commander:

The return of the first and second batch has been completed in the hope that this will deter those whose behaviour is bad, or those who were mistakenly chosen. In spite of this, mistakes have been repeated. If the delegation command had to return people and withhold certificates according to orders, half the delegation would have had to return. However, in the interest of our revolution and our people, the delegation command invested all its efforts in absorbing as many as possible up to the last moment and this will be attested to by Colonel Abu Majdi himself, and those who accompany him. For example, one of the members of the Popular Front, whose name is Sa'id Razaq, came back late from leave and arrived at the college at 04:30 in the morning.

On the next day they celebrated the end of the course and the commander of the college decided to hold back his certificate. We all agreed to this, including Abu Majdi. However, after the certificates were distributed, the commander of the college went back on his decision and gave the man his certificate.

Going by my experience in command of this large delegation, I ask your permission, Commander of the Struggle, to submit to you a number of simple proposals and I request that you study their usefulness, for the sake of the good name of the revolution and our people in foreign countries.

Following are the proposals:

1. The opening of a training course for those who are to be sent abroad before their departure, in which they will study the latest developments in the Palestinian problem and the aims behind the dispatch of military delegations abroad, over and above the studies themselves.

2. The conducting of early checks, by the instruction administration, of those intended to participate in courses as regards their suitability, and the dispatch of only those who pass the checks.

3. The subordination of the officers to the course command so that their personal ability as commanders can be checked without taking into account the considerations of organizations or preferences according to former opinions.

4. Choice of people of high quality, who are capable of representing us outside, will be the responsibility of the direct commander.

5. Explanation, before the trip, to candidates for courses abroad with regard to arrangements and rules in the absorbing college.

6. Lowering the level of the courses abroad to those which cannot be conducted within the training directorate.

7. If the need arises to send people to courses of all types and specialities, it is preferable to lower the number in order not to harm the quality and to allow a better selection.

8. If a large number of courses are chosen, it is advisable to appoint a delegation commander who is not connected with any course, so that this will

be his only function. It is also advisable to use officers who have already participated in a course at the same college and who know its rules.

9. The military delegations in foreign countries must be equipped with a large number of books in foreign languages, especially in the language of the host country — in political, historical and cultural subjects. They should also have PLO stickers and slogans in booklets and publications, etc.

10. Similar material should also be sent by post.

Sir, the Supreme Commander, may God protect him, I am sending this report on behalf of the PLO delegation to the Soviet Union, and pledge our adherence to wise behaviour which will guide us to victory and the establishment of our independent state; long live the PLO under your leadership, the sole legal representative of the Palestinian people.

Signed — Colonel Rashad Ahmed, Commander of the Delegation.

Document 27A-2

بمادة السلاح لجميع الدورات بشكل جيد ومنتظم مع البرامج المقررة لعدم ٤٢
الكلية من ساعات التدريب لكل مادة وكل اختصاص . وقد اطلعت قيادة البعـ
ـثة على الخطط الدراسية لكل دورة وأبدت ملاحظاتها وقد تجاوبت قيادة الكلية
هذه الملاحظات وأدخلتها على الخطط التدريبية حسب إمكاناتها وخاصة الـ
المطلوب التدريب عليها وبعض المواضيع النظرية التي تتناسب مع ظروفنا وطـ
أعمالنا مثل القتال في المدن – القتال في الجبال – الدفاع عن الساحل البحري
الذي لإيطاليا [illegible]

٤ـ بعد انتهاء المدة المخصصة لجميع دورات البعثة جاء موعد تنفيذ المشروع النهائي
والمقرر فيه اشتراك جميع أفراد البعثة . تبلورت المشروع في شقيه
أ ـ مشروع القيادة والأركان « على الخرائط »
ب ـ مشروع تكتيكي .

تمت مناقشة المشروع من قبل قيادة البعثة وقيادة الكلية كما طرح قائد
البعثة أن تتقدم البعثة بجميع وسائل لعمل مشروع القيادة والأركان لكل
اختصاص اختصاصه ودوره في المعركة ثم في النهاية يتم المشروع التكتيكي
لكن قيادة الكلية أبدت ملاحظاتها حيث أن التنفيذ بالأسلوب الذي تريده
قيادة البعثة غير ممكن لأنه يحتاج إلى إمكانيات كبيرة والكلية في هذه الفترة
لا تستطيع تنفيذه بنفس الأسلوب وحرصها على الاستفادة بأي شكل من جهة
ما وافقت قيادة البعثة على رأي الكلية وتم التنفيذ على الوجه التالي :
١ ـ مشروع القيادة والأركان على مستوى لواء
مثلت جميع القطع التابعة من قيادة اللواء : تم تشكيل الأركان للواء
من الدورات المختلفة وكان إجمالي المشتركين ١٧ ضابط واستمر العمل
على الخرائط ثلاثة أيام متصلة ، كانت حصيلة العمل فيه ممتازة حسب تقييم
الضباط المشرفين من الكلية والإشراف اليومي من المدربين فما له الكلية خصوصاً
وقد حقق مشروع القيادة والأركان مراحل المعركة التالية
أ ـ السير إلى منطقة المعركة التصادمية « مع تنفيذ المعركة التصادمية »
ب ـ ثم الهجوم من التماس المباشر .
جـ ـ ثم الدفاع .
٢ ـ في اليوم الرابع من المشروع تم تنفيذ المشروع التكتيكي من قبل أفراد المعسكر
وهو سرية مشاة معززة بسرية دبابات في الهجوم من التماس المباشر

يتبع

Document 27A-1

الأخ رئيس اللجنة التنفيذية لمنظمة التحرير الفلسطينية

القائد العام لقوات الثورة الفلسطينية

الأخ ياسر عرفات حفظه الله .

الموضوع / تقرير عن البعثة الفلسطينية في الاتحاد السوفيتي .

تحية الثورة وبعد

بتاريخ ١/٩/١٩٨٠ وصلت البعثة إلى " سمفربل " الاتحاد السوفيتي

لحضور الكليات الحربية لعقد الدورات .

عدد أعضاء البعثة ١٩٤ مائة وأربعة وتسعون ضابط وصف ضابط .

الدورات كالتالي :-

١- قيادة كتائب دبابات

٢- قيادة سرايا دبابات

٣- قيادة سرايا مشاة

٤- قيادة سرايا استطلاع

٥- قادة فصائل مشاة

٦- قادة فصائل استطلاع

٧- قادة فصائل م/د

٨- قادة فصائل صواريخ " مولتكا "

٩- قادة فصائل م/ط .

فصائل المشاركة كالتالي :-

١- حركة التحرير الوطني الفلسطيني " فتح " .

٢- جيش التحرير الفلسطيني

٣- الكفاح المسلح

٤- الجبهة الشعبية .

٥- الجبهة الديمقراطية

٦- القيادة العامة

٧- الصاعقة

٨- الجبهة العربية

٩- جبهة النضال

١٠- جبهة تحرير فلسطين

يتبع

Document 27A-4

والدول المضيفة فقد كانت ذلك علامة أولدت ايجابي لصالح شعبنا وثورتنا
بقيادة تلك الحكمة
أما عن السلبيات في البعثة
أ- على صعيد التكتيك
ا- النقص في المترجمين العرب ، وقد واجهت قيادة البعثة في لبنان
متاعب كثيرة بذلك ، وأمام الالحاح المستمر اضطرت الكلية أن تستدعي
مترجمين لتغطية النقص ولكنهم مع الأسف لم يكونوا قادرين على
الترجمة العسكرية الصحيحة ولكنها حلت جزءاً من مشكلة الترجمة
ولم تستطع الكلية أكثر من ذلك
ب- ضعف بعض الأهلية في الدورات المختلفة والمتعادية مع المعلم
الجيد وتم التغلب على ذلك ولكن بجهد كبير
ج- النقص في وسائل الايضاح التكتيكية
د- التبليغ المسبق المناسب للدورات الدروع والصواريخ والدفاع الجوي
بعد انتهاء الصف المقرر بحوالي شهر تقريباً وأمام موعد السفر
القريب تكامل أعداد المتعلمين اضطرت الكلية إلى التعامل مع كثير من
المسائل بالتوضيح
هـ- نظراً لتزامن البعثة الفلسطينية مع وجود بعثات أخرى ونظراً
لعدم توفر الأماكن الكافية فقد اضطرت الكلية الى وضع عشرة
طلاب في غرفة واحدة لحوالي ثلثي البعثة ، وهذا بدوره كان عاملاً
في خلق بعض المشاكل والتسيب والجهد المكثف ثم التغلب عليها
ب- على صعيد البعثة
ا- عدم الوعي من المنتسبين للدورات بالابعاد السياسية في إيفاد البعثات
العسكرية للخارج مما جعل الملل مستشري في البعثة وهم يعتبرونه دورة
عادية تكتيكية ويضيعون التعلم طالبين السفر بحجج غير منطقية إذا
قسناها بالمفهوم العسكري الصحيح رغم امكانية التغلب عليها ببساطة
شديدة ، ولو عاد كل منهم بذاكرته الى اليوم الأول الذي التحق فيه ثائر
السيرة والنضال بالبعثة وأحيل توجيهاته قبل السفر لتغير الموقف
تماماً . وقد تمكنت قيادة البعثة بتقريرها وأحل لسيادتكم عن طريق
ممثل المنظمة في موسكو الأخ العميد/ شاعر بتاريخ ٢٢/٩/١٩٨١

فيح

Document 27A-3

وقد مثلت منحكانة صنوف الأسلحة العضوية والحفر وبتشكيل جو إدراكه الحقيقي
وتنفذ المشاريع بنشاط وحيوية المناضل الفلسطيني رغم ظروف الطقس القاسية البرد
وكان مشروعاً ناجحاً تماماً نال الاعجاب من جميع المعلمين والمشاهدين من البعثات
الأخرى في الكلية الذين أظهروا ثقتهم بالكلية لمشاهدة المشروع والاستفادة منه
في التكتيك العام

ثانياً: عن ايجابيات البعثة

أ- على صعيد التدريب

١- الاستفادة من مواضيع الدروس بشكل جيد ... وقد شهد المعلمون
أن البعثة الفلسطينية أحسن بعثة من القدرة الرائعة على الاستيعاب
خلافاً للبعثات الأخرى

٢- هنا يتقدم شهادة المعلمين لبعثة الدم/ق. أنهم وصلوا من التدريب إلى تحرير
مواقعهم واحتلال مواقع العدو في معارك تكتيكية في الميدان المطلوب.

٣- شهد المعلمون الذين اعتقدوا دورة الدم/ط عند حضورهم إلى مدينة [illegible]
المعاني أنهم بأكفاء جيدين

٤- ونتيجة لظهور البعثة الفلسطينية وعنفوانها الجيد عند مناقشة القضايا السياسية
في دروس المنهاج السياسي والذي يعتبر المرحلة الموضوعية من المذاهب
الخاصة لهذه الدورات خصوصاً ويركزون عليه.

ب- على صعيد العلاقات

١- بناء علاقات جيدة ضمن إطار الكلية مع المدرسين والعاملين.

٢- التعرف على عادات وتقاليد شعوب الدول المضيفة

٣- الشرح المستفيض عن القضية الفلسطينية ودور منظمة التحرير الفلسطينية
الممثل الشرعي والوحيد للشعب الفلسطيني والثورة المسلحة حتى تحقيق أهدافها
وإقامة الدولة المستقلة.

٤- التعرف على البعثات الأخرى وحركات التحرر وبناء العلاقات الجيدة بينهم
وقضيتنا سواء من خلال اللقاءات الشخصية أو من خلال الاجتماعات والندوات
الرسمية ومناسباتنا الوطنية.

ولقد بلغ تفهم بعثة جنوب أفريقيا لثورتنا وقضيتنا الفلسطينية أن قدمت
قائدة البعثة في حفل تخرجهم [illegible] جميع البعثات وإدارة الكلية [illegible]
[illegible] الثورة الفلسطينية والتضامن [illegible] أكثر ما تحدث عن نفسه

يتبع

Document 27A-6

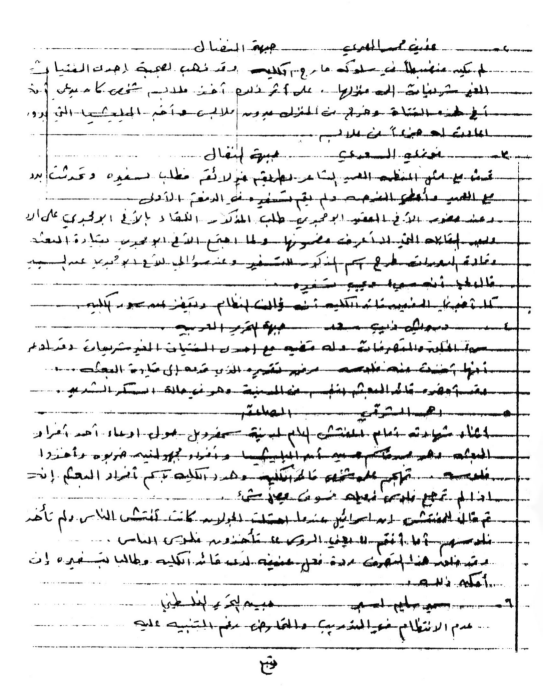

٢- عفيف محمد المصري   جبهة النضال

لم يكن منضبطاً في سلوكه ما رجع للكلية وقد ذهب بصحبة إحدى الفتيات

الغير شرعيات الى منزلها ، على أثر ذلك أخذ ملابس شخص كان موجوداً في

أي هذه الفتاة وخرج من المنزل بدون ملابس وأخذ الملابس التي

العائدة له جزءاً من ملابسه

٣- توفيق السعدي   جبهة النضال

تحدث مع ممثل المنظمة العسكرية بشأن طريقته في الأكل فطلب تسفيره وتحدثت بعد

مع العسكري وأعطي الفرصة ولم يتم تسفيره في الدفعة الأولى

وعند حضور الأخ العقيد أبو مجدي طلب المذكور اللقاء بالأخ أبو مجدي على أن

يطلب إقالته التي لا أعرف مضمونها ولما اجتمع الأخ أبو مجدي بقيادة المعهد

وقيادة البعثات طرح حكم المذكور التسفير وعند سؤال الأخ أبو مجدي عن السبب

قال له إنه [illegible] يجب تسفيره .

كما أخبر المفتش الكلية أنه قال إن النظام [illegible] الكلية .

٤- [illegible]   جبهة التحرير العربية

سوء الخلق والتصرفات وله قضية مع إحدى الفتيات الغير شرعيات وقد ادعى

أنها أخذت منه فلوسه [illegible] تقريره الذي قدمه إلى قيادة البعثة ...

فقد قائد البعثة بنفسه [illegible] وهو في حالة السكر الشديد .

٥- احمد الشرقي   الصاعقة

أثناء شهادته أمام المفتش [illegible] أحد أفراد

البعثة [illegible] فضربوه وأخذوا

فلوسه . [illegible] قائد الكلية [illegible] أفراد البعثة إنه

إذا لم ترجع [illegible] شيء .

ثم قال المفتش إن إسرائيل عندما احتلت الجولان كانت تفتش الناس ولم تأخذ

فلوسهم أما أنتم [illegible] تأخذون فلوس الناس .

وقد طلب هذا الشخص [illegible] لدى قائد الكلية وطالبا بتسفيره إن

أمكن ذلك .

٦- [illegible] سليم [illegible]   جبهة التحرير الفلسطينية

عدم الانتظام في التدريب والتمارض رغم التنبيه عليه

توقيع

Document 27A-5

٤- عدم الانضباط الجيد من قبل الطلبة من غالبية التنظيمات المعنية في الدورات مما
قيادة البعثة الى تسفير عدد قليل أذكرهم مع الاسباب الداعية لتسفيرهم وهم :-

الدفعة الأولى

١- الملازم/ عبد المنعم البدري — جبهة التحرير الفلسطيني

[illegible] قادة سرايا استطلاع — طلب تحويله الى دورة ما [illegible]
[illegible] قيادة البعثة وممثل منظمة التحرير تقسم طلب بطلب
التسفير [illegible] لتلقي العلم العسكري [illegible] وتم
الطلب التسفير الى قيادة البعثة.

٢- عبد جواد حنا — الجبهة الديمقراطية

طالب بافتعال مشاكل تنظيمية بين الجبهة الديمقراطية وجبهة النضال [illegible]
مع الرفيق [illegible] من جبهة النضال

٣- [illegible] حنا بكر — الصاعقة

طلب التسفير [illegible] لأسباب [illegible] لا تسمح باستمرار الدراسة وتم ذلك
بعلم قيادة البعثة وممثل المنظمة

٤- محمود حنا محمود — الصاعقة

طلب التسفير لأسباب صحية لا تسمح باستمرار الدراسة ومتابعة الدورة وتم ذلك
بعلم قيادة البعثة وممثل المنظمة [illegible]

٥- [illegible] البيطار — الصاعقة

طلب التسفير لأسباب صحية لا تسمح باستمرار الدراسة ومتابعة الدورة وتم ذلك
بعلم قيادة البعثة وممثل المنظمة.

٦- ملازم/ ابراهيم [illegible] — جبهة التحرير الفلسطيني

طلب التسفير لأسباب صحية لا تسمح باستمرار ومتابعة الدورة وعندما حضر
الأخ [illegible] الرائد [illegible] وحضر حاول اقناعه ولكنه دون جدوى

الدفعة الثانية

١- علي [illegible] — جبهة التحرير الفلسطينية

فشل في قيادة [illegible] الصواريخ المعنية عليها وكان مثالاً سيئاً من الانضباط
العسكري حيث كان يتميز بسوء [illegible] الكلية مخالفة النظام.
هذا [illegible] قيادة البعثة من قيادة الكلية [illegible] علاقة [illegible] والأراء
المزاجية

يتبع

Document 27A-8

ومتابعة القائد المباشر منه مع الانضباط الجيد.

٥- اطلاع العسكريين في دورات الخارج على نظم وقوانين الكلية الخاصة بهم قبل السفر.

٦- تنفيذ ترقية الدورات الخارجية والاكتفاء بالدورات الخارجية عن ترقية داخلية للكليات

للضباط بسرعة الشديدة.

٧- في حالة ضرورة ارسال الدورات بجميع المراحل واختصاصاتها يفضل أن يكون

الحكم قليل بحيث لا تكون قد مرينا من ترقية الدورة في نفس الوقت الفترة

متاحة لاحد لمثل الجيد.

٨- في حالة ارسال دورات باعداد كبيرة يفضل تعيين قائد لهذه متفرغ معهم مع

في أي دورة.

٩- كما يفضل العسكريين من الضباط الذين سجلوا دورة أخرى دورة في نفس الدولة

وعلم بالقوانين والانظمة.

١٠- تزويد مكتبات العسكريين في الخارج بعدد لا بأس به من الكتب باللغات الاجنبية

والأفضل لغة البلد المضيف سواء كتب سياسية أو تاريخية أو تراثية

وكذلك تزويدهم بالمجلات وجميع منشورات منظمة التحرير الفلسطينية ومختلف

ارسال الصحف والنشرات عن طريق البريد وبشكل منتظم.

١١- القائد العام حفظه الله

اسمح لي أن أتقدم بهذا التقرير باسم البعثة الفلسطينية في الاتحاد السوفيتي

معبرين عن أننا سنظل عند حسن ظنكم وقيادتكم الحكيمة حتى تحقيق النصر

والعودة لدولتنا المستقلة.

عاشت منظمة التحرير الفلسطينية بقيادتكم

الممثل الشرعي والوحيد لشعبنا الفلسطيني

وإنها لثورة حتى النصر

مقدم / رشاد أحمد النبريصي

قائد البعثة « مزوبل »

الاتحاد السوفيتي.

Document 27A-7

٧ـ مجموعة منشقة فتح

تم تصفية بعض عناصرها بعد اغتيال المفتي محمد أنه له مشكلة مع إرادة أبو شيت
وقد تمثلنا النقص بها لسفر تكلفة آخر المؤسسة ـ ويقبض بوظيفة أبو حمزة عقد لواء
ومغنى نقدم عنه لقيادة الجيش.

قضية المولويات الذين وقد علمت بإرسالكم للتقرير عنها عن طريق الأخ
نقل المنظمة في معسكر العبيد إثر تاريخ ٨/١٠/١٩٨١ ـ

ثالثاً: الوضع العام

لم يتم تنفيذ البند الأول والثاني على أكمل وجه في ذلك راجع لذوي الحوال
السوفيت والنوريين لم يسمح لإختيارهم وبالرغم من ذلك فقد تكررت الأخطاء
على مستوى قيادة الجيش أو تنفيذ المستفيد من بعيد والحرمان من التطورات
مع الأوامر والتعليمات لم تنفذ أصلاً العملية وتكون أمام مصلحة ثورتنا
وشعبنا فقيادات قيادة الجيش كانت جهودها وعلاقاتها للمستجاب الكثيرة لكل
وقفت منها آخر لحظة وكان على ذلك شاهد مسؤول الأخ الأول العقيد أبو جودة
ومن معه منها لما ذهب أحد أفراد الجبهة الشعبية في إجازة واسمه سعيد
عن أحمد لم يعط المالكية الذي يستلم الرابعة والنصف صباحاً. وكان اليوم الثاني
هو يوم حل الترحيل فقرر قائد الكتيبة حرمانه من التنزيلات وعاقبناه حبساً على ذلك
وعاقبه بالأخ أبو جودة وتكون دون تنفيذ التنزيلات وعلى قائد الكتيبة عن قرار
مسؤول المركز مشاركته.

ومن خلال هذه التجربة في قيادة الجيش هنا العدد الكبير أرجو أن تسمح لي بإعطاء
الخبرة والشغال لأن اكتب الاقتراحات البسيطة. أرجو أن تدرس والأخذ بتجنيد
الاعتماد ما هو مفيد منها من أجل مصلحة ثورتنا وشعبنا في الخارج.

اقتراحات :ـ

١ـ إجراء دورة تثقيفية للدارسين بالخارج قبل الإيفاد عن آخر التطورات للتصفيت
بشرح الأهداف الفلسطينية من وراء البعثات العسكرية للخارج.

٢ـ إجراء توجيهات أوليه من قبل مديرية التدريب للمعنيين في الدورات للإدارة
مع التنسيق الجيد المستمر مع الذين يتنازون هذه التوجيهات.

٣ـ إخضاع الضباط المعنيين لقيادة الدورات للاختبار القدرة الشخصية
على القيادة دون النظر إلى التنظيمات أو الأقدمية ((الكفاءة))

٤ـ اختيار الشخص الجيد القادر على التمثيل الخارجي وتكون المسؤولية

يتبع

[Document 28]: Report of PLO delegation to East Germany

The visit took place during April 1982.

The delegation arrived at the East Berlin airport at 13:00 and was met by the Deputy Defence Minister, General Fleissner; the Chief of Staff, General Helmuth Borowke; Colonel Karl Keides; and the interpreter, Captain Roland Kuchbuch.

After a brief rest in the VIP room at the airport, General Fleissner handed us our visit schedule:

14 April — no formal talks.

15 April — talks about training with General Borowke and Colonel Bonowke, the man in charge of recruitment and training in the military training centre. In the afternoon, a colonel from General Fleissner's office will survey the military assistance to be delivered to us, and will determine with us the time and location of delivery. Once agreed, a final protocol will be prepared for signature.

16 April — Visit to the recruitment and training centre of the ground forces to review the training programme, training aids, ranges, naval equipment, training in grenade launching and anti-aircraft training. Later on, discussions will be held with air defence and coastal defence experts to determine our needs.

17 April — Talks with the Department of Foreign Trade and sightseeing.

18 April — Visit to Berlin.

19 April — Signature of the protocols, official banquet, special tour of the city and then departure to Hungary.

The Visit:

On 15 April we held discussions on training; General Borowke, accompanied by Colonel Bonowke, Karl Keides and Captain Roland came in. The Palestinian delegation included Captain 'Abd al-Na'im.

General Borowke: In view of the talks held last October between General Fleissner and the deputy commander of the PLO, we had agreed to accept PLO trainees into our military, and absorb them in our military schools. I wish to point out that in training our officers, we stress the following:

1. Political indoctrination: a general survey of sociology and politics and clarification of the general purpose of training. All this is done under the supervision of an army officer.

2. Technical and tactical training.

3. Physical fitness.

We also teach mathematics, physics and the German language. The Marxist-Leninist theory is the foundation of our training. Do you object to that?

Answer: Not at all!

Our query: Will our trainees be trained separately or together with German officers? We would like them to be mixed with the Germans and to undertake the same pattern of training.

Answer: There is no special training camp for the Palestinians. Therefore, they will train with German officers, although as a separate group, because of their limited knowledge of German and because the Germans also study Russian.

Our delegation stressed once more our request that the training be mixed with German officers.

General Borowke: We have another problem. We have explained to the deputy commander of the PLO that our training period is three years. In our artillery course we train in fast and comprehensive deployment. The deputy commander has asked us to speed up the training and we agreed to concur down to the battery level.

Our delegation asked about the numbers of our candidates and their skills.

Answer: In our previous talks we agreed about the numbers, and agreed that they would be trained to operate Soviet weapons.

Our delegation asked that the numbers be increased and that relations be further strengthened between Palestinians and the German army and people.

Answer: In principle, we will maintain the number of trainees we agreed upon and we will determine the programme of training accordingly. We will inform you of all details through the embassy[42] as regards any increase in the number of trainees and we will specify that in the protocol.

Our delegation: How about altering the specialization of trainees already agreed upon in the protocol?

Answer: If we distribute them in various units, this would increase expenditures. However, with regard to certain specializations, we will dispatch the trainees to the Soviet Union.

Our delegation: If you approve an increase in numbers, we would like the following specializations: 10 trainees in armour and 10 in engineering.

Answer: We agree, and we will let you know via the embassy before May 30.

The protocol was approved.

Our delegation expressed its gratitude about the understanding shown for our needs and the response to our requests. We submitted an invitation to the minister of defence on the part of the deputy commander of the PLO to visit us. General Fleissner had suggested that we invite him during our rest at the airport, and asked us to inform the deputy commander of the PLO that the minister would visit Syria in September, and would like to meet the commander general of the PLO and his deputy in Damascus. Our delegation also asked to meet with the defence minister in order to deliver to him personally the greetings and the invitation of the commander and his deputy.

Thursday afternoon

Colonel Karl Keides from the Ministry of Defence declared that he was authorized by General Fleissner to discuss military assistance. Before he began, he apologized that the minister would be unable to meet us; our delegation showed understanding.

18 April 1982, 10:00

The foreign trade official brought along the prices of the items we want to purchase:

(1) A light coastguard vessel, armed with a missile — $118,000.

In the original, a variety of ammunition and guns — 27mm, 57mm, 100mm, 122mm, 130mm — are listed with their prices.

---

42. In the Soviet bloc, the Palestinian envoys are accredited as full ambassadors and their legations enjoy the rank of embassies.

Delivery

Some items can be delivered immediately, and others within four weeks of payment in bank. The above prices include loading aboard ships in Rostock, Germany. The prices will be increased by 10 percent if the deliveries are brought to Tartus.

Monday, 11:00

Signature of the protocol and its annexes in the presence of General Fleissner. Then an official banquet and exchange of presents.

Monday, 19:00

Dinner at the residence of the Palestinian ambassador with General Fleissner attending, along with the deputy defence minister and Chief of Staff General Borowke. The general delivered a speech expressing his admiration for the quality of our delegation, its courtesy, and its military, political and professional skill.

Document 28A-1

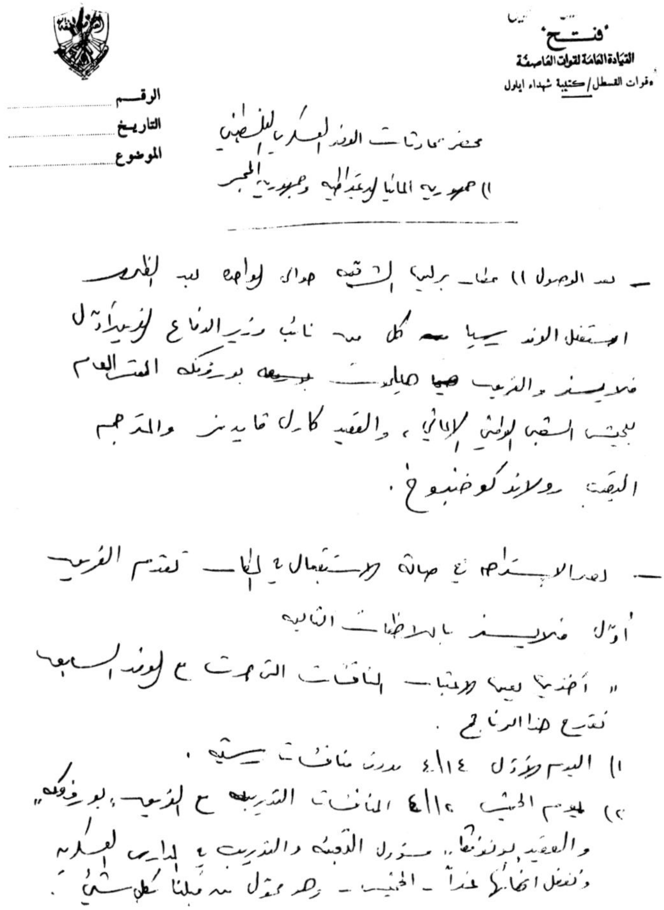
فتح
القيادة العامة لقوات العاصفة
قوات القسطل/كتيبة شهداء ايلول

الرقم
التاريخ
الموضوع

محضر محادثات الوفد العسكري الفلسطيني
مع جمهورية المانيا الديمقراطية وجمهورية المجر

- بعد الوصول الى مطار برلين الشرقية حوالي الواحدة بعد الظهر
استقبل الوفد رسميا من قبل نائب وزير الدفاع الفريق أول
فلايسنر والفريق [illegible] بروفكه المفتش العام
للجيش الشعبي الوطني الالماني، والعقيد كارل فايدنر والمترجم
[illegible] كوخنبوخ.

- بعد الاستراحة في صالة الاستقبال في المطار تقدم الفريق
أول فلايسنر بالملاحظات التالية
" أخذنا بعين الاعتبار المناقشات التي تمت مع الوفد السابق
لتقديم هذا البرنامج.
1) اليوم الأول 14/10 بدون مناقشات سياسية.
2) اليوم الثاني 15/10 المناقشات التدريبية مع الفريق بروفكه
والعقيد [illegible] مسؤول التعبئة والتدريب في ادارة العمليات
[illegible] غدا الخميس [illegible] كل شيء.

Document 28A-2,3

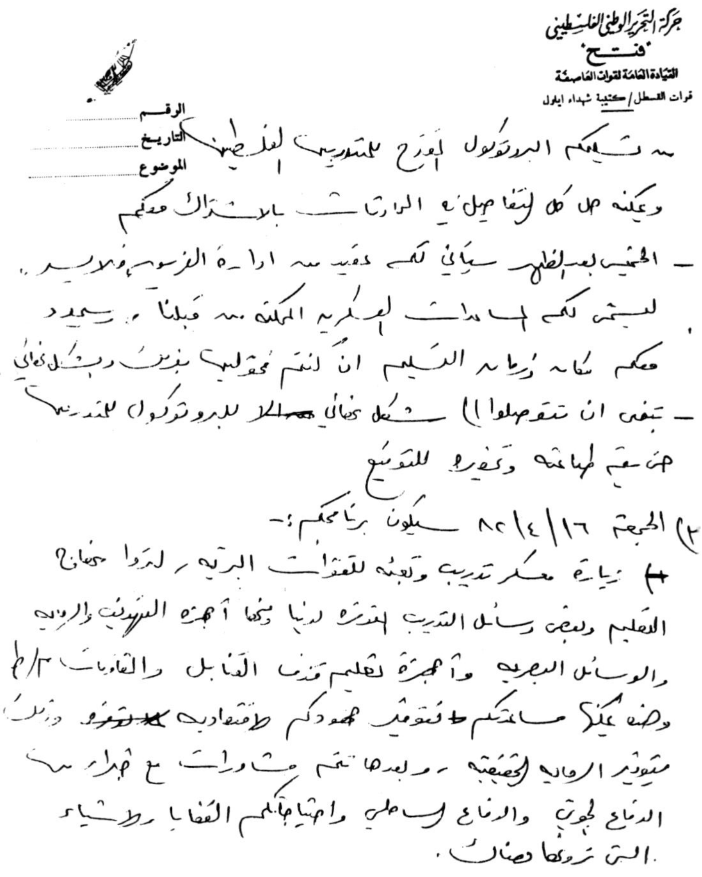
حركة التحرير الوطني الفلسطيني
"فتح"
القيادة العامة لقوات العاصفة
قوات القسطل/كتيبة شهداء ايلول
الرقم
التاريخ
الموضوع

من شأنكم البروتوكول المقترح للتدريب الفلسطيني
وعليه حل كل التفاصيل في الزيارات بالاشتراك معكم
- الخميس بعد الظهر سيأتي لكم وفد من ادارة الفروع [illegible]
لبحث لكم المساعدات العسكرية الممكنة من قبلنا ، ويحدد
معكم مكان وزمان التسليم ان كنتم [illegible]
- نرجو ان تتوصلوا الى شكل نهائي للبروتوكول للتدريب
من شقيه لمناقشته وتحضيره للتوقيع
٢) الجمعة ١٦/٤/٨٢ سيكون برنامجكم:
+ زيارة معسكر تدريب وتعبئة للقوات البرية ، لتروا منهاج
التعليم وبعض وسائل التدريب المتوفرة لدينا ومنها أجهزة التلفزيون والراديو
والوسائل التجريبية وأجهزة لتعليم قذف القنابل والقاذفات [illegible]
وضعنا [illegible] لتوفير جهودكم [illegible]
متوفر الوسائل الحقيقية ، وبعدها تتم مشاورات مع خبراء من
الدفاع الجوي والدفاع الساحلي واحتياجاتكم القضايا والأشياء
التي تريدونها هناك .

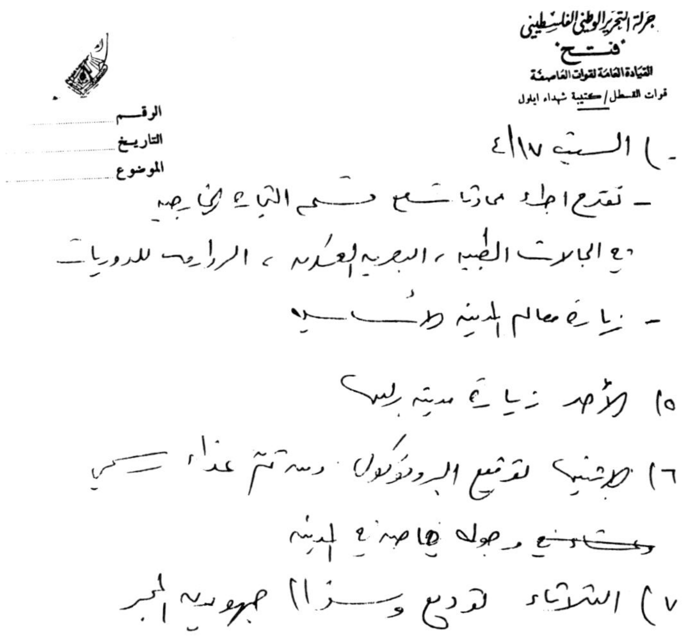
حركة التحرير الوطني الفلسطيني
"فتح"
القيادة العامة لقوات العاصفة
قوات القسطل/كتيبة شهداء ايلول
الرقم
التاريخ
الموضوع

٣) السبت ١٧/٤
- نقترح اجراء مباريات [illegible] في قسم [illegible]
في المجالات الطبية ، البحرية العسكرية ، الزراعية للدوريات
- زيارة معالم المدينة [illegible]
٥) الأحد زيارة مدينة [illegible]
٦) الاثنين لتوقيع البروتوكول ويتم غداء [illegible]
[illegible] ودخول [illegible] في المدينة
٧) الثلاثاء لتوديع [illegible] جمهورية [illegible]

Document 28A-4,5

حركة التحرير الوطني الفلسطيني
"فتح"
القيادة العامة لقوات العاصفة
قوات القسطل/ كتيبة شهداء ايلول

الرقم ....
التاريخ ....
الموضوع ....

- أحب أن أعرف هنا ملاحظة يا رفاق
هل أنه سيكون هناك تدريب الرياضيات والفيزياء
مع اللغة الالمانية ايضاً لتتم طلعة قاعدة للتدريب عليها.
- سيكون النجاح لدى الشقي هو القاعدة التثقيفية هل هناك
مانع لديكم أو اعتراض على هذا النوع التدريب ؟؟

جواب : كلا لا مانع

سؤال من الوفد :- هل المتدربين سيكونوا لوحدهم أم
مع الضباط الالمان . بالنسبة لرغبتنا نحن نتمنى ان يكون ذلك
مع الضباط الالمان وبنفس المقاع دورة التدريب .
جواب : انه لا يوجد مقر خاص ~~للتدريب~~ للتدريب الفلسطينيين
لذا فانهم سيتدربون مع الضباط الالمان وكذلك كمجموعة
ذاتية ، وذلك لان اتقانهم الالمانية لن يكون كالعرب
الالمان كما انه لا يوجد هنا مترجمين للعربية . لذا سيكونوا مع اخوانهم

حركة التحرير الوطني الفلسطيني
"فتح"
القيادة العامة لقوات العاصفة
قوات القسطل/ كتيبة شهداء ايلول

الرقم ....
التاريخ ....
الموضوع ....

-- متى الدفعة الاخرى ان يتم التدريب مع الضباط
الالمان ان امكن .

الفريق بوزمك : هناك قضية أخرى ، لقد شرحنا لنائب القائد
العام بان التدريب لدينا مدته ثلاث سنوات ، حيث المدفعية
تدرس الاستخدام الكامل والفني والتكتيكي ، وقد طلب منا ان
نضع في التدريب كل ولمدة ستة شهور ، وأفهمنا بالموافقة من
مستوى القيادة وهناك حالات جديدة في القيادة أن يتلقوها .
ولدي سؤال : ماذا بالنسبة لضباط تأهيل الحديثة للمدفعية ؟
ماذا تريدون ؟!
جواب الوفد - نريد تخريج هندسة مدفعية ان كان ذلك ممكناً
الفريق : اننا ندرب الضباط على كيفية استخدام اي شيء
من ادارة منطقة مدفعية كاملة عامة الاستخدام الفني
والاصلاحات البسيطة ، نحن لا ندرب في الصيانة ، انه
خاص في القوات يطلب اليه استخدام المدفع فقط

Document 28A-6,7

حركة التحرير الوطني الفلسطيني
"فتح"
القيادة العامة لقوات العاصفة
قوات القسطل/ كتيبة شهداء ايلول

الرقم ....
التاريخ ....
الموضوع ....

الموضوع : (محادثات التدريب)

حضر الوفد بورونكه ورافقه العقيد بولونكا والعقيد كارل فايدنر والترجمان النقيب رولاند كوجيشوخ . والوفد الفلسطيني + الرائد [illegible]

الوفد ~~بورونكه~~ بورونكه

استنادا الى الاتفاقات التي اجراها الرفيق [illegible] مع الرفيق [illegible] القائد العام في تونس اول تم الاتفاق على تبادل مدربين من منظمة التحرير في جيشنا وجيش [illegible] ولذلك ان [illegible] بخصوص باب التدريب للضباط عندنا يؤكد [illegible] اختصاصات رئيسية :

١) تدريب سياسي :- معرفة عامة عن العلوم الاجتماعية والسياسية وهذا [illegible] ان يكون كل [illegible] ضابط عسكري .

٢) تدريب فني وتكتيكي وتعبوي

٣) التدريب البدني واللياقة البدنية لكون الضابط قدوة لجنوده

[illegible]

حركة التحرير الوطني الفلسطيني
"فتح"
القيادة العامة لقوات العاصفة
قوات القسطل/ كتيبة شهداء ايلول

الرقم ....
التاريخ ....
الموضوع ....

- طلب من الوفد باضافة تعليم اصلاح المدافع والرشاشات حتى يمكنه نقل الـ ١١ المتدرب عدد ٢ المدفعية .

جواب الوفد : نوافق ، حتى تعلم صنع بعض الادوات من الحديد المتوفر لديه ومستعينا بالمناظ الدفيه ، ونقدم تدريب ضباط لصف للاعمال الصيانية الكاملة .

سؤال الوفد : هل هذا يشمل جميع انواع المدفعية ؟

جواب الوفد : نعم سيكون مدافع ١٢٢ ملم وشتمل السيطرة بانواع المدافع ٨٢ ملم ، ١٢٠ ملم ، ١٣٠ ملم/ د ١٢٠ ملم .

وفي اخر نصف ~~[illegible]~~ للتنسيب فانه سيكون له تخصص بنوع المدفعية التي تكون وحدته . كما سيتم تدريبهم ٨ الاجهزة البصرية .

سؤال الوفد :- عن العدد والاختصاصات للتنسيب ؟

جواب الوفد : عا بخصوص العدد فانه يتفق عليه في المحادثات السابقة والصواريخ سنقوم بالتدريب ٢ [illegible] السوفيتية .

[illegible]

Document 28A-8,9

حركة التحرير الوطني الفلسطيني "فتح"
القيادة العامة لقوات العاصفة
قوات القسطل/كتيبة شهداء ايلول

الرقم
التاريخ
الموضوع

طلب من الوفد : في حالة الموافقة على الزيارة
نطلب الاختصاصات التالية عدد عشرة أفراد دروع +
عشرة أفراد هندسة .

الوفد : موافقون على الاختصاصات وسنبلغكم
عن طريق السفارة قبل ٢٠ آب [نص البروتوكول
في ذلك] وقدمت مسودة البروتوكول للدراسة والموافقة .

الوفد الفلسطيني : تقدم بالشكر على تفهم ظروفنا وحاجاتنا
وأكد على دعوة الأخ نائب القائد العام لوزير الدفاع لزيارتنا
((أعلم الوفد فلاسيز قد أشار إلى هذه الدعوة في الاستراحة بالطائرة . وأجابنا
ابلاغ الأخ نائب القائد العام بأن السيد وزير الدفاع سيزور سوريا في أيلول ويود
لو يقابل الأخ القائد العام ونائبه في دمشق))
كما تمنى الوفد أن تتاح له فرصة زيارة وزير الدفاع
لنقل تحيات القائد العام ونائبا القائد العام وتؤكد على الأهمية .

حركة التحرير الوطني الفلسطيني "فتح"
القيادة العامة لقوات العاصفة
قوات القسطل/كتيبة شهداء ايلول

الرقم
التاريخ
الموضوع

وستزيد العلاقة لتوثيقها بين الجيشين
الفلسطيني والألماني وتدين الشعبين ولدينا عدداً كبيراً من الطلبة .
جواب الرئيس : نتبنى أيضاً قائمة مباريات تدريب الثاني وأقدم
عليكم ما يلي .

~~مناقشة~~ مبدئياً العدد المتفق عليه في المباريات
السابقة يبقى كما هو ومن ثم ندرس امكانياتنا فيما تطلبونه
(مدرسين ، مدارس وكل التفاصيل المتعلقة بالتدريب) وسنخبركم
عن طريق السفارة هنا ~~وبشكل~~ في وقت واضح وصريح . وعلى كل
زيارة العدد ستتم عليه للبروتوكول [نص الملحق في الزيارة]

سؤال من الوفد : من امكانية تبديل الاختصاصات المتفق عليها
في البروتوكول .

جواب الوفد : لقد أبلغكم سيزيد الانفاق الاقتصادي منذ
لا نستطيع أن نعلمكم كما لهم . ووضعت الاختصاصات الحالية
حسب تقديم من الاتحاد السوفيتي .

Document 28A-10,11

التاريخ ....
الموضوع ....

الخميس - بعد الظهر

العقيد كارل فايدنر

المقدم كاستينك أمين مكتب وزير الدفاع

ترحيب واستعداد انهم متحمسين من قبل الزعيم أول فلايسنر

بإجراء محادثات حول المساعدات

قبل البدء تقدموا باعتذار - [طلبتم زيارة الجنرال فاندلش

وزير الدفاع، ولقد بلغ رغبتكم، ولكن الوزير آسف جداً

حيث لم يتمكن، مشغول بواجبات الزامية ويعرب عن اسفه

الشديد = هناك وزير دفاع مفضولا = ويرجو تقبل التحيات

١) الرفاق القائد ... ونائب القائد ... ونقترح انه زيارة

للزعيم أول فلايسنر يوم ١٩/٤ للغداء معه] .

الوفد الفلسطيني - تفهم ظروف وزير الدفاع. وشكره

أخوي وابلاغه تحيات القيادة وترحيبنا به في منطقتنا

العقيد فايدنر : تم الاتفاق مع الوفد السابق في تشرين ان

نبحث مع وفد الخبراء تفاصيل المساعدات، وطلب وزير

القيادة العامة لقوات العاصفة
قوات القسطل/كتيبة شهداء ايلول

الرقم ....
التاريخ ....
الموضوع ....

~~الحزب~~

الدفاع ان نقدم كشفا متفقا عليه

بالمساعدات مراحل لتوقيعها باسم الحزب والدولة .

- لقد وجه الزعيم أول فلايسنر اهتمامنا مع الوفد

الرئيسي ونقدم الشكر بشكل صريح اهتمامنا في الحزب الوطني

بالمساعدة هذه .

١- رشاشات M.BH1 عدد ٨٠٠ رشاش
ذخائر للرشاشات عدد ٧٢٠ ألف طلقة

٢- مدفع م/ط ٥٧ ملم عدد ٦ مدافع
طلقات مدافع ٥٧ ملم عدد ١٢ ألف طلقة

٣- مناظير قياس ٧×٤٠ عدد ٢٠-٢٤٠ منظار

٤- أدوية ومعدات طبية عدد ٣٠٠ قيمة (٥٠) ألف مارك الماني .

٥- القيمة الإجمالية ٢,٢ مليون مارك الماني

٦- تم تسعيرها بالتخفيف من جهة المانية .

٧- نقترح مناقشة قضية التسليم والتوقيع ومباشرة ومسؤولية
(من تسلمه وأين واذا كان بحراً فإلى أي ميناء)

Document 28A-12,13

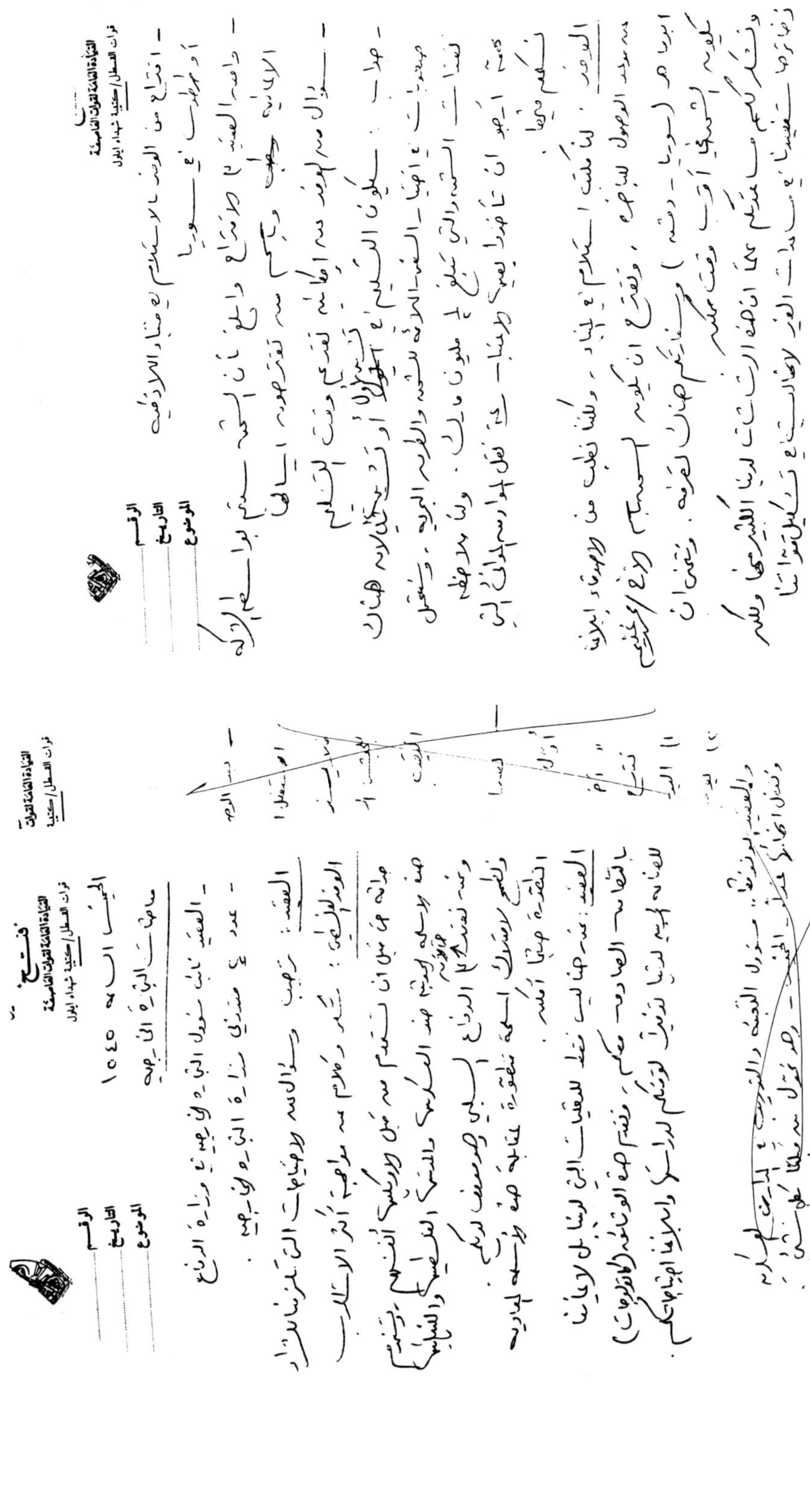

فتح

القيادة العامة لقوات العاصفة

قوات العاصفة / كتيبة شهداء ايلول

الرقم

التاريخ

الموضوع

فتح

القيادة العامة لقوات العاصفة

قوات العاصفة / كتيبة شهداء ايلول

الرقم

التاريخ

الموضوع

Document 28A-14,15

فتح
القيادة العامة لقوات العاصفة
قوات القسطل/كتيبة شهداء ايلول

الرقم ....
التاريخ ....
الموضوع ....

الوفد : لابد من الاطلاع عليها بشكل
سريع لنقدم لقيادتكم فكرة مسبقاً عما رأيناه نحو
تحديث قواتنا ودعمها .

الجمعة ١٦/٤/٨٢

زيارة ميدان التدريب والرماية والآت وأجهزة
الإيضاح والاطلاع على مناهج وطرق التدريب
واعتقد انه كان هناك كلاماً مهماً جداً مع الاصدقاء
بما فيهم خبراء الدفاع الجوي والدفاع الساحلي
حيث انه تم شرح ظروف شعبنا وقواتنا والمشاكل
التي تعترضنا جواً وبحراً مع العدو الصهيوني
ولقد أعجب الرفاق بأقلنا وتأثروا جداً عسكريا
وسياسياً بكلام الوفد بوعي وفهم وصدق وصراحة
اثرت في الجميع . وأضيف ان متطلباتنا تعتمد على ما رأيناه

والقصد بالوفد: مسؤول التعبئة والتدريب في الاجهزة العسكرية
ونقل انطباع هذا الجيش - وهو تحويل من قبلنا [illegible]

[illegible]

فتح
القيادة العامة لقوات العاصفة
قوات القسطل/كتيبة شهداء ايلول

الرقم ....
التاريخ ....
الموضوع ....

أو إلى الساعة ... وكان يوم كسب
أصدقاء جدد للشعب والثورة .

السبت ١٧/٤/٨٢

- عرض مقترح البروتوكول بما فيه المحور الذي سنطلب
فيه طلب زيادة المتدربين في مقاعد للدروع والهندسة .
- أبلغنا انهم أخذوا الترتيبات لاستقبال المتدربين
الفلسطينيين يوم (٢٧-٢٩) أيلول من بعد
وسنجمع البرنامج قبل ... (كما نص البروتوكول)
- لقد طلب زيارة المعالم المهمة في برلين
١٧/٤ جولة حول برلين وزيارة حائط برلين
والقلعة والبرج .

والقصد بالوفد: مسؤول التعبئة والتدريب في الاجهزة العسكرية
ونقل انطباع هذا الجيش - وهو تحويل من قبلنا [illegible]

[illegible]

Document 28A-16,17

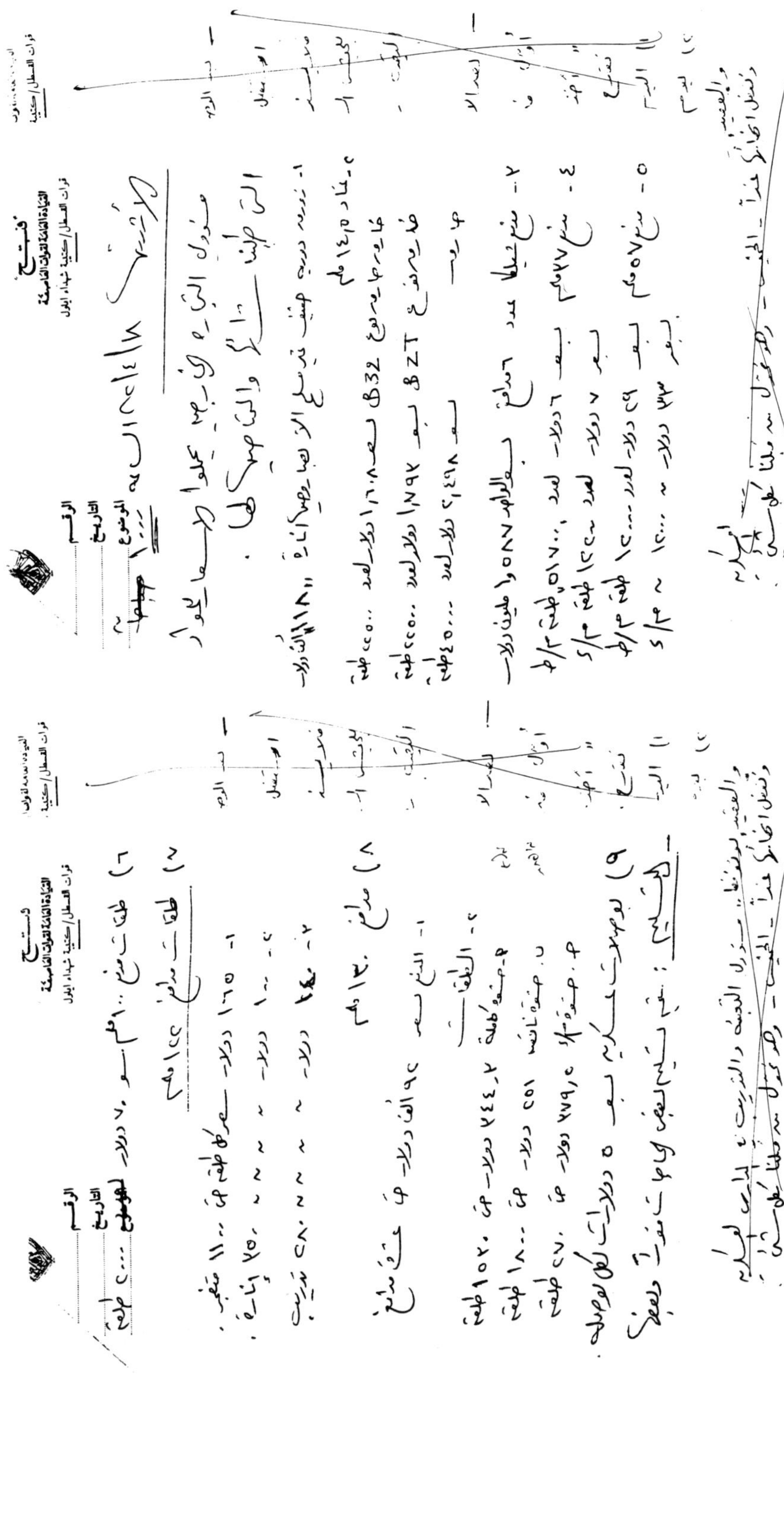

Document 28A-18,19

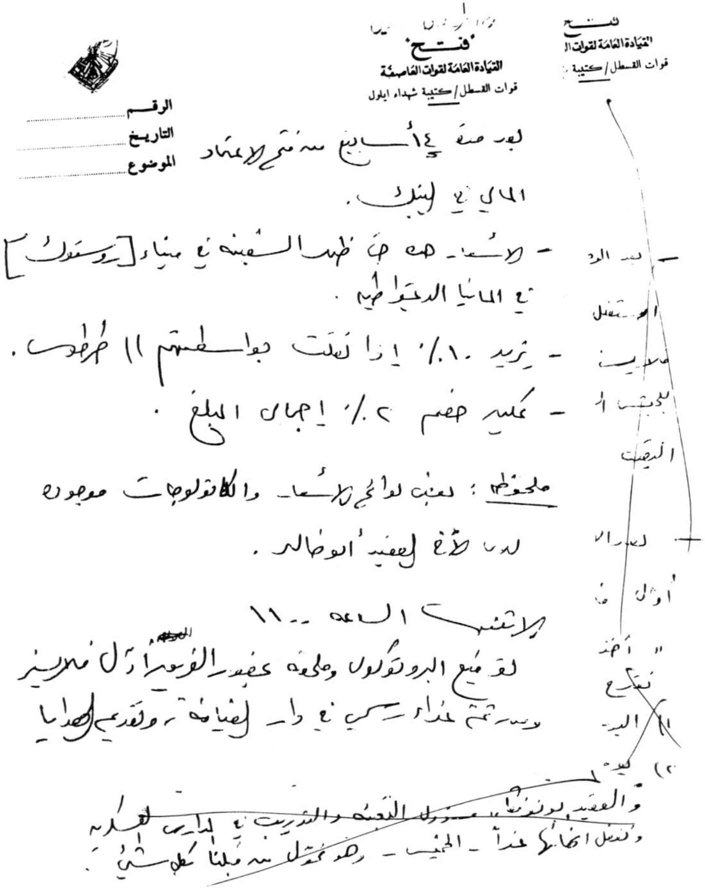

فتح

القيادة العامة لقوات العاصفة

قوات القسطل/كتيبة شهداء ايلول

الرقم

التاريخ

الموضوع

لقد مضى ١٤ أسبوع من فتح الاعتماد المالي في البنك.

- الأسلحة هي في طريق الشحن في ميناء [روستوك] في المانيا الديمقراطية.
- نزيد ١٠٪ إذا نقلت بواسطتهم الى بيروت.
- تكلفة خصم ٢٪ إجمالي المبلغ.

ملحوظة: لوائح الأسلحة والكتالوجات موجودة لدى الأخ العقيد أبو طالب.

الرشيدية الساعة ١١:٠٠

لقد تم البروتوكول [illegible] الفريق أول [illegible] [illegible] وتقديم الهدايا

والعقيد [illegible] مسؤول التعبئة والتدريب في [illegible] ونفضل [illegible] غداً - الخميس - [illegible] من قبلنا [illegible].

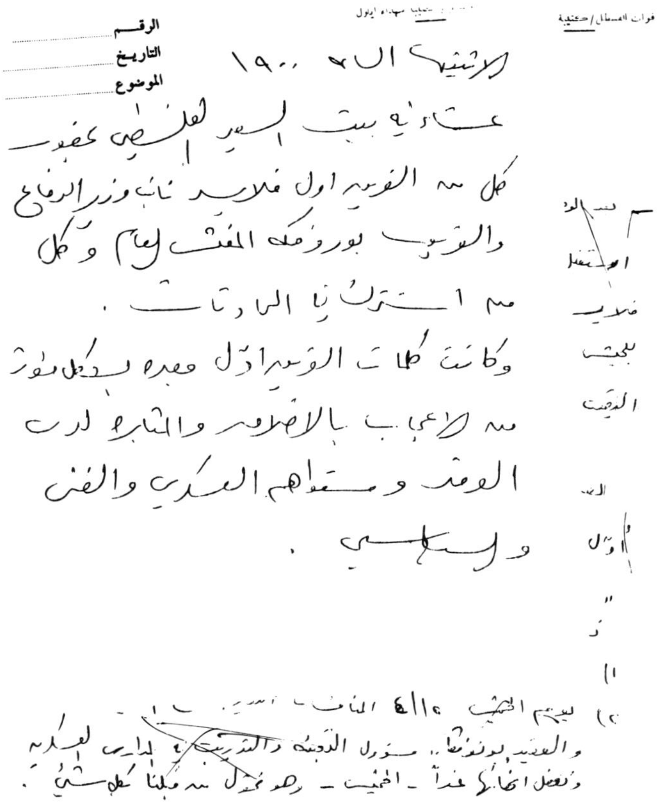

قوات القسطل/كتيبة شهداء ايلول

الرقم

التاريخ

الموضوع

الرشيدية ٢ ١٩:٠٠

عشاء في بيت السفير الفلسطيني بحضور كل من الفريق أول [illegible] نائب وزير الدفاع والفريق [illegible] المفتش العام وكل من اشترك في المباحثات.

وكانت كلمات الفريق أول معبرة [illegible] من الإعجاب بالأصدقاء [illegible] الوفد ومستواهم العسكري والفني والسياسي.

[illegible] ١٩:٠٠ [illegible]

والعقيد [illegible] مسؤول التعبئة والتدريب [illegible] ونفضل [illegible] غداً - الخميس - [illegible] من قبلنا [illegible].

[Document 29]: Yugoslavian chemical warfare handbook

Printed by the Staff College of the Yugoslavian Ground Forces in 1979, the booklet was seized in a PLO command post in Sidon.

KOMANDNO-ŠTABNA AKADEMIJA KOPNENE VOJSKE

- Katedra ABHO KŠA KoV -

Seminarske vežbe sa slušaocima KŠA KoV

TEMA-23: PROGNOZA UČINAKA HEMIJSKIH UDARA

Prilog: K

Karta JNA 1:50.000 Slavonski Brod-1 br.375/1

Document 29-2,3

RAD SA HEMIJSKIM RAČUNAROM

Pomoću hemijskog računara može se vršiti prognoziranje
a) - Gubitaka ljudstva u primarno zahvaćenom rejonu (PZR) u %.
b) - Dubina prostiranja primarnog (početkog) oblaka para sarina u km.
c) - Domet para primarnog oblaka aerozola VX otrova u km.
d) - Domet para - aerozola sekundarnog (naknadnog) oblaka u km.
e) - Postojanost sarina i iperita na zemljištu u časovima.
f) - Postojanost VX otrova u danima na zemljištu.

U prognoziranju gubitaka ljudstva na PZT, kao i u ponašanju BOt na zemljištu (kao što je dato pod b,c,d,e i f), da bi se dobili potrebni podaci (parametri), u radu sa hemijskim računarom mora se voditi računa i uzeti u obzir:

- stepen zaštite ljudstva (objekata po kojem je izvršen HU;
- vrsta vojnog otrova: sarin, iperit ili VX otrov;
- vrsta lansirnog uredjaja: artiljerija, avijacija ili rakete;
- stepen iznenadjenja i
- dati meteorološki podaci.

Seminarske vežbe sa slušaocima u načinu upotrebe hemijskog računara pri prognoziranju gubitaka ljudstva i ponašanju BOt-a na zemljištu, kao što je dato pod (a,b,c,d,e, i f); dobijeni podaci služe kao osnov za taktičku procenu situacije i preduzimanje adekvatnih mera.

V e ž b a br.1

Situacija:

U 08.00 20.09. artilj.vatrenim udarom od 30 sekundi izvršen je hemijski udar (HU) po 1/1.pp u rejonu s.Kršnici - Rastik (k.151). Bojni otrov sarin. U momentu HU zahvaćeno ljudstvo bilo je van zaklona, jedinica iznenadjena.

Podaci o meteorološkoj situaciji:

Prizemni vetar iz pravca severoistoka, duva brzinom 2-3 m/sek. po pravcu stalan. Prosečna dnevna temperatura zemlji-

- 2 -

šta danju 20°C, a noću 10°C. Vertikalna stabilnost (strujanje) vazduha danju konvekcija, a noću inverzija.

Z a d a t a k:

1.- Na kartu JNA 1:50.000 Slavonski Brod ucrtati PZR (600 x 300 m)

2.- Pomoću hemijskog računara izvršiti prognoziranje gubitaka ljudstva u privremeno zahvaćenom rejonu.

3.- Prognozirati i proceniti ponašanje sarina na zemljištu:

a) dubinu prostiranja primarnih (početnog) oblaka para sarina;

b) domet para sekundarnog (naknadnog) oblaka para sarina u km - ucrtati granice:

c) postojanosti sarina na zemljištu u časovima.

R e š e n j e:

Stalan - 1/5
Promenlj - 4/5

NP 20 KT
1KT = 1000 t TNT
20 = 20000 t TNT

Document 29-4,5

-/3 -

V e ž b a   br.2

Situacija:

U rejonu s.Stipanovići po okb izvršen je HU raketom "R"-65 zahvaćena 1.tč, bojni otrov VX, ljudstvo u tenkovima, iznenadjeno, u opremi bataljona su tenkovi T-34.

Podaci o meteorološkoj situaciji:

Prizemni vetar duva brzinom od 2-3 met/sek, duva iz pravca severozapadd, promenljivog pravca, temšeratura zemljišta 20°C, zemljište odkriveno, vertikalna stabilnost (strujanje) vazduha danju konvekcija, a noću neutralno, temepratura zemljišta noću je oko 10°C.

Z a d a t a k:

1.- Na kartu JNA 1:50.000 ucrtati PZR, jedinačna raketa 70 ha.

2.- Pomoću hemijskog računara izvršiti prognozu gubitaka ljudstva u PZR, proceniti taktički položaj jedinica u PZR, kao i jedinica koje će se naći u naknadno zahvaćenom rejonu.

3.- Prognozirati ponašanje VX otrova na zemljištu i to:
- domet primarnog oblaka aerozola VX;
- domet aerozola sekundarnog (naknadnog) oblaka VX i na karti ucrtati granice odparavanja oblaka VX;
- odrediti postojanost VX na zemljištu (PZR) u danima.

R e š e n j e:

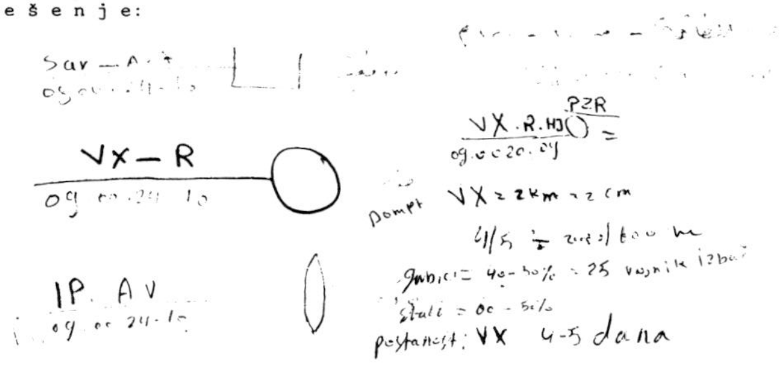

- 4 -

V e ž b a   br.3

Situacija:

U trajanju od 10 min. u 09.30 20.09 izvršen je divizioni artiljerijski vatreni udar, Bot iperit. HU izvršen je po rejonu s.Vrankovac (tt.263, zahvaćena 1 hab iz PAG-1, ljudstvo u momentu HU 50% bilo je van zaklona, a ostalo u odkrivenim rovovima, jedinica iznenadjena.

Podaci o meteorološkoj situaciji:

U rejonu HU duva severozapadni vetar pod uglom 340°, brzina vetra u prizemnim slojevima 2-4 m/sek. temperatura zemljišta 10-12°C danju, a noću oko 8°C, vertikalna stabilnost (strujanje) vazduha konvekcija danju, noću neutralno, po pravcu vetar stalan, u rejonu (PZR) zemljište odkriveno.

Z a d a t a k:

1.- Na kartu JNA 1:50.000 ucrtati PZR sa podacima: veličina PZR, vrsta BOt, lansirno sredstvo i vreme izvršenja HU.

2.- Pomoću hemijskog računara izvršti prognoziranje gubitaka kod zahvaćene jedinice, gubitke izraziti u % i brojčano. Proceniti taktički položaj zahvaćene baterije, kao i jedinice koje će se naći u naknadno zahvaćenom rejonu.

3.- Prognozirati stanje u PZR i ponašanje BOt na zemljištu:
- domet para sekundarnog(naknadnog)oblaka para iperita:
- postojanost BOt iperita na zemljištu u časovima,

R e š e n j e:

Document 29-6,7

JP. A
12cc ... cg II

- 5 -

V e ž b a   br.4

Situacija:

Grupom od 4 aviona lovaca - bombardera u 10.00 20.09. izvršeno je grupno bombardovanje po koloni 1.had - 122 mm koji se našao na maršu na deonici puta s.Slobodna Vlast - s.Imrejevci. BOt sarin, ljudstvo u vouilima, nije iznenadjeno, dat je signal NHB opasnosti. Zemljište pretežno odkriveno, u rejonu HU, dok u širem rejonu - po karti.

Podaci o meteorološkoj situaciji:

U rejonu HU prizemni vetar duva iz pravca 180°,brzina 5-6 m/sek po pravcu promenljiv. Temperatura zemljišta danju u proseku iznosi 18-20°C a noću 8-10°C. Vertikalna stabilnost (strujanje) vazduha danju konvekcija, a noću neutralno.

Z a d a t a k:

1.- Na kartu JNA 1:50.000 ucrtati PZR,uneti podatke o vrsti BOt,lansirno sredstvo, vreme izvršenja HU.
2.- Pomoću hemijskog računara izvrštiti prognoziranje gubitaka kod had-105 mm,gubitke izraziti u % i brojčano. Proceniti taktički položaj zahvaćenih delova.
3.- Prognozirati stanje u PZR i ponašanje BOt na zemljištu:
- dubinu prostiranja primarnog oblaka para sarina,
- domet para sekundarnog (naknadnog) oblaka sarina i na karti ucrtati zonu otparavanja (osu i granice).
- postojanost sarina na zemljištu u časovima.

R e š e n j e:

- 6 -

V e ž b a   br.5

Situacija:

Grupom LB od 4 aviona u 12.00 20.09. izvršen je napad po koloni 2.pb, kolona bataljona se našla na deonici puta s.Major - s.Levonjska Varoš, Napad izvršen polivanjem, BOt iperit. Ljudstvo u vozilima, nije dat signal NHB opasnosti. Karakteristike zemljišta - po karti.

Podaci o meteorološkoj situaciji:

Prizemni vetar duva iz pravca 50-55°, brzina 2-4 m/sek, po pravcu stalan. Temperatura zemljišta danju u proseku oko 17-20°C, a noću 8-10°C. Vertikalna stabilnost vazduha danju konvekcija, a noću neutralno.

Z a d a t a k:

1.-Na kartu JNA 1:50.000 ucrtati PZR i uneti ostale podatke (vrsta BOt,lansirno sredstvo i vreme izvršenja HU).
2.- Pomoću hemijskog računara izvršiti prognoziranje gubitaka ljudstva u PZR,i proceniti tak.položaj 2.pb.
3.-Izvršiti prognozu ponašanja BOt na zemljištu:
- domet para sekundarnog (naknadnog) oblaka iperita,
- postojanost iperita na zemljištu.

R e š e n j e:

ch OR P = 20 km2
BS = 600

V. 10 - R
1200 22 cg

7,07 x 30 = 212 ljudi

Površina zone 1,5 km P = 7,07 km2

PZ
BS = 600 - 20 =
BS = 1 km 30 ljud.

Document 29-8

- 7 -

V e ž b a   br.6

Situacija:

U 13,00 20.09. raketnom artiljerijom (dvbr) izvršen je HU plotunom po odbrambenom rejonu 1.pb. HU zahvaćena 2/1.pb u rejonu s.Poligalovci (tt.211) Babar, BOt sarin,višecevni bacači raketa M-91.

Ljudstvo u odkrivenim rejonima, iznenadjeno. Karakteristike zemljišta - po karti.

Podaci o meteorološkoj situaciji:

Prizemni vetar duva iz pravca 240-245°, po pravcu promenljiv, brzina vetra 2 do 3 m/sek. Temperatura zemljišta danju oko 20°C, a noću oko 10°C.

Vertikalna stabilnost danju konvekcija, a noću neutralno.

Z a d a t a k:

1.- Na kartu JNA: 1:50.000 uneti PZR sa datim podacima.
2.- Pomoću hemijskog računara izvršiti prognoziranje gubitaka ljudstva u PZR, i proceniti takt.položaj 2/1.pb.
3.- Izvršiti prognoziranje ponašanja BOt na zemljištu i to:
a) dubina prostiranja primarnog (početnog oblaka sarina:
b) domet para sekundarnog (naknadnog) oblaka sarina, na karti ucrtati osu i granice zone odparavanja;
c) odrediti postojanost sarina na zemljištu u časovima.

R e š e n j e:

1,1 km P = 3,8 km²

20 km²

30 : 20 : 1,5 kamion po km²

1,5 x 3,8 = 5,70 Kamjona izbačnizborbe

mb, 20 : 6 = 3

[Document 30]: Snapshot of PLO personnel at a Soviet tank course

PLO personnel join other foreign students training in a model of a Soviet tank.

[Document 31]: PLO representative in East Germany

Sa'iqa group request to the Syrian foreign minister to issue a special passport to Muhammed Amin al-Askari, who was appointed head of the organization in East Germany.

طلائع حرب التحرير الشعبية

قوات الصاعقة

القيادة العامة

الرقم ....

التاريخ ....

الرفيق وزير الخارجية

تحية عربية :ـ

يرجى الموافقة على منح الرفيق / محمد امين العسكرى / جواز سفر خاص مع تأشيرة خروج لعدة ستة أشهر كون الرفيق المذكور يعمل لدى القيادة العامة رئيس فرع المنظمة في المانيا الديمقراطية ولضرورة العمل •

ودمتم للنضال

[Document 32]: Visit by Zimbabwe delegation to PLO

The message, dated 17 March 1981, urges Fatah officials to make arrangements to welcome the 12-member delegation.

32

حركة التحرير الوطني الفلسطيني
فتح
قسم حركات التحرر

الرقم ....
التاريخ ....

الأخ مدير الشؤون الإدارية
تحية الثورة

مراجعة [illegible]
٣/١٨

وبعد، يصل إلى لبنان ١٢ من الضيوف من زيمبابوي
يرجى تأمين مهمة استقبالهم من طريق المطار
يوم ١٩/٣/ الساعة [illegible] ومرافقتهم
إلى الفندق ودفع للضرورة للوصول،

مع تحياتنا لكم
وثورة حتى النصر

أخوكم حليم [illegible]
٨١/٣/١٧

[Document 33]: Fatah names military attaché for Hungary

Major Majid Sa'id al-Saghir is appointed by Fatah as the PLO military attaché in Hungary (6 January 1982).

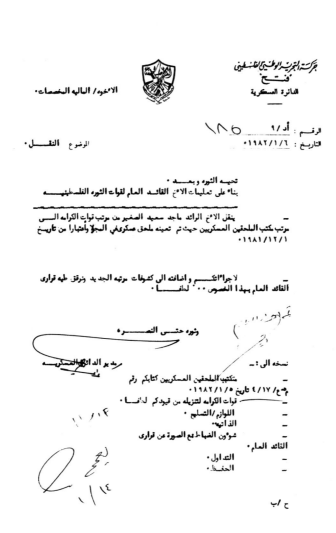

حركة التحرير الوطني الفلسطيني
"فتح"
الدائرة العسكرية

الاخوه/ الماليه المخصصات٠

الرقم : أد/٩/ ١٨٥
التاريخ : ١٩٨٢/١/٦٠

الموضوع النقل٠

تحيه الثوره وبعد٠
بناء على تعليمات الاخ القائد العام لقوات الثوره الفلسطينيه

- ينقل الاخ الرائد ماجد سعيد الصغير من مرتب قوات الكرامه الى مرتب مكتب الملحقين العسكريين حيث تم تعينه ملحق عسكري في المجر اعتبارا من تاريخ ١٩٨١/١٢/١٠

- لاجراءاتكم واضافته الى كشوفات مرتبه الجديد ونرفق طيه قرارى القائد العام بهذا الخصوص ٠٠ لطفا٠

وثوره حتى النصر٠

مدير الدائرة العسكريه

نسخه الى :-

- مكتب الملحقين العسكريين كتابكم رقم م ع/٤/١٧ تاريخ ١٩٨٢/١/٥٠
- قوات الكرامه لتنزيله من قيودكم لطفا٠
- اللوازم/التسليح٠
- الذاتيه٠
- شؤون الضباط مع الصورة عن قرارى القائد العام٠
- التداول٠
- الحفظ٠

ح/ب

[Document 34]: Instructions in Chinese for handling explosives

This document was seized at a PLO command post in southern Lebanon.

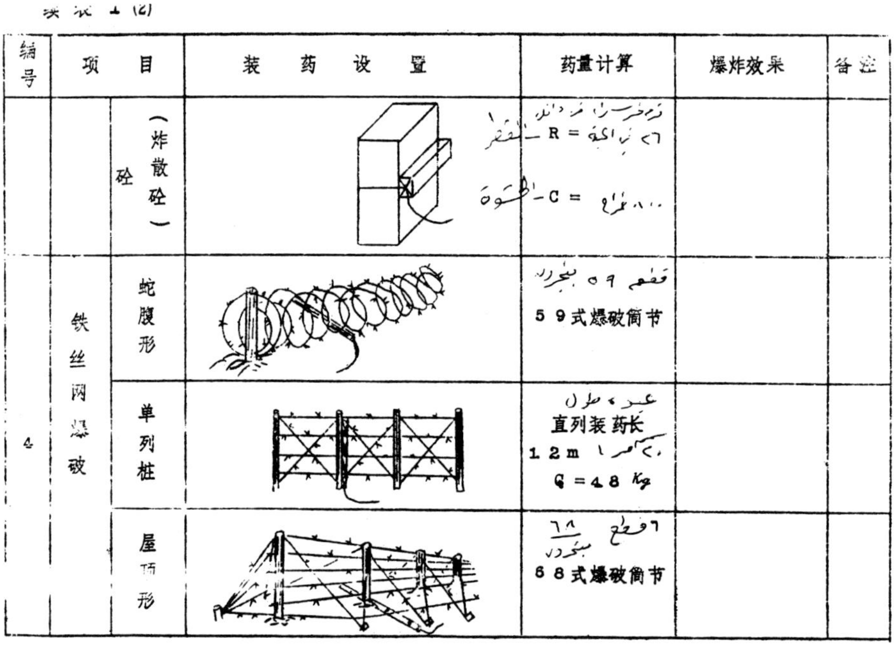

续表 1 (2)

编号	项目		装药设置	药量计算	爆炸效果	备注
		砼（炸散砼）		[illegible] R = [illegible] [illegible] C = [illegible]		
4	铁丝网爆破	蛇腹形		[illegible] 5 9式爆破筒节		
		单列桩		[illegible] 直列装药长 1.2m [illegible] C = 4.8 Kg		
		屋顶形		[illegible] 6 8式爆破筒节		

续 表 1 (1)

编号	项目		装药设置	药量计算	爆炸效果	备注
2	钢材爆破	钢板		F = ; C =		
		钢管		F = ; C =		
		钢索		d = ; C =		
3	钢筋混凝土爆破	砼（内部）		R = ; C =		
		砼（炸断）	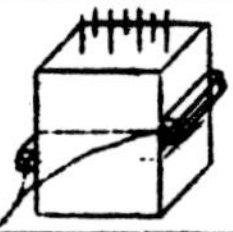	F = ; C =		

爆破实炸作业方案

编号	项目		装药设置	药量计算	爆炸效果	备注
1	木材爆破	方木		F = ; K = ; C =		
		圆木		F = ; C =		
		密集木桩	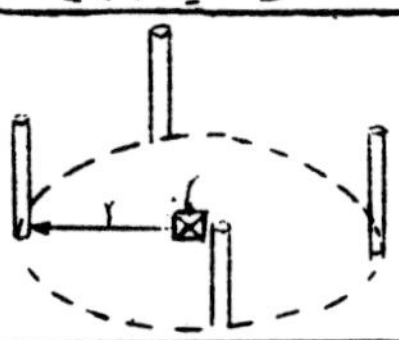	D = ; r = ; $C = 30KDr^2$		
		钢轨		C = 400 克 (TNT)		

[Document 35]: PLO political activity in Cuba

This letter, dated 17 March 1982, was sent by a member of the extremist Popular Front, who was studying medicine in Cuba while engaging in political activity on behalf of his group. The rival Fatah group unsuccessfully tried to sabotage a celebration organized by the Front in Havana. The writer reported about the "blind hatred" of the Fatah representative in Cuba towards the Front and gave details of his studies, which included: didactics, history, political economy, socialism and capitalism, the world and the Cuban Labour Movement; he specified that, in addition to his professional training, he would complete a political training course as well.

الرفيق العزيز ابو حسام

تحية رفاقية وبعد

بمناسبة الذكرى الثالثة عشرة لانطلاقة جبهتنا
اوجه لكم اجمل التهاني الثورية متمنياً لكم مزيداً
من العمل وتحقيق الانتصارات. كيف صحتك يا ابو حسام
وكيف عملك عله [redacted] ماشي الحال وكيف الأوضاع
على صعيد المنطقة، كيف ام حسام والأولاد عساهم جميعاً
بخير وبصحة جيدة، كيف صحة الحاجة ام سعيد عساها
بخير وقوية، كيف الإستعدادت العسكرية عندكم
لمواجهة الإحتمالات القادمة، على صعيد نشاطنا
اقمنا احتفالاً كبيراً وكان ناجحاً حيث شارك فيه
شخصيات ذات مستوى رفيع وقد ظهر على التلفزيون،
وكان اضخم احتفال يقام على صعيد كوبا، وقد حاولت
الفتح من خلال ضغط مكتب منظمة التحرير على الكوبيين على
الغاءه، وقد نقل الإحتفال من مسرح الجامعة الى
بيت الصداقة والتضامن بين الشعوب وقد باءت

Document 35A-2

احتفال فتح بالفصل الدراسي ، ولم ندعوا فتح لحضور الإحتفال
لتجنب المشاكل ، لأنه كل سنه يحاولون تخريب احتفالتنا
انا بخير وبصحة جيدة ومبسوط كثير والحمدلله ما في
مشاكل . الدراسه جيده وممتازه ، وكانت علاماتي
في الإمتحانات الفصل الأول ٤ مواد خمسه من خمسه ،
و٢ ماده أربعه من خمسه ، وقد بدأ الفصل الثاني
في ٢٢ شباط والآن الدراسه اسهل من الفصل السابق ،
لقد انجزنا حتى الآن دراسة المادة الديالكتيكية والتاريخيه
والإقتصاد السياسي الرأسمالي والإشتراكي والآن ندرس
الحركة العماليه الكوبيه والعالميه ، يعني الواحد بتخرج
من هنا طبيب ودورة حزبيه .
على صعيد الإتحاد العام لطلبة فلسطين تحاول الفتح عرقله
عمله . الحرية تصلنا باستمرار . الآن بدأ الشغل العملي
المضبوط في المستشفيات والواحد عم يكتسب
خبره بالبلد في جميع النواحي ، والحياة هنا في
كوبا مستقر على جميع الأصعدة . كيف جميعكم

Document 35A-3

الأقارب والرفاق عندكم . ما هي الأسباب وراء عدم
بناء ملاجئ في الداخور ، كيف العلاقة مع منظمة
امل بعد الإشتباكات الأخيره ، وكيف تطور
الأسلحة عندكم وخصوصاً في الفترة الحاليه .
هذه الصيغة سيزور خليل نضار لبنان وسيطلعك
عن الوضع بالتفصيل على ساحة كوبا . مسؤول الفتح
عنا في سنيا اخوا هو محمود ابو العفاجم وهو من مخيم نهر البارد
وهو يكره الجبهه على الإجمال لأنه كما تعرف هم عدة جماعات
ودائما يبتعدون في عملهم عن الوحدة الوطنيه .

سلامي وتحياتي للجميع
المشتاق لكم

١٧ آذار ١٩٨٢

[Document 36]: PLO representative in Havana reports on Cuban assistance
The document was printed on the stationery of the PLO Permanent Mission in Havana. Our slightly abridged English translation follows.

Dear Comrades,
I should like to take this opportunity to express once more our gratitude to the Cuban Communist Party, and to all of you, for your solidarity with our revolution, and the gratitude of the Palestinian fighters under the leadership of Yasser Arafat. The Palestinian problem started following World War One. Palestine was then under the British Mandate, which lasted 30 years, until 1948, and dominated the country as a colonialist and imperialist regime. That regime helped the Zionist organization by issuing certificates for massive Jewish immigration to the country, in order to set up a Jewish state in our land, Palestine, while all manner of terror was being used.

The importance of Palestine, as a bridge between three continents, stems from the economic wealth of the Middle East, especially in oil. Therefore it has always been a target for the imperialists.

Prior to the Palestinian revolution, 15 May meant nothing. This was a black day in human history, because on that day the Zionist State of Israel was established on the land of Palestine. That state was founded with colonialist British and American assistance. They took our land and expelled our people, resorting to force and other fascist means, which instilled fear in the hearts of our people.

Our revolution, which has marked great victories since its inception in 1965, has turned around the image of the Palestinian objectives. Henceforth, the Palestinian people is part of the conflict in the Middle East. Without the implementation of its rights, there can be no peace in this area.

The Fifteenth of May is our international day of protest for all revolutionary forces, including your own, who support our organization, the PLO, as the exclusive representative of the Palestinian people who seek to establish an independent liberal state. Our victories, which we have won, thanks to the assistance of the socialist countries, the Organization for African Unity and the Islamic countries, constituted the decisive factor in defeating the aggressive forces of imperialism. We are in the same boat with all the anti-imperialist forces.

We take this opportunity to express our respect and admiration for revolutionary Cuba, led by Fidel Castro, and for your goals. We will follow a road similar to yours until we reach our common path. We must cite Comrade Arafat: "War starts in Palestine and so does peace." We can characterize our activities in the Middle East by stating that, in October 1973, the Arabs launched a war against the Zionist State of Israel for the first time. That war has encouraged revolutionary forces, and given an opportunity to the Arab people to join the war. It was a war of honour and liberty. However, a few days after the war was launched, it became evident that President Sadat of Egypt had planned not to liberate Palestine but to give imperialism the upper hand. Thus, following the cease-fire and Egypt's shameful stand vis-à-vis American policy, the plot was revealed to eliminate the Palestinian organizations. During that period of time, blows were dealt to us in Lebanon, which persist to this day. But despite these serious attacks, the Palestinian revolution, hand-in-hand with the national-progressive forces in Lebanon, was determined to defend Arab Lebanon from the Israeli Zionist attacks. Following the October War, President Sadat declared that all solutions to the Middle East conflict were in the hands of the United States. He also visited occupied Jerusalem, thus hurting the feelings of all Arabs and especially the Palestinian people. That step was taken in collusion with the Zionist enemy, for the signature of the so-called peace treaty was indeed an instrument expressing his agreement with the Zionist enemy, while ironically denying the rights of the legitimate and exclusive representative of the Palestinian people. Therefore, that agreement is illegal insofar as President Sadat did not represent the Palestinian people and as that agreement was concluded between himself and Israel only. The dangerous outcome of that agreement, and the ongoing link between Egypt and Israel, constitute a threat to peace in the world and to all nations which fight for their national freedom. This agreement shields the imperialists' interests in our Arab area which is rich in oil and it has a bearing on the African continent where many organizations fight for their freedom.

The success of the popular revolution in Iran, under the leadership of Khomeini, has had a great impact through its support of the Palestinian revolution under the leadership of Arafat, the supreme commander of the Palestinians. Iran will directly oppose Israel and imperialism to enable our people to achieve its objective of establishing its own independent homeland.

Concurrently with the signature of that treacherous agreement, the Zionist state began bombing civilian targets of our people in southern Lebanon. So, they killed women, children and aged people, both Palestinian and Lebanese. The Zionists have thrown their support to the rightist-fascist forces in Lebanon who oppose any joint Palestinian-Lebanese positions.

We are declaring here, on behalf of the Palestinian people, that we shall pursue the road of armed struggle until the final liberation of our occupied land. We shall continue to fight in all possible ways, with the backing of UN resolutions, of the Islamic organization and the OAU. We are certain that the war inside and outside the occupied areas will be fierce and well-organized. We shall not give up our weapons and we shall pursue the revolution until we fulfil the hopes of our people, namely, the return to their land and resettlement there under freedom, just like all other peoples of the world. If we believe in revolution, we shall be able to frustrate violence and Camp David. We shall also be able to eliminate all traitors, including those in the Arab world.

We wish to ask for your help in our war against the imperialist-Zionist plot, which is attempting to liquidate our people and all forces of liberation in the world.

The victories in Vietnam, Laos, Cambodia, Africa and Latin America are our own, for we stand beside all peoples who fight for their liberty everywhere in the world. We support the Vietnamese and Nicaraguan people. The pursuit of our armed struggle is our way to freedom. We are all united until we topple imperialism and Zionism, until we liquidate the Camp David treason.

Long live the PLO, the only representative of the Palestinian people!
Long live the Cuban Revolution!
Long live Yasser Arafat!
Long live Fidel!
Revolution until victory!

Document 36-1

ORGANIZACION PARA LA LIBERACION
DE PALESTINA
MISION PERMANENTE EN CUBA
LA HABANA

COMPAÑERAS Y COMPAÑEROS:

Quisiera aprovechar esta ocasion , para manifestar , una vez mas , nuestro agradecimiento al PARTIDO COMUNISTA DE CUBA , y a todos ustedes por ofrecer esta magnifica oportunidad de solidaridad con nuestra Revolucion y con nuestro pueblo , manifestando al mismo tiempo , el saludo revolucionario de los combatientes palestinos , de nuestro maximo dirigente YASSER ARAFAT.

El problema palestino se inicio despues de la Primera Guerra Mundial , por lo cual Palestina estuvo bajo el mandato Britanico que siguio durante 30 años hasta 1948 , bajo esta dominacion el Colonialismo y el Imperialismo apoyaron al Movimiento Sionista a traves de una inmigracion masiva de los judios para poder crear un estado judio sobre nuestra Patria Palestina utilizando todos los medios de terror y de opresion.

Debido a la importancia de Palestina como entrada a los tres Continentes, y a los recursos del Medio Oriente especialmente el Petroleo , y esto que persiguen los imperialistas , para explotar los pueblos en la Zona , como conocemos prefectamente la naturaleza del Colonialismo como forma de Racismo y de la descriminacion racial . Por otra parte "El sionismoa y el antisemetismo son dos caras de la misma medalla."

Document 36-2

..2/

ORGANIZACION PARA LA LIBERACION
DE PALESTINA
MISION PERMANENTE EN CUBA
LA HABANA

COMPAÑERAS Y COMPAÑEROS :

Antes del surgimiento de la Revolucion armada Palestina , el 15 de Mayo, no significo nada , pero hoy todos los pueblos que apoyan nuestra causa y nuestra Revolucion Palestina , manifiestan su solidaridad Revolucionaria .

Este dia negro en toda la Historia de la Humanidad , porque fue establecido el estado Sionista de Israel , sobre nuestra Patria Palestina, que debido al apoyo de los colonialistas ingleses y norteamericanos se se apoderaron de nuestra tierra y expulsaron al pueblo por la fuerza utilizando todos los medios y formas fascistas de barbarie y violencia sembrando el terror a cada pasi de nuestro pueblo .

El surgimiento de la Revolucion en el 65 y el logro de las Victorias han podido cambiar el concepto múndial sobre la causa palestina , quien se adjudico la responsabilidad del conflicto del Medio Oriente y sin el derecho del pueblo Palestino nunca se podra establecer la paz en esta Zona.

El 15 de Mayo es una manifestacion Internacional de todas las fuerzas Revolucionarias y ustedes progresistas que apoyan nuestra OLP , unico Representante legitimo del pueblo Palestino , quien persigue el estableci-

Document 36-3

..3/

ORGANIZACION PARA LA LIBERACION
DE PALESTINA
MISION PERMANENTE EN CUBA
LA HABANA

miento de un estado independiente .

Estas victorias obtenidas a traves de nuestra propia fuerza y del apoyo de los paises socialistas guiados por la URSS , los paises NO ALINEADOS , LA UNIDAD AFRICANA Z y los paises de la Conferencia Islamica han sido un factor decisivo para destruir las fuerzas agresoras y de explotacion , porque consideramos que estamos juntos en la misma trinchera con todas las fuerzas antiimperialistas.

Aprovechamos esta ocasion para expresar nuestro respeto y admiracion por la posicion de CUBA REVOLUCIONARIA , hacia nuestra causa , dirigida por el PCC y su maximo dirigente FIDEL CASTRO , y al pueblo cubano por toda la ayuda moral y material que nos han brindado .

Afirmamos juntos que estamos en el mismo camino hasta lograr nuestros objetivos comunes . Repetimos lo dicho por nuestro Compañero YASSER ARAFAT: " LA GUERRA SE ESTALLA EN PALESTINA , LA PAZ COMIENZA EN PALESTINA" .

Podemos limitar las acciones en la Zona del Medio Oriente despues de la Guerra de Octubre de 1973 , cuando los arabes en la primera vez fomentaron la Guerra contra el estado sionista de Israel , donde dio empuje a todas las fuerzas revolucionarias y al pueblo arabe para participar en esta

Document 36-4

...4/

ORGANIZACION PARA LA LIBERACION
DE PALESTINA
MISION PERMANENTE EN CUBA
LA HABANA

Guerra de dignidad y liberacion , pero despues de varios dias del inicio de la Guerra se vio clara la posicion del Presidente Egipcio ANUAR EL SADAT , demostrando que el plan de la Guerra no tenia el objetivo de la Liberacion sino de provocar la situacion favorable al Imperialismo .

De ahi despues del cese de la Guerra y la descartada posicion egipcia hacia la politica norteamericana empezo , practicamente el complot de la exterminacion de la Revolucion Palestina . Se iniciaron las acciones sangrientas en el Libano , que siguen hasta nuestro tiempos actuales donde se movieron las fuerzas derechistas fascistas apoyadas por el regimen sionista el imperialismo y la reaccion arabe.

A traves de estas fuertes agresiones siguio la Revolucion Palestina , junto a las fuerzas nacionalistas y progresistas libanesas , la defensa del Libano Arabe y contra los ataques israelies firmando su posicion de fracasar todos esos intentos de agresion .

No podemos ver la situacion en el Libano contra nuestra Revolucion separada de la posicion de EL SADAT , despues de la Guerra de Octubre y su afirmacion de que toda la solucion del problema del Medio Oriente esta en manos de los Estado Unidos .

Document 36-5

..5/

ORGANIZACION PARA LA LIBERACION
DE PALESTINA
MISION PERMANENTE EN CUBA
LA HABANA

Con esta objetivo realiso su visita a Jerusalem ocupada , echando por tierra todo el sentimiento del pueblo arabe en general y particularmente del pueblo Palestino Este paso de capitulacion con el enemigo sionista y en firma al llamado "TRATADO DE PAZ " , no es mas que aceptar la ocupacion sionista de nuestra Palestina , burlando asi el derecho de la ORGANIZACION PARA LA LIBERACION DE PALESTINA , unico representante legitimo del pueblo Palestino . Este tratado ha sido ilegalmente acordado , ya que EL-SADAT no ha tenido la autorizacion de hablar en nombre de los palestinos , solamente se ha considerado un tratado por separado entre el e Israel.

Los peligrosos resultados de esta tratado yvsu reflejo esta en contra e del Movimeinto de Liberacion Arabe e Internacional debido a esta alianza sionista con el regimen de EGIPTO y amenaza la paz mundial y el avance de todos los pueblos del mundo que lucahan por su liberacion nacional.

Por otra parte esta encaminado a proteger los intereses del Imperialismo en nuestra Zona Arabe, quien es rica en petroleo. Ademas repercute en el Continente Africano porque ataca los Movimientos de Liberacion y a la vez apoya a los lacayos del Imperialismo y la reaccion.

Document 36-6

..6/

ORGANIZACION PARA LA LIBERACION
DE PALESTINA
MISION PERMANENTE EN CUBA
LA HABANA

Pedemos señalar de que el triunfe de la Revelucien pepular en IRAN dirigida per AYATHOLAH KOMEINI va a jugar un papel impertantisime en peye a la causa de nuestre pueble palestine dirigide per YASSER ARAFAT, maxime dirigente de les Palestine y se va a cenvertir en un estade de enfrentamiente directe centra Israel, les intereses imperialistas y tedas las fermas de expletacien en nuestre Zena para que nuestre pueble pueda ejercer su derecho inalienable y establecer su estade independiente

Paralelamente mientras fimaren el tratade de traicien, el estade sienista cemenze a bembardear la zenas civiles de nuestre pueble en el Sur del Libane, matande cruelmente a mujeres, niñes y viejes palestines y libaneses indefenses.

Pedemes afirmar que, el bembardee de les sienistas, elles utilizan materiales de Guerra de fabricacien nerteameribana, apeyande asi las fuerzas derechistas y fascistas libanesas que atacan las pesicienes palestinas-libanesas prevecando una gran cantidad de agresienes sienistas derechistas reaccienarias apeyadas per el imperialisme yanqui y sus lacayes luege del fracase inelvidable para les sienistas frente a les cembatientes palestines.

Document 36-7

..7/

ORGANIZACION PARA LA LIBERACION
DE PALESTINA
MISION PERMANENTE EN CUBA
LA HABANA

Afirmamos aqui en nombre del pueblo palestino de seguir el camino de la lucha armada hasta la liberacion total de nuestra tierra ocupada , respaldados por todas las resoluciones de las Naciones Unidas , el Movimiento DE LOS NO ALINEADOS , de la Conferencia Islamica y la Organizacion de la Unidad Africana , utilizando todos los medios necesarios

Estamos convencidos que la lucha dentro y fuera del territorio ocupado va a ser mas fuerte , mas organizada , expresando a traves de la O.L.P. que no dejaremos el fusil que continuaremos a la Revolucion hasta ver realizados las aspiraciones de nuestro pueblo del retorno a su Patria, y el establecimiento de su estado en su tierra para vivir libre como todos los pueblos.

Llevando la fe revolucionaria podremos hacer fracasar la agresion y Camp David y destruir todos los traidores y lacayos de la Zona Arabe.

Aprovechamos la ocasion de la Celebracion de la VI CUMBRE DE LOS NO ALINEADOS EN CUBA , de la cual somos parte integrante como fuerza revolucionaria internacional , apoyados por el Campo Socialista encabezado por la U.R.S.S. y

las fuerzas democraticas del mundo para hacer un llamado de apoyo

tra lucha frente a este intento imperial sionista y reaccionario que

Document 36-8

..8/

ORGANIZACION PARA LA LIBERACION
DE PALESTINA
MISION PERMANENTE EN CUBA
LA HABANA

que persigue la exterminacion de nuestro pueblo y todos las fuerzas de liberacion en el MUNDO.

Las victorias en VIETNAM , LAO , KAMPUCHEA , y las victorias en Africa , y en America Latina , es una victoria nuesta , manifestamos AQUI DELANTE DE UDS : QUE ESTAMOS AL LADO DE TODOS LOS PUEBLOS QUE LUCHAN POR SU LIBERACION EN TODAS PARTES DEL MUNDO , ESTAMOS CON EL PUEBLO DE VIETNEM, CON EL PUEBLO DE NICARAGUA Y SU VANGUARDIA EL FRENTE SANDINISTA DE LIBERACION .

SEGUIR LA LUCHA ARMADA ES NUESTRO CAMINO PARA LA LIBERACION

ESTAMOS TODOS UNIDOS HASTA DERROCAR EL IMPERIALISMO , EL SIONISMO Y LA REACCION , HASTA FRACASAR LA TRAICION DE CAMP DAVID Y TODOS LOS LACAYOS DE IMPERIALISMO EN ETODO EL MUNDO .

VIVA LA OLP UNICO REPRESENTANTE DEL PUEBLO PALESTINO

VIVA LA REVOLUCION CUBANA

VIVA YASSER ARAFAT

VIVA FIDEL

REVOLUCION HASTA LA VISTORIA.

[Document 37]: Spanish-language sabotage handbook

A top-secret handbook in Spanish (presumably from Cuba) teaching techniques of sabotage against civilian targets — cars, trains, telephone and electricity systems and gasoline supplies.

MUY SECRETO.
HOJA #117.

SABOTAJE DE LAS VIAS DE COMUNICACIONES POR CARRETERAS

Construcción de obstáculos en las carreteras

Con el fin de evitar el transporte por carreteras de tropas y municiones, hacia las zonas donde operan las guerrillas, los grupos clandestinos de las regiones urbanas y sub-urbanas, pueden realizar una serie de sabotajes que retrasarían el avance de tropas, y darían tiempo a las guerrillas a evadir el combate, o a fortificarse mejor para hacer frente al enemigo.

Estos sabotajes se pueden realizar con medios locales combinándolos con trampas explosivas.

Debido a las características clandestinas que tienen los combatientes urbanos y sub-urbanos, es recomendable que estos trabajos se realicen durante la noche y de ser posible un día anterior al movimiento del enemigo, para así sorprenderlo. Por eso la rapidez en la construcción de dichos obstáculos es una cuestión primordial.

Teniendo en cuenta los factores antes mencionados, exponemos una serie de normas para la construcción de obstáculos en las carreteras, las cuales hacen menos complejo el cumplimiento de estas misiones.

1.- Debemos aprovechar los árboles que crecen a la orilla de las carreteras y que pueden ser volados con explosivos, o serruchados con el propósito de atravesarlos en medio de la vía. Al realizar esto se recomienda que no se utilicen árboles demasiado grandes, ya que en caso que vayan a ser volados se requeriría más cantidad de explosivo, o más tiempo de trabajo manual.

2.- A estos arboles medianos o pequeños, que se utilicen como obstáculos, deben colocárseles trampas explosivas, que estarán sembradas a la orilla de las carreteras, con un alambre de disparo enmascarado y amarrado al árbol. Esta medida traerá como resultado que, cuando el enemigo trate de limpiar el camino se encontrará con las minas, y esto le ocupará tiempo en la desactivación de las mismas.

Document 37-2,3

MUY SECRETO.
HOJA #118.

3.- En los casos en que no existan explosivos para la construcción de estas trampas, se pueden éstas simular, colocando alambres que vayan desde los árboles hasta la orilla de la carretera. Esto causará un efecto sicológico en el enemigo, porque debemos recordar que lo mas importante en este tipo de obstáculos son las minas (reales o simuladas) y no el árbol en sí, ya que el enemigo, al limpiar la carretera, raras veces lo hará a mano, sino que generalmente utilizará un vehículo para remolcar el árbol a otra parte. Si hay trampas explosivas instaladas, necesitará un transporte blindado (tanque, tanqueta, etc.) para poder limpiar la carretera rápidamente sin preocuparse de las explosiones, o tendrá que utilizar las unidades de **západores**. Todo esto, como hablabamos en el párrafo anterior, representaría para él trastornos y demoras para llegar al objetivo.

Otro método de sabotaje que se puede llevar a cabo en las carreteras, es la obstrucción de la vía mediante el riego de grampas, clavos u otros objetos que sirven para ponchar los vehículos. Esto trae como resultado que los vehículos civiles y militares que transiten por el lugar se verán imposibilitados de continuar la marcha, por lo que demorarán más tiempo en llegar hasta el objetivo.

Es necesario que todas estas acciones que realicen los combatientes urbanos y sub-urbanos estén en estrecha coordinación con las acciones que deban realizar las guerrillas; ya que ésto no tendría sentido si las guerrillas no estuvieran realizando alguna acción en esa zona, o si el enemigo no necesitara utilizar urgentemente la carretera como vía de acceso hacia el lugar donde se encuentran las guerrillas.

MUY SECRETO.
HOJA #119.

D I B U J O No. 1

Illustration Missing from Original Captured Document

Document 37-4,5

MUY SECRETO.
HOJA #120.

SABOTAJE A LOS VEHICULOS MOTORIZADOS.

Teniendo en cuenta que el transporte es uno de los medios-fundamentales en el que se basa la economía de un país, ya-que una ciudad sin transporte sería una ciudad muerta, en -la que los obreros no podrían asistir a sus fábricas, etc., los combatientes de las organizaciones clandestinas en las-áreas urbanas y sub-urbanas pueden realizar una serie de sabotajes, tanto de las empresas privadas (nacionales o ex---tranjeras) como en las empresas estatales. Estos se irían-produciendo lentamente, sin riesgo alguno y con medios que-están al alcance de cualquier obrero. No podemos decir que este tipo de sabotaje sirva para conseguir por si mismo el-derrocamiento del régimen existente, pero si podemos decir-que el mismo forma parte de un conjunto de acciones que se deben llevar a cabo con el fin de afectar la economía del -país. A continuación señalaremos una serie de métodos que-sirven para inutilizar y destruír en forma considerable los vehículos motorizados :

1.- Echarle azúcar al tanque de la gasolina. Con este método logramos que todos los conductos que van del tanque al carburador se tupan, lo cual obligará a desmontar el tanque, toda la tubería y el carburador; esta reparación durará alrededor de dos días.

2.- Echarle agua al tanque de la gasolina. Este método ---trae como consecuencia que de inicio el vehículo tenga-que hacer un trabajo mayor, debido a que el octanaje de la gasolina es menor. Esto afecta su funcionamiento y-finalmente el vehículo llega a pararse, por lo que hay-que hacerle una reparación que consiste en el desmonte-del tanque y la limpieza del mismo.

3.- Aflojar los tornillos del tubo de salida del aceite para que éste se derrame. Este procedimiento sirve para-ir desangrando lentamente el depósito donde se encuen--tra el aceite, del cual se abastecen todos los mecanismos del motor del vehículo. Este se reseca de tal forma que la fricción entre los distintos metales hace que el vehículo se funda.

MUY SECRETO
HOJA #121.

4.- No abastecer las piezas móviles del vehículo con la --grasa que requieren. De esta forma la fricción y la -falta de grasa harán que las mismas se destruyan.

5.- Manejar el vehículo incorrectamente : con poco aire --en las gomas, para gastarlas; forzando los frenos constantemente sin dejar de acelerar; sin haberle dado el-tiempo y recorrido necesario al cluth, acelerar fuertemente el carro, estando en primera, o manejarlo despacio en segunda o tercera para desgastar el motor.
Todas estas formas incorrectas de conducir hacen que -el vehículo sufra grandes desgastes en su interior, --los cuales no se notan al momento, pero con la continuidad del tiempo hacen que el mismo llegue a paralizarse.

Formas de incendiar un automóvil.

Entre las formas más rápidas de incendiar un automóvil están las siguientes :

1.- Estando el carro apagado acelérelo varias veces hasta-que el carburador se rebose, después levántele el capó e introduzca papeles de periódico encendidos. La desventaja que tiene esta forma es que el que realice el sabotaje tiene que introducirse dentro del vehículo y-por la rápidez con que se origina el fuego, el combatiente puede ser descubierto al tratar de alejarse, --por lo que se recomienda que esta acción se efectúe en la noche.

2.- Colocar dentro del tanque de la gasolina una pequeña bomba incendiaria de tiempo. Este método ofrece más -ventaja que el anterior, ya que el combatiente que va-a realizar este sabotaje tiene tiempo suficiente para-desaparecer del lugar, antes de que el vehículo se incendie.

Document 37-6,7

MUY SECRETO.
HOJA #122.

D I B U J O No. 2

Illustration Missing from Original Captured Document

MUY SECRETO.
HOJA #123.

SABOTAJE A LA RED DE COMUNICACIONES

TELEFONICAS

Dentro de los sabotajes que podemos realizarle a la red-telefónica vemos, de acuerdo a sus características, que-los podemos sub-dividir en tres partes diferentes :

1.- A la red de hilos telefónicos o telegráficos exteriores.

2.- A la red de cables telefónicos o telegráficos soterrados.

3.- A la central telefónica o telegráfica.

SABOTAJE A LA LINEA EXTERIOR

Este sabotaje se puede llevar a cabo mediante la voladura o corte de los postes, con el fin de que al caer rompa el tendido.

Los lugares principales para la destrucción de estas líneas son, sobre todo, los cables que van directamente a-los lugares de mando (cuarteles, jefaturas de policía, -etc.) cuando este sabotaje se realiza solamente en la — parte urbana, donde es imposible la ruptura de los postes o el corte de los mismos, se cortan o arrancan los -alambres, o se provoca un corte-circuito en la línea.

Uno de los métodos más sencillos de sabotaje contra la -línea telefónica o telegráfica en la ciudad, es el corto circuito; solamente es necesario amarrar una piedra o un pedazo de hierro a un cordel largo y fuerte y tirarlo — por encima de los alambres. El cordel se enredará con — los alambres y después sólo hay que tirar de él. Se recomienda que esta operación se haga en medio de dos postes, ya que allí es donde los alambres son más frágiles.

Document 37-8,9

MUY SECRETO.
HOJA #124.

SABOTAJE EN LA LINEA SOTERRADA.

La línea soterrada se compone de varios alambres asilados-entre sí, y aislados de la tierra, formando un cable. En-algunos lugares estos cables se meten en tubos de hierro o envolturas de cemento, que los protegen.

El llevar a cabo este tipo de sabotaje es una cosa delicada y peligrosa, ya que para lograr la destrucción de este-tendido hay que excavar la mayoría de las veces, y que por lo general, estos cables se encuentran soterrados a lo largo de una calle concurrida.

Teniendo en cuenta lo antes expuesto es que las normas para la realización de este sabotaje serán dos : primero : - cuando existe tiempo suficiente para su realización, o un-manto adecuado que nos permite excavar sin ninguna interrupción; segundo : cuando el trabajo hay que hacerlo en forma clandestina, protegido solamente por la vigilancia de los-compañeros del grupo de acción.

1.- Procedimiento esmerado:-
Se debe excavar la tierra hasta donde se encuentra el-alambre (generalmente está a una profundidad de 80 cms) después que se haya encontrado debemos quitar con un -corta-pluma la primera capa aisladora; a continuación-se debe serruchar el cable y quitar la segunda capa -aisladora.
Una vez hecho este trabajo se procederá a rellenar el-hoyo. Repetimos de nuevo que este trabajo se hace en esta forma únicamente cuando el que lo realiza tiene -un manto adecuado que se lo permita.

2.- Procedimiento rápido:-
Primeramente se debe proceder a desenterrar el cable y luego serrucharlo; antes de tapar el hoyo debemos cerciorarnos que los alambres no se toquen entre sí, para evitar esto, podemos colocar una piedra entre uno y -otro, después se debe rellenar el hueco y camuflagear el lugar.

MUY SECRETO.
HOJA #125.

La interrupción provocada será de un promedio de tres o -cuatro días. El punto más débil de este sabotaje, o sea, donde se puede llevar a cabo con más facilidad, es donde-el cable cruza un río, debido a que en estos lugares pasa por debajo del puente o por un costado y es más fácil interrumpirlo en esa zona.

SABOTAJE A LA CENTRAL TELEFONICA

De las tres formas en que se sub-dividió el sabotaje a la red de comunicación telefónica, ésta es la más difícil y-compleja, debido a las características propias de las centrales telefónicas, las cuales siempre tienen un turno de trabajo rotativo, o sea, que las veinticuatro horas del día se encuentra personal dentro de la misma. A medida-que se va agudizando la lucha y por el enemigo conocer -- que eso es un objetivo de ataque de las fuerzas revolucionarias, por lo general designa custodia para el mismo, lo que hace más difícil el cumplimiento de la misión.

Teniendo en cuenta todos estos factores, podemos decir --que el sabotaje a una central telefónica, se puede llevar a cabo en dos formas.

1.- Con penetración.

2.- Mediante un golpe de mano.

1.- Con penetración:-
Esta forma consiste, en la cooperación de un miembro-activo o colaborador de la organización, que funcione dentro de la central; a través de esta persona se puede pasar algún tipo de artefacto explosivo para colocarlo dentro de la instalación de las distintas pizarras telefónicas que existen y que, por lo general, -se encuentran en lugares apartados de donde opera el-personal. De esta forma no se corre el riesgo de que pueda resultar accidentado algún obrero.

2.- Mediante un golpe de mano:-
Esta forma consiste en el estudio minucioso del objetivo, su vigilancia y el asalto posterior, con el fin

Document 37-10,11

MUY SECRETO.
HOJA #126.

de destruir toda su instalación y de ser posible incendiarla para destruirla completamente.

D I B U J O No. 3

Illustration Missing from Original Captured Document

MUY SECRETO.
HOJA #127.

SABOTAJE A LA RED FERROVIARIA.

El sabotaje a la red ferroviaria lo dividimos en tres tipos : Sabotaje de la Vía; Sabotaje de estaciones y Sabotajes de material rodante. Como bien se da a entender, cada clasificación tiene sus características propias; he — aquí la sub-división táctica que se le ha hecho :-

SABOTAJE DE LA VIA : (RAILES)

El sabotaje de los railes de ferrocarril se debe llevar a cabo mediante el uso de explosivo, el cual, dándole una buena utilización, puede causar grandes daños al enemigo.

Con el fin de volar la vía ferrea se deben escoger lugares preferentemente abiertos y en curvas. Las cargas de explosivo deberán colocarse siempre en los raíles exteriores. La cantidad de vía que es necesario volar para lograr el descarrilamiento de un tren, está en dependencia de si es en una curva o no. Si la voladura se produce en una curva, debido a que el maquinista no ve la línea y — continúa manteniendo la misma velocidad, solamente es necesario de 30 a 40 cms., de línea férrea volada: ahora — bien si es en la línea recta, donde el maquinista tiene tiempo de ver la voladura y aplicar el freno de emergencia o aminorar la velocidad, es necesario volar mucho más tramo.

Cuando la organización no cuenta con mucho explosivo como para llevar a efecto este tipo de operación, puede utilizarse, sobre todo en las pendientes, grasa, que se untará en todos los raíles a lo largo, de por lo menos, 150 mts., con el fin de que todo el tren patine dentro del tramo — afectado y se interrumpa su avance.

Document 37-12,13

MUY SECRETO.
HOJA #128.

SABOTAJE DEL MATERIAL RODANTE

Para el sabotaje al material rodante (trenes), se utilizará como primera forma una carga explosiva que se enterrará en la vía férrea (entre los dos raíles) y que se hará detonar mediante cables, en el momento que pase la locomotora. En los casos que se sepa que en determinado vagón viaja alguna persona importante, explosivo, etc., se puede volar la carga explosiva en el momento en que ese vagón pase por encima de la misma. Otra de las formas de descarrilamiento del material rodante es mediante el aflojamiento de los pernos, tornillos, tuercas, que sujetan los raíles y largueros. Esta operación se debe realizar en ocho largueros continuos, retirando las tuercas de la junta de unión de los raíles (de 4 à 6 tuercas juntas).

Posteriormente se separarán las aletas de los raíles, forzándose el raíl hacia dentro con una barreta, trabando la junta entre las dos puntas. Este procedimiento es lento y trabajoso, pero su resultado es efectivo en cuanto al descarrilamiento de los trenes.

Otro de los métodos efectivos para lograr el descarrilamiento de un tren es colocar en el eje del vagón central del tren una lata conteniendo 1 Klg. de explosivo. Este método es seguro, pero tiene el inconveniente que hay que colocar la carga directamente al objetivo, que de seguro estará vigilado, por lo que se deberá actuar con mucha cautela. Cuando hay poco tiempo se pueden llevar dos latas de 600 gr. de explosivos cada una, soldadas a un alambre; éstas se colocarán directamente sobre el eje del vagón.
En este caso se recomienda que el alambre quede lo más corto posible, con el fin de que en el momento de la explosión las cargas se encuentren lo más adosadas posibles al eje. (Estas minas detonarán por retardo).

Existen otros métodos para sabotear los trenes y en los que no se necesita explosivo. Por ejemplo, echarle arena o polvo, desperdicios de hierro (esmeril) en la caja de la lubricación de los ejes, que se encuentra situado en la rueda de los trenes, y que es fácil abrir con la mano. Este método no da resultado instantáneo, pero después de un largo recorrido, los ejes, producto de la fricción, sufrirán un serio desgaste.

HOJA #129.

Como para la realización de este sabotaje no es necesario ningún procedimiento técnico, cualquier persona lo puede poner en práctica; por ejemplo, un obrero ferroviario, dedicado al cuidado de los vagones o a la carga y descarga de los mismos, etc.

SABOTAJE A LAS ESTACIONES FERROVIARIAS

Las estaciones ferroviarias presentan las siguientes características :-

1.- Un edificio central donde se encuentran las oficinas, y algunas veces existen pequeñas instalaciones de control.

2.- Lo que podemos llamar red de las vías: tramos de vías, aguja, controles, vías circulares para cambiar de dirección los trenes.

3.- Instalación de señales de entrada y salida.

4.- Mástiles de conductores eléctricos, así como una red de comunicaciones, en la cual entran desde los teléfonos civiles hasta la oficina de telégrafo, que radica en toda estación ferroviaria.

Tomando en cuenta estas características antes mencionadas, podemos plantear que el sabotaje a una estación ferroviaria se puede llevar a efecto de la misma forma que en la estación telefónica, o sea, mediante la penetración o un golpe de mano.

Durante el golpe de mano a una estación, la consecutividad de las demoliciones deben ser en la forma siguiente :

Si existe poco tiempo, volar la aguja con una carga explosiva de 1 Klg. y luego la estación de control.

Si existe mucho más tiempo, volar además el mástil prin

Document 37-14,15

MUY SECRETO.
HOJA #130.

cipal de conducto de combustible, así como los tramos - centrales y cruces de la red de railes.

Destrucción de las agujas:- Colocando una cuña de madera o de hierro en la palanca de laaguja, la misma queda trabada y el tren, al cambiar de vía salta de la misma. Este método solamente se puede llevar a cabo cuando.— existen miembros de la organización o colaboradores, debido a que la aguja solamente la puede manipular el personal asignado.

D I B U J O No. 4

Illustration Missing from Original Captured Document

MUY SECRETO.
HOJA #131.

SABOTAJE EN LA RED DE ELECTRICIDAD.

El sabotaje a las redes eléctricas lo podemos realizar - con dos métodos :

Método directo y Método indirecto.

El Método Directo.-

Es el que contempla el sabotaje a las redes de instalación (destrucción de tendidos de alta tensión, que van - de la ciudad al campo o voladura de los mástiles o torres de sostén) y el sabotaje a las estaciones de transformadores (sabotaje a los tendidos de alto voltaje en los pueblos, destrucción de los aisladores, creación de cortocircuito, o tumbar los postes con explosivo o serrote).

El Método Indirecto.-

Es el que contempla el sabotaje en los talleres de electricidad (sabotaje a las turbinas, compresores, así como a los muros de las represas).

El método para la realización del sabotaje "Directo" o "Indirecto" se llevará a cabo en la misma forma que el sabotaje en la red de comunicaciones por teléfono, con la - única salvedad de que al realizar dichas acciones se deben tomar extremas medidas de seguridad para no quedar — electrocutado por cables de alta tensión que se destruyan. Además existe un punto que es el sabotaje a las estaciones de transformadores, el cual es completamente distinto, que el que se realizaría en una central telefónica, debido a sus características propias que señalaremos a continuación.

Sabotaje a una estación de transformadores.-

Una estación de transformadores se compone de los objetivos siguientes :-

Una casa, la cual podrá ser de uno o dos pisos; en uno - de los pisos se encuentra el dormitorio de los empleados, y en el otro el cuarto de los controles.

Para evitar los accidentes producidos por el alto volta-

Document 37-16,17

MUY SECRETO.
HOJA #132.

Je, por regla general estas estaciones están rodeadas por una cerca de alambre, reforzadas con alambre de púas a — una altura de dos o dos metros y medio, que encierra toda el área. Dentro de esa cerca, en lo alto de unos mástiles, se encuentra una instalación de reflectores para iluminar el área y facilitar el trabajo de noche.

El fluído eléctrico es conducido mediante tendidos de alta tensión, que están suspendidos en mástiles. El último mástil, por lo general, siempre se encuentra próximo a la cerca de alambre (a una distancia de 100 metros).

La instalación de los transformadores está compuesta de transformadores, enfriadores, chuchos, y aisladores. Todos estos objetos se encuentran al aire libre, en lo que podemos denominar patio de la estación.

Analizando las características que presenta este tipo de objetivo, podemos decir que para sabotearlo y causarle considerables daños debemos hacerlo mediante un golpe de mano. El personal que realice este tipo de operación, — una vez adentrado en el objetivo y en dependencia del — tiempo con que cuente, deberá actuar basándose en el siguiente orden de prioridad:-

Si existe poco tiempo:-

Se deberá destruír en primer orden los transformadores. Estos transformadores constituyen el núcleo general de toda la instalación: como existen generalmente pocos — transformadores el trabajo será bastante rápido, los mismos se pueden destruír mediante disparos de armas largas o mediante la colocación de una carga de 4 Klg. de explosivo. Después de destruídos los transformadores se deben destruír los enfriadores. Para la destrucción de este objetivo se empleará el mismo método que para los — transformadores.

Si existe mucho tiempo:-

Además de los dos objetivos antes señalados, también se deberá destruír los aisladores, los chuchos que se encuentren en el cuarto de control. Antes de emprender la retirada se deberá volar el mástil más próximo a los cables de alta tensión, debido a que ese es el que lleva el fluído eléctrico a toda la estación.

MUY SECRETO.
HOJA #133.

D I B U J O No. 5

Illustration Missing from Original Captured Document

Document 37-18,19

MUY SECRETO.
HOJA #134.

SABOTAJE A UNA INSTALACION DE TANQUES DE GASOLINA.

Las instalaciones de gasolina se encuentran, por lo general, cerca de una estación de ferrocarril y están conectadas a ella por una vía férrea.

Este tipo de instalación se compone de :-

La casa de los operarios de los tanques, que se encuentra por lo general en la planta alta de una construcción de dos pisos; en la planta baja, detrás de una rampa se encuentra la instalación de descarga de los camiones cisternas; más afuera, en lo que podemos llamar el patio de la estación, se encuentran los tanques al aire libre, con una capacidad de unos cuantos miles de galones. Cerca de estos tanques se encuentran otros tanques soterrados que se comunican por medio de un túnel.

Después, pegado al chucho ferroviario, se encuentra una instalación para descargar los carros tanques del ferrocarril; la instalación por lo general, cuenta con un teléfono para su comunicación externa y está cercada en una forma corriente.

El sabotaje a esto tipo de objetivo se debe realizar mediante un golpe de mano, el cual, debido al carácter de su sorpresa, puede destruir la instalación en pocos minutos ayudado por las características del combustible y el fuego.

Durante este ataque, se debe seguir un orden de prioridad que es el siguiente :

Si hay poco tiempo:-

Se destruyen los tanques de combustible, tanto los que se encuentran soterrados, como los que están al aire libre, así como también las instalaciones de carga de los camiones cisternas y los carros tanques del ferrocarril. Estos tanques se pueden destruír mediante la instalación de una carga explosiva de 4 Kg., situada en la base del tanque. En caso de que el tanque no vuele, sino que simplemente se derrama el combustible, entonces se podrá completar el trabajo, dándole fuego.

MUY SECRETO.
HOJA #135.

Para la destrucción de los tanques soterrados, que generalmente se encuentran a una profundidad de tres metros bajo tierra, se debe colocar una carga explosiva, con preferencia sobre la chapa del tanque. En caso de que el tanque esté lleno, la explosión causará la reventación de la envoltura de hierro, ya que el líquido no se puede comprimir, en este caso después se completará el trabajo con el fuego. En caso de que el tanque se encuentre mediado, lo más probable es que la parte vacía se haya llenado de una mezcla de aire, con peligro de explosión, lo que ayudará en la destrucción. En todos los casos la carga explosiva debe colocarse adosada al tanque del combustible.

D I B U J O No. 6

Illustration Missing from Original Captured Document

[Document 38]: Sandinista Booklet

This Booklet dislayed in a PLO office in southern Lebanon, states the goals of the Nicaraguan Revolution; it is dated June 1980.

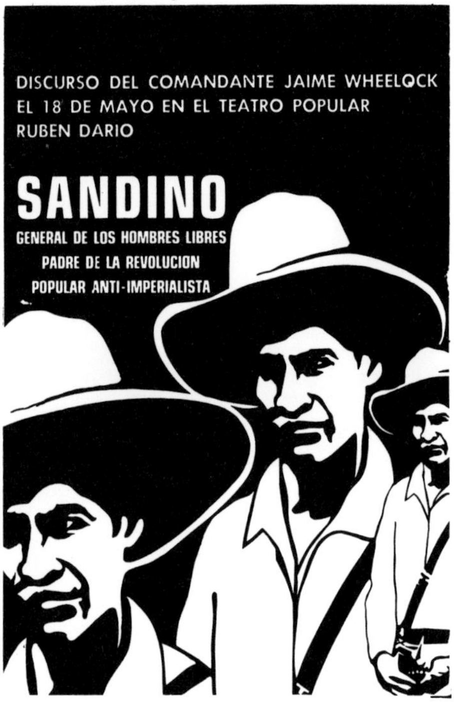
DISCURSO DEL COMANDANTE JAIME WHEELOCK
EL 18 DE MAYO EN EL TEATRO POPULAR
RUBEN DARIO
SANDINO
GENERAL DE LOS HOMBRES LIBRES
PADRE DE LA REVOLUCION
POPULAR ANTI-IMPERIALISTA

1980 – AÑO DE LA ALFABETIZACION
MANAGUA – NICARAGUA

Las enseñanzas de Sandino fecundaron en el FSLN para culminar la obra revolucionaria.

- El amor puro e incondicional por la Patria.
- La confianza en el pueblo humilde para defensa de la Nación.
- El odio a los agresores externos y los vendepatrias.
- La lucha armada para arrojar a los invasores.
- La unidad Nacional Antiimperialista.

La Revolución
Nicaragüense es Nacional
Y Fundamentalmente
Antiimperialista

COLECCION JUAN DE DIOS MUÑOZ
SERIE ORIENTACION SANDINISTA 1

VI. THE INTER-ARAB, INTER-ISLAMIC AND THIRD WORLD CONNECTIONS [Documents 40-60]:

The Communist world, which provides the PLO with most of its ideological, political and military backing in a shared spirit of revolution, is only one section, admittedly the most important, in the worldwide network of ties which the Palestinian organizations have forged. They are also supported by many Arab countries, by the Islamic world and by much of the Third World.

Of these three elements, the Arab world is the most committed to supporting the PLO, due to feelings of brotherhood and joint participation in the long Arab-Israeli conflict. The Rabat Summit of 1974 recognized the PLO as the sole representative of the Palestinian people. Even Arab countries which do not accept the PLO's radicalism and are indeed frightened of the menace that the revolutionary PLO poses to their regimes, are duty-bound to assist the PLO militarily, financially and politically — or at least to pay lip-service to the PLO cause. Parallel to the active involvement of Syria, Algeria and Libya, Egypt and Saudi Arabia give support in less direct, but no less significant, ways. Egypt champions the Palestinian cause politically via the autonomy talks and various other channels; Saudi Arabia, the PLO's greatest financial benefactor, supports it in the political arena and militarily, through the delivery of American weapons. In any case, no Arab country, which wishes to maintain its respectability as a committed member of the Arab League, can afford to disclaim publicly its interest in the PLO cause.

The second nexus is the Islamic world. Not only are the Arab countries (21 of them) members of the Islamic community, constituting its most wealthy and influential bloc, but they also lead the 40-odd-member Islamic Conference, which has been convening annually since 1969 and wielding considerable political clout in world affairs. The backing of the Islamic world, with its 800 million believers, lends to the Palestinian problem in general, and the PLO in particular, much more leverage than it would otherwise have. Thus, such countries as Indonesia, Pakistan, Bangladesh, Iran and Turkey embrace the PLO cause and often actively participate in training PLO personnel.

Other Third World states, which either have a strong Muslim minority, like India, or allow subversive groups to operate, like many countries in Africa, Asia and Latin America, are also part of the international web of PLO activity.

[Document 39]: Libyan officer in charge of PLO air defence

Popular Front for the Liberation of Palestine
General Command
No. 4128/ZA'AH
Date: 26 April 1982

Administrative Order

1. Capt. Hamduni, attached from the Libyan armed forces, was appointed assistant to the commander of Al-Na'ama stronghold for air defence matters, valid as of today.

2. Capt. Hamduni continues to supervise the air defence forces in all military districts. He was assigned the following by the secretary-general:
   a) To train the air defence units of the Front in all strongholds.
   b) To raise the level of training and tactics.
   c) To guarantee their needs in weapons, ammunition and equipment in coordination with the air defence headquarters of the armed forces in Tripoli.

3. Capt. Hamduni will supervise the air defence forces attached to Fatah.

4. Capt. Hamduni will conduct a comprehensive and documented survey of the following items in the air defence forces:
   a) Arms and equipment.
   b) Military installations and instruments.
   c) Vehicles and technical equipment.
   The reports will be submitted according to regulations to the secretary-general within 15 days.

5. It is the task of the commander of the Al-Na'ama stronghold to:
   a) Guarantee Capt. Hamduni a place to stay and properly attach him to the stronghold.
   b) Guarantee residence for Capt. Hamduni's men inside the stronghold.
   c) The assignment of Capt. Hamduni will be fully integrated with the table of organization of Al-Na'ama stronghold in everything relating to personnel, military finance, administration and the munitions centre.

d) Capt. Hamduni will be put in charge of air defence in the stronghold and will set down a full programme for approval by the stronghold commander, with a copy to the central military officer.
e) All air defence equipment and personnel in the stronghold will be subordinate to Capt. Hamduni. Daily activity will be his responsibility.
f) It is necessary to ensure that Nakib Hamduni has a fire control position in the stronghold at times of enemy attacks.

6. During visits of Capt. Hamduni in other strongholds, which have air defence systems in the front, it will be his responsibility:
   a) To ensure that the air defence equipment is in operational order.
   b) To ensure that such equipment is properly and effectively deployed.
   c) This will be done in cooperation with the stronghold commander and the soldier responsible for air defence in the stronghold.
   d) Once every month Capt. Hamduni will submit a periodical report about the air defence situation in the strongholds, along with his proposals.
   e) Capt. Hamduni is not permitted to transfer personnel or weapons from one stronghold to another, but will submit his proposal to the officer responsible in the front, and if required, an order concerning the matter will be issued by the secretary-general.

(signature)
Secretary-General

Copies:

File
Fara military hq
Front positions
Colonel Zallah

Document 39A-2

الجبهة الشعبية لتحرير فلسطين
القيادة العامة
الامانة العامة

الرقم /   /
التاريخ / / ١٩

-٢-

جـ - ضم جميع ملاك النقيب حمدوني لملاك موقع الناعمة سواء مما يتعلق بفرع الافراد او المالية العسكرية او التسليح المركزي .

د - اعطاء النقيب حمدوني مسؤولية الدفاع الجوي في الموقع من خلال وضع خطة متكاملة يتم التصديق عليها من قبل قائد الموقع وترفع نسخة عنها الى المسؤول العسكري المركزي .

هـ - يتم وضع جميع الوسائط المضادة للطائرات وعناصرها في داخل الموقع تحت آمرة النقيب حمدوني وتكون على مسؤولية في قيادة العمل اليومي .

و - يؤمن للنقيب حمدوني موقع لادارة النيران اثناء الغارات الجوية المعادية (في موقع الناعمة)

٦- عند قيام النقيب حمدوني بزيارة المواقع الاخرى في الجبهة والتي لديها وسائط الدفاع الجوي تكون مسؤولياته :-

أ- التأكد من حسن سير عمل الوسائط المضادة للطائرات

ب - التأكد من التوزيع الجيد لهذه الوسائط وفاعليتها

جـ - يتم ذلك بالتعاون مع قائد الموقع والعنصر المسؤول عن الدفاع الجوي في الموقع

د - يقوم النقيب حمدوني برفع تقرير دوري عن وضع الدفاع الجوي في المواقع وفاعليته والاقتراحات المطلوبة وذلك كل شهر مرة .

هـ - لا يحق للنقيب حمدوني اجراء اية مناقلات للعناصر او الاسلحة ((من موقع الى موقع)) بل يرفع اقتراحه الى المسؤول العسكري في الجبهة واذا كان في ذلك مصلحة يتم اصدار امر بذلك من الامين العام .

الامين العام

المرسل اليهم :-

- المصنف
- فرع القيادة العسكرية
- مواقع الجبهة
- العقيد صالح

Document 39A-1

الجبهة الشعبية لتحرير فلسطين
القيادة العامة
الامـــانة العامـــة

الرقـم / ٤١٢٨ / ص أ ع
التاريخ ٢٦/ ٤/ ١٩٨٢

أمـــــر اداري

١ـ يتم تعيين النقيب حمدوني المفرز من القوات المسلحة الليبية معاونـــا لقائد موقع الناعمة لشؤون الدفاع الجوي واعتبارا من تاريخه اعلاه .

٢ـ يستمر النقيب حمدوني بالاشراف على قوات الدفاع الجوي في عمـــوم القطاعات العسكرية وبتكليف من الرفيق الامين العام .

أ ـ للنهوض بتشكيلات الدفاع الجوي للجبهة بجميع المواقع

ب ـ رفع قدراتها التدريبية والتعبوية .

جـ ـ لتأمين لوازمها من اسلحة وذخائر وعتاد وبالتنسيق مع قيادة الدفـــاع الجوي في القوات المسلحة بطرابلس .

٣ـ يقوم النقيب حمدوني بالاشراف على قوات الدفاع الجوي المفرزة لـــدى (فتح)

٤ـ يقوم النقيب حمدوني بعمل جرد كامل وموثق لقوات الدفاع الجـــوي بما يتعلق :ـ

أ ـ الاسلحة والعتاد

ب ـ التجهيزات العسكرية والادوات .

جـ ـ الاليات والمعدات الفنية .

وترفع هذه الكشوف حسب الاصول الى الامين العام خلال مدة لا تتجاوز ١٥ خمسة عشر يوما .

٥ـ يقوم قائد موقع الناعمة بترتيب الامور التالية

أ ـ تأمين مقر للنقيب حمدوني وربطه مع الموقع بشكل جيد

ب ـ تأمين مقر الاقامة للقوة التابعة للنقيب حمدوني داخل الموقع .

[Document 40]: Training of PLO members in Arab and Islamic Countries.
See chart in Document 26 on page 96-102

[Document 41]: Promise of military assistance by Syria and Saudi Arabia

THE PALESTINE NATIONAL LIBERATION MOVEMENT

FATAH

'ASIFA FORCES GENERAL COMMAND

Date: 25.7.81

Protocol of the 6th meeting of the military council dated 25.7.81.

Present:
Commander-in-Chief:
Abu 'Ammar (Arafat)
Abu Jihad
Abu al-Walid, et al.
The Political Situation

The Commander-in-Chief reviewed the recent political situation, and praised the determination of the Palestinian and Lebanese fighters in the recent battle. "General Callaghan presented an official request for a cease-fire and our response was that we agreed in principle to a cease-fire, but for this we must receive authorization of the joint command."

We have a condition, we do not recognize the border enclave of Major Sa'ad Haddad.

We will regard all aggression emanating from the border enclave as Israeli aggression.

Arafat reviewed the meeting of the Executive Committee and his meeting with the National Movement, and the final decision that the National Movement and the Palestine resistance groups will agree to a cease-fire.

In addition, the military committee was informed about the dispatch of three anti-aircraft batteries by Syria, following the visit of Abu al-Walid and his meeting with Hekmat al-Shehabi.[43] The meeting was also informed about the

43. The Syrian Chief of Staff

visit of the Saudi Arabian ambassador, in which the latter reported that King Khaled is pressuring the United States to oppose the conquest of Lebanon by Israel. In addition, he made it clear that we are committed to the UN and the Security Council to observe the cease-fire, but not to Philip Habib.

Arafat reported that we have information indicating that the Lebanese authorities want to hand over the bridges in the south, and Qala'at Shakif[44] to the Lebanese Army or to UN forces. But we will prevent the execution of this plan.[45]

After that Abu al-Walid reviewed the meetings of the Joint Arab Defence Council in which he took part and said:

"All the participants in the Council are apprehensive of a continuation of the fighting but they refused, at the end of the meeting, to emphasize the need for joint Arab action or to call for the convening of an Arab summit, for fear that it might incite the USA or Israel."

The Palestinian delegation demanded that all the countries bordering on Israel open their borders.

The Jordanian delegation rejected this demand. The Jordanian delegation proposed to assist the confrontation states. On this subject a lengthy discussion ensued and the names of the countries interested in taking steps to open the borders were recorded. Syria supported the opening of the borders in order to carry out operations in the conquered territories but opposed the idea of shelling.

The Libyan delegation opposed the participation of the Sudanese delegation and left the meeting. The remaining Arab delegations condemned the organization for not holding consultations with them before approaching the Defence Council for coordination.

The Defence Council failed to take any steps for the Steadfast Front and the resistance.

Saudi Arabia promised to fulfil all our requests for the supply of arms and ammunition.

44. The Beaufort stronghold, conquered by the PLO from the UNIFIL forces.

45. This illustrates the determination of the PLO to defy the authority of the Lebanese government within the sovereign territory of Lebanon.

Document 41A-1,2

حركة التحرير الوطني الفلسطيني
"فتح"
القيادة العامة لقوات العاصفة

الرقم ______
التاريخ ______
الموضوع ______

[illegible]	الموضوع	الإجراء

الموقف السياسي

شرح الأخ الناطق العام الموقف السياسي الأخير وأشاد أيضاً بموقف المقاتل الفلسطيني واللبناني بالمعركة الأخيرة، وقال لقد تقدم الجنرال كالاهان بطلب يحتوي لوقف إطلاق النار وقلنا له أننا من ناحية المبدأ لا نعترض على وقف إطلاق النار ولا بد من أخذ موافقة القيادة المشتركة ولكن لنا شرط وهو أننا لا نعترف بالشريط الحدودي ولا بالرائد سعد حداد ويجب أن يعتبر أي تعدي من الشريط الحدودي هو تعدي من اسرائيل. وأوضح كيفية اجتماع اللجنة التنفيذية واجتماعه مع الحركة الوطنية واتخاذ القرار المناسب بموافقة الحركة الوطنية وفصائل المقاومة الفلسطينية على وقف إطلاق النار.

وكذلك أوضح للمجلس العسكري عن ارسال سوريا لثلاثة طائرات ٢٠٠٠ [illegible] على أثر زيارة الأخ أبو الوليد واجتماعه مع [illegible]
وتكلم عن زيارة السفير السعودي وإبلاغه أن الملك خالد يضغط على أمريكا [illegible] لإسرائيل باحتلال الجنوب.
وكذلك أوضح أننا نلتزم بوقف إطلاق النار أمام الأمم المتحدة ومجلس الأمن الدولي وليس أمام فيليب حبيب.
وقال أنه لدينا معلومات أن السلطة اللبنانية ترغب بتسليم [illegible] في الجنوب وكذلك قلعة الشقيف إلى الجيش اللبناني أو إلى القوات الدولية. إلا أننا سنمنع تنفيذ هذا المخطط.

حركة التحرير الوطني الفلسطيني
"فتح"
القيادة العامة لقوات العاصفة

الرقم ______
التاريخ ______
الموضوع ______

ينفذ من قبل	الموضوع	[illegible]

الأخ أبو الوليد

ثم أوضح الأخ أبو الوليد عن اجتماعات مجلس الدفاع العربي المشترك [illegible] فقال
أن جميع اللذين شاركوا بالمؤتمر يشعرون باستمرار المعارك، ورفضوا من نهاية المؤتمر أن يشيروا الى ضرورة العمل العربي المشترك أو الى دعوة القمة العربية خوفاً أن يشكل ذلك استفزازاً لأمريكا وإسرائيل.
وقد طلب الوفد الفلسطيني فتح الحدود من جميع الدول المحيطة بإسرائيل فاعترض وفد الأردن على هذا الطلب، واقترح الوفد الأردني تقديم الدعم المادي لدول المواجهة، وجرى على هذه التسمية جدال طويل وحتى أخيراً الدول المعنية بعدم [illegible] الوصول الى أي اجراءات لفتح الحدود.
وكان الموقف السوري ضد مع فتح الحدود للعمل داخل الأراضي المحتلة أما [illegible] فلم يعترض عليه.
أما الوفد الليبي فقد اعترض على وجود الوفد السوداني وانسحب من الاجتماع
[illegible] الدول العربية فقد [illegible] المنظمة على عدم اعطاء [illegible] [illegible] لمجلس الدفاع من أجل التنسيق.
والتقييم الأخير لمجلس الدفاع هو أنه فاشل ولم يتخذ أي اجراء لصالح الصمود والتصدي.
وقد وعدت السعودية أن تقدم لنا جميع ما نطلبه من أسلحة [illegible]

[Document 42]: M-16 rifle crates

These rifles, made in the United States, were captured in Lebanon. The United States sells such equipment to Saudi Arabia.

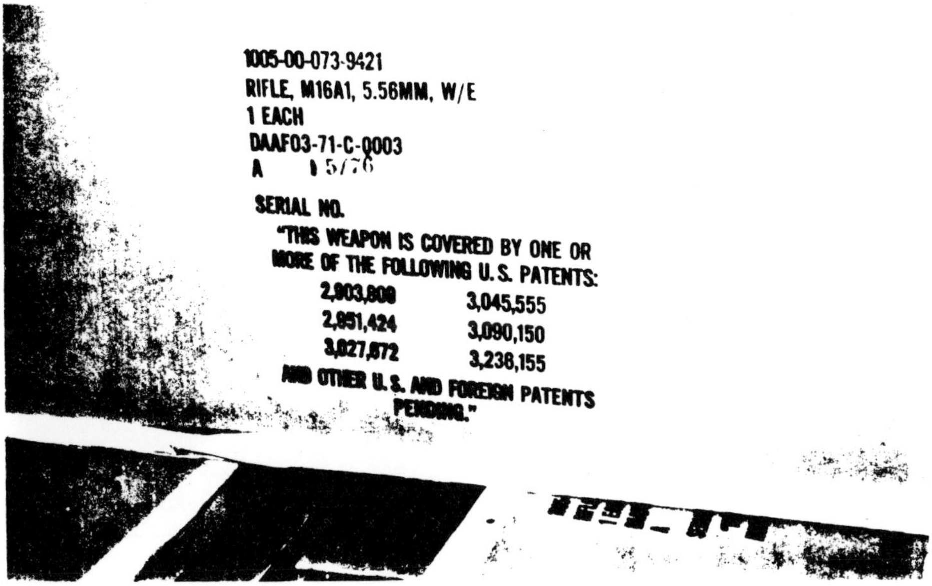

[Document 43]: Ammunition shipping tag: Missouri-Saudi Arabia

This US military shipping tag, attached to crates of ammunition, was found in a PLO arms cache in Lebanon.

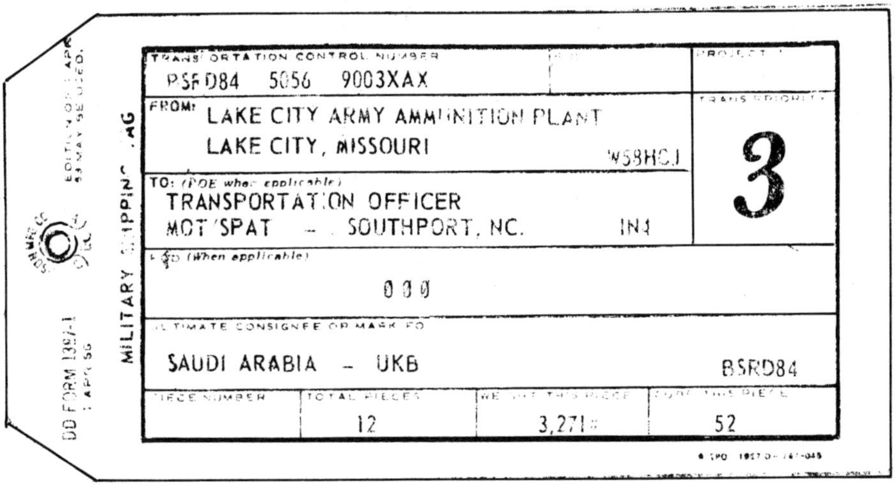

MILITARY SHIPPING TAG

DD FORM 1387-1

TRANSPORTATION CONTROL NUMBER: PSF D84 5056 9003XAX

FROM: LAKE CITY ARMY AMMUNITION PLANT
LAKE CITY, MISSOURI W58HCJ

TO: (POE when applicable)
TRANSPORTATION OFFICER
MOT SPAT - SOUTHPORT, NC. IN4

3

(When applicable)
0 0 0

ULTIMATE CONSIGNEE OR MARK FO

SAUDI ARABIA - UKB BSRD84

PIECE NUMBER	TOTAL PIECES	WEIGHT THIS PIECE	CUBE THIS PIECE
	12	3,271	52

[Document 44]: PLO position manned by Egyptians, Syrians and Libyans

This handwritten document implies that 23-25 persons, mostly Syrians and Egyptians, manned an underground cave where two Katyusha rocket launchers and three 82mm mortars were located. The commander of the position is Abu-Ra'd, who is in charge of 15 people armed with B-7 rocket launchers and a group of Libyans assigned to a Landrover vehicle.

يوجد بداخل المغارة راجمة عدد ٢ عدد الصواريخ لكل راجمة
٤٨ صاروخ محمولة آلية ٦ دواليب وراجمة أخرى على
سيارة تويوتا عدد ١٢ صاروخ و هاون ٨٢ عدد ٣
ومن الجهة الشمالية المغارة مغارة قيادة عدد غرف ٤ مجهزة
بالكياس رمل مع رشاش كرينوف و مسؤول هذه المغارة ابو
رعد عدد عناصره ١٥ عشر مسلحين ٤ بقواذف ب٧
و مجموعة من الليبيين مخصصين للاندروفر مع باسلحتهم الكاملة وهم
مسؤولين من القوات المسلحة الليبية لحرب العصابات وهم فدائيين
صواريخ سام ٧

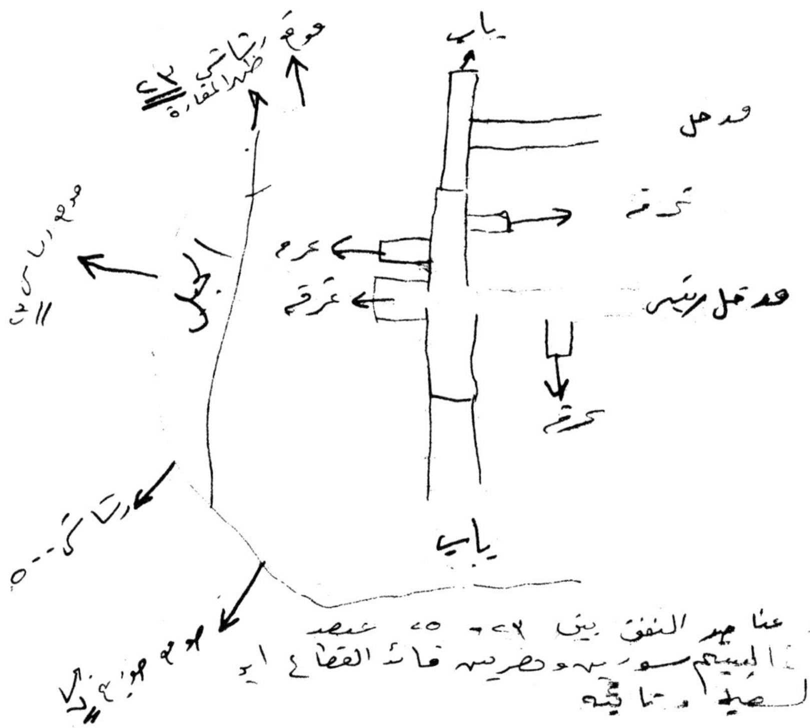

عدد عناصر النفق بين ٢٣ و ٢٥ عنصر
اغلبيتهم سوريين ومصريين قائد القطاع ابو
...

[Document 45]: PLO rest and recreation in Cairo

According to this order, signed by Colonel Zaki Abu-Hayye of the Palestine Liberation Army in Lebanon, 12 NCO's were given airplane tickets to go to Cairo for rest and recreation. The date is 10 February 1982.

منظمة التحرير الفلسطينية
رئاسة هيئة اركان جيش التحرير الفلسطيني — الرقم /١٦٨٧/ ٢
شعبة التنظيم والادارة — التاريخ / ١٠/ ٢/ ١٩٨٢
فرع الافراد

جيش التحرير الفلسطيني
قيادة قوات التحرير الشعبية
الرقم: ٢/٥٩٧
التاريخ: ١١/ ٢/ ١٩٨٢

==============================

أمر اداري

يصرف تذاكر سفر بالطائرة من بيروت الى القاهرة والعودة لصف الضباط والجنود المدرجه اسماؤهم ادناه حيث صدق لهم باجازات خارجية الى ج م ع ، حسب مشروع الاجازات الدفعه الرابعه المجموعة الثالثة وهم :-

م	الرتبه	الاسم والشهرة	الوحده	تاريخ القيام بالاجازة	ملاحظات
١	مساعد أول	ابراهيم حسن كسوحه	الفوج الاول المدرع	١٥/ ٢/ ١٩٨٢	
٢	"	محمد سلامه ابو غرقود	"	١٥/ ٢/ ١٩٨٢	
٣	رقيب أول	محمود ابراهيم وشاح	"	١٥/ ٢/ ١٩٨٢	
٤	عريف	خالد سعيد العصي	"	١٥/ ٢/ ١٩٨٢	
٥	جندى	محمد احمد احمد	المقر العام	١٥/ ٢/ ١٩٨٢	
٦	"	عبد الوهاب البدرى عبد الوهاب	"	١٥/ ٢/ ١٩٨٢	
٧	رقيب أول	فايق عبد الله وشاح	"	١٥/ ٢/ ١٩٨٢	
٨	جندى	ابراهيم عبد الرحيم ابو عبيد	"	١٥/ ٢/ ١٩٨٢	
٩	رقيب	سليمان محمد ابو راشد	"	١٥/ ٢/ ١٩٨٢	
١٠	رقيب أول	محمود عطيه كتيع	قوات التحرير الشعبية	١٥/ ٢/ ١٩٨٢	
١١	جندى	فواز سعد سعد	"	١٥/ ٢/ ١٩٨٢	
١٢	رقيب	عدنان محمد عباس	الكتيبه (٤٢٢) صاعقة	١٥/ ٢/ ١٩٨٢	

- يتم الحجز لهم حسب تاريخ القيام بالاجازه .

العقيد / زكي ابو حيه
نائب مدير امور جيش التحرير الفلسطيني بلبنان
التوقيع /

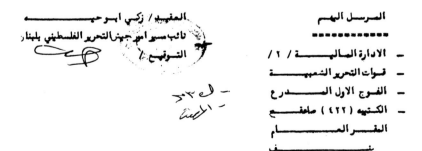

المرسل اليهم
============
- الادارة المالية / ٢ /
- قوات التحرير الشعبية
- الفوج الاول المدرع
- الكتيبه (٤٢٢) صاعقة
المقر العام
نسف

[Document 46]: PLO member sent to Gaza via Cairo

On 6 March 1982, Abu Ismail was ordered, in accordance with a decision of the Sidon office of the PLO, to issue a laissez-passer to Mahmud Dhib Iskandrati so that he could reach Gaza via Cairo. Presumably, he was to infiltrate illegally through Israeli-held northern Sinai (this was before Israel's withdrawal) and then into the Gaza Strip.

بسم الله الرحمن الرحيم

٦/٣/١٩٨٢

الأخ ابو اسماعيل

تحية الثورة

اما بعد

بناءً على تقرير الأمن المركزي بمنطقة صيدا ارجو

تزويد حامله الأخ محمود ذيب اسكندراني بتصريح لمغادرة

لبنان بغية الوصول الى غزة عن طريق القاهرة حيث

انه مأذون من قبل السلطات [illegible]

ارجو ان يكون امره سريا

مع الاحترام

ابو صالح - المسؤول

[illegible]

[Document 47]: PLO trainees in Damascus

Dated November 1981, this document lists 21 officers and NCO's from the Kastel Brigade who took 100mm anti-tank gun courses in Damascus.

.. [illegible] ..

القيادة العامة لقوات العاصفة

قيادة قوات القسطل

المرجع :

التاريخ : / ١١ / ١٩٨١م

ملف الدورة لدراسته

الأخ / مدير العمليات المركزية حفظه الله

تحية الثورة وبعد

نعدد لكم أسماء منسبينا للتدريب على المدفع ١٠٠ ملم م/ط المنعقدة في دمشق

وهم :-

✓ ١- النقيب : سلامه ابراهيم الطويسي ---- ٢١٥٠

✓ ٢- الملازم أول : خميس ابراهيم محمود

✓ ٣- الملازم أول : احمد محمد غنايم

✓ ٤- الملازم ثاني : احمد عبد الغني ابو عطير

✓ ٥- الملازم ثاني : عبد اللطيف احمد عبد اللطيف حمدان

✓ ٦- الرقيب أول : خالد حميد سويدان

✓ ٧- الرقيب أول : عزيز ابراهيم شعبان

✓ ٨- العريف : ناصر محمد ابو خروب

✗ ٩- المناضل : ماهر سليمان شحاده

✓ ١٠- " : محمد محمد عطا

✗ ١١- " : وائل حسن زغلوه

✓ ١٢- " : سليمان محمد خزاعي

✓ ١٣- " : علي عيسى محمد جبر

✗ ١٤- " : عيسى احمد صالح

✓ ١٥- " : غزال يحيى حسين غزال

✓ ١٦- " : عبد موسى علي يعقوب

✓ ١٧- " : عماد حسن محمود احمد

✓ ١٨- " : زايد عبد سليمان الخليان

✗ ١٩- " : تيسير محمد الغايب

✓ ٢٠- " : كامل خليل بخيت الخليان

٢١- ملازم ١ محمود سليمان محمد سليمان

يرجى اتخاذ الترتيبات لاستقبالهم في مكان عقد الدورة .

وانها لثورة حتى النصر

عن/ العقيد

قائد قوات القسطل

الحاج اسماعيل

ركن العمليات

نسخة الى :-

- السجل
- الملف

[Document 48]: PLO members from India, Pakistan and Bangladesh

This Fatah document, dated 12 May 1982, orders the "fellow-fighters" from Pakistan, India and Bangladesh not to use a certain route on their way from Lebanon to Syria and back.

حركة التحرير الوطني الفلسطيني
" فتـــح "
القياده العامه لقوات العاصفه

الرقـــم / أد / ٢ / ٤ ٠ ٥
التاريخ / ١٣ / ٥ / ١٩٨٢ م

تعميـــم

تحية الثورة وبعـــد !

- لوحظ ان الاخوه المناضلين يسلكون طريق الكحاله في الذهاب والعـوده الى ســوريا أو منطقة البقاع وخاصه الاخوه / الباكستانيين والهنـود والبنغاليين مما يترتب عليه أوضاع غير أمنيـة .

- لـذا يرجى ابلاغ الجميع عدم سلوك هذا الطريق حيث ان الطريق المتبع طريق عرمون وذلك حرصا " على عدم التعرض للمخاطر مع تحميل المسؤوليـه لكل مخالفه وتحت طائله العقاب .

- لاجراءاتكم وتعميمه على كافة وحداتكم ..... لطفـــا .

وثورة حتى النصر ،

/ مدير الدائره العسكريـــة

نسخه الى :-
- الذاتيـة .
- قسـم الهويات .
- شؤون الضباط والمرتبـات .
- التـداول .
- الحـفظ .

ش / ف

[Document 49]: Ten PLO members from Bangladesh

The list includes 10 Bangladesh nationals who were recruited to Company No. 2 of the September Martyrs Battalion, which is part of the Kastel Brigade.

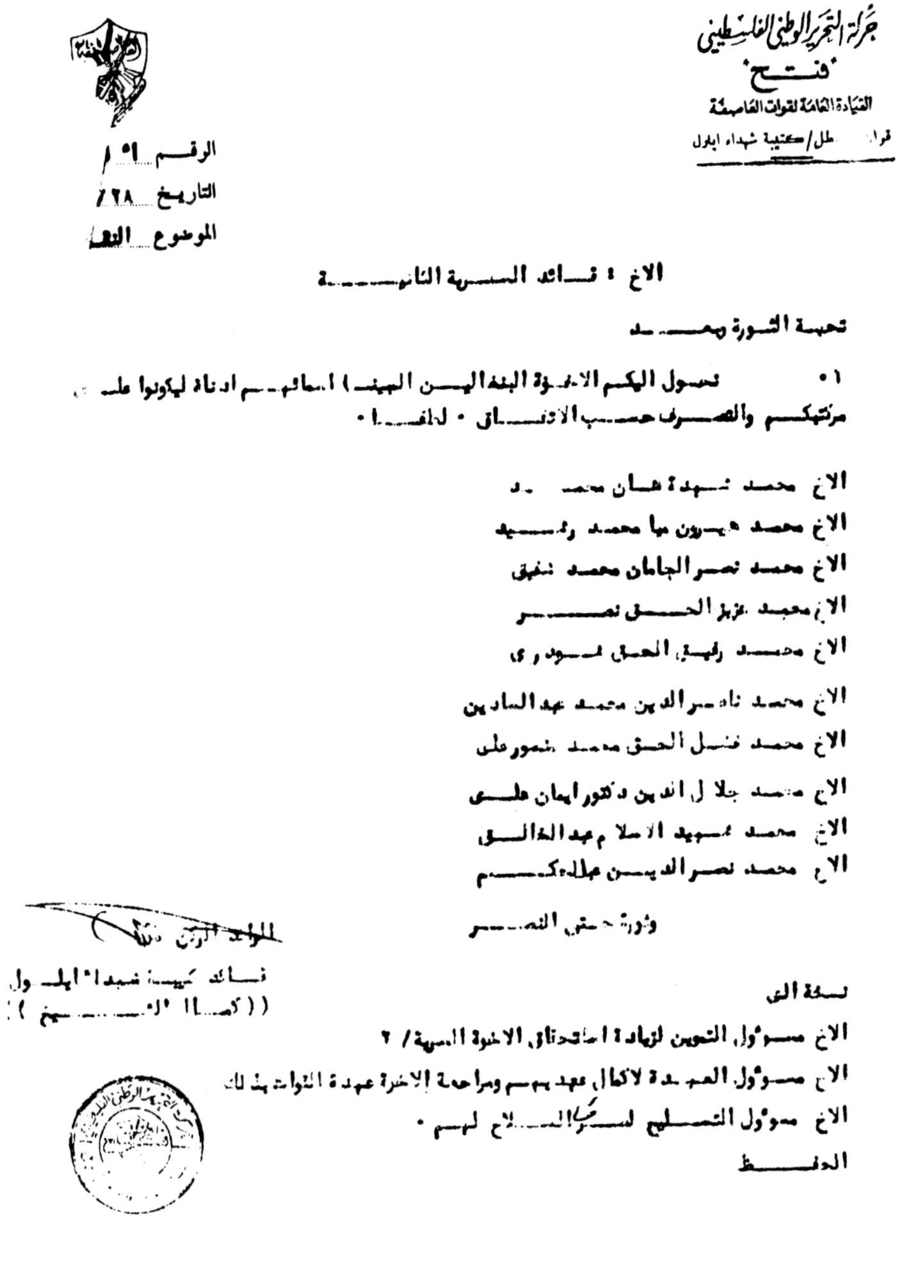

حركة التحرير الوطني الفلسطيني
"فتـــح"
القيادة العامة لقوات العاصفة
قوات [illegible] طل/كتيبة شهداء ايلول

الرقم ١٠٩م
التاريخ ٢٨/
الموضوع النقل

الاخ : قائد السرية الثانية

تحية الثورة وبعد

١. نحول اليكم الاخوة البنغاليين الهنـ (اسمائهم ادناه ليكونوا على [illegible] مرتبكم والصرف حسب الاتفاق . لاتفا .

الاخ محمد شهدة شان محمد
الاخ محمد هارون ميا محمد رشيد
الاخ محمد نصر الجامان محمد شفيق
الاخ محمد عزيز الحق نصر
الاخ محمد رفيق الحق مسعودي
الاخ محمد ناصر الدين محمد عبد السادين
الاخ محمد فضل الحق محمد منصور على
الاخ محمد جلال الدين دكتور ايمان على
الاخ محمد سعيد الاسلام عبد الخالق
الاخ محمد نصر الدين عبد الكريم

وثورة حتى النصر

المقدم [illegible]
قائد كتيبة شهداء ايلول
(([illegible]))

نسخة الى
الاخ مسؤول التموين لزيادة استحقاق الاخوة السرية / ٢
الاخ مسؤول العهدة لاكمال عهدتهم ومراجعة الاخيرة عهدة القوات بذلك
الاخ مسؤول التسليح لتسليم السلاح لهم .
الحفظ

[Document 50]: Twenty more PLO members from Bangladesh

A second list of 20 Bangladeshis who joined the Kastel Brigade of Fatah on 9 April 1982.

حركة التحرير الوطني الفلسطيني
" فتح "
القيادة العامة لقوات العاصفة
قيادة قوات القسطل

٥/١٢

الرقم : أ/١/٣/ ١٠١ ٨
التاريخ : ٩/٤/١٩٨٢م

الموضوع / النقل

الاخوة / كتيبة شهداء ايلول

تحية الثورة وبعد

ينقل اليكم الاخوة البنغاليين و المذكورين تاليا من مرتبنا / قيادة القوات - معسكر التدريب و الذين انهوا الدورة التدريبية اعتبارا من تاريخه وهم :-

٠١	محمد عبد العزيز عبد السبحان ميا	٠٢	فاكير فاروق احمد بابور علي فاكير
٠٣	محمد شفيق الاسلام شمس الدين احمد	٠٤	محمد حسين عرب مونشي
٠٥	محمد نذر الاسلام محمد جواد الله	٠٦	توفايل احمد ان ميا
٠٧	نور الاسلام محمد عبد الاوال	٠٨	محمد عبد المنان عبد الجبار
٠٩	محمد عبد الرحيم عبد الرحمن فقير	١٠	محمد نور النبي صفي الله ميا
١١	محمد نذر الاسلام مطهر علي	١٢	محمد عبد الرشيد محمد رستم علي
١٣	محمد محفوظ مصدق الرحمن	١٤	محمد منصور ايماد علي
١٥	محمد فكر الاسلام احمد الله	١٦	محمد جعفر علي حاجي حسن علي
١٧	مؤمن الله شيخ احمد بنسي	١٨	محمد ممتاز الدين محمد ناصر الدين
١٩	عنايت جمعه محمد عبد الغني	٢٠	محمد نايم صديق علي

لاجراءاتكم و اضافتهم لقيودكم ... لطفا

وثورة حتى النصر

ادارة قوات القسطل

نسخة الى / :
= = = = = = = = = = = = = = =

المالية
الذاتية + ٢٠
السجل
الحفظ

[Document 51]: PLO member from Somalia
Identity card of Somali national found in Lebanon.

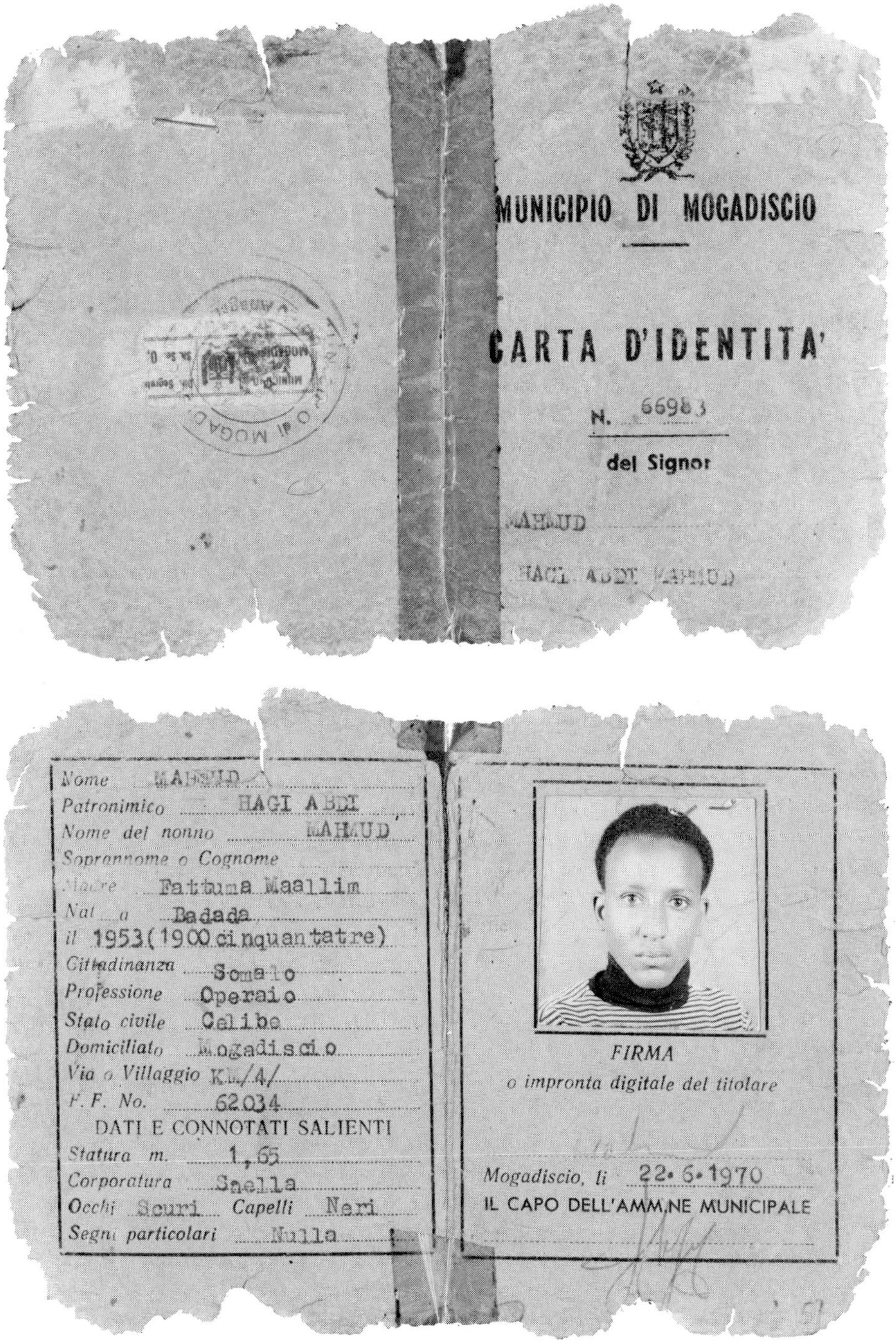

MUNICIPIO DI MOGADISCIO

CARTA D'IDENTITA'

N. 66983

del Signor

MAHMUD

HAGI ABDI MAHMUD

Nome MAHMUD
Patronimico HAGI ABDI
Nome del nonno MAHMUD
Soprannome o Cognome
Madre Fattuma Maallim
Nat. a Badada
il 1953 (1900 cinquantatre)
Cittadinanza Somalo
Professione Operaio
Stato civile Celibe
Domiciliato Mogadiscio
Via o Villaggio KM/4/
F. F. No. 62034

DATI E CONNOTATI SALIENTI

Statura m. 1,65
Corporatura Snella
Occhi Scuri Capelli Neri
Segni particolari Nulla

FIRMA
o impronta digitale del titolare

Mogadiscio, li 22.6.1970
IL CAPO DELL'AMM.NE MUNICIPALE

[Document 52]: PLO officers train in India

A 27 March 1981 order from Fatah headquarters to five of its units to dispatch one officer each for training in basic engineering in India.

حركة التحرير الوطني الفلسطيني
"فتح"
القيادة العامة لقوات العاصفة
قيادة قوات الكرامة

رقم ع ٢ / ٥ / ٢٢٨
التاريخ ٢٧ / اذار / ١٩٨١

الاخوه / قيادة كتيبة الجليل
الاخوه / قيادة كتيبة الكرمل
الاخوه / قيادة كتيبة نسور العرقوب
الاخوه / قيادة القوه المحموله
الاخوه / قيادة وحدة الهندسه الاولى

الموضوع / الدورات الخارجيه

تحية الثوره وبعد .

١- خصص لكل منكم مقعد واحد في احد الدورات التاليه والتي ستعقد في الهند :-
قادة فصائل — [redacted] تاسيسيه للضباط — هندسه تاسيسيه للضباط

٢- يرجى تنسيب واحد من كل منكم وموافاتنا باسماء منسبيكم حتى ١٩٨١/٥/١ .

٣- يشترط في المنسب ان يكون لائق صحيا ولديه معرفه في اللغه الانكليزيه وعمره لا يتجاوز الثلاثين وبرتبة ملازم .

وثوره حتى النصر

العقيد الركن
قائد قوات الكرامه
ابو هاجم

نسخه الى :-
السجل
الحفظ

[Document 53]: PLO officers train in Pakistan

The picture shows an officers' class which trained at the School of Armour in Nowshera, Pakistan, in 1980. Two PLO officers are among the graduates.

[Document 54]: PLO member spies against Iran

A copy of this document, written in Persian, was found in a PLO command post in southern Lebanon.

Top Secret

From: Iranian Embassy in Beirut

To: Foreign Ministry, Director General of Asian-African Affairs, Mr. Louasani

cc: Political Director-General, Mr. Sheikh al-Salam

It has come to my attention, that in the future you may appoint Mr. Ahmed Mawahdi to a position at one of our embassies. I thus feel myself obligated to convey to you the following information. I assure you, no personal grudge is involved.

1. The man is an indirect spy for the KGB who worked through Fatah.
2. During his service in Beirut, he totally ignored the interests of the Islamic revolution, and acted as an agent.
3. As a result of his mistaken policy, he misled about 60 percent of the workers due to his improper conduct.
4. During his period of service, he caused consternation among the Shi'ites who were faithful to the Islamic revolution.
5. I have attached photocopies of his reports.

Once again I note that I do not expect that you either accept or reject this information, but it is, I repeat, for the sake of God.

(signed)
Syed Mehsan Musawi,
Temporary Chargé d'Affaires

Document 54A-1

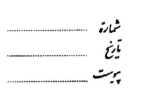

سفارت جمهوری اسلامی ایران

بیروت

شماره ....

تاریخ ....

پیوست ....

خیلی محرمانه

وزارت امور خارجه

ب/ مدیر کل سیاسی آسیا و آفریقا – برادر لواسانی

معاونت سیاسی – برادر شیخ الاسلام

از آنجا که اطلاع یافتم ممکن است از آقای احمد موحدی بعنوان کاردار در دیگر نمایندگیها استفاده گردد بر خود تکلیف دیدم تا مطالبی را بعرض برسانم و خداوند را شاهد میگیرم که هیچ غرض شخصی با نامبرده نداشته و فقط برای خدا سخن میگویم .

بدیهی است که مطالب زیر در خدمت ۷ ماه کاری با ایشان رسیده‌ام و نظرات شخصی اینجانب می باشد .

۱– ایشان جاسوس غیر مستقیم K.G.B هستند (از طریق سازمان الفتح) .

۲– درمدت مأموریتشان در بیروت تنها چیزی که برای نامبرده مطرح نبود انقلاب اسلامی و منافع آن بوده است و در تمام طول مدت بعنوان یک عامل عمل میکرده است .

Document 54A-2

شماره ....

تاریخ ....

پیوست ....

سفارت جمهوری اسلامی ایران

بیروت

ـ ۲ ـ

۳ـ در مدت ماموریتشان در اثر اتخاذ سیاست غلط وابستگی وعدم فعالیت در مسیر زنده نگهداشتن انقلاب در اذهان طرفداران آن تقریباً ۶۰ درصد آراء دوستان انقلاب منحرف گردیده است واکثراً علت را رفتار ناشایست نامبرده ذکر می نمایند .

۴ـ ایشان با کارهایشان در مدت ماموریتشان باعث قطع امید شیعیان مخلص وعاشق انقلاب از انقلاب اسلامی گردیده اند . واین مسئله باعث شده تا تبلیغات سوء دشمنان به اثرات سوء خود نائل آیند .

۵ـ فتوکپی بعضی از گزارشات وی را که بخط خود می باشد جهت استحضار بپیوست تقدیم میدارد .

مجدداً یادآوری می نمایم که هدفم از این گزارش این نیست که تمام مطالب مرا بپذیرید ویا . . . . . بلکه فقط هدفم اجرای تکلیفم در برابر انقلاب بوده است وبس .

خداوند مارا از لغزشها حفظ بفرماید .

سرپرست موقت ـ سید محسن موسوی

[Document 55]: PLO meetings with subversive groups

Pages of an office diary captured in Tyre in June 1982. The notes read:

February 26: Final exams for the Salvadorian course
April 6: The course for the comrades from Haiti began today
April 29: Abu Hamid, Damascus, 446608
May 16: The comrades from South Africa left today
June 4: A group of five persons arrived from Turkey
June 8: The course started for the comrades from Turkey
June 11: A group arrived from Africa, 10 people from Malawi
June 23: The training started for the comrades from Malawi
July 4: The course of the comrades from Turkey was completed
July 6: The Turkish group left

[Document 56]: PLO subversion in Niger and Mali

This document, dated 30 October 1981, was discovered in a PLO base in southern Lebanon in June 1982. It provides evidence of the PLO's alliance, or at least complicity, with Libyan-led subversive activities in Niger and Mali. The revolutionary movement of the Touareg people, supported by both Libya and the PLO, claims to represent a non-Arab minority in Niger and Mali, and the fact that the document is written in Arabic attests to Arab involvement in this activity. Excerpts from the document follow.

Because of our geographical situation, we find it necessary to appeal for aid and support from all peace-loving nations, particularly the people of North Africa and especially the brotherly Libyan Arab people. This is in view of the declaration by Brother Qaddafi that he will always stand by the underprivileged nations.

The main goals of our revolution are as follows: . . . .

3. Our basic goal is: the complete liberation of our homeland.

4. The establishment of a state that will adopt the popular socialist regime of the masses and ensure a popular government. Our constitution and legislation will draw on the Islamic principles of the "Shari'a."

5. One of the revolution's principles is to bring back our natural resources and exploit them for the benefit of the masses.

6. Our revolution aims at achieving full unity with our brethren in North Africa, especially with the Arab Libyan people.

7. One of our goals is to strengthen the relations of goodwill with the Arab sister states and with Africa and the Islamic world and with all peace-and-freedom-loving nations.

Our revolution aims at making an active contribution to the destruction of racism, Zionism and the imperialist hegemony in any shape and form.

Those who participated in the planning of this project and are now in Tripoli are waiting only for the final authorization of their proposals by the appropriate Libyan authorities, in order to turn immediately into an executive committee of the organization, defining the area of responsibility of each participating member in accordance with the structure of the above-mentioned apparatus. Thereby it will be possible for the revolution to make a real breakthrough, abandon the situation of uncertainty and hesitation that it has known for the past two years and move towards the stage of realizing its principles and goals as originally determined.

Because of the serious plight of our people, we ask our Arab Libyan brother to assist us, to quickly reach this stage of creating a basic apparatus of a revolutionary liberation organization.

At this point we wish to remind our Libyan brethren that the above region (Mali and Niger) is now in a dangerous state of political and economic vacuum as a result of the all-out bankruptcy of the governments that were created by imperialism in the area.

It may prove very dangerous if North African countries — especially Libya — ignore the fate of this vital region, which, from the historical, geographical and human points of view, represents an inseparable part of North Africa. There can be no doubt that the fate of this region will determine the final fate of North Africa, West Africa and Central Africa.

From our point of view, we have committed ourselves to support the Arab Libyan revolution, under the leadership of Qaddafi, who has taken upon himself all the political, economic and diplomatic tasks, in order to stand by our people. We take this opportunity to declare that we stand by our Arab Libyan brethren. We do this because the covenant between us and them is not a creation of changing circumstances but, as we said, it is historical, fateful and eternal.

Published in Tripoli
Date: 3 October 1981

Document 56A-2

ـ ٢ ـ

فمشاركة هذه الجماعة فى عمل ثورى تؤدى حتما الى فشله وسحب ثقة الشعب منه اذ ان ابد الله ديبوى وجماعته ليسوا ثوريين وليست الثورة هدفهم ، بل ان عملهم يهدف الى مجرد الانتقام الشخصى من نظام كونتشى ومحاولة الوصول الى كراسى الحكم •

ومما لا شك فيه ايضا ان هدف ابد الله ديبوى هو تخريب حركتنا الثورية التى بدأناها منذ الاستقلالات المزيفة سنة ١٩٦٠م ، وكذلك التجسس على هذه الحركة وعلى الجماهيرية العربية الليبية التى احتضنتها •

ومن الدلائل الصريحة على ذلك ان احد هذه الجماعة اعترف اخيرا بحضور جماعة قائلا " ان لهم منظمة سياسية فى باريس وابدجان ، وانهم لم ياتوا الى الجماهيرية الا بقصد محاولة استخدام مناضلينا عند الحاجة لتنفيذ مخططاتهم الشخصية التى لا علاقة لها بثورتنا الشعبية

ومما يدل على ذلك ايضا ان احد قادة هذه المنظمة الذى رجع اخيرا من جولة فى اوربا الغربية طلب من الموظفين النيجريين الذين دخلوا الى الجماهيرية اخيرا قادمين من النيجر أن يعطوه قائمة كاملة بأسمائهم وتوقيعاتهم ليقدمها الى الصحافة الفرنسية والافريقية ، زاعما ان هذه الصحافة طالبت منه هذه المعلومات كشرط اساسى لكتابة المقالات عن الوضع فى النيجر•

ولا شك ان المقصود من وراء هذا هو التجسس على الحركة الثورية لشعبنا بل وعلى الجماهيرية نفسها •

ـ ومما يستغربه مناضلونا الثوار أنهم تواجدوا على الجماهيرية افواجا ودخلوا فى المعسكرات من أجل الثورة ، وفجأة يأتى أربعة (٤) أشخاص غرباء عن الثورة فيتولون قيادتها والتحكم فى مصيرها • وهذا قد خلق بلبلة كبيرة واستنكارا صارخا فى صفوف الشعب وفى صفوف الجنود •

ـ واخيرا يلاحظ ان قادة هذه الحركة لا يقيمون فى الجماهيرية وانما ياتون اليها لبضعة ايام فقط للحصول على الفلوس ثم يواصلون جولاتهم السياحية الدائمة فى فرنسا وسويسرا وايطاليا وساحل العاج ونيجريا ... الى اخره ، تاركين وراءهم شئون المنظمة مهملة •

وفى النهاية نؤكد ان انتقادنا لقادة هاتين المنظمتين ينبثق من حرصنا الشديد على خلق جهاز ثورى أصيل لا مجال فيه للتفرقة القبلية او اللغوية او الجهوية ، حيث تكون هذه المنظمة مفتوحة لكل المناضلين المخلصين من ابناء المنطقة مع استبعاد العناصر الأنتهازية الرجعية التى لا هدف لها الا المتاجرة باسم الثورة او التى تحاول الاندساس فى صفوف حركة التحرير لمجرد التجسس لقوى اجنبية معادية لثورتنا وللجماهيرية العربية الليبية التى بذلت كل الجهود لاعانتنا على تحرير بلادنا واسترجاع ثرواتها المنهوبة •

وانطلاقا من كل ما ذكر تظهر ضرورة مراجعة الامور وذلك بالعمل على تأسيس حركة تحريرية جديرة بهذا الاسم ، وتكون على مستوى المسئولية الخطيرة التى وضعها شعبنا على عاتق مناضليه الاحرار بكفاح ترتفع الى مستوى الاعانة الجبارة التى ما انفك اشقاؤنا الليبيون يقدمونها الى شعبنا المهضوم •

وفى الفقرة التالية نفصل مبادىء هذه المنظمة المقترحة واهدافها الاساسية :

Document 56A-1

بسم الله الرحمن الرحيم

المشروع المقترح لتنظيم حركة ثورية من اجل تحرير شعب الازواد (مالي والنيجر)

١) الاسباب الداعية الى ضرورة انشاء تنظيم ثوري جديد

لقد انشئت في الماضي منظمتان لغرض تحرير المنطقة:

١) جبهة تحرير الصحراء العربية الوسطى وقد تكونت هذه المنظمة سنة ١٩٨٠م وفشلت في عملها للاسباب التالية:

- في مؤتمر الخمس الذي تكونت فيه هذه المنظمة وقع اختيار مسؤولين لا يمثلون الشعب لا في اشخاصهم ولا في اهدافهم. ولم يقع الاستماع الى ممثلي الشعب - فضلا من قبولهم كأعضاء في المكتب التنفيذي.

ومن الامثلة على ذلك ان الشخص الذي عين امينا عاما للمنظمة لم يكن حاضرا في هذا المؤتمر ولم يكن معروفا لدى الشعب ولا لدى ممثليه.

- لقد انحرف قادة المنظمة عن هدفها الاساسي وهو تحرير سكان منطقة النيجر ومالي، فربطوها بمشاكل تعتبر داخلية لموريتانيا وأهملوا الاهداف الحقيقية المتلخصة في تحرير النيجر ومالي.

- أظهرت المنظمة عدم الاهتمام بالمعسكرات وبمشاكل الاخوة الموجودين بها.

- منذ بدأ التجنيد في السنة الماضية كان هناك جماعة من الاخوة الذين تطوعوا لجمع الشبان الذين يحملون جنسية نيجرية أو مالية. وقد قام هؤلاء الاخوان بجهد المجهود داخل الجماهيرية بل وجازفوا [illegible] بحياتهم ودخلوا سرا الى كل من النيجر ومالي لتحريض الشباب على القدوم الى الجماهيرية للانخراط في العمل الثوري.

ومن المؤسف ان المنظمة لم تقدم اي عون لهؤلاء الاخوة المتطوعين بل عملت في النهاية على سجن بعضهم وطرد بعض آخر من الجماهيرية لانهم قد انتقدوا خطها المناقض مع مبادئ الثورة.

- خلق قادة المنظمة سلاحا خطيرا واستعملوه للتفرقة بين المناضلين وتقسيمهم بدعوى ان هذا حساني وذاك طارقي وهذا من جهة وذاك من جهة اخرى وهذا من قبيلة كذا وذاك من قبيلة اخرى..

ونتيجة لكل هذه العوامل فقد فقد قادة هذه المنظمة ثقة الشعب وثقة المجاهدين واعتبروا سلوكها سلوكا تآمريا ضد طموح الجماهير نحو الثورة والتحرير.

٢) منظمة جبهة التجمع الجماهيري لتحرير النيجر

- ان السيد "عبد الله ديوري" وجماعته لهم ماض أسود يعرفه كل أفراد شعبنا ومن البديهي ان لا يقبلهم الشعب في اي عمل كان وبالخصوص في العمل الثوري.

Document 56A-4

ـ ٤ ـ

وبديهي ان تحقيق هذا الهدف المباشر شرط جوهري لانطلاق العمل الثوري ونجاحه •

٢) من اهداف الثورة توحيد كل الطاقات والجهود من أجل عمل ثوري موحد ، واستبعاد كل اسباب الاختلاف والانقسام •

٣) هدفنا الاساسي هو تحرير وطننا تحريرا كاملا وشاملا •

٤) تهدف ثورتنا الى تأسيس دولة تتبنى النظام الجماهيري الشعبي الوحدوي الاشتراكي وتؤمن بالسلطة الشعبية ، وتستمد دستورها وشريعتها من مبادئ الشريعة الاسلامية •

٥) من اهداف الثورة استرجاع كل ثرواتنا ومواردنا الطبيعية واستغلالها لمصلحة جماهير الشعب•

٦) تهدف ثورتنا الى تحقيق الوحدة الكاملة مع اشقائنا شعوب شمال افريقيا وخاصة مع الشعب العربي الليبي الشقيق •

٧) من اهدافنا تقوية العلاقات الأخوية مع البلاد العربية الشقيقة وافريقيا والعالم الاسلامي ومع كل الشعوب المحبة للسلام والحرية •

٨) تهدف ثورتنا الى المساهمة الفعالة في القضاء على العنصرية والصهيونية والهيمنة الامبريالية بجميع اشكالها •

وبعد الانتهاء من شرح مبادئ المنظمة التحريرية المقترحة واهدافها نتحدث في الفقرة التالية عن الهيكل الاساسي لأجهزتها •

ج) الهيكل الاساسي لأجهزة المنظمة المقترحة :

لكي تتحدد المسئوليات في المنظمة حتى يكون نشاطها جديا وفعالا في كل الميادين والمشاكل التي يمكن ان تعترض سيرها فاننا نقترح ان تقسم ميادين العمل فيها حسب طبيعة المشاكل المختلفة وذلك على النحو التالي :

ـ الامين العام للمنظمة
ـ مسئول التنظيم والتوعية
ـ مسئول الشئون العسكرية
ـ مسئول العلاقات الخارجية
ـ مسئول الشئون المالية
ـ مسئول الشئون الاجتماعية واغاثة السكان
ـ مسئول الاعلام
ـ مسئول التموين
ـ مسئول النقل
ـ مسئول التخطيط والمتابعة
ـ مسئول التعليم والثقافة
ـ مسئول الصحة

لقد تبين من كل ماذكر بيان الاسباب الحقيقية التي دعت الى طلب مراجعة الامور لتصحيح الاوضاع كما اتضحت مبادئ المنظمة المقترحة واهدافنا الاساسية ، وكذلك هيكل اجهزتها المختلفة بعد تكوينها •

Document 56A-3

ـ ٢ ـ

ب) مبادئ واهداف الحركة الثورية المقترحة :

تتلخص المبادئ الاساسية لثورتنا فيما يلي :

١) ان ثورتنا هي ثورة شعبية نابعة من ارادة الشعب الذي صمم على تحمل مسئولياته في مكافحة الاستعمار والظلم والاضطهاد والقبلية والتمييز العنصري واسترجاع حقه في الحرية والسيادة على ارضه وثرواته .

٢) ثورتنا هي ثورة جذرية وشاملة على جميع الاوضاع الشاذة التي خلقها الاستعمار ولا يزال يرعاها ، وليست مجرد معارضة يكون هدفها الاساسي مجرد اسقاط انظمة او تغيير حكومات في النيجر ومالي .

٣) تؤمن ثورتنا بأن شعبنا هو جزء لا يتجزأ من شعوب شمال افريقيا جغرافيا وتاريخيا وبشريا وحضاريا ، ويتصف بكل خصائص شعوب شمال افريقيا ، وزيادة على ذلك فهو يمثل همزة وصل مابين شعوب الشمال الافريقي وشعوب غرب افريقيا .

٤) تؤمن ثورتنا وتتمسك بضرورة وحدة العمل الثوري وتنسيقه في المنطقتين الشرقية والغربية (النيجر ومالي) .

٥) ترفض ثورتنا وتستبعد تعدد المنظمات والنزعات في اطار العمل الثوري السياسي والعسكري .

٦) تؤمن ثورتنا وتتمسك بمبادئ حقوق الانسان وحرية الشعوب وحقها في تقرير مصيرها بنفسها واسترجاع حريتها وسيادتها وكرامتها ، وترفض رفضا باتا جميع اشكال الاستعمار والهيمنة الامبريالية والصهيونية والتفرقة العنصرية والقبلية .

٧) تؤمن ثورتنا بمبدأ يعد من تراثنا الثقافي والاجتماعي منذ اقدم العصور ، وهو مبدأ الديموقراطية والمساواة والتضامن الاجتماعي .

٨) تؤمن ثورتنا ايمانا عميقا بضرورة وحدة شعوب شمال افريقيا التي تعتبرها حتمية تاريخية وجغرافية وحضارية واقتصادية للمحافظة على وجودها وكرامتها في خضم الصراع الدولي .

٩) وانطلاقا من البطولات التاريخية والجهود الجبارة التي حققها شعبنا في سبيل نشر الاسلام وحضارته في الصحراء وافريقيا الغربية فان ثورتنا تتمسك وتحرص على تأكيد القيم والمبادئ الاسلامية وتساهم في تقوية روابط الامة الاسلامية المجيدة .

١٠) وانطلاقا من واقعنا الجغرافي وحتمياتنا التاريخية والحضارية والاقتصادية فان ثورتنا منحازة الى وجيه آمالها في التأييد والمساندة نحو كل الشعوب المحبة للحرية والسلام وخاصة شعوب شمال افريقيا وعلى الاخص نحو الشعب العربي الليبي الشقيق في ظل ثورة الفاتح العظيمة التي اعلن قائدها الملهم الأخ / العقيد معمر القذافي وقوفه باستمرار الى جانب الشعوب المظلومة .

اما الاهداف الاساسية لثورتنا تتلخص فيما يلي :

١) هدفنا المباشر هو تكوين جهاز ثوري منظم لحركتنا التحريرية مع تحديد المسئوليات المعينة التي يجب على كل عضو من أعضاء المنظمة المقترحة ان يتحملها ، بحيث لا يكون هناك مجال للغموض ولا للاهمال واللا مبالاة .

Document 56A-5

— ٥ —

وبهذه المناسبة نقترح لهذه المنظمة اسم : الحركة الشعبية لتحرير الطوارق (النيجر ومالي) .

هذا وان الاخوة الذين شاركوا في تحضير هذا المشروع والذين هم موجودون في مدينة طرابلس لا ينتظرون الا الموافقة النهائية من السلطات العربية الليبية المختصة على مقترحاتهم ليكونوا فورا المكتب التنفيذي للمنظمة مع تحديد مسئوليات كل عضو منها ، وذلك على ضوء هيكل الاجهزة المذكورة اعلاه . وبذلك سيمكن أن تنطلق الثورة انطلاقا صحيحا وتخرج من مرحلة التردد والشكوك التي عرفتها في السنتين الماضيتين لتدخل في مرحلة تجسيم مبادئها وأهدافها المحددة سابقا .

ونظرا للظروف الخطيرة التي يعيشها شعبنا فاننا نرجو من اشقائنا العرب الليبيين ان يعينونا على الاسراع في قطع هذه المرحلة الضرورية مرحلة تكوين الجهاز الاساسي للمنظمة الثورية التحريرية .

وبهذه المناسبة فاننا نستطيع ان نؤكد لأشقائنا العرب الليبيين بأن هذه الحركة اذا انطلقت بنجاح فانها ستحرر هذه المنطقة ذات الاهمية بمواردها البشرية والحضارية والاقتصادية والاستراتيجية . كما انها بدون ادنى شك ستضمن لأشقائنا الليبيين في القارة الافريقية حلفاء طبيعيين ومضمونين نظرا لان هذا التحالف ينبع من وحدة الاصل والجغرافية والتاريخ والحضارة والاهداف والمصير المشترك .

وبهذه المناسبة ايضا نذكر اشقائنا الليبيين بأن المنطقة المعنية (مالي والنيجر) تعيش الان في فراغ سياسي واقتصادي خطير نظرا للافلاس الشامل للحكومات العميلة التي نصبها الاستعمار في المنطقة . وانه لمن الخطير جدا ان تتهاون دول شمال افريقيا وخاصة الجماهيرية العربية الليبية في مصير هذه المنطقة الحساسة المهمة والتي هي في واقعها التاريخي والجغرافي والبشري جزء لا يمكن بحال من الاحوال ان يتجزأ من الشمال الافريقي .

ومما لا شك فيه ان مصير هذه المنطقة سيحدد المصير النهائي لشمال افريقيا وغربها ووسطها .

ومن جهتنا فاننا قد تعهدنا بأن نؤيد الثورة العربية الليبية ثورة الفاتح العظيمة بقيادة الأخ العقيد معمر القذافي الذي تحمل كل المخاطر السياسية والاقتصادية والدبلوماسية من أجل الوقوف الى جانب شعبنا المهضوم .

وبهذه المناسبة نعلن اننا نقف اليوم وسنقف غدا الى جانب اشقائنا العرب الليبيين ، وفي اليوم الذي ستسمح لنا فيه قوة ووزن سنبقى درعا واقيا الى جانب اشقائنا الليبيين وذلك لان التحالف بيننا وبينهم ليس وليد الظروف الطارئة المنظورة ، ولكنه كما قلنا تاريخي ومصيري وخالد .

=========

حرر بمدينة طرابلس بتاريخ

٣ اكتوبر ١٩٨١م

====

[Document 57]: PLO subversion in Niger and Mali

Found in the same file as Document 56, this document, signed by Abu Iyyad, the number-two man in the PLO, refers to the PLO contribution to these African operations.

IN THE NAME OF ALLAH THE MERCIFUL
THE POPULAR FRONT FOR THE LIBERATION OF PALESTINE
GENERAL COMMAND

Date: 20 December 1981

Following the meeting held between us on 18 December 1981, we are sending you this report, which shows the correct picture and presents the most important conclusions we reached concerning the mission you decided upon. . .

There is an urgent need to send the group back where it came from... we are asking you to make the necessary arrangements for the trip.... They turned over the ID's to comrade Abu-Jasit due to their relations with foreign elements, especially the Embassy of Mauritania, which had sent a man to them.... We are sending you a list of the comrades who are in serious economic circumstances. They number 24 men. We request that you facilitate their journey and grant them leave so they can return to their families. We request that you allocate monthly wages to all the comrades and expedite the situation regarding courses, since many of the comrades have become disgusted with this matter.

Abu Iyyad

Document 57A

بسم الله الرحمن الرحيم

الجبهة الشعبية لتحرير فلسطين
القيادة العامة

الموضوع: تقرير
التاريخ: ٢٠/١٢/١٩٨١م

الرفيق الامين العام

تحية والثورة والنضال وبعد

بناء على الاجتماع الذى جرى بيننا بتاريخ ١٨/١٢/١٩٨١م نرفع اليكم هذا التقرير لننقل اليكم الصورة الصحيحة واهم ما توصلنا اليه فى المهمه التى كلفنا بها من قبلكم بعد المحاولات والاقناع والتحقيق فى الوضع بصفة عامة نؤكد لكم انه من الضرورى ايجاد وسيلة لتسفير المجموعة التى ابت الا ان تصر على السفر والرجوع الى حيث اتو بغض النظر عن الاسباب ونرجو توفير لهم الاجراءات الضرورية للسفر واعطائهم مستحقاتهم وجعلهم فى المكان اللائق بهم .

ونحيطكم علما انه لايمكن القضاء على الشغب وايجاد جو مستقر الا بعد تسفيرهم وعددهم ٢٢ فرد المزوجة بالاضافة الى عناصر الموجودة فى وحدة ١٧ ايلول الذين سلموا هوياتهم الى الرفيق ابو جاسم نتيجة لوجود ارتباطات بجهات خارجية وخاصة السفارة الموريتانية التى اوفدت شخصا اليهم له الرياء فى نفس المجموعة .

وكما نرفع اليكم ايضا لائحة باسماء الرفاق ذوى الظروف الاجتماعية الصعبة وعددهم ٢٩ [illegible]ا نرجو تسهيل سفرهم ومنحهم اجازات الى عائلاتهم .

وكما نرجو منح الرواتب الشهرية الى جميع الرفاق والتعجيل فى عملية التخرج نظرا لوجود ملل فى بعض الرفاق .

ونعاهدكم اننا سنواصل الطريق معا طريق النضال الشريف خدمة للقضايا المصيرية للاهل ضد الاستعمار والصهيونية حتى تحرير الارض والانسان .

والسلام عليكم ورحمة الله تعالى وبركاته

التوقيع/ ابو اياد

[Document 58]: PLO collusion with Sahara rebels

A handwritten document on the stationery of the Popular Front for the Liberation of Palestine indicates collusion between the PLO and the Front for the Liberation of the Central Arab Desert, that is, the Sahara. (There is no date on the original document.)

POPULAR FRONT FOR THE LIBERATION OF PALESTINE
GENERAL HEADQUARTERS
MILITARY HEADQUARTERS

When the plot was uncovered, a battle broke out on the night of 15 May. 300 soldiers were killed. Three officers from the Niger forces seized Sgt. Sidi Muhammad, the two officers and the soldiers who launched the coup. But the Imam, who is secretary-general of the Front, succeeded in escaping via the desert to Mauritania. There, together with his deputy, Muhammad Musa, he met up with the Polisario fighters, and then reached Libya where they remained.

The current activity of the revolutionaries is continuing deep inside Mali. The revolution has organized a widespread underground movement based on mobilizing the masses, ideological indoctrination and a financial fund, which was set up in order to raise 10 million francs to release the leader, Zaya ben Tehir, who had sought refuge in Algeria. Ben Bella extradited him to Mali where he was imprisoned from 1963 until 1979. Now he lives under supervision in Mali. The revolution is pursuing underground mobilization. Each new recruit takes an oath on the Qur'an to keep allegiance to the revolution and never to uncover its secret.

The founding conference of the Front took place in 1979 with the participation of all its leaders. There the Front's organizational framework was laid out, and camps and offices were opened in Libya in coordination with Algeria.

The goals of the Front for the Liberation of the Central Arab Desert are:

1. Liberation of the Central Arab Desert from the colonialism of Mali and Niger, and its reunification.

2. Annexation of the Desert to the Arab homeland and unification with any Arab country so willing.

3. Making Arabic the official language of the Desert.

4. Establishing a free, democratic state, its slogan being "Freedom, Islamic Socialism and Unity."

5. War against colonialism, imperialism, Zionism and racial discrimination.

6. Liberation of the citizens of the Desert from all their shackles.

7. Liberation of the national economy from foreign domination.

8. Evacuation of foreign bases from the north.

الجبهة الشعبية لتحرير فلسطين

القيادة العامة

القيادة العسكرية/ التحصين

الرقم:............

التاريخ: / / ١٩

يكشف بخطه قصارت معركة ليلة ١٥/مايو تقتل ٢٠ فيه ٧ وثلاثة
ضباط من القوات الليبرية حيث تمكنوا من القبض على النقيب سعيد محمد ولد
واثنين من ضباط والعناصر الذين قاموا بعملية انقلاب وتمكن الامام الذي
هو الامين العام للجبهة تمكن من الفرار عن طريق الصحراء الى موريتانيا واستقر
هناك والنائب محمد موسى الى ثوار البوليزاريو ثم الى الجماهيرية واستقر هناك
لقد استمرت عمليات الثورة السرية في جميع اراضي مالي وأصبحت الثورة
حركة سرية وواسعة النطاق بتغطية الجماهير وتوجيهها وعملت جهدها على
ذلك لتمكينها من دفع الاعمال ... فرنك من اجل اطلاق سراح الزعيم زيد بن طاهر
الذي لجأ الى الجزائر وسلمه بن بلة الى حكومة مالي ووضعته في السجن منذ عام ١٩٦٢م
ولم يفرج عنه حتى عام ١٩٧٩م وهو الان في ~~اقامة~~ الجبهة المرافقة في داخل
مالي. لقد استمرت الثورة في حركة شعبية سرية قياده على العنصر الجديد في
ان يعلن الثوار على الاعلان عن الثورة وان لا يفتش سرها الا وقت عام ١٩٧٩م
عقد اول مؤتمر تأسيسي للجبهة حضره جميع القيادات حيث كون الهيكل التنظيمي
للجبهة وفتح المعسكرات في الجماهيرية العربية الليبية واكتفى بالتنسيق مع
الجزائر.

١- اهداف الجبهة الشعبية لتحرير الصحراء العربية الوسطى.

١) تحرير الصحراء العربية الوسطى من الاستعمار المالي والنيجيري وتوحيد اراضيها.

٢) - ضم الصحراء العربية الوسطى الى الوطن العربي واعلان الوحدة مع اي دولة عربية تريد ذلك.

٣) - جعل اللغة العربية اللغة الرسمية للصحراء العربية الوسطى.

٤) - تكوين دولة حرة ديمقراطية شعارها الحرية والاشتراكية الاسلامية والوحدة

٥) - محاربة الاستعمار ~~الجديد~~ والامبريالية والصهيونية والتمييز العنصري.

٦) - تحرير المواطن الصحراوي من جميع القيود والاغلال

٧) - تحرير الاقتصاد الوطني من السيطرة الاجنبية

٨) - طرد القواعد الاجنبية الموجودة في الشمال -

[Document 59]: Kurdish Poster

The poster was found in PLO offices in Sidon, in June 1982. It features a map of Kurdistan (covering territories in Turkey, Iraq and Iran), Kurdish women freedom-fighters, and a slogan of the Kurdish Communist Party.

VII. THE PLO'S MODUS OPERANDI [Documents 61-74]

Although the PLO's major preoccupation in Lebanon was Israel, its occupation of southern Lebanon presented it with day-to-day problems of administration, extension of services, coordination with local Lebanese authorities and UN forces, and confrontation with portions of the local Lebanese population, the Haddad forces and, on occasion, UNIFIL as well.

The following selection will illustrate the wide range of PLO concerns in southern Lebanon, from planning operations against Israeli population centres and American bases, recruiting Palestinian and international youth to its ranks, organizing local defences, collecting intelligence, convening ideological meetings and engaging in propaganda.

The PLO's gratuitously brutal behaviour toward the people of southern Lebanon will be explored in the final section of the book. But much of the legacy of resentment and bitterness which the PLO left behind resulted from its "normal" operational activities in meeting the "needs of the revolution." For example, if it was "necessary" to mobilize 12-year-old children to fill in for their fallen fathers, no overriding moral consideration could dissuade the organization from such a decision. When it located its military positions in apartment houses, schools and hospitals, it probably did so out of a conviction that it would thus gain immunity from counterattack. If it evicted UN observers from certain military positions (notably the Beaufort), it was convinced it "deserved" to control these positions in order to better "protect" southern Lebanon against Israel. And if it expelled civilians and took over their property in the southern villages and towns, that was done as an "interim" move toward victory for the revolution. The terror, blackmail, rape, murder, expropriation and other excesses were only means to achieve the goals of the revolution which were considered supreme.

[Document 60]: Guidelines for shelling Israeli population centres

This document of the unified PLO command, dated 13 May 1981, details a meeting attended by Arafat and representatives of all PLO groups. It says, among other things:

Due to the approaching election,[46] Begin has to display some signs of vitality. This has been confirmed by a cable from our representative in Belgium who visited the Belgian Foreign Ministry where he was told that Israel was on the verge of a vast operation against the Palestinian revolution.... This operation would last two days after which the powers would interfere and impose a cease-fire lest it escalate into war.... European countries have asked Begin to refrain from this operation in southern Lebanon, but in vain.... After discussing the military steps that are to be adopted in the south, the following was decided:

a) If hostilities break out we cannot sit by and watch, we have to initiate contact with the enemy and deal him a blow that would cause the greatest number of casualties and damage.

b) Four rocket launchers will be earmarked for the central and eastern war zones, aimed at totally destroying Kiryat Shemona.

c) Two 130mm guns will be set to shell Kiryat Shemona.

d) 20 "Grad" missiles will be infiltrated into the border region in order to shell Safed.

e) Squads of fighters will be set up to fight the Israelis from house to house in Nabatiye and pursue the battle around the Arnoun Fort in order to prevent its conquest. A suicide squad of ten first-rate fighters will be posted in the fort and in the cultivated lands of Bani Sakhr.

---

46. The elections were to be held on 30 June 1981.

Document 60A-1

جبهة التحرير العربية
~~مكتب عضو الرفيق~~
العمليات

جبهة التحرير العربية

رقم
تاريخ ١٤/٥/١٩٨١

اجتمـــــاع العسكـــرى الأعلـــى

١٣ / ٥ / ١٩٨١

الحضـــــور :
===========

الأخ أبـــو عمـــار
الاخ أبـــو جهـــاد
العميـــد أبـــو الوليـــد " العمليـــات المركزيـــه "
الرفيـــق أبـــو عـدى " العربيـــــه "
الرفيـــق علـــي اسحق " الفلسطينيـــه "
العقيـــد عبد الرزاق المجايـــده " التعبئـــه "
العقيـــد الركـــن عبد الله صيام " قوات مشتركـــه "
أبـــو ابـــراهيـــم " القيـــادة العامـه "

الرفيق ابو جمال " النضـــال "
الاخ الحاج اسماعيل " قيادة الجنـوب "
المقدم ابو موسى " العمليات المركزيـة "
العقيد الركن ابو الزعيم " الاستخبارات العسكرية "
العميـــد ابو المعتصم " احتياط فتـــح "
مـــــدوح " ديمقراطيـــه "
ابـــو احمد فـــؤاد " شعبيـــه "

الاخ القـــائـــد العـــام :
=====================

الى ان الموقف السياسي يميـل الـى الانفراج سـورى ـ اسرائلي وان تنفيس الموقف سيكون علـــى
ـــاب الموقف الفلسطينـــي والمقاومـــه الفلسطينيـــه .
ـي اســوأ ســوف تتطـــور العمليـــه الاسرائيليـــه المحتملـــه على قوات الثـوره الفلسطينيـــه فـــي قطـــاع الجولان
نبطيـــه الـــى ضـــرب بعض قواعـــد الصواريخ السوريه بواســـطة صواريخ اسرائيليـــه جـــو ـ أرض ٩٠ كـــم
ـــى انه لا تحدث خسائر فـــي صفوف الاسرائيليـــن غيـــر قابلـــه علـــى الاحتمـــال خاصه وأن الاجـــواء
نتخابيـــة والمعارضه الاسرائيليـــه لا تسمـــح بذلـــك .

Document 60A-2

جبهة التحرير العربية
~~مكتب~~ ...
العمليات

رقم ...
تاريخ ١٤/٥/١٩٨٦

لما ان بيغن لا بد من تنفيذ عمليه تنفس تحديده وتغييره في الانتخابات هذا ومما يؤكد ذلك
قيه ممثلنا في بلجيكا حيث زار وزارة الخارجيه البلجيكيه واطلع على ان اسرائيل ستقوم بعمليه كبي
ربعه محدوده ضد الثورة الفلسطينيه لتوسيع الشريط الحدودى ومدة هذه العمليه يومان بعده
.خل الدول لمنع تطور القتال وتوقف اطلاق النار . وقد تدخلت الدول الاوربيه لدى اسرائ
نها لم تؤثر على بيغن لمنعه من القيام باى عمليه على جنوب لبنان .

وبعد مناقشة الاجراآت العسكريه التي ستتخذ في الجنوب تم الاتفاق على .

- اذا حصل قتال فلا بد من ديمومته وعدم التوقف وادامة الاتصال مع العدو وضربه بقوه بهدف ا
كبر الخسائر الماديه والبشريه في صفوفه .

- تخصيص ٤ راجمات صواريخ في القطاع الشرقي والقطاع الاوسط بهدف تدمير كريات شمونه تدميـ
ـراً كاملاً .

- مدفع ١٣٠ ملم لقصف مستعمره كريات شمونه ايضاً .

- ٤٠ صاروخ كراد تهرب الى داخل الشريط الحدودى لضرب صفد .

- تم نقل كتيبة الصاعقه التي كانت متوضعه على الحدود الاردنيه السوريه الى القطاع الشرقي علو
ضع سريه في العيشيه مع ٢ مدفع ٣٧ ملم من الصاعقه .

- إنشاء مجموعات متميزه ومحربه في القتال تبقى داخل المنطقه [illegible]
مقاتلة الاسرائيليين في حال دخولهم مع القتال من بيت الى بيت في المنطقه وادامة القتال حوا
نون وعدم السماح باحتلالها وتشكيل قوه من ١٠ مقاتلين اشداء من كل تنظيم تستخدم هذه
ه انتحاريه في القلعه وفي حرش النبي ضاهر .

- اعتبارا من تاريخه يتم دوام ممثلي المجلس العسكرى الاعلى في الجنوب مع الحاج اسماعيـ

ابو احمد فؤاد   العقيد فخرى شقوره

(٢)

Document 60A-3

جبهة التحرير العربية
مكتب [illegible]
العمليات

رقم [illegible]
تاريخ ٢٤/٥/١٩٨٢

[illegible] ح   المقـدم ابـو موسى

- فرز تصليه دبابات مع اربع راجمات على تلة معدون في الريحـان

- تلغيم سهل الحرمق ((المدمشقـه - خط التابلاين))

الـرفيـق ابو عهد

١٢/ ٥/ ١٩٨٢

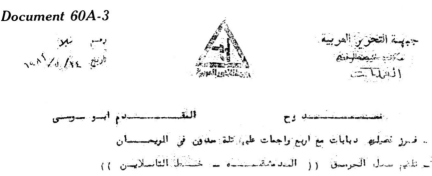

[Document 61]; Target chart of Israeli population centres

A target chart for artillery positioned in Kafr Rumman in southern Lebanon. The computed targets are: Kiryat Shemona, Misgav Am and Metulla.

بطـاقـة نيـران مـدفع غـراد من مـربض كفـر رمان

رقم الهدف	الهـدف	المسافة بالامتار	الارتفاع بالديه	الاتجاه الرئيسي	المستوى
١٠١	الخـالصـه	١٩ _ ٧٠٠	٦ _ ٧٠	٢٦ _ ٢٠	٢٩ _ ٨٦
١٠٢	عين ابو جل / الخالصه	٢٠٦٠٠	٨ _ ٣٠	٢٦ _ ٣٠	٢٩ _ ٨٦
١٠٣	مسكاف عـام	١٥٩٠٠	٤ _ ٢٠	٢٦ _ ٥٠	٣٠ _ ٢٢
١٠٤	المطـلـه	١٣٨٠٠	٣ _ ٣٣	٢٣ _ ٩٠	٣٠ _ ٠٠

الاهـداف مـأخـوذه عـن خـارطـة تـربيـع فلسطيـن. ١ / ٥٠٠٠٠

صنعـت ١٩٧٥

الانحـراف المغنـاطيسـي جـاهـز -

نـوع الصـاروخ " معـدل "

[Document 62]: Artillery assignments against Israeli targets

PLO No. 145/m
THE UNITED COMMAND ARTILLERY *27 July 1981*

TOP SECRET AND MOST URGENT

From: The commander of artillery of the United Command in the south
To: All units

Greetings for the revolution!

1. Following are the targets and their particulars:

No.	Target	Artillery Unit[47]	Quantity
1.	Misgav Am	Artillery Battalion 1	20
2.	Kiryat Shemona	Sa'iqa	20
3.	She'ar Yashuv	Artillery Battalion 6	20
4.	Dan	The Popular Front	20
5.	Kfar Yuval	The Liberation Front	20
6.	Hagoshrim	The Democratic Front	20
7.	Ma'ayan Baruch	The Front	20
8.	Kfar Giladi	Liberation Front	20
9.	Metulla	Artillery Battalion 1	20
10.	Nahariya[48]	The Missile Unit	11
11.	The Military Airport, Betzet[49]	Artillery Battalion 3	20
12.	Marj'ayun[50]	Artillery Battalion 1	20
13.	Qlei'a	Artillery Battalion 1	20

2. The firing will take place in two stages:
a) Phase 1 — 21 July 1981, at 11:00
b) Phase 2 — 22 July 1981, at 08:00

47. Practically all PLO groups were given a share in the shelling.
48. Practically all major towns in the north were targeted for shelling.
49. This is the only "military" target mentioned in the list; it is, in fact, a seldom used field-strip in western Galilee.
50. The last two targets are Lebanese villages in Major Haddad's area.

3. The following codes will be used:

a) After Phase 1 is completed — "A thousand greetings to our imprisoned fighters."

b) After Phase 2 is completed — "Shame and stigma on our enemies."

c) When on standby for execution — "You'll be punished while alive."

4. We must keep off the air immediately before and during execution.

5. Our firing methods, routine schedules and movements must be altered so as to escape detection by the enemy.

Colonel (Signature)

Document 62A

الرقم: ١٤٥ / م

التاريخ: ٢١ تموز ١٩٨١

من: قائد مدفعية القوات المشتركة في الجنوب

إلى: الجميع

تحية الثورة وبعد

اولاً. بأسماء الاهداف وتخصيص الواجبات:

التسلسل	الهدف	الوحدة	المقياس	المجموع
١	مصانع عام	ك م ١	٢٠	٢٠
٢	كريات شمونه	الصاعقة	٢٠	٢٠
٣	شعار يا شوف	ك م ٦	٢٠	٢٠
٤	دان	ج ش	٢٠	٢٠
٥	كفار يوفال	ج ن	٢٠	٢٠
٦	هاغوشريم	ج د	٢٠	٢٠
٧	معيان باروخ	ج ق ع	٢٠	٢٠
٨	كفر جلادي	ج ث ف	٢٠	٢٠
٩	المطلة	ك م ١	٢٠	٢٠
١٠	نهاريا	جبهة الصواريخ	٢٠	٢٠
١١	مطار البصة العسكري	ك م ٣	٢٠	٢٠
١٢	مرجليوت	ك م ١	٢٠	٢٠
١٣	القليعة	ك م ١	٢٠	٢٠

ثانياً. يتم الرمي على مرحلتين:

أ. المرحلة الاولى الساعة ١٩٠٠ يوم ٢١ تموز ١٩٨١

ب. المرحلة الثانية الساعة ٠٨٠٠ يوم ٢٢ تموز ١٩٨١

ثالثاً. تستخدم الرموز التالية:

أ. الف تحية لحملتنا داخل السجون ——— نفذت المرحلة الاولى

ب. الخزي والعار لاعدائنا ——— نفذت المرحلة الثانية

ج. وتلم في الحياة قصاص . ——— اعتذر عن امكانية التنفيذ

رابعاً. يرجى عدم استخدام الاجهزة اللاسلكية عند التنفيذ او قبله.

خامساً. يرجى تغيير اسلوب الرمي واسلوب الحركة والتحضير وتغيير التوقيتات الروتينية تجنباً لرصدنا من قبل العدو.

وثورة حتى النصر

أخوكم
المقدم الركن
التوقيع

[Document 63]: Target chart for firing in the central sector

This is the heading for a 1:50,000 scale map of southern Lebanon and northern Israel with 141 targets marked for firing; 16 of the targets are towns and villages in the Galilee; the other targets are in southern Lebanon.

خطة الرمي في القطاع الأوسط

مع جدول بالأهداف مرفق ربطاً

مقياس: ١/٥٠،٠٠٠

<u>المستند</u>

خريطة: الناقورة - بنت جبيل - حولة ١/٥٠،٠٠٠

خريطة: صور - النبطية - مرجعيون ١/٥٠،٠٠٠

لائحة الأهداف

[Document 64]: Precaution against Israeli counterattacks

This battle-order, dated 28 May 1981, is from the Sidon area commander of the September Martyrs Battalion of the Kastel Forces of Fatah to the commander of the United Command in the south. It illustrates the PLO policy of locating military units in civilian zones. We have translated two excerpts.

The unit has a multiple mission:

1. To ward off the enemy's attempts to dislodge the revolution from the Sidon area;

2. To hold on to all existing positions and defend them;

3. To be on constant alert to confront aggression on the part of the Zionist enemy, the separatist forces[51] and their allies;

4. To maintain a reserve unit for the entire area...

The built-up areas in the town of Sidon and the surrounding villages are excellent areas for shelter. The trees provide complete camouflage and concealment for vehicles and personnel.

Positions should be taken up in the built-up areas in Sidon, the refugee camps and the villages.

---

51. The term usually used by the PLO and the Lebanese left to designate the Christian forces in Lebanon. and sometimes Haddad's troops in particular.

Document 64A-1

حركة التحرير الوطني الفلسطيني
فتـح
القيادة العامة لقوات العاصفة
قوات القسطل – كتيبة شهداء أيلول
قيادة منطقة صيـدا

الرقم ع/١/١/...
التاريخ : [illegible] أيار ١٩٨٢
الموضوع : امر القتال رقم (٤)

الاخ قائد القوات المشتركة لمنطقة الجنوب .

تحيـة الثورة والعودة :

اليكم تقدير الموقف في صيدا والمنطقة المحيطة بموجب امر القتال رقم (٤) :
خرائط المراجعة (١ : ٥٠٠٠٠) اصدار ١٩٧٥ دمشق تيهم ميركاتور .

١ . المهمـة :

١ . التصدي للعدو المحتمل ومنعه من تحقيق اهدافه في احتلال الثورة من منطقة صيـدا .
٢ . التمسك بكل نقاط التمركز الحالية للقوات والدفاع عنها .
٣ . الجاهزية الدائمة لمواجهة احتمالات العدوان من قبل العدو الصهيوني والانعزالي وحلفائهما .
٤ . ابقاء احتياط بقوام (مجموعة قتالية متحركة لردف محور زفتا – النبطية) .

٢ . طبيعة الارض :

أ . الغطاء :
تشكل المناطق المبنية في مدينة صيدا والقرى المحيطة بها مناطق مغطاة بشكل جيد من الاشجار وتوفر امكانية الاختفاء والتمويه للافراد والآليات بشكل كامل (تقريبا) ما عدا مرتفع (١٨١) احداثي (٣٧١٦ – ٢٨٤) ومرتفع (٦٥٦) احداثي (٣٧٠٤ – ٢٨٢) ومرتفع ١٢٧ احداثي (٣٧١٢ – ٢٨٢) حيث تنعدم التغطية في هذه التلال عدا ما تناثر من بنايات قليلة .

ب . الارض التكتيكية :

١ . المناطق المبنية وخاصة في صيدا – عبرا
٢ . ... مغدوشة تشكل مناطق حيوية للدفاع عن صيدا والمخيمات والساحل .

Document 64A-2

(٢)

٣ • تشكل المنطقة الجنوبية في عبرا الجديدة ومرتفع شرحبيل اهمية كبرى للدفاع عن المنطقة الساحلية الممتدة من الرميلة – جامع الزعتري وتتمتع بسرعة منشأة ميكانيكية وفصيلة دبابات •

حـ • الارض الحيوية :

١ • تشكل منطقة مغدوشة نقطة حيوية للدفاع عن محور الزهراني – صيدا

٢ • منطقة الميه وميه – مار الياس – عبرا الجديدة – شرحبيل مناطق حيوية للحفاظ على تواجد الثورة في صيدا ومخيماتها بشكل حر وقوي •

د • الطرق والممرات :

١ • طريق الزهراني – صيدا طريق من الدرجة الاولى صالح لكل انواع العربات

٢ • طريق النبطية عرب صاليم – صربا – مغدوشة طريق من الدرجة الاولى يصلح ويحتمل كل انواع العربات (وصعوبة في منطقة حرش الفوقا) •

٣ • النبطية – عرب صاليم – جرجوع – جباع – مجيدل – جزنايا – اللوبية – عين الدلب – صيدا طريق صعب وضيق لا يصلح لمرور الدبابات وخاصة ما بين جباع – واللوبية •

٤ • طريق النبطية – حومين الفوقا – صربا – طنبوريت – درب السيم طريق درجة اولى • وجيد يصلح لمرور كافة الاليات حتى عنقون ومن ثم صعب وضيق لا يصلح الا لمرور المركبات المتوسطة وبصعوبة •

• الطرق الداخلية الفرعية في منطقة صيدا جيدة وصالحة لمرور كافة العربات بما فيها الدبابات •

الاستنتاجات

من خلال دراستنا للارض نستنتج ما يلي :

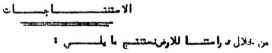

Document 64A-3

(٣)

جـ • تشكل [illegible] التي تحيط بالمناطق [illegible] وخاصة [illegible] ([illegible])

[illegible]

و • الا[illegible] لقوات العدو [illegible] على المناطق [illegible]

[illegible]

[illegible] في المناطق المحتلة [illegible]

[illegible]

Document 64A-4

(٤)

٣ ـ تطوير التقدم بقوة (لواء مشاة ميكانيكي + كتيبة دبابات) على محور (النبطية ـ الزهراني ـ صيدا) .

٤ . ان يقوم العدو بعمليات انزال بحرية بقوة (كتيبة مغاوير بحرية) على الساحل الشمالي لصيدا ومنطقة الزهراني بهدف عزل صيدا وصور في وقت واحد .

٥ . ان يقوم العدو بعمليات انزال لوحدات الصاعقة بالطائرات العمودية حول مدينة صيدا او في منطقة بعيدة عنها (٤ ـ ٨ كم) والتقدم لضرب مرابض المدفعية ومراكز الدبابات المتواجدة في المنطقة .

٦ . القيام بغارات جوية واسعة ومكثفة على مناطق تواجد الدبابات ومرابض المدفعية ومقرات القيادة لقوات الفلسطينية وحولهما .

٧ . القيام بعمليات ازعاج وتخريب بواسطة مجموعات خاصة يتم انزالها من البحر او الجو لقطع الطرق وعلى مقربة من الاليات ووسائط الاتصالات .

الاستنتاجات .

١ . يجب ان تكون [illegible] اسلحة م/ط بشكل منسق [illegible] الاكثر احتمالا .

٢ . يجب ان توضع مراقبات جوية والتشديد عليها الى [illegible] .

٣ . يجب وضع مراقبات بحرية وان تكون على اتصال وتمهد الاسلحة الداعمة للمواقع الامامية على الشاطئ .

٤ . القوات الصديقة :

Document 64A-5

(٥)

ب . القوات المطلوبة للدفاع عن صيدا :

١ . سرية مشاة .

٢ . بطارية هاون ١٢٠ ملم .

٣ . كتيبة دبابات ت/ ٣٤ .

٤ . كتيبة م/ط .

وتكون القوى المطلوبة من :

١ . خمسة (٥) سرايا مشاة .

٢ . مرتين (٢) م/د (١٠٦ ملم ، ٥٥ ملم) .

٣ . ثلاثة (٣) سرايا م/ط (١٤ ملم رباعي ، ٢٣ ملم ، ٣٧ ملم)

٤ . [illegible] (٣) راجمات [illegible] / ٢٢ .

توزيع القوى المطلوبة للدفاع عن صيدا والمنطقة [illegible] :

---

١ . محور الجية – صيدا – جنوب صيدا :

أ . سرية مشاة

ب . كتيبة دبابات ت/ ٣٤ .

ج . فصيلة م/د ١٠٦ ملم .

د . فصيلة م/ط ٣٧ ملم .

هـ . قسم هاون ١٢٠ ملم عدد (٢) .

٢ . مرتفعات [illegible] :

أ . فصيلة م/ط (رباعيات دوشكا ١٤ ملم ، ٢٣ ملم) عدد (٢) [illegible] .

ب . قسم هاون ١٢٠ ملم عدد (٢) .

٣ . المهمة [illegible] :

Document 64A-6

(٦)

ب . فصيلة م/د (١٠٦ ملم) .

ج . فصيلة م/ط (رشاشات ٢٤ ملم) .

٥ . موقع [illegible] (٣١٥ ١٨٣٥ ٢٤٢٥) جنوب وجنوب غرب الدالهمية :

أ . سرية مشاة .

ب . فصيلة دبابات ت/٣٤ .

ج . فصيلة رشاشات (١٤,٥ ملم) .

٦ . منطقة جسر الد[illegible] :

أ . سرية مشاة

ب . فصيلة دبابات ت/٣٤ .

ج . فصيلة م/ط (١٤,٥ ملم) .

د . فصيلة م/د (١٠٦ ملم) .

٧ . [illegible] :

أ . سرية مشاة .

ب . فصيلة دبابات ت/٣٤ .

ج . فصيلة م/ط ١٤,٥ ملم .

د . قسم هاون ١٢٠ ملم .

٨ . منطقة الدفاع عن محور (المحور الاول ـ المنصورية [illegible] ـ جامع الزهري) :

أ . سرية مشاة + فصيلة [illegible] .

٩ . منطقة دفاع جامع الزهري ـ [illegible] :

أ . سرية مشاة .

١٠ . منطقة دفاع [illegible] الغازية [illegible] المتاخمة [illegible]) :

أ . سرية مشاة .

Document 64A-7

(٧)

الاستنتاجات

نستطيع الاستنتاج مما تقدم [illegible] القوى والوسائط المتوفرة [illegible]:

١ . انه لا يمكننا الدفاع [illegible] بشكل جيد [illegible] الطول وما [illegible]

٢ . [illegible] القوى والوسائط المتوفرة [illegible]
و [illegible] والمنظمات .

٣ . يبقى الوضع [illegible] القوات المتواجدة [illegible] .

٤ . يطالب في حالة بقاء هذه القوى والوسائط على ما هي عليه ان يتولى [illegible] الداخلية مهمة الدفاع المحلي [illegible] ;

٥ . الروح المعنوية والتدريب :

أ . يتحلى مقاتلونا بروح معنوية عالية جدا وبقدرة على تحمل التضحية والاستعداد للقتال .

ب . العمل في الاونة الاخيرة [illegible] كبيرة من افراد التعبئة العامة للكتيبة وان ما الحق بها
بشكل اعتيادي مما يؤثر على القدرة القتالية . وهذا ما يضعف قيمة [illegible]
العدوية .

ملحوظة :

يتضح مما تقدم ان الدفاع عن منطقة [illegible] في امر القتال رقم (٤) [illegible]
فيمكنكم بانه يتعذر [illegible] بحسب القوى والوسائط المتوفرة لذا نرجو من الاخوة مساندة القوات التي ترابط
في الجنوب وايضا ما يلي :

١ . زيادة الملحقين من قوى ووسائط لتساند منطقة [illegible] العسكرية .

٢ . بانتظار تعليمات جديدة سيتم وضع خطة تأخذ بعين الاعتبار القوى والوسائط المتوفرة والتي
لا تكفي للقيام بالمهمات الموكولة لي بموجب امر القتال رقم (٤) .

واقبلوا فائق الاحترام

[Document 65]: "RPG kid"

One of a few hundred "RPG kids", aged 10-15, who were trained by the PLO to operate the rocket-propelled-grenades. Some two hundred of them were arrested by the IDF and released shortly thereafter.

In the terrorist camps, children aged 12 and upwards were recruited into the fighting force, equipped with personal weapons and sent off to fight the Zionist enemy. Testimony is now being collected from teachers about the "sons of fighters" — teenagers armed with Kalashnikovs. The "student fighters" did not hesitate to threaten teachers and fellow students, or to fire these weapons periodically into the classroom.

Anyone travelling around southern Lebanon these days is likely to come across young boys and girls, mostly in their teens, without fingers. This phenomenon is particularly noticeable in the villages. The terrorists regarded the village youth as potential fighters in Haddad's militia or in the Lebanese Army. They would often kidnap children and return them to their homes with their fingers amputated.

[Document 66]: Palestinian child in full military gear

[Document 67]: Order to mobilize 12-year-olds
The document was found in Sidon.

THE PALESTINE NATIONAL LIBERATION MOVEMENT
FATAH
GENERAL COMMAND OF 'ASIFA FORCES
KASTEL FORCES/SEPTEMBER MARTYRS BATTALION

No. 727/4/1 A
Date: 4 June 1982
Subject: Mobilization and Annexation

To: Commanding Officer, Company 3

Following is the text of a letter from the Kastel Forces Command, No. 1325/2/1 A, dated 3 June 1982.

1. In accordance with what was discussed at the meeting of the Military Council of 27 May 1982, it has been decided to draft the sons of the fighters, beginning on 1 June 1982, and until 30 September 1982, as follows:

a) The sons of the fighters in the armed forces, the Yarmuk forces, the Karame forces, the Kastel forces, and the "Ajnadin" forces.
b) Those under 12 years of age will not be accepted.
c) A monthly allowance of 400 Lebanese pounds will be paid to each one.
d) They will be stationed at the camps of the abovementioned forces, and will be provided with the necessary technical personnel.
e) All other units must send their representatives to the locations nearest the abovementioned forces.
f) For action.

(signed)
Major Abu 'Uthman, Staff Officer
Commander, September Martyrs Battalion

Document 67A

حركة التحرير الوطني الفلسطيني
"فتح"
القيادة العامة لقوات العاصفة
قوات القسطل/كتيبة شهداء ايلول

الرقم ١٠/١/٩٤/ ٧٥٧
التاريخ ١٩٨٢/٦/٤
الموضوع التجنيد والالحاق

الاخ قائد ......السرية الثالثة

تحية الثورة وبعد

بناءً على نص كتاب الاخوة قيادة قوات القسطل رقم ١٠/٢/١٣٢٥ تاريخ ١٩٨٢/٦/٣

---

١. بناءً على اجتماع الاخوة المجلس العسكري بتاريخ ١٩٨٢/٥/٢٧ تقرر تجنيد ابناء المقاتلين اعتبارا من تاريخ ١٩٨٢/٦/١ ولغاية ١٩٨٢/٩/٣٠ وحسب ماهو مبين ادناه .

أ) يتم تجنيد ابناء المقاتلين في القوات العسكرية . قوات اليرموك . قوات الكرامة . قوات القسطل قوات اجنادين .

ب) لا يقبل اقل من هم دون الثانية عشرة عاما .

ج) يصرف مخصص شهري للواحد بمعدل (٤٠٠) اربعمائة ليرة لبنانية شهريا .

د) يكون التجمع في معسكرات القوات المذكورة وتجهز بالكوادر الفنية المناسبة لها .

هـ) على جميع الوحدات الاخوى ارسال منسبيهم الى اقرب مكان للقوات المذكورة .

و) لذا يرجى العمل بموجبه والتقيد بدقة ...... لطفا .

وثورة حتى النصر

نسخة الى
- الحفظ

م/ الرائد الركن
قائد كتيبة شهداء ايلول
((احمد ابو كمال))

[Document 68]: Order to mobilize 16-39-year-olds

The document, dated 8 May 1981, stipulates that in order to strengthen the front against the enemy, all men aged 16-39 are to be called up to the PLO within 48 hours; thereafter, the revolution will set up roadblocks and hand over all eligible men who have not responded to the call.

الموقف الحالي / موقفنا موضوع التعبئة وضرورة تطبيقها حتى يتسنى لنا
الامكانية للتصدي للعدو بشكل أكثر فعالية وتم الاتفاق على دعوة
مواليد (١٦ سنة - ٣٩ سنة) وشكلت لجنة تعبئة لهذا الغرض على
أن يتم الاستدعاء خلال ٤٨ ساعة بعدها تقوم الكفاح المسلح
بنصب حواجز وإلقاء القبض على كل فلسطيني ضمن هذا العمر على أن
تقوم المنظمات باستدعاء مليشياتها خلال هذه الفترة.
تحركات العدو الإسرائيلي / أن المكان الرئيسي للعمليات سيكون مرج عيون
الدامور / المصنع سالكاً الطريق العام بهدف قطع الطريق أمام القوات
السورية مع ضربة طيران شديدة إلى الأهداف السورية على كافة
الأراضي اللبنانية وخاصة الصواريخ تترافق مع الهجوم
الإسرائيلي على المنطقة / النبطية / أنصار / أبو الأسود بعد أن
تقوم قوة محمولة بالهبوط على (جسر القاسمية / أبو الأسود
الزهرانية) وهذه العملية تتم خلال خمسة أيام بعدها
تدخل الاتحاد السوفييتي وأمريكا لإيقاف القتال ودعوة الأطراف
المعنية إلى طاولة المفاوضات.
أ- ستكون حرب محدودة بين سوريا وإسرائيل والمقاومة الفلسطينية
[illegible] كما نريد.
ب- أن هذه الحرب هي حرب تحريكية مشابهة لحرب تشرين.
جـ- دخول سوريا والمقاومة كوفد موحد مع إسرائيل على طاولة
المفاوضات ضمانات [illegible] إلى تسوية شبيهة كمب ديفيد.

[Document 69]: Plans to attack American airbases

Cover and table of contents of a military training book entitled "Sabotage," written by Colonel 'Afallah Muhammad 'Atallah (Abu al-Za'im), PLO military intelligence chief. The cover illustration shows an explosion blowing apart a Star of David, symbol of the State of Israel. The table of contents is preceded by a note about "American airbases," giving a generalized description of such bases, and specifying that one kilogram of TNT would cause serious damage if used at certain weak points. Any penetration of American airbases is to be preceded by reconnaissance and observations.

اعداد العقيد الركن

عطاالله محمد عطاالله

(ابو الزعيم)

Document 69A-2

القواعد الجوية الامريكية

بها مدرج واحد وممرات تؤدي إلى المدرج الرئيسي واماكن للتخز
للطيارين ومراكز للاتصال ومحطة كهرباء منفردة وانابيب نفط ومس
ومستودع ذخيرة ومحولات كهربائية ومحطات رادارية ونقطة مر
واماكن تزويد للوقود واجهزة الضغط واجهزة مفرغة للتزويد السريع وا
لها حوالي ١ كغم واهداف اساسية مثل محطة الكهرباء ومركز المرا
وانابيب النفط ومستودع الذخيرة وبالنسبة لاساليب التدمير كلها معروف

اساليب التسرب او الدخول لها . أهم شيء هنا الاستطلاع

فهرست

[Document 70]: PLO to escalate violence in southern Lebanon

The document originated in the security staff of PLO joint forces in southern Lebanon.

THE SECURITY OF THE SOUTH.

24 February 1981

We learned from our representative that following the Islamic Conference[52] the Fatah movement will escalate the situation in southern Lebanon both domestically and externally.

Internally — Fatah will create problems between the Palestinian resistance and the Amal movement[53] by inciting against some of the resistance groups on the one hand and extending assistance to Amal on the other.

Externally — Fatah will initiate military operations through the border enclave,[54] and launch continuous shelling on the villages of the enclave and on (Israeli) settlements.

As of now, there is some difference of opinion between Fatah and the Syrians, because the Syrian regime supports other (PLO) organizations against Fatah. Thus, an armed clash is possible between the Syrians and Fatah. Syria might then either evacuate its forces or concentrate them in order to create a threat against Fatah (lest it exploit) the vacuum that would emerge after Syria's retreat.

Revolution until victory!

---

52. Islamic Conferences have been held annually since 1969. In March 1981 the Conference met in Ta'if, Saudi Arabia, and called for a Jihad (Holy War) to liberate Jerusalem.
53. The Shi'ite militia, which supported the "left" and the PLO in principle but clashed with them with increasing frequency in the months before Operation Peace for Galilee.
54. That is, the zone controlled by Haddad's forces.

Document 70A

رقم الصادر ع ل / ١٠٦ / ٨١ امن الجنوب

تاريخ المعلومات ٢٤/ ٦/ ١٩٨١

مصدر المعلومات

تسلم المعلومات

تحية الثورة

عنوان التقرير

افادنا مصدرنا بأن حركة فتح بعد المؤتمر الاسلامي تسعى الى توتير الوضع في جنوب لبنان على المستوى الداخلي والخارجي .

ـ على المستوى الداخلي تعمل على خلق عدد من المشاكل بين المقاومة الفلسطينية وحركة أمل من خلال التعبئة ضد بعض فصائل المقاومة ومساعدة حركة أمل بما تطلبه .

ب ـ على المستوى الخارجي ـ فتح العمليات العسكرية عبر الشريط الحدودي و[illegible] القصف المستمر لقوى الشريط والمستعمرات .

وهناك خلافات حاليا بين حركة فتح والسوريين لأن النظام السوري يدعم بعض التنظيمات ضد جبهة حركة فتح واحتمال أن يحدث صدامات بين المنظمات الفلسطينية ودنا احتمال صدام مسلح بين المنظمات والسوريين وستقوم سوريا بسحب أو تجميع القوات المتواجدة على الساحة اللبنانية وذلك لتهديد حركة فتح بالفراغ الذي سيترتب بعد السحب السوري .

ودمتم للنضال

وصورة حضرة التحرير

VIII. EYEWITNESS REPORTS AND COMMENTS [Documents 75-124]

As the dust of battle began to settle, and the hundreds of thousands of Lebanese refugees who had been expelled by the PLO made their way back to their homes, horror stories began to surface about terrifying experiences under the PLO occupation. In some places, where the Lebanese population was almost totally annihilated, only a few survivors are left to tell the story. In other areas, notably Nabatiye, Damour, Sidon and other towns, which have been rapidly recovering from the destruction of seven years of fighting and where the original population has been streaming back, the stories of PLO terror are told with sighs of relief. Some of these eyewitness reports have been told to journalists, others to the local Lebanese authorities and still others to Israeli soldiers who participated in Operation Peace for Galilee. Some reports were submitted in writing, while others were conveyed in television, radio and newspaper interviews.

Where possible, we have included names and other information about the witnesses. We contacted some of them in order to reconfirm their stories. The majority, however, are anonymous people from all walks of life who felt the need to share their horrors with the world at large. Many of the stories were confirmed by independent sources, including PLO men detained by Israel. Some of the accounts may be inaccurate or exaggerated, but there can be no doubt about their basic authenticity. We have sifted through thousands of testimonies and selected a few samples in order to do justice to this otherwise undocumented aspect of the PLO occupation of Lebanon.

[Documents 71-99]: Eyewitness reports on PLO conduct in Lebanon

[Document 71]: An elderly Lebanese woman, Sidon, 6 July 1982

The interview was broadcast on Israel Television on 23 July 1982 (translated from Arabic).

This is my house, anyone who passed by it could not help marveling at it. The garden was full of flowers, it was a living paradise, until they (the PLO) came, shot us, killed us and destroyed our houses.

[Document 72]: Major Khalil Yasin Khalil Abu Ghanim, formerly in charge of transportation for Fatah, now in Israeli custody.

The interview was broadcast on Israel Television on 23 July 1982 (translated from Arabic).

Due to the general chaos in Lebanon, they (the PLO) intervened in the everyday life of the Lebanese; they interfered in his livelihood, in everything. They desecrated his honour, his life, his children.... In addition to that, their very presence in Lebanon, which necessitated Israel's reprisals in self-defence, caused damage to the densely-populated areas where they had entrenched themselves.... This, of course, generated a lot of bitterness among the Lebanese. One must say that the Lebanese people want to see no more of our fighters, for they know that the current disaster in Lebanon was caused by force of arms. This is what happened in Lebanon. They did in Lebanon what they had done in Jordan.

[Document 73]: Yihya Jawad Kharob Fatlawi, a PLO member

The interview was broadcast on Israel Television on 23 July 1982 (translated from Arabic).

I was born in Baghdad on 1 January 1961.... The PLO and its people, including officers, perpetrated many thefts and kidnappings and even murders in Lebanon. One of these "operations" was carried out by a group of Fatah members who robbed the casino. They killed one person, assaulted many others.... Once they raped the wife of a local doctor. All this took place in Sidon and everybody knew about it. Many other things were perpetrated by members of the organizations.... I learned to handle a Kalashnikov rifle with its silencer; this is the kind of weapon I use...

I have a distant relative in Sidon. I went to see him and he offered to employ me in intelligence, in a liquidation squad to kill people. We worked together, the two of us, and other persons too, to eliminate Iraqis who opposed the Iraqi government. He dispatched me to collect information within several organizations which employ Iraqis and Palestinians who oppose the Iraqi government.... We have also mounted attempts against the lives of some Iranians who were members of Fatah and opposed our activities.

Q: Who are the people you killed?
A: Abu Sadam al-Iraqi, who was a captain in Libyan intelligence and maintained contacts with the PLO, especially with the Popular Front — General Command. He had his own group of anti-Iraqi activists which operated against Iraq...

We also killed Hussein al-Sharif, the head of the Iranian students in the Middle East, who maintained contacts with Fatah, as well as his deputy, someone called Khazem.

Others had been murdered before I joined the gang and after I left that intelligence squad.... They also killed ‘Izzat al-Fahd, Khaled al-‘Iraqi and ‘Adel Wasfi. Other people like Sadef al-Ja‘fer, from the Communist party, collected information about the victims.

[Document 74]: Miriam and Diana Fakhr-a-Din, young women, Sidon
The interview was broadcast on Israel Television on 23 July 1982 (translated from Arabic).

We knew that they (the PLO) killed people and threw their corpses in the courtyards. Some of them were mutilated and their limbs were cut off. We did not dare to go out for fear that we might end up like them. Many of the murdered were dumped in parks and forests. Nobody knows where they are buried, not even the families...

Once we heard of a girl in our school who was raped and then they slaughtered her.... They set up many roadblocks. They were filthy people.... So we were prohibited to leave the house lest we be raped too. Because if we had gone out, they would have constituted a temptation for them.... They did many filthy things. We did not even dare go to the beach because they molested us, weapons in hand. They shot and used abusive language, all the words that one could imagine.

We could not go to the movies, because they would fight among themselves about who would sit next to a certain girl. So any girl who wished to go to the movies had to take along with her ten of her friends, so that they would not bother her.

They would roam the streets in jeeps and make fun of people and girls. Life was impossible with them. Lately, a case was published in a newspaper in Sidon. They raped a girl and threw her body next to a very famous statue here. The picture was published in the newspaper. They tortured her horribly and then buried her body. So, we did not dare go out of the house. When we went somewhere, for example to my father's clinic, they would stop their jeep and start trailing us and bothering us, and we were intercepted in any direction we went. They would say, "Hi sweetheart, come here, don't be afraid, let me — you" and so on....We could do nothing. Even if we wanted to shout for help we would be afraid because they were armed. And there are many more things of this sort.

[Document 75]: An elderly man, Sidon
The interview was broadcast on Israel Television on 23 July 1982 (translated from Arabic).

My son drove a car and accidentally crashed with another car driven by a Palestinian. The latter's car was new and its bumper was badly damaged, something estimated at 100-120 Lebanese pounds. The PLO member came here and phoned his family; they all came with their Kalashnikov submachine guns; they came to my house at Ein Hilwe,[55] and we immediately assured them that they would be fully compensated. They said, "If you do not pay 1,000 pounds, we'll arrest you. Get it?" I paid 3,500 pounds and begged that they leave me in peace.... We did not dare to venture out of the house at night, even not one step outdoors. The moment darkness set in, we closed down and went home.... You know why? Just because of this trouble.... All troublemakers that God created have somehow found their way to Lebanon.... They come here and for any minor problem, draw their pistols or threaten with their Kalashnikovs. They used to shout, "Get out of here, man!" I would hold them and beg, "Put down your rifle! A round may be shot by mistake and blood will be spilled."

[Document 76]: Yussuf Abu-Mar'i and his wife Zakya, Sidon
The interview was broadcast on Israel Television on 23 July 1982 (translated from Arabic).

Husband: This is my son's house. He was sitting here, in front of it when members of the "Front"[56] came in. They called his name and asked whether we had armed people inside. He said, "No." They insisted that armed men

55. A suburb of Sidon. Part of Ein Hilwe is populated by local Lebanese, another part is a Palestinian refugee camp.
56. The Popular Front.

were hiding inside; they put him against the wall and ordered him to stay there. Then, they shot him in the back, right here. His mother and his wife, who had become concerned about him, rushed out and found him killed.... They wanted to throw his corpse in the garden and bury him...

Wife: We were outside and we heard that some Palestinians had penetrated into our house. We did not believe it, but before long we realized that they were assaulting us. I was right here and the children hid in the field. I was looking for the kids, but I could not find them. They killed my elder son right by the door. He was at home, he opened the door to go downstairs, when he ran into them. They ordered him to raise his hands and shot him.... My other son went out to hide the children. He was 14. When he came back to see his brother, they killed him too. I went upstairs, I found them lying on the floor, one here, the other there. They were dead, both of them. This is what happened. They killed and killed, all we saw here was bodies of the dead. I asked Saint Mary to give me forbearance. They killed the son of my daughter too. They were all young.

[Document 77]: A couple from a village near Tyre
The interview was broadcast by Israel Television on 23 July 1982 (translated from Arabic).

Wife: They attacked the village like ants. There were thousands of them, a mixed batch, Palestinians and others.... Then, they left the killed behind.... We were allowed to go out at 5 o'clock pm and we found our children killed, our houses robbed. They took our sheep and other herds and killed our children; they ransacked our houses. When I returned home I found nobody, my husband was not there. I only found the boy killed and two others dead upstairs. They took away my husband and I stayed alone in the house...

Q: What did you tell them when you saw the children slain?

A: They asked, "Why are you crying? We are going to evacuate the bodies!" I said, "If you do, you are in for more turmoil!" What an idea to take them out! We covered them and took them in.

Husband: They took me into custody for 40 days, first in Rashidiye and then in Faqahani.

[Document 78]: A PLO member from Bangladesh
The interview was broadcast on Israel Television on 23 July 1982 (translated from Arabic).

My name is Purisbel. I came from Bangladesh to work in a hospital and they enlisted me in the George Habash organization. They paid me 600 Lebanese pounds monthly.... The PLO was a multi-national affair: they had terrorists from Somalia, Libya, Iraq, Pakistan and Bangladesh.... There were terrorists from many countries. They were stationed in this entire area, especially here in the village of 'Abra.

[Document 79]: Hamed Ahmed Muhammed 'Isa, a Lebanese

The interview was broadcast on Israel Television on 23 July 1982 (translated from Arabic).

Originally I was Palestinian but now I am a Lebanese national. I was born in Lebanon. I went to Germany in 1970 where I lived illegally until 1974-5. I met a German girl, Ruth Merkel. I befriended her and I lived with her family. When I decided to ask for political asylum, they wanted me to extend the validity of my passport. So I went to the Lebanese consulate, where someone from the PLO called Hamdi Harb was present. The Lebanese consul told me that no passport could be extended to Palestinians unless by PLO consent. The PLO official asked me to follow him to his office and he offered me a job with youth [in Lebanon].... I was told to discuss politics with them and any other topic I might be ordered to.... I consented.... Thus, I established contacts with Arab youth; we used to sit together and discuss matters...

The day came when I wanted to go back to Germany. I went to the PLO offices to report my trip.... I arrived in Germany in the company of a young man called Nazih and while in West Berlin another man, named Ahmad Tuffel, met us. He took us around Berlin.... Ahmed Tuffel brought along his friends: Merwan, and a German boy with whom they spoke German.... and so, we walked around for some time...

One day, Ahmed took us to the offices of the organization in East Berlin and the man in charge was at home.... Ahmed came to report that we were entrusted with a mission. We asked what it was and he said, "some kind of bombing." We said, "We came here to have a good time; if we are caught we'll be in trouble." He said, "Don't worry." We insisted that we did not want to do it. He said, "OK, leave the task to me," and we went on roaming around the city with him...

Then, I went to order my return ticket to Lebanon since my vacation was over. I went home and saw Ahmed again. He said, "We are going out for our mission." I said that I refused to go because I was going back to Lebanon. He said, "OK leave it to me," and he went downstairs. Downstairs a dark-skinned boy was waiting for him, holding a briefcase, which he handed over to Ahmed. I asked what it was but he said, "Don't worry..."

There were Germans who collaborated with our organization, such as Wolfgang Iwot, Tatlev Mercury, but not the Merkel family. Another was called Hiblmar Krist and another was Karl Kamele.... They are Communists.... They published articles for us in the newspapers because they knew German better than us.... They also organized political gatherings...

At 21:00 that night a bomb exploded in a restaurant, wounding 25 people, 8 of them seriously; a one-year-old baby is still in critical condition. The bomb was so powerful that all the traffic was blocked, the bomb had been hidden in the briefcase, and a woman was seen leaving the restaurant briefly prior to the explosion...

Q: Why would they want to blow up an Italian restaurant in West Berlin?

A: According to Ahmed, that restaurant was frequented by foreigners: Americans, Pakistanis; that is, foreigners. Therefore, they decided to blow it up.

Q: You were born in Lebanon. Lebanese blood flows in your veins. What do you think has happened to Lebanon since the coming of the PLO?

A: Lebanon was a paradise. Now, they inflicted upon it destruction, expulsion and chaos. This is what happened in Lebanon. Beirut used to be called "Paris No. 2", everybody here lived in affluence and abundance! But since the organization came here in 1967, Lebanon has been all but destroyed.

[Document 80]: Umm-Atallah, a Christian woman, Damour

The interview was broadcast on Israel Television on 23 July 1982 (translated from Arabic).

Oh God, oh God, you are the Almighty, return to us our homes! My Lord, it was my children who built this house. My family used to live here. Oh my God! They assaulted Damour and murdered people there. My son and my nephew were killed; my second sister, her son and grandson, her daughter and her daughter-in-law, her daughter's mother-in-law and her second grandson, and the son of my third sister [were all murdered]. After they invaded Damour, they went in and killed everybody in the house, with the assistance of a group of the Na'ama neighbourhood inhabitants: Palestinians, Syrians and other people from Na'ama...

We went to the palace of [Camille] Chamoun, and we were sent by boat to Jounieh. When we left Damour it was a big torch in flame. This is what happened. When they entered Damour, every house which was not burnt or destroyed, they set afire and robbed. They robbed and stole, because it was full of expensive furniture. Our houses were particularly well furnished. They stole furniture and took money, so we left behind us money and jewelery. After they stole and robbed, they went back and burnt down everything. All in order to let out their frustrations and wrath on the Christian Lebanese, cut men and women into pieces. They literally cut them down with axes before they killed them...

These past seven years I have been told not to go back to Damour, but I said that God is almighty, nothing is impossible for God. Since the Israelis arrived here, I am saying and repeating that they were sent by God. It is God who sent us the Israelis, God the Almighty.

[Document 81]: Tawfik Shamtef from the village of 'Abra

The interview was broadcast on Israel Television on 23 July 1982 (translated from Arabic).

The moment they moved into 'Abra, they took over the strategic spots. They broke down our olive trees and other nice places and trees. Every house which looked strategic to them, they took over, turned it into a position and conducted observations and other military activities from there. We tried to talk them out of it politely, but they would not listen. They saw a new house which had just been completed, and its owner just occupied it, and they confiscated it. They urged us to keep our mouths shut and to remain indoors. So, we took our children and sheltered them in a protected room; we were hardly in that room, when they started shelling us with cannon. Two girls from the Safi household were killed, and my father was wounded and died.

Then they started shelling the streets and the rest of the houses and we had no one to ask for help. We had no choice but to take our wounded to a nearby hospital under fire. This is what happened to us. We located the wounded according to their cries for help; I and other young people who were in the village went to collect the wounded and the dead. We met the village mukhtar who, himself, had removed a dead girl. Her hands were cut off and part of her head was missing. The houses were set on fire, people were caught in the fire, burning and unable to escape, all crying and weeping. We picked up some crying women but they shot at us and the walls around us were full of bullet holes. We wanted to load them into cars and rush to hospitals but we could not go far; they blocked the roads with their jeeps and forbade us from going any further. Nevertheless, we succeeded in bringing to the hospital a few of the wounded.

[Document 82]: Hasan-a-din and his father, from the village of Haruf
The interview was broadcast on Israel Television on 23 July 1982 (translated from Arabic).

Son: On Ramadan of two years ago, that is 1980, exactly on the night of the 21st, at 3:30, my only brother was kidnapped by armed people. Three days later, he was found dead at the "Musila" station, that is about 15 kilometres from Nabatiye.

Father: I say again: my late son, Sayyid Ali, was an imam in the mosque and was delivering sermons as part of his religious duties. Many times he was asked by the local youth, "What can we do?" He answered, "You have to fast and pray to God and you must bless His name, so that you act in unison and preserve your land to which you have a full right." These words were transmitted by spies — by some of the aliens who were here, the terrorists, if you wish — to them [the PLO] and they interpreted them as they wished. Therefore, they acted against him, and it is evident that his words cost him his life. This is what I believe and, beyond that, only Allah knows.

[Document 83]: Hasan Abd-al-Hamid, from the village of Rujeib
The interview was broadcast on Israel Television on 23 July 1982 (translated from Arabic).

There were families who were forced out of their homes. Girls, women and children were crying at night when their personal belongings were thrown out of the windows to the street.... At night, they used to bring girls upstairs to their offices, where they had a spare office; you can see it there. The girls were begging, "In the name of Allah, leave us alone; Allah will preserve the honour of your women, do not desecrate ours!" A few minutes later, the cries would subside...

[Document 84]: A doctor at al-Hilal Hospital, Sidon
The hospital had been the personal property of Dr. Rashid Khouri, a member of the Lebanese parliament, but was taken over by the PLO in 1976. The interview was broadcast on Israel Television on 23 July 1982.

This is a hospital of the Palestinian Red Crescent. It has been here for a few years now in order to help all Palestinians here, and especially the Fatah people. Fatah actually ran the hospital and gave treatment to certain people in particular. But at the same time, they used it as a storehouse for weapons, ammunition, as a gathering place for the terrorists, and so forth.... The shelters were full of weapons and ammunition and people were afraid to go to the shelter, lest a direct hit during an air-raid might blow it up. It is true that Palestinian wounded were brought here, but on one instance they brought an Israeli soldier who was wounded.[57] According to the French doctor who was here, the soldier was not in critical condition, for he had been only slightly injured in his foot and hand. When the French doctor left, he left him in very good condition, and his life was not in danger.... But when the command post, which was here, ran away, the Israeli troops arrived and found the corpse of the dead soldier. The Israel army debriefed the French doctor, and he insisted that when he left the hospital the soldier was alive. It turns out that the group who was occupying the hospital simply killed the wounded soldier before they retreated. The French doctor also said that the Israeli soldier had assured his captors that nothing would happen to them when the Israeli troops got here, because he would report that he had been well-treated by them. But they killed him, discarded his body and left.

It is true, yes, that the government hospital was hit [by Israel], but this hospital is located in a very dangerous spot, right in the "Nasser Camp." Almost all the Palestinian organizations have bases there: the Arab Front, Fatah, the Armed Struggle and what have you. They used to roam around the hospital, and when shelling or an air-raid began, they would rush with their weapons into the hospital in order to seek shelter. Then, they would shoot at the airplanes from the hospital. They thought they were protecting themselves that way, but in fact they caused us and our hospital damage.

When clashes occurred between the "National Front" and the Palestinians and Amal movement, they used to bring Amal's wounded from the villages to Al-Hilal Hospital. Here, they [the PLO] would arrest them, and when we Lebanese came from the Government hospital to enquire about them, we were prohibited from taking them back to the hospital. They simply kidnapped those young men.... This is what I wanted to tell you; they did very bad things to them...

Q: What was it?

A: We found 11 corpses here; they were dead with their hands bound. We could not even identify them, because when we found them they were already in an advanced stage of decomposition. They were totally decomposed, they smelt badly and we could not stand there...

---

57. Presumably during the Israeli operation in Lebanon in June 1982.

[Document 85]: Marcelle Fakhuri, 20, and her mother Suraya, 44, Beirut
Marcelle was interviewed while distributing sweets to Israeli servicemen on the outskirts of Beirut. The interview appeared in Yediot Aharonot, *27 July 1982 (translated from Hebrew).*

I am Catholic. I live in East Beirut. They [the PLO] slaughtered my uncle and his two sons. They killed him as I was looking on, they raped my best girlfriend and killed her husband. I am happy, now that they are punished. What they did to us could not be worse.... They simply took them to the nearby valley and opened automatic fire on them. They knew that we hated them, therefore they harassed us.

About a year ago they arrested my uncle, he was 45, the brother of my mother, Suraya. They simply cut his throat with a knife and he agonized for a few days before he died. Then they tied my girlfriend and her husband. They cut his flesh with their knives and they raped my friend. That was not the first or only time they did that. Many other women were raped and they ran away from this area...

When I came home, I saw my friend beaten and crying, and her husband had been mutilated. They behaved with us like animals and I hate them for that.... I joined the Christian forces and I served with them for a while. But when the Israeli army came in, my mother and I returned to our home.... Now I am happy because somebody is taking revenge for the spilled blood of my family....To this day I have turned down all propositions to marry because I hated to see another man of my family murdered. Now, when peace comes, I'll be able to marry, finally. I have decided not to marry as long as there is no peace.

[Document 86]: John Nasser, 49, a Maronite priest, Ayshiyeh village
Interview appeared in Ma'ariv, *14 July 1982 (translated from Hebrew).*

I want to shout out to the whole world that the comparison should be made between Nazi crimes and the deeds of that bloodthirsty animal band, that vile organization they call the PLO.

On 19 October 1976, a thousand armed terrorists attacked our village in force. They burst into the houses and dragged out the villagers — 100 families in all, men, women, and children, old and young alike. The majority they locked in the village church, while some 65 of our brothers and sisters were still outside. We heard shots, burst after burst of gunfire. Panic seized those of us imprisoned in the church, but we could do nothing because armed terrorists stood over us, threatening to shoot us down without mercy. For two days the villagers were held prisoner in the church. When the doors were finally opened, the atrocity was revealed; 65 bodies of men, women and children were lying in a pool of dried blood. Amongst them my brother Ibrahim, my niece and nephew, my brother-in-law Joseph and 15 other relatives.... For many hours cries of grief filled the air. Then convoys of trucks came into the village; the terrorists emptied the houses of their contents, nothing was left. The villagers of Ayshiyeh buried their dead, and went in the clothes they were wearing to take refuge in other villages, near and far. Ayshiyeh is my Oradour.[58] Our beloved unhappy Lebanon is full of Oradours. It must be told. The world must know. I am prepared to fulfil my sacred duty to our slaughtered brothers, to face the cameras and tell it all.

[Document 87]: Mahmoud al-Masri, Shi'ite religious leader, Ansar

In 1980, Sheikh al-Masri led civilians who resisted the entry of the terrorists into his village. In a forceful sermon, he announced that it was the moral and religious duty of Muslims to oppose the terrorists, who had imposed a rule of terror on many towns and villages. The interview appeared in Ma'ariv, *14 July 1982 (translated from Hebrew).*

[I said in my sermon] that they abuse and humiliate our brethren, rape our wives and daughters, loot our property. We will not let them in here.... We set up two roadblocks at the gates of the village and armed friends were posted there. Under cover of the night, the terrorists stormed Ansar in force. They subjected the village to heavy fire in order to teach its inhabitants a lesson. They then turned first to my house, burst in, tied me and my wife up; after they raped my daughter before our eyes, they shot her, leaving her naked body with the breasts cut off on the threshold of the house.

[Document 88]: A town leader, Nabatiye

The official who recorded this testimony noted in the margin that the witness was frequently overcome with tears. Interview appeared in Ma'ariv, *14 July 1982 (translated from Hebrew).*

A gang of about 10 young terrorists, all heavily armed, burst into my house. They tied me up together with my sons. Then, they seized my wife and daughters, and raped them in front of me and my sons.

58. A French village where 600 civilians were murdered by the retreating Nazis in June 1944.

[Document 89]: Imam Sayid-a-Din Badr from the village of Haruf
Interview appeared in Ma'ariv, *14 July 1982 (translated from Hebrew).*

The terrorists tried to force me to give a sermon in praise of the PLO. I refused. On my return home from prayer, my young son was missing. Some days later, the boy's mutilated body was brought to me by a shepherd who had found it in the field.[59]

[Document 90]: Salah Safro, 65, Mukhtar of Burj-Bahal, a village near Tyre
Interview appeared in Ma'ariv, *14 July 1982.*

Hundreds of terrorists are still hiding like mice in their holes and that is why the mayor [of Sidon] is afraid to tell the truth.... Let the mayor come to me, I'll be delighted to talk frankly to him.... It is fear itself which has brought the national tragedy of Lebanon.

Burj-Bahal is the only village in the whole district which the terrorists did not take over. The 400 villagers collected money, bought a cannon and rifles. We placed the cannon in the village square in a position left to us by the Israeli army during the Litani Operation. We divided the rifles between the men and women of the village. When the terrorists saw that they were faced with armed opposition, they went away. For seven years the terrorists stayed away from Burj-Bahal. On the first day of Operation Peace for Galilee, they burst in, entrenched themselves on the rooftops and shot into the air, trying to draw Israeli fire onto the village to destroy it and thus take revenge on us. But the Israeli pilots are smart, they dropped one bomb only on Burj-Bahal, destroying our cannon with a direct hit...

The terrorists are just like Nazis. On a business trip to Sidon, one day, I heard of a man condemned by their courts for collaboration with Israel. A search of the man's house had turned up shekel banknotes and a pair of Israeli-made shoes. In order that the case should serve as a warning, it was decided to stage his execution in public, in the central square of the city. The prisoner's arms and legs were chained to the bumpers of four cars. At an agreed signal, a pistol fired by a Fatah officer, the four cars took off, two forward and two

59. The murder and mutilation of the Imam's son caused such a furor throughout the area that Yasser Arafat himself had to come to Haruf. On his orders, thousands of residents were brought to the reception in the village square. As a dramatic gesture to the crowd, Arafat gave his personal revolver to the eldest brother of the murdered boy, saying, "Take my gun and go revenge your brother's blood, shed by the Zionists."

backwards, simultaneously tearing the four limbs off the condemned man. While the body was still in its death throes, the four cars dragged it around the square, parading it before the crowd of shuddering citizens.[60]

For seven years we lived a living death — and the world did not know. We came back to life when you Israelis came in and rid us of the terrorists.

[Document 91]: Ahmed Hassan, the village of Dawir
The witness had not yet recovered from his wounds as he related his story; the interview was published in Ma'ariv, *14 July 1982 (translated from Hebrew).*

Two terrorists who had been living in our house gathered up their belongings in a panic [upon the arrival of the Israelis] but before they left, they turned on the threshold; one of them, known as Abu-Salah, a boy of about 20, said we would not be privileged to greet the Zionist soldiers. With that, he trained his Kalashnikov on us. I thrust my wife against the wall and threw myself on my two daughters. The terrorist fired, wounding me in the arm and leg.[61]

[Document 92]: Sa'ad Milhem, 78, Ein Hilwe
Milhem's home was destroyed during the fighting; the interview appeared in Ma'ariv, *14 July 1982 (translated from Hebrew).*

They barricaded themselves in the mosque, from where they were shooting. We were about 50 persons, old people and mothers with children. When the Israeli soldiers were nearby, two terrorists came up. One was called Abu Namir; he lived near me. They told us to get up and go outside and threatened that if we didn't go out towards the soldiers, they would kill us in the mosque. Some 50 women, children and old people set out, with the terrorists shooting from the rear towards the oncoming Israeli forces.... We fell to the ground. The terrorists yelled at us to get up and started to shoot at us. Many were killed or wounded. But by then, the Israeli soldiers had taken the mosque and so I stayed alive.

---

60. The incident has been verified by residents of Sidon. One of them said, "People fainted in that square, but no newspaper wrote about what happened; the world did not hear of it." An Israeli soldier who fell into PLO hands suffered the same fate, according to an American television report.
61. Many other victims reported that they had been shot by terrorists, who had lived in their homes, as soon as the Israelis arrived.

[Document 93]: Dr. Ghassan Hamud

The witness owns and directs the Hamud Hospital, the largest and most modern of Sidon's 11 hospitals. The interview appeared in Ma'ariv, *14 July 1982, and* Ha'aretz, *27 July 1982 (translated from Hebrew).*

Many parents brought their daughters, some of them no more than children, for a virginity check. In many cases it became clear that the girl had been raped and impregnated. I knew that many parents sought out midwives in the camps to carry out abortions...[62]

I cannot confirm that this disgusting and criminal behaviour was ever brought to my attention.[63] But anything is possible, and likely, when speaking of the Palestinian revolution, the dirtiest, richest, most corrupt and most brutal revolution in the history of nations.... Every junior officer drives the city streets in a new Mercedes, armed with a sub-machine gun, or in an expensive Rangerover "Safari" car, from which peeps the barrel of a machine gun...

They always presented themselves as national heroes, and boasted how they had spilt their blood in battle against the Zionist enemy, in the holy Arab cause of the liberation of Palestine. But the truth is that more than 90 percent of their injuries were incurred during in-fighting between the various factions. These are freedom-fighters? These are animals!

The terrorists would arrive at the hospital in a long convoy of cars. They would start behaving badly in the parking lot, forcing us to remove our cars to make way for them. Once my brother, an engineer who serves as the hospital administrator, refused to move his car and they simply rode over it with a heavy military vehicle and crushed it.... The PLO patients and their escorts spread terror throughout the hospital. A sick or wounded terrorist kept his arms beside him. Whenever he wanted to call a medical attendant to his bedside he would shoot at the ceiling.[64]

---

62. There is an increasing amount of evidence about an abortion industry in the refugee camps. These abortions were often fatal, due to primitive methods and unsanitary conditions.
63. The story to which Dr. Hamud refers says that whenever the PLO's supply of blood ran low, blood would be pumped from the other patients for the use of the terrorists. Eyewitnesses spoke of dead bodies found drained of blood. The staff of the government hospital in Sidon has called for an international inquiry committee to investigate PLO "crimes against humanity."
64. Other staff members at the hospital confirmed that since their institution was the best and most prestigious in Sidon, it was popular with PLO officers, who would force the management to admit them through violence and armed threats. Whenever they brought in one of their wounded, they would compel the medical staff to abandon other patients in mid-treatment to attend to their men.

[Document 94]: Khalil Shamraya, 30, Sidon

The witness owns a chain of clothing stores; the interview appeared in Ma'ariv, *14 July 1982 (translated from Hebrew).*

About one month before the Israeli entry into southern Lebanon, the two sides, civilians and PLO, sensed that Israel had reached the limits of its endurance.... For the first time since the terrorists took over, the civilian population raised its head. We were convinced that you were about to attack and people were even betting on the exact day of your arrival. We knew that if we didn't drive the terrorists out of our civilian areas and banish them to the refugee camps, they would turn all Sidon into a battlefield. A delegation of residents dared to present itself to the PLO at Ein Hilwe, and demanded the removal of the command post and arsenals to the camps. The terrorists responded with more terror. They rampaged through the town, shooting and beating on all sides and spreading threats of death...

Our faith that the Israelis would come gave confidence to the town's people. A commercial strike was announced. The merchants closed up their shops and the civilian population closeted itself at home. The terrorist response was not long in coming. They set fire to the main business street.... But now, never mind; it is not the first time that our property has gone up in flames; perhaps though, it will be the last.

Among the abuses of the PLO terrorists in the commercial centre over the years, there were break-ins, collection of protection money, daily acts of robbery and plunder. Terrorists would come to the store, dress themselves from head to toe, take whatever caught their fancy and depart after firing a rain of bullets into the shop or breaking the display window.... During the early years of terror, a few shopkeepers dared to resist. Then, two of them were kidnapped from their homes, tried as "enemies of the Palestinian revolution," executed and their bodies thrown into the sea. In other cases, booby-trapped cars exploded near the stores of the people concerned. Resistance quickly dwindled. You ask where the police were? Don't you know that the courts were not functioning, that there was no police force and that no one had any right to try a Palestinian for anything? A Lebanese, if he was smart, never complained to anyone. If he was stupid, he went to the PLO's security police. Soldiers of the Lebanese Army were afraid to leave their bases in uniform because at the first checkpoint — whether manned by followers of Jibril, Hawatmeh, Habash, or Fatah — they would be killed. Don't you know that Arafat's gangs simply eliminated the rule of law and allowed sheer anarchy to reign?

[Document 95]: A police officer, Sidon

The interview appeared in Ma'ariv, *14 July 1982 (translated from Hebrew).*

The Lebanese police was forced to enter into humiliating negotiations with the PLO and accept its ultimatums; the Lebanese police would limit itself to directing traffic and conducting "social" investigations of family disputes and neighbourhood strife.... They called us the "social police" and took upon themselves what they called "strategic security functions and political security." They disarmed us and forbade us to make arrests. They set up a police force of their own [Al-Amm a-Sha'bi] and equipped it with vehicles and equipment confiscated from us. The terrorist organizations divided the city into four police districts. The police ceased to function. The law courts were closed. Gangs of armed ruffians terrorized the population of southern Lebanon by humiliation, oppression, abuse, degradation, rape and murder. Our men were kidnapped and imprisoned at Qaishqatini. There, they were tortured and murdered.[65]

[Document 96]: Dr. Labib abu-Dahr, Sidon

Dr. Labib owns the ultra-modern Labib hospital in Sidon. He studied at the medical school of the American University in Beirut, and worked as a surgery intern in New York City before opening his hospital in 1974. He belongs to a prominent Sidon family. The interview appeared in Ha'aretz, *16 July 1982 (translated from Hebrew).*

I used to be blacklisted by the PLO. They wanted to blow up my facility and I had to hire armed men to watch the building and bodyguards for myself...

They had positioned two anti-aircraft guns right next to the building, one of them among the trees in the garden, the other near the eastern fence of the hospital. They are crazy. I asked them, "What do you want, that the Israelis destroy my hospital with their bombs?" They laughed like mad. Do you know why they positioned their guns near the hospital? Exactly for the same reason that they positioned their cannons near clinics, schools, churches and mosques. You call that "liberation fighters?" They are sheer criminals! They turned Sidon into their dominion and we, the local population, were exposed to their whims. You did well when you expelled them from the city; now you ought to evict them from the entire country. I hope that you Israelis will do it.

---

65. Another policeman, Hassan Samieh Jabar, said that he had been kidnapped by an armed gang of terrorists back in mid-1981, imprisoned and tortured. He rolled up his sleeves and showed arms full of burn marks. He said that the terrorists had used his body as an ashtray, even extinguishing cigarettes on his genitals.

[Document 97]: Majida, a Palestinian refugee, Ein Hilwe
Interview appeared in Ha'aretz, *28 July 1982 (translated from Hebrew).*

Almost all the men in the camp were members of one PLO organization or another. Almost all families made their livelihood from their association with the organizations, which paid salaries to us. But my husband has never killed anyone, he never left the camp, he always trained. The commanders are responsible for my personal disaster. I asked my husband to run away with our baby [when hostilities began], and my husband was prepared to go. But the commanders said that whoever tried to run away would be shot. May Allah curse all Arab countries: Jordan, Syria and Egypt! What did they do for the revolution? Nothing. Allah will yet punish them all.

[Document 98]: 'Abbas al-Haf, 55, a Palestinian refugee, Ein Hilwe
Interview appeared in Ha'aretz, *28 July 1982 (translated from Hebrew).*

I was not arrested [by the Israelis] because everyone knows that I am not a terrorist. I cannot be a terrorist because I am old and sick.... When I came here in 1948, there were much fewer people, only 10,000, and we were better off. We had some housing and UNRWA provided us with food stuffs.

In 1970, the situation got worse, when new refugees came in from Jordan, where they were expelled by King Hussein in Black September. But the situation became still worse in 1976, and in March 1978, when new refugee waves came in — those who had run away from the Phalangists, the Israeli army and Major Haddad's militias.

This past year there were some 50,000 people in the camp. We had electricity and water but no sewer system. Can you imagine a camp of 10,000 housing 50,000? Besides our tough living conditions, the PLO made life impossibe for us. Young Palestinians, who had migrated to oil-rich countries and sent money to their families, were arrested when they came to visit and were forced to join the PLO. University students, too, were compelled to join the organizations for at least a year.

We had a vocational school in the camp where we could learn carpentry, mechanics and electricity, but a year ago the PLO appointed a new director to the school, Dr. Mehsen. At the end of the school year, he refused to deliver diplomas to the students unless each graduate joined the PLO and fought for at least one year. Thus, about 800 of our students gave themselves up to the Israelis. They said the truth; they said they wanted their diplomas.

While the condition of the refugees was terrible, the PLO chiefs led quite a good life. Every week you could see them driving better and more modern cars which they had stolen. The Arab countries have allocated millions of dollars over the past 34 years to the Palestinians, but they did not use that money to build a sewer system in Ein Hilwe. The leaders spent the money in luxurious hotels in Paris.

This camp did not have to be destroyed, it could have remained intact. Leaflets were dropped from Israeli planes urging us to leave the camp, but the PLO would let no one go. My neighbour, Salem, tried to escape, but they shot him in the back and tied him to a pole until he died. In the camp some 300 people were killed. Who is to blame for their death? Please write: only the PLO who blocked their escape. Now there are again some 10,000 people left in the camp. Many PLO members are either under Israeli custody or ran away to Shtura and the Beqa'a. The women and children now live in schools, stores or just outdoors.

I have forgotten my anger against the Jews who caused me to leave my home in 1948. I have come to be reconciled with that development and I rebuilt my life at Ein Hilwe. Now my life has again been destroyed and I am no longer young or healthy. My hatred for the PLO by far surpasses the hatred I once felt towards the Jews. You can write in your newspaper in England.[66] everything I told you. You can write my name: Abbas al-Haj. Please write that the PLO has inflicted on the Palestinians their greatest disaster. Please write that the Israelis have thrown bombs on our houses and destroyed them. But houses can be rebuilt. The PLO has ruined our souls and our future, and those cannot be restored.

---

66. The Israeli journalist had to pass as a British correspondent in order to enter the camp; his Arab companions warned that they could not guarantee his safety otherwise.

[Document 99]: Salah Mar'i Khalil, 13, and Burhan Ahmed, 12, Nabatiye

On the day of the interview, the Red Cross was making arrangements to send the boys back to their parents in Syria. The interview appeared in Newsview *(Tel Aviv), 6 July 1982.*

We are Palestinians who lived, until six weeks ago, in a camp near Damascus. On our way to school we were intercepted by PLO people who told us that they would take us for a trip to Lebanon. We were not allowed to tell our parents or even say goodbye, and a day later we were in Nabatiye in a PLO training camp for children, who were trained in the use of the Russian Kalashnikov assault rifles. When the training was over, we were assigned to "active military duty," our parents still unaware of our fate. When the Zionist forces approached, we were manning a roadblock. Mar'i was injured in the arm by an Israeli bullet; we sought refuge in a cave. Our PLO mentors escaped and we remained until the shooting was over. We decided to surface, because Mar'i's arm was so painful and he was losing a lot of blood.

An Israeli army doctor patched the wounded arm after removing the bullet. Then the army took us over and provided us with a roof, clothing and food.

[Documents 100-112]: Comments and Topical Reports

[Document 100]: Dr. Khalil Turbiya, Beirut

Dr. Turbiya is one of the most renowned surgeons in Lebanon, and owns a private hospital. He visited Israel as a guest of the Israeli Committee for Aid to Lebanon. The interview was broadcast on Israel Television on 22 July 1982.

The chaos and destruction inflicted upon Lebanon is not our concern alone. It matters to the entire world. Lebanon is a major point in world history, and now a turning point in world thinking. I am not inclined to just answer questions, so let me talk from the top of my head, as this is the first meeting between us. Any improvisation on my part would be much more spontaneous and would directly emanate from the heart. I am going to make use at the same time of my heart, my conscience and my thinking...[67]

We would like to strive so that what happened in Lebanon will never occur again here or anywhere else, for no country in the world is likely to bear what we had to. Those who said there was a civil war between Muslims and Christians distorted the issue. We cannot renounce any one of our Lebanese citizens — exactly as we cannot renounce one inch of our territory — regardless of whether he is a Druze, a Muslim or a Shi'ite.[68] Muslims Shi'ites and Druze are dearer to me than the Christians, although I am a Christian believer and so is my son, but we are all Lebanese brethren and we love our country. Unfortunately, we incurred very difficult situations that could have decimated any other country. We were subjected to fear and to horrible acts of terror, which perhaps I could tell in detail later...

We want Lebanon's image in the world to be one of the civilization that contributed the first alphabet to humanity and whence the first ship sailed to the open sea.... But in recent years, our image was tarnished and we were turned into murderers and criminals in the process of defending our country against those who have burst into it...

As to the Palestinian organizations, I would like to refer to them on a personal level, because I'm a common man who has nothing to do with politics. All my life I have striven to contribute from what I learned in the US [medicine] and all I wanted was to serve my country.... When the Palestinians left Palestine, we hosted them very kindly in our houses and I personally treated them in the hospital.

---

67. Here, as elsewhere, passages lauding Israel were deleted due to their irrelevance to our subject matter.
68. Shi'ites are certainly Muslims, too, but in Lebanon, the term "Muslim" usually refers to the Sunni, while the Shi'ites, also called Mutawalis, are perceived as a separate community.

I treated them with all due respect, exactly like all the rest. At Tel al-Za'tar[69] we had some family property and I went to inspect it. I found there three armed people who immediately pointed their Kalashnikovs at me and said that I could not enter. I asked: Why can't they let me enter my land? They said that they decided to confiscate it for their benefit. I said to them, "If your goal is to recuperate your lost land [Palestine], then why do you confiscate the lands of others? Where is the logic? You only stand to lose if you behave that way. Everyone must retrieve his rights by moral and scientific methods. Look at the Israelis: they waited 2,000 years before they could return to their land and they used their best scientific brains to achieve that. They accomplished what they wanted in a scientific and honest fashion."

The apparent splits among the Lebanese are in fact non-existent. Only courageous Lebanese say what they think, while those who hide — we know nothing of their thinking, no matter whether they are Muslim, Christian, Shi'ite or Druze. When they are freed of outside pressure, they have the courage to say what they think, exactly as I have the courage now. When they speak the truth, they do not attack one another...

I am a Maronite Christian very deeply rooted in the land. For seven years I served in Al-Basto, which is the Sunni stronghold. I acquired many friends there, of whom I am very proud... I still visit them on every occasion and they continue to come to my house. Our household is one and we know how to host our guests in Lebanon.... So, we shall never leave Lebanon, we shall never give up one inch of it or one of its inhabitants.

Q: What do you think about Jumblatt's charge that Sarkis and Butrus are traitors?[70]

A: I do not want to go into political intrigues which are all related to competition over government seats. I reflect Lebanese truth, not Lebanese politics. This is precisely the politics which destroyed the country. We do not care what Jumblatt thinks or what Butrus and Sarkis want. Had Sarkis thought in the right direction our situation would have been different. I am saying this with regard to my president whom I respect very much. All successive Lebanese governments have worked for narrow-minded interests. Therefore, we need today a new policy to direct our country on a new basis, so that the civilized image of Lebanon can be restored...

69. A PLO stronghold in Beirut taken over by the Phalangists in 1976 after a bitter and bloody battle.
70. Walid Jumblatt is the son of the Druze leader Kamal Jumblatt, founder and head of the "Socialist Party" until his assassination in 1979. Elias Sarkis was president of Lebanon from 1975 to 1982. Fouad Butrus was foreign minister in Sarkis' administration.

East Beirut and West Beirut are not a problem for the Lebanese. Only today, I have a letter for one of my Muslim colleagues who works in the hospital of the American University. The letter will get to him despite the shooting.... Those who shoot from the East westwards, and from the West eastwards, are well-known mercenaries. They have started the war and they will pursue it, they are paid to do it and they are not Lebanese. These people do not know what Lebanon is and these people would not be mourned by Lebanon. In every house there is a rest room; those are the rest rooms of Lebanon... They will end by leaving Lebanon; they have no choice and we have no room for them. They are besieged now.[71]

And let me tell you frankly that we are grateful to Begin. We call him "Begin" without anv titles, because of the democratic regime in your country. We think he is a real man; who else could evict them [from Beirut]?

We are a civilized people, but they expel us from our country. They are armed groups who inflicted much suffering upon other people. They are able to arm another million persons; how could we possibly evict them from our country? How could we live under those circumstances? I want the entire world to know that. Just imagine, I am a doctor and I have a hospital. Occasionally I have to rush to the hospital to save lives; do I have to take leave of my family, each time I leave, as if I would never return home? Do I have to drive alone on the road in a state of war and terror?

Their terror is there to be seen by all. Why should we sacrifice our lives for it? What do they want to achieve? They brought in gangsters, murderers and other criminals from around the world, for the purpose of "retrieving Palestine." Will Palestine be retrieved if Lebanon is destroyed? Will they go back to Palestine after they ruin Lebanon? We are duty-bound to tell the world that we cannot yield to the sword. The era of the sword is over: we now live in a new era of civilization, of know-how, technology, brains and progress. There is no other way.

---

71. On the day of the interview the Israeli siege around PLO-held West Beirut was running into its eighth week.

[Document 101]: Interview with Bashir Jemayel

Bashir Jemayel, 34 years old, was elected president of Lebanon on 23 August 1982, and assassinated a few weeks later. At the time of the interview, he was the strongman of the Maronite Christians. The interview was broadcast by ABC News on 27 June 1982 and by ABC's news program "20/20" on 9 July 1982.

Jemayel: As far as we are concerned, we're looking for the liberation of our country. We are looking that all the foreigners get out — Syrians, Palestinians, and Israelis, and even the UNIFIL — we don't need any foreign armed presence in this country. As Lebanese, as a strong central government, as a strong central army, as once again the nation is reunited, we will take care of the security of our own country. We don't need anybody in this country and Arafat should understand that.

Interviewer: (Jemayel told me he received a telephone call last night. It was from his arch enemy, Yasser Arafat.) What did you and Yasser Arafat talk about?

A : I told him that it's enough. I told him that he destroyed the Lebanese army, he destroyed the Lebanese state, he destroyed the Syrian army, he destroyed to a certain extent the Syrian state. I told him that he made fun of the Saudis, of the Kuwaitis, of the Arabs, of the West, of everybody. It may work, but now he is dealing with the Israelis and this will not work. And he will not be able to do with the Israelis what he has been doing with the Lebanese army and the Syrian army. He should understand all that, and stop the whole zoo he is doing now in West Beirut to save more than twenty or thirty or 40,000 Lebanese people, who may be killed if he would continue to play his tricks and if he will continue to say with Habash and other people that Beirut will be Stalingrad.

He may do Stalingrad in his own village, in his own country. He doesn't have the right to speak and to make any Stalingrad or any other Stalingrad in West Beirut. This is what I told him.

Interviewer: How was the conversation? It seemed incredible to me, knowing the background, that you could speak.

A : He said that this is not the proper time to speak about all that on the phone. Well, but for the time being, it is not possible to meet in any case because you know what's the situation and he has to take his own decisions, first of all, to save thousands and thousands of Lebanese from death. The situation in West Beirut is really awful; it's because of the Palestinians, and it's a Palestinian responsibility, and he will have that on his conscience, in case he has any conscience; he will have all the responsibility for what is going on in West Beirut today.

And what was going on in Lebanon for eight years, he will have sooner or later to pay the price for that. I even don't know if it will not be a good idea to have later on a Nuremberg to put on trial all the people — Lebanese and foreigners — who have been responsible for what's going on now in the country, and to pay the responsibility for the 100,000 Lebanese killed. After all, someone is responsible for all that. Who is this someone? This must be found.

Interviewer: Is Israel your ally?

A : In politics, there is nothing permanent; you don't have permanent allies and permanent enemies. We are taking the maximum advantage and benefit of the changing of the balance of power and equilibrium of power in the Lebanon.

Here, our resistance was for eight years already, and now Shlomo Argov was assassinated, or they tried to assassinate Shlomo Argov in London.[72] The Israelis reacted. I didn't ask them to come. I didn't; I was not responsible for their entry here. It was done; it was not done for the advantage of the Lebanese, but definitely, for us, this was the only way to finish with all the problem.

Interviewer: Why didn't you join the fight?

A: It is not my fight. I told you, the Israelis are not doing that for me. The Israelis don't need me, maybe, on the ground. They have the strongest army in the world, or in this part of the world. They know exactly what they are doing and they are doing it for their own purposes.

My aim and my goal and my target is that this country be freed. We will establish a new political regime for both Christians and Muslims, a new basis of equilibrium, equal chances, equal rights, equal opportunities for everybody, a real modern state, democratic state, liberal state, with a real democracy, parliamentary system, a liberal system in economics, and for the private property and so on and so forth. We are going to start building up this

72. Argov was the Israeli ambassador in London. The attempt on his life on 4 June 1982 triggered the Israeli reprisals against PLO positions in Lebanon, which escalated into a full-fledged Israeli incursion to mop up all southern Lebanon from the PLO presence.

new country. And our turn in these developments will be that, in due time, we will have the legal authority in the hands of the real people of Lebanon and we can start again building from the very beginning the new country.

And when the country will be stabilized, it will be stabilization all around. Because the Lebanon was weak, the Syrians are here, the Israelis are here and the war is not over yet. I will dare to say that the war has not started yet. The actual war has not started. The fight for Beirut has not started yet and the fight in the Beqa'a has not started yet, and I don't know if the fire in the Beqa'a will not lead to a major conflict between Israel and the Syrians.

A weak president means a weak Lebanon; a weak Lebanon means destabilization for the whole area. Under President Reagan, under the new administration, I feel absolutely secure. I feel that both of us, the Americans and their national interests in Lebanon, and in the Middle East, are one and, in the fight between the major superpowers, definitely we are on the side of the Occident and of the West, and this has started to be understood now.

Interviewer: Will the fighting ever stop?

A : Definitely, it will have to stop. Definitely, we are living now the last hours of eight years of war. Definitely, we are starting now to think about after the war.

In short, if I must figure something, I will say that we have, out of a population of three million inhabitants, more than 100,000 killed, more than 300,000 wounded and almost half of the population uprooted from its villages and its homes and places.

Interviewer: In eight years of fighting?

A : In eight years of fighting. And now, a lot of people are coming back to all the south because the Israelis are here. Today a lot of people are coming to all the villages where the Israelis are entering and the situation — I'm not going to say that it's becoming normal; but since then, this country is being reunited every day more and more.

We always kept saying that Lebanon is easy to eat, but almost impossible to digest. The Syrians and the Palestinians didn't understand that; they kept playing tricks in Lebanon, they kept playing with fire in Lebanon. We kept telling them, don't. They never understood, and here we are.

Interviewer: (Until very recently, it was Jemayel who was never understood. When 20/20 first interviewed him a year and a half ago, he was a political unknown outside his own country — a man with a cause virtually no international diplomat or newsperson even wanted to hear).

A : Until now, US public opinion didn't know that we are fighting the same combat and the same fight, for the same values and the same interests.

Interviewer: As the United States?

A : As the United States. And I think that this is why we were destroyed.

Interviewer: A year ago, or less, American officials wouldn't even return your telephone calls. What have they discovered?

A : I must say, to be fair, that when we started to be organized, the US started to understand us more and more. And the more united and the more organized we were, the more the US was giving us a more responsible ear and they were listening more and more to what we had to say. You are right to say that a few months ago they would even not return my calls; I must say that today it's basically a different situation.

[Document 102]: United Nations General Assembly speech by Lebanese UN Ambassador Edouard Ghorra

Ambassador Ghorra delivered this speech on 14 October 1976.

[The Palestinians] transformed most — if not all — of the refugee camps into military bastions around our major cities.... Moreover, common-law criminals, fleeing from Lebanese justice, found shelter and protection in the camps.... Palestinian elements belonging to various splinter organizations resorted to kidnapping Lebanese, and sometimes foreigners, holding them prisoners, questioning them and even sometimes killing them.... They committed all sorts of crimes in Lebanon, and also escaped Lebanese justice in the protection of the camps. They smuggled goods into Lebanon and openly sold them on our streets. They went so far as to demand protection money from many individuals and owners of buildings and factories situated in the vicinity of their camps.

[Document 103]: Speech by Syrian President Assad

President Hafez Assad delivered this speech to the Council of District Governments on 20 July 1976. He criticized PLO violence and intervention in Lebanon.

What connection does Syria have to the events now taking place in Lebanon? My fellow citizens, I want you to pay close attention to this matter. There are people on the outside who want to infiltrate the ranks and ask: What do the events in Lebanon have to do with us? Why is Syria getting embroiled in the events in Lebanon?.... Historically, Syria and Lebanon are one country and one people. History teaches us that [those living in] Syria and Lebanon are one people, and they thus have genuine common interests involved, leading to genuine common security concerns and close relations between people in the two countries. Thousands of families in Syria have branches in Lebanon, and thousands of families in Lebanon have branches in Syria. Thus, as a result of this common history, geography and these events, about one-half million Syrians lived in Lebanon before the recent incidents. They worked at various occupations there as merchants, doctors, labourers, attorneys, and the like These people have returned to Syria as a result of recent events. There are now at least one-half million Lebanese refugees in Syria. 150,000 of our Palestinian brothers living in Lebanon have now come to Syria. Thus, about one million people have entered Syria as a result of these events. I believe we all can see the serious problem created by the entry of some one million people into a country whose population is less than nine million.

With respect to the fighting between the PLO and the Christians, Assad said:

I asked brother Yasser Arafat to consider how these circumstances constitute a danger to continued united action, and what a serious matter it is for the Palestinian fighters to get so basically involved in this fighting. I told him then, and I still say to him: I cannot understand the connection between the Palestinians' fight in the heights of Mount Lebanon and the liberation of Palestine. Whoever wants to liberate Jounieh and Tripoli does not want to liberate Palestine, even if he says he does.

This is what they told me in 1970. Remember, brothers, what was said in Jordan in 1970. At that time, they coined the slogan: 'Power, all power to the Resistance; Power, all power to the Revolution; Palestine will be liberated through Amman.' This is now happening once again in Lebanon. At that meeting, Yasser Arafat promised me that he would not take part in the fighting. He came to Lebanon in order to tell that to the others. I do not want to get into a lot of details here, but I do want to say that this was not implemented at all. At any rate, the fighting ceased after a number of days. But as you remember, it stopped [only] after Dean Brown[73] arrived in Beirut.

[Document 104]: Interview with a Palestinian refugee in Lebanon

This interview of Basam Jaber Darwish Dweikat, originally from the West Bank, was broadcast on Israel Television on 23 July 1982 (translated from Arabic).

I am from the village of Rujeib, 3 kilometres east of Nablus. I studied in an elementary school in the village, then completed high school in Al-Najah College in Nablus. In 1973, I got permission to leave Israel for Lebanon. I enrolled in the university and completed a BA degree in law. Now I am working on my masters degree.[74]

Every commander has to think very well whether he is helping his people or hurting it. People like Saddam Hussein[75] or Yasser Arafat brought no benefit to their peoples.... They caused damage and did nothing useful.... Yasser Arafat was actually cheated, if I can say that. All the Arab countries cheated him, as did many other countries. Arafat would not have started a war against Israel if he knew that he relied only upon his PLO fighters. He would not have started a war where Syria sits by and does nothing, while at the same time alleging — I insist, "alleging" — that its presence in Lebanon is aimed at defending the Palestinian revolution. But in fact this is not true. Syria beat the Palestinians once before,[76] but now she beat them even more seriously. Therefore, Arafat was bound to lose. He lost because he counted on people that he should not have counted on. I would have preferred if he had rather relied on Sadat. That was better than relying on Hafez al-Assad. I am responsible for what I am saying, for Sadat neither promised nor delivered, but Assad promised and never delivered. Even the UN has promised much to the Palestinians, but delivered nothing. If they [the PLO] had learned something from the lesson of Jordan,[77] then what is happening today in Lebanon could have been avoided.... Our proverb says that "the believer does not fall twice in the same trap."

They behaved in Lebanon exactly the same way they had in Jordan. This only proves that their conduct has become second nature to them. Therefore, I am saying that this could happen in any Arab country. Finally, I would like to say

---

73. A U.S. State Department trouble-shooting official appointed by President Ford.
74. Basam was employed by the PLO as a judge in one of its "popular courts."
75. The president of Iraq.
76. In 1976, Syria attacked the Palestinians in Lebanon before turning against the Christians.
77. He is referring to "Black September" in 1970, when the PLO was expelled from Jordan after trying to take over the country.

a word to my comrades in Lebanon: one must remain a human being before anything else. One must not forget his human nature. The Lebanese people have incurred a lot of suffering from us. They have made a great sacrifice for us and they suffered a great deal. We must now take the initiative and alleviate this burden from them by removing our evil-doing away from them. If there are still armed fighters around, I beg them to lay down their weapons and leave Lebanon so that it can live in security. They are good people and they deserve to live securely.

[Document 105]: Christian journalist reports from Lebanon

French author François Cellier wrote this report after visiting Lebanon with a delegation of Christian journalists and writers, from 29 June to 1 July 1982 (translated from French).

Our delegation was made up of 44 people: about a dozen international representatives (including myself representing France), plus representatives of the major American Christian television stations, radio channels and newspapers; an American congressman; and two soldiers who escorted us. The purpose of our mission to Lebanon was to ascertain the facts, and to hear the point of view of Lebanese Christian political and military leaders.

We left Jerusalem on 29 June, and our first stop was Kibbutz Ayelet Hashahar, near Metulla. Late in the afternoon, we visited the famous castle of Beaufort. It is a ruined fortress, perched high in the hills, dominating the Galilee and the valleys of Lebanon. The fighting there was very intense, as this citadel crammed with cannons and machine-guns seemed impregnable, and yet it fell to Zahal — the Israel Defence Forces!

That evening we had a press conference with Major Sa'ad Haddad, commander of the Free Lebanon Forces. He is a friendly and brave man and a sincere Christian. He reaffirmed his feelings of friendship and gratitude towards Israel; he is a true precursor of an Israeli-Lebanese peace. We spoke to the people under his protection: Lebanese Christians and Arab refugees. They told us how glad they were to be rid of PLO oppression.

We now returned to our kibbutz. At five o-clock in the morning we set out for Beirut, visiting Qlei'a, Marj'ayun, Nabatiye, Damour and Sidon. The ruins and bullet-ridden or gutted houses and buildings testified to the intensity of the fighting that had taken place. The people we met on the way expressed their relief at having been liberated. At Damour, a man told us that he had spent ten days in a refrigerator in order to elude detection and save his life. Everywhere we saw the PLO's propaganda posters, and we realized how great a psychological influence it must have had. At Sidon, there was a great deal of damage, but we also saw the Lebanese population making a spectacular return to life, and resuming their commercial activities in front of gutted shop facades.

From the outlying hills around Beirut we observed the airport, a strategic point of combat. Mingled among columns of tanks and trucks of the Israeli army and the Lebanese Defence Forces, we arrived in the outskirts of the capital. Despite all the dust and noise and military activity, we did not feel aware of any warlike tension. It was as if everything was finished.... We visited various quarters of Beirut under Lebanese escort (our Israeli escort had passed us on to them) and we were then taken to the Monastery of St. Nicholas (Anamun Kesruan), where we spent the night.

Before beginning the series of press conferences with Christian leaders, we visited the area bordering the PLO enclave in West Beirut. The Lebanese soldiers took us to the top of a damaged building, where we quietly observed their fortified area. Throughout this visit we heard only one or two gunshots. Everything was calm, but there was a strong atmosphere of tension. The few Lebanese who still lived in this area, near to the PLO, told us how much they had suffered and how happy they now were, but also expressed their regret at not being completely liberated from the PLO presence. One of them even told me that he would even have preferred another hundred or two hundred civilians having been made victims in a final assault, providing the PLO was destroyed, so much had they suffered from them...

Late in the afternoon we met Mr. Pierre Jemayel, head of the Kataeb Democratic Party, at Saifi. The press conference took place, after the Lebanese joined our delegation, in an atmosphere of solemnity, owing to the lordly demeanour of this old political leader.

The main point to emerge from this conference — when divorced from the political form of expression — was that Pierre Jemayel acknowledged that Israel, for its own reasons, had put an end to a desperate situation, permitting Lebanon to regain its sovereignty. Mr. Pierre Jemayel did not hesitate to denounce the hypocrisy of the Western states who, for seven years, had allowed disaster to overtake his country without raising a finger. Only Israel had done anything.

We next visited the home of President Camille Chamoun, head of the Lebanese Front and the National Liberal Party, in Ashrafieh. He received us cordially and I began the discussion by asking his opinion about a prophecy of Isaiah concerning Lebanon, a text more than two thousand seven hundred years old:

Is it not yet a very little while, and Lebanon shall be turned into a fruitful field, and the fruitful field shall be esteemed as a forest?

And in that day shall the deaf hear the words of the book, and the eyes of the blind shall see out of obscurity, and out of darkness.

The meek also shall increase their joy in the Lord, and the poor among men shall rejoice in the Holy One of Israel.

For the terrible one is brought to nought, and the scorner is consumed, and all that watch for iniquity are cut off.

(Isaiah XIX, 17-20)

When I read it aloud, he said he knew this passage and recognized its providential present-day significance.... It is a text which bears a hope of liberation for his country with the aid of Israel.

After this press conference, we visited the headquarters of Mr. Bashir Jemayel, head of the Lebanese Resistance Forces. He is likely to become the future strongman of the country, for he seems determined to realize his patriotic ambitions. He honestly admitted that the action of the Israel Defence Forces has permitted a solution to the Lebanese problem, and expressed his gratitude. He thought that one day a process of normalization could take place between the two countries.

In the evening, a picturesque supper was prepared for us by Father Boulos Naaman, head of the Maronite community in Lebanon and the Middle East. The press conference here had a markedly Christian character, for we were able to pray with him and his monks for peace in Lebanon, and we sang hymns with them. Two of our delegates, famous singers — Merv and Merla Watson — displayed their talents at the end of the meal, and then a group of monks astonished us with Aramaic chants more than two thousand years old, the very ones Jesus and his disciples must have sung.... Father Boulos Naaman gave us an objective historical account of the development of the situation. He told us that, that very morning, he had officiated at the burial of the eleventh of his priests to be slaughtered (this one was killed by the Druze). All the priests were elderly men, all had attempted to carry out a mediation effort between the opposing factions, and their Christian ministry of conciliation had cost them their lives. Boulos Naaman declared himself most favourable to the Israeli intervention, but he regretted that it had not pushed back the Syrian army beyond the Lebanese borders instead of concentrating its attention on the PLO abscess in West Beirut.

After two or three hours rest on camp beds in the cells of these hospitable monks, we left Beirut on our return journey, passing through Sidon, where we again talked to Arab and Christian civilians and even to some Arab children aged twelve to fifteen, who by force or persuasion had been drafted into the ranks of the PLO. Again, we were reminded that women and children had served as hostages or as a shield for PLO gunmen firing at Israeli soldiers. As the Israelis were unable to fire back, they lost many lives due to this stratagem.

Then our bus broke down! We had to disperse ourselves throughout the length of the Israeli military convoy which stretched for kilometres. With our baggage and cameras, we jumped into trucks or half-track vehicles, in an attempt to reach Haifa airport to catch our Arkia airplane, which was waiting to take us to Jerusalem, where, at 6 p.m., we were to have a press conference with Prime Minister Menahem Begin. Only a small group of us succeeded in reaching the Knesset in time for an excellent TV interview with the prime minister. For my part, I arrived just in time for a reception which had been arranged at the headquarters of the International Christian Embassy.

Next morning, I was present at the conclusion of the press conference given by M. Gutmann, Secretary-General of the French Foreign Ministry, M. Delaye, adviser to Minister Claude Cheysson, and Israeli Foreign Minister Yitzhak Shamir. I was able to give M. Gutmann a brief account of my impressions of Beirut. At this point M. Bonnefous, the French ambassador in Israel, broke in, telling M. Gutmann, "Pay no attention to them. The Christian Embassy isn't credible: they are not to be taken seriously." In other words, we are regarded as pro-Israeli!

This, unfortunately, is the attitude which prevails amongst French officials.... It's a pity, for President Mitterand was not ashamed to declare himself the friend of Israel. Moreover, Mr. Begin is well-disposed towards us, as well as Major Haddad, and as for Messrs. Camille Chamoun, Pierre and Bashir Jemayel and Father Boulos Naaman, they all related to us seriously, aware of our credibility both in the present and with regard to the future. We believe that our mission, which will be relayed to more than 50 million television viewers and readers of the international press, will have a genuine impact, and that the road of peace which we have travelled from Jerusalem to Beirut will remain open. This is what both the Israeli and the Lebanese peoples and their leaders want. One day our Western officials will have to acknowledge that if the Israeli intervention served Israel's interests, it also served the interests of the Lebanese people whom it freed from the PLO, and also the interests of the nations of the free world, where the cancer of terrorism was developing to the point of becoming a fatal and incurable affliction.

In conclusion of this chronological account of our "Cedars of Lebanon" operation, here is the substance of the opinions expressed by the Christian leaders:

The attention of the world community has been focused on the situation of the PLO and not on the desperate situation of the Lebanese people — Christians, Druze and Muslims.

The activities of the PLO in Lebanon have ruined the Lebanese people and state without anything having been gained for the Palestinian people.

Lebanon's problems cannot be solved until the foreign forces have left Lebanon.

The vast scale of the PLO's military preparations is inexplicable, unless the PLO was preparing for a major offensive against Israel, which was thwarted by the Israeli intervention.

The PLO military buildup in Lebanon, which included Soviet arms, was on an enormous scale. It was probably intended for a major operation, masterminded by the Soviets.

The figures given for the destruction and casualties caused by the Israel Defence Forces have been grossly exaggerated.

It is clear that the PLO centres in Lebanon provided the instruction, logistics and equipment for numerous terrorist organizations, including the Red Brigades in Italy, the Bader-Meinhof and Neo-Nazis in Germany, the ETA Basque separatists in Spain and many other organizations. The Peace for Galilee operation of the Israel Defence Forces has finally destroyed the headquarters of terrorism and international subversion.

At the present time (2 July 1982), the Europeans ought to preserve a vigilant neutrality in order not to complicate a typically Oriental situation — i.e. one that is infinitely complex and impenetrable to Western logic. Those most competent to solve the problems of the Middle East are always the Jews and the Arabs themselves... with the intelligent mediation of the United States, within the framework of the Camp David Accords, which have already produced the precedent of the Israel-Egyptian peace treaty.

[Document 106]: Nabatiye workshop for booby-traps
The IDF spokesman issued the following report on 27 June 1982.

A workshop in which PLO terrorists had produced a variety of booby-traps was discovered by the Israel Defence Forces (IDF) in the southern Lebanese town of Nabatiye. Many of the devices found in the workshop were common, everyday objects in which explosives had been concealed. They were made in such a way that ordinary manipulation of the object would set off the concealed explosive.

Two major types of sophisticated booby-traps were discovered:

* Devices implanted in various weapons, including mines, rifle magazine clips, high-explosive bricks and other military hardware;

* Devices implanted in common objects, such as cigarette packages, household electric-connection boxes and cans of food.

The PLO terrorists also frequently disguised their sabotage and other destructive weapons. For example, road mines were camouflaged to look like clumps of earth.

Following are some of the booby-traps found spread over the battlefield area and explanations of how they operate:

1. Disguised anti-personnel mines:
   Anti-personnel mines, type 3-PMA (made in Yugoslavia) and M-59 (made in France), were disguised by PLO terrorists to look like clumps of earth. These mines were non-symmetrically shaped and painted a brown earth-colour.

   The purpose of disguising these weapons was:

   * To make it almost impossible to detect and discover the mines simply by looking at them;
   * To facilitate the planting of the mines over large areas without having to dig in the ground;
   * To increase the effective radius of damage by the addition of an outside cover made of material that splinters.

2. Booby-traps activated by movement (example: a surgical syringe):

   The mechanism contains the body of a regular medical syringe into which an iron ball was inserted. The upper part of the syringe is covered by a rubber seal containing the uncovered end of two insulated electrical wires. The device is connected to an explosive brick.

   When ready to explode, the iron ball is at the bottom side of the syringe. The trap is activated by moving the syringe so that the iron ball touches the electrical wires and closes the electric circuit which activates the charge.

3. An explosive device activated by the movement of a mercury ampoule:

   The mechanism in this black plastic box was originally designed for the automatic operation and control of lighting systems. After dismantling the mechanism and removing it from the box, the PLO terrorists replaced it with plastic explosive powder.

   A mercury ampoule placed in the box contains the tips of the electrical wires. Before use, the mercury is in a position which does not allow a connection between the electrical wires. However, any movement of the mercury ampoule results in closing the electrical circuit, thus causing the device to explode.

Anti-personnel mine M-59 (back cover).

Anti-personnel mine M-59 (front cover).

A booby-trap activated by the movement of an improvised electrical starter.

The black plastic box.

4. Booby-trapped Kalashnikov magazine:

   A pair of rifle magazines was filled with plastic explosive powder connected to an as yet unknown electrical mechanism. Five bullets were placed in the magazine so that the trap was not recognizable. The release of the bullets activates the explosive powder inside the magazine.

5. Disguised booby-trapped sabotage bricks (type T-500):

   An explosive brick is wrapped in styrofoam containing a large quantity of nails and shaped with plaster to look like a stone. A surgical syringe at the bottom of the device acts as a trigger. The explosion is triggered by raising the stone-shaped brick, or by arranging it so that a spring inside the surgical syringe activates an electric circuit and triggers the explosion.

   Raising the stone-shaped brick, or setting a spring inside it, activates an electric circuit that triggers the surgical syringe and sets off an explosion.

6. A booby-trapped explosive brick:

   The hollow-centred brick contains a trigger and a mechanism for its release. By raising the brick, the trigger is released and the booby-trapped device explodes.

7. A booby-trapped cigarette package:

   The cigarette package is emptied of its contents, and filled with explosive powder and an as yet unknown triggering device. Opening the package activates the explosive charge. (Dark stains caused by the explosive powder enable detection.)

8. Booby-trapped food cans:

   An empty food can is filled with explosive powder and steel nails. A surgical syringe acts as a trigger. The device is activated by raising or moving the tin can.

A booby-trapped cigarette package (note the dark stain at the bottom).

[Document 107]: PLO arms dumps in civilian facilities
The IDF spokesman issued the following report on 27 June 1982.

The Palestine Liberation Organization (PLO) terrorists hid tons of arms and ammunition in private homes, mosques and other civilian locations in southern Lebanon. These arms were discovered by the Israel Defence Forces during Operation Peace for Galilee.

Initial estimates show that thousands of PLO weapons were captured, including more than 100 tanks (Soviet T-34/54/55 tanks), machine guns, RPG bazookas, artillery guns of various sorts, radar-guided machine guns and tons of ammunition.

These crates of Soviet-made light arms were among the weapons caches discovered during Operation Peace for Galilee.

This Soviet-made 130mm artillery gun, found east of Rashidiye, was among the weapons captured in southern Lebanon, which had been used by the PLO to shell Nahariya in northern Israel.

This 106mm recoilless rifle, mounted on a jeep, was among the vast quantities of military equipment found in the PLO terrorist arsenal in southern Lebanon.

[Document 108]: PLO Attacks on Jewish targets
The IDF spokesman issued the following report on 20 June 1982.

The following is a partial list of attacks on Jewish targets in various countries carried out by Arab terrorist groups or with their encouragement:

GERMANY

9 November 1969:	A time bomb was discovered in Berlin's Jewish Community Centre; it was planted by Habash's Popular Front.
13 February 1970:	A Jewish old age home in West Germany was set on fire; 2 inmates died and several others were injured.
4 November 1972:	A letter-bomb was received at a branch office of the Zionist youth organization in Frankfurt.
19 August 1975:	A shipment of letter-bombs was addressed to the head of the Jewish community in Berlin. The package exploded in a German police car without causing any damage.
15 October 1978:	Two explosive charges were discovered in West Germany near a Jewish community centre building and a Jewish store. The charges were laid by Sa'iqa.

15 January 1980:	An explosive charge went off in a Jewish-owned restaurant in West Berlin, killing a 19-month-old-baby, wounding 24 other people and damaging the building.

FRANCE

3 August 1974:	A booby-trapped car exploded in Paris near the offices of the Jewish Welfare Organization for France. The device was planted by Habash's Popular Front.
10 July 1976:	An explosive charge went off in the Paris offices of B'nai Brith.
27 March 1979:	A bomb placed in a Jewish restaurant in Paris by Sa'iqa exploded and 26 people were injured.
27 March 1979:	An explosive device was detonated in a Jewish-owned drugstore in Paris.
7 April 1979:	Paris police dismantled a time-bomb hidden in the satchel of a motorcycle parked outside a cinema showing a film during "Jewish Culture Week." Sa'iqa claimed responsibility.
4 October 1980:	An explosive device detonated near the synagogue on Rue Copernic in Paris, killed 3 and wounded 20 other people.
25 November 1980:	A travel bureau in Paris, which organized trips to Egypt and Israel, was attacked by a terrorist. The Jewish manager and his wife were murdered and a local employee injured.

SWITZERLAND

11 November 1972:	Letter-bombs were sent to Jewish organizations in Geneva and to the homes of an Israeli delegation there.

GREAT BRITAIN

18 August 1969: An explosion at Marks and Spencers in London, causing no injuries, was perpetrated by Habash's Popular Front.

11 November 1972: 14 letter-bombs were received by prominent Jews and Jewish organizations. A Jewish diamond merchant was severely injured when one of the letter-bombs exploded.

30 December 1973: Lord Sieff, a leader of British Jewry, was injured in an assassination attempt perpetrated by Habash's Popular Front.

BELGIUM

27 July 1980: Hand grenades were thrown by terrorists, apparently members of Fatah, at a group of Jewish youths and children near the Agudat Israel offices in Antwerp. One French boy was killed and a number of other young people were wounded. The attack was aimed at Jewish organizations and institutions in Antwerp and Brussels.

20 October 1981: A booby-trapped car exploded opposite the Portuguese Synagogue in Antwerp, 20 minutes before the opening of Simchat Torah services, killing 3 people and wounding 100.

HOLLAND

5 September 1975: 4 terrorists with Syrian passports, members of Sa‘iqa, were arrested in Amsterdam. They had intended to take 12 train passengers hostage, in order to force a halt to Dutch support for Jewish immigrants.

ITALY

25 September 1976: A bomb was thrown into the HIAS (Hebrew Immigrant Aid Society) office in Rome.

7 October 1981: A bomb exploded outside the main Rome post office — a place frequented by Jewish emigrants from Russia — wounding 2 people.

SPAIN

3 March 1980	A terrorist, belonging to the Abu Nidal group, murdered a Spanish attorney and his daughter in Madrid. The attack was aimed at the honorary president of the Madrid Jewish community.

AUSTRIA

29 September 1973:	Sa'iqa terrorists took over a train carrying Jewish emigrants from the Soviet Union, while it was stopped at the Marchegg border station. 3 Jews were held hostage, and the terrorists demanded that Austria close the Schoenau Castle immigrant transit camp in exchange for their release.
22 April 1979:	An explosive device went off in the Jewish community building and synagogue in Vienna, causing no injuries.
26 April 1979:	Attempts were made by Fatah to sabotage the central fuel storage tanks and to murder the head of the Jewish community in Vienna.
1 May 1981:	Heinz Nittel, chairman of the Israel-Austria Friendship Association was shot and killed by members of the Abu Nidal group.
29 August 1981:	Terrorists from the Abu Nidal group attacked a synagogue in Vienna with hand grenades and sub-machine guns. 2 Jewish people were killed and 19 others wounded, including 2 Jewish children and 2 Austrian policemen.
4 February 1982:	An explosive device was detonated at the entrance of the house of the Chief Rabbi of Vienna, causing property damage but no injuries.

UNITED STATES

26 July 1977:	An explosive charge was discovered at the house of the head of the American-Israel Public Affairs Committee (AIPAC) in Washington. No one was injured.

CANADA

21 November 1972:	4 letter-bombs were discovered addressed to Jews in Toronto.

TURKEY

2 January 1980:	The manager of the El Al office in Istanbul was murdered by 3 terrorists, while parking his car near his home.

IRAN

23 August 1969:	An explosive charge went off in a Jewish school, causing slight property damage.
12 May 1977:	2 Iranians attempted to break into the Jewish Agency offices, apparently acting on behalf of the Iranian underground.

CYPRUS

12 March 1973:	A Jewish merchant was murdered by a Jordanian student belonging to Fatah (Black September). The assassin escaped.

VENEZUELA

12 January 1978:	An explosive device went off near the office of the Federation of Jewish Organizations, causing property damage.

GUATEMALA

23 May 1980:	A Jewish community leader was murdered.

ARGENTINA

20 September 1972:	The Buenos Aires synagogue was sabotaged.
3 October 1979:	An explosive device was detonated in the playground of the Jewish school in Buenos Aires, causing property damage.

7 August 1980:	An explosive charge was detonated near the Jerusalem Synagogue in Bueno Aires.

COSTA RICA

29 April 1973:	A Molotov cocktail was thrown at a synagogue.

MALAYSIA

4 October 1972:	Letter-bombs were sent by Fatah (Black September) to destinations in Israel and abroad. Recipients included HIAS, Jewish leaders in Rhodesia, and Hadassah in New York.

EGYPT

29 April 1980:	An explosive device went off at the synagogue in Cairo.
16 February 1981:	3 Palestinians, members of Fatah, and 2 Egyptians were arrested on suspicion of planning to blow up a synagogue and the Israeli embassy building.

[Document 109]: Attacks on diplomatic personnel in West Beirut by PLO and allies

The IDF spokesman issued the following report on 25 May 1982.

Despite the presence of Syrian occupation troops in Lebanon under the guise of the fictitious "Arab Deterrent Force," that hamstrung country continues to be plagued by violence.

West Beirut, which is completely dominated by Syrian and PLO personnel, has become the hub of a pattern of hostilities directed, on numerous occasions, against foreign diplomatic personnel and missions.

Since September 1980, more than 40 attacks have been perpetrated against foreign embassies in West Beirut.

A detailed listing of these attacks follows:

27 September 1980	Missiles fired at American embassy hit second and fourth floors.

3 October 1980	Missiles fired at Iraqi and Iranian embassies heavily damaged both buildings.
9 October 1980	Four explosions occurred: 1. Bomb exploded in car of Danish ambassador next to his home in Al-Rusha (also residence of US military attaché). 2. Bomb exploded at entrance to home of Swiss ambassador (in building in Al-Rusha which also serves as residence of Canadian ambassador). 3. Bomb exploded at residence of Yugoslav ambassador. 4. Bomb exploded at residence of Greek consul.
11 October 1980	Car belonging to Belgian embassy's second secretary was broken into, while parked near "Beirut" theatre.
27 December 1980	Missile fired at garden of French embassy, causing an embassy car to explode.
7 January 1981	Lebanese government received urgent cable from Swiss government, demanding increased security for Swiss embassy and its diplomatic corps — in aftermath of threats received at embassy.
6 February 1981	Jordanian consul and attendant kidnapped from consul's home in West Beirut, after two bodyguards were murdered.
27 February 1981	Two employees of Iraqi embassy murdered in course of attack on ambassador's car.
1 March 1981	Tunisian diplomat kidnapped by armed individuals, later released.
10 March 1981	Vehicle escorting French ambassador hit by gunfire.

2 April 1981	Iraqi diplomat murdered in vicinity of Iraqi embassy.
7 April 1981	Missiles fired at French embassy in West Beirut.
25 May 1981	Missiles fired at American embassy.
3 June 1981	First secretary of Iraqi embassy wounded by gunfire.
7 June 1981	First secretary of Bulgarian embassy wounded by gunfire.
26 June 1981	Missile fire directed at Kuwaiti embassy.
26 June 1981	Press adviser at French embassy kidnapped.
27 August 1981	Missile fire directed at Saudi Arabian embassy.
28 August 1981	RPG rocket fired at Saudi Arabian embassy in Beirut, causing heavy damage to building.
4 September 1981	Assassination attempt on life of French ambassador and his chauffeur, at entrance to ambassador's home.
	Rockets fired at offices of Libyan legation.
19 September 1981	Coordinator for UN Development Programmes attacked and robbed. Car belonging to German embassy's cultural attaché stolen.
21 September 1981	Car belonging to Iranian consul in Beirut stolen.
17 October 1981	Assassination attempt on life of Iranian consul; car hit by ten bullets.
15 December 1981	Rigged car exploded next to Iraqi embassy,

	killing 51 people (32 Iraqis and 19 bystanders, mostly Lebanese and Palestinians) and wounding about 70; Iraqi ambassador among those killed.
December 1981	Explosive device went off in car of Egyptian diplomat.
26 December 1981	Tunisian embassy's social affairs attaché wounded by gunfire.
13 January 1982	First consul at Algerian embassy kidnapped from home, later found dead in southern Beirut.
31 January 1982	Bomb exploded at entrance to Moroccan embassy, damaging property.
18 February 1982	Explosion near Turkish Cultural Centre in West Beirut.
15 March 1982	Lebanese civilian, serving as British embassy's second secretary, kidnapped; released following day (apparently in return for ransom).
15 March 1982	Explosion next to Egyptian embassy in West Beirut.
16 March 1982	Explosion next to Egyptian embassy in West Beirut.
30 March 1982	French ambassador stopped at Syrian roadblock in eastern Lebanon.
12 April 1982	Rockets fired at American embassy in Beirut.
15 April 1982	Employee of French embassy and pregnant wife murdered in West Beirut.
19 April 1982	Explosive charge went off at entrance to Agence France Presse news agency in West Beirut.

9 May 1982	Second floor of home of French diplomat residing in West Beirut hit by missile.
24 May 1982	Rigged car exploded at French embassy building in West Beirut; 14 persons killed (including French security men); 21 persons wounded.
24 May 1982	Yugoslav ambassador's car attacked by three armed men in Beirut.

Altogether, more than 30 foreign embassies have been the victims of bombings and sabotage attempts since the start of hostilities in Lebanon (according to *Al-Nahar al-Arabi wa-Dawli*, Beirut, 23 January 1982). More than 100 cars belonging to foreign diplomats have been stolen. According to some sources, the diplomatic corps in Beirut has had to endure many thefts and humiliations. Recently there has been an exit of foreign diplomats from the Kuwaiti, Jordanian, United Arab Emirates and German embassies. The British embassy has reduced its staff.

Those embassies which have remained in Lebanon have created elaborate security systems and have imported their own security men to safeguard their offices. The American embassy posted marines to guard the embassy from within. The French embassy deployed paratroopers in the embassy compound in anticipation of an attack. Arab embassies have used local armed factions to protect their offices.

Most ambassadors in Beirut travel exclusively in bullet-proof cars and are escorted by armed guards. The diplomatic corps is now characterized by diplomats who are either beginning or ending their careers in the foreign service.

Since the start of 1982, the Lebanese government has established a special security contingent to guard foreign embassies. However, in view of the continuing violence and bloodshed in Lebanon, all indications are that this effort, too, will fail.

[Document 110]: Interview with Congressman Charles Wilson
The Texan democrat was interviewed on Israel Radio on 26 June 1982.

Congressman Wilson: The biggest surprise that I had was the enthusiasm — the universal enthusiasm — with which the Lebanese welcomed the Israeli army.

Q: What do these Lebanese, whom you met, want today from Israel?

A: I guess the easiest way to describe what they want from Israel is security. They, I think, have some self-doubts about their ability to get their act together, assuming that the Israelis and the Syrians and the PLO leave. But their main emotion right now is an immense relief to get rid of the PLO. I found that everywhere, and I didn't go expecting that. They would say, "Now we're safe. Now we can go home."

Q: There have been reports that thousands of Lebanese are now returning from the Beirut area to southern Lebanon, now under Israeli control. Did you see this?

A: Yes, I saw an astonishing number. Where there were traffic jams, I'd get out of the car and talk to them. But the friendliness toward the Israelis — it's almost like a liberating army. One fellow in our car was sick. Our car was obviously an Israeli car. He got out of the car and kids would bring him lemons. One little Arab got out of his car to come back and hold a wet rag on his head. I mean it was astonishing. I expected this somewhat from the Christian population, but I didn't expect it from the Muslim population.

Q: Mr. Wilson. you're now going back to the American Congress. What message are you going to be taking with you?

A: Well, I'm going to take that message. I'm not prepared to pass judgement in my own mind on the wisdom of the invasion at this point. But it's a funny thing; there's no doubt that it was good for the Lebanese. It remains for history to decide whether it was good for the Israelis or not - but it was good for the Lebanese. But I'm going to try to offset some of the unfair publicity that has accrued in the United States — basically on television. I stopped at Sidon, where, as you know, the damage was severe — probably the most severe... and in talking to a group of people, some of whom had lost their homes, some of whom had lost relatives — they said it was awful, but they said that, all in all, to be free of the PLO, it was worth it — and that was a profound realization to me. I intend to try to get the word out at home that the citizens — the Lebanese themselves — are glad it happened. I had an argument last night with a French reporter, as I usually do with French reporters. He admitted that the people he had talked to were glad that the Israelis came, but that they should have come another way. And I said, "How's that?" And he said, "Without bombs." And I said, "And I suppose that in 1944 we could have invaded Normandy without bombs, too, you know."

Q : What was your impression of the situation of the people regarding health care, food, water, etc?

A : No problems. The Israelis are doing a good job in that regard. A lot needs to be done, and I hope that my country can help in repairing the war damage and rebuilding the homes, but as far as sanitation, food and water are concerned, I don't believe there's a problem. It was interesting to note, too, that in East Beirut, old damage was just as severe as this damage, maybe more so. The damage that was incurred in East Beirut in the various wars between the various Lebanese factions and the Syrians, might be more widespread.

[Document 111]: PLO takeover of the Lebanese media
The Lebanese daily, Al-'Amal, *published this survey on 29 June 1982. It was the fifth in a series of articles on PLO and Syrian domination of Lebanon.*

Since their emergence in Lebanon, the PLO organizations have been more active in propaganda than in the military domain. In 1964, the Lebanese daily *Al-Muharrir*, in collaboration with the Qawmiyun al-Arab movement, which included Muhsin Ibrahim, Na'if Hawatmeh and George Habash[78], began publishing a daily half-page column under the heading, "News from the Homeland," which dealt with Palestinian affairs and the Palestinian resistance. That column was so well received in some Lebanese circles, that other newspapers, too, began publishing items relating to Palestinian organizations. Thus, any PLO activity in Israel or against its interests became a propaganda issue in those newspapers. In those days, the pro-Saudi newspaper *Al-Hayat* became a Palestinian organ and publicized Palestinian activities.

In those days, Palestinian propaganda was based on the following newspapers, journals and other media:

1. *Filastinuna — Nida' al-Hayat (Our Palestine — the Call of Life)* — because of the difficult conditions of the Palestinian people, no Palestinian organ-

78. Leaders of PLO constituent groups.

ization had succeeded in publishing any organ which would reflect its aims. But later on, in 1959, a semi-official monthly — *Filastinuna-Nida' al-Hayat* — began publication in Beirut, under the supervision and guidance of Fatah. For five years, this journal played a decisive role in expressing the views of Fatah before the "armed struggle" was launched. All the articles in the journal dealt with the Palestinian entity and the need to set up a fedayeen movement.[79]

2. *Al-'Asifa (The Storm)* — this Fatah monthly appeared between 15 May 1965[80] and October 1967. It published news about operations of the 'Asifa group and reactions by Arab and Israeli newspapers.

3. *Filastin (Palestine)* — was a supplement of the Lebanese biweekly *Al-Muharrir*; it appeared between November 1964 and 1967. It was the organ of the Qawmiyun al-Arab movement and was directed at the intelligentsia, rather than the general public. It published many articles on the Arab-Israeli conflict, supported the PLO and lent salience to Palestinian identity. It did not show much interest in guerrilla warfare until the appearance of the two fedayeen organizations: *Abtal-al-Thawra* (The Heroes of the Revolution) in 1966 and *Shabab-al-Tha'r* (The Youth of Revenge) in 1967.

4. *Akhbar Filastin* (News of Palestine) — a political weekly, appeared in Gaza from 1965 to 1967, as an organ of the PLO, concentrating on PLO news.

In 1967, the Palestinian movement gathered momentum and so did the number of newspapers reflecting its views;

Lebanese publications

1. *Al-Hadaf* (The Target) — a political daily bought by the Popular Front for the Liberation of Palestine via Ghassan Kanafani.[81] After July 1969, *Al-Hadaf* was published as a weekly.

2. *Al-Huriyya* (Freedom) — the weekly organ of the Qawmiyun al-Arab starting in 1959. It later became the organ of the Popular Front for the Liberation of Palestine, and then of the Democratic Front for the

79. "Fedayeen" (suicide fighters) is a religiously loaded term in Islamic history. In Fatah, it came to designate guerrilla squads who launched acts of terror against Israel or Israeli interests under Palestinian inspiration, guidance or initiative.
80. May 15 is "Palestine Day", commemorating the anniversary of Israel's independence.
81. One of the best-known writers and ideologists of the PLO until his murder a few years ago.

Liberation of Palestine and the Amal (Labor) communist party of Lebanon. Since 1973, it has been advocating Palestinian national unity outside the framework of the PLO, between revolutionary elements who understand the problems of the Palestinian struggle.

3. *Ila al-Amam* (Forward) — a political weekly of the Popular Front for the Liberation of Palestine — General Command. In 1970 the Popular Front bought the concession to publish this journal.

Palestinian Publications

1. *Fatah* — A daily started in June 1970 as the organ of the PLO; since July 1970 it has served as the organ of the PLO's Central Committee. The daily first appeared in Amman, and then moved to Damascus. In August 1971 it became a weekly. In May 1973, it yielded its place to *Filastin al-Thawra* (The Palestinian Revolution).

2. *Al-Qa'ida* (The Base) — a monthly published by the mass organization department of the PLO from September 1971, dealing with organization and trade union affairs.

3. *Filastin al-Thawra* — a political weekly, considered the main journal of the PLO.

4. *Asda' al-Thawra al-Filastiniyya* (The Echoes of the Palestinian Revolution) — propaganda weekly published by Sa'iqa.

5. On behalf of the Popular Front for the Liberation of Palestine:
   Al-Jamahir (The Masses) — first published in Jordan in 1970, during the struggle between the PLO and Jordan.

6. On behalf of the Democratic Popular Front for the Liberation of Palestine:
   a) *Al-Shararah* (The Sparkle) — monthly organ of the Front's Central Committee; it first appeared in Jordan in 1969.
   b) *Al-Muqawamah* (The Resistance) — a news daily published from October 1971 to August 1972.

7. On behalf of the Popular Front for the Liberation of Palestine — General Command:
   a) *Al-Jabhah* (The Front) — monthly published since January 1969.
   b) *Ailul 17* (17 September) — a news monthly geared to propaganda, first published in 1971.

8. On behalf of the Pioneers of the Popular War of Liberation — Sa'iqa:
   a) *Al-Tala'i* (The Pioneers) — a political weekly published by the Central Propaganda Committee of the Sa'iqa forces from November 1969. In June 1971, it became the organ of the PLO's Central Committee and then of its Executive Committee. Published pictures and cartoons for the most part. Informative. Continued to be published as an internal bulletin of the Sa'iqa group.
   b) *Sawt al-Tala'i al-'Ummaliyya* (The Voice of the Pioneer Workers) — a monthly dealing with workers' problems.

9. On behalf of the Palestinian Liberation Army and the Popular Liberation Forces:
   a) *Sawt Filastin* (The Voice of Palestine) — military biweekly published by the indoctrination department of the Liberation Army. It later became a monthly dealing with military studies.
   b) *Al-Jundi* (The Soldier) — news biweekly, published since 1972.
   c) *Al-Thawri* (The Revolutionary) — news biweekly published, since 1969, as the organ of the Popular Liberation Forces.

10. On behalf of the PLO:
    a) *Fatah* — news weekly published since May 1969.
    b) *Al-Masira* (The Trajectory) — weekly published by the political indoctrination department in the Sa'iqa headquarters since January 1972.
    c) *Al-Thawra al-Filastiniyya* (The Palestinian Revolution) — political journal published by the organization and guidance office of the Popular Liberation Front; it started as a biweekly and then appeared once every three weeks.

11. On behalf of the Popular Liberation Front:
    Al-Tha'ir al-'Arabi (The Arab Revolutionary) — political publication published by the organization and guidance office of the Popular Liberation Front. Started as a biweekly and then appeared once in three weeks.

12. On behalf of the Popular Revolutionary Front for the Liberation of Palestine:
    Al-Shararah (The Sparkle) — published as an internal bulletin of the Lebanese chapter from 1971 to 1974.

13. On behalf of the Popular Struggle Front for the Liberation of Palestine:
    a) *Al-Nidal* (The Struggle) — news monthly published from 1967 to 1969.

b) *Al-Nidal al-Sha'bi* (The Popular Struggle) — news monthly published from 1969 to 1973.
c) *Nidal al-Sha'b* (The People's Struggle) — news monthly published in 1973.

14. On behalf of the Popular Organization for the Liberation of Palestine:
    a) *Al-Haqiqah* (The Truth) — educational monthly published in 1968 and 1969.
    b) *Al-Munadil* (The Struggle) — news biweekly.
    c) *Anba' Baladina al-Muhtallah* (News of our Occupied Country) — news biweekly.

15. On behalf of the Arab Palestine Organization:
    a) *Al-Muqatil al-Thawri* (The Revolutionary Fighter) — news publication which appeared in 1969 only.
    b) *Al-Kalimah al-Mas'ulah* (A Responsible Word) — news monthly published since 1970.

16. On behalf of the Militant Organizations for the Liberation of Palestine:
    Al-Ru'yah al-Qawmiyyah (The National Opinion) — propaganda and information journal published in 1970.

Secondary Publications

1. On behalf of the PLO:
   Hassad al-'Asifa (The Yield of the Storm) — weekly news journal published in Lebanon since 1967.

2. On behalf of the Popular Front for the Liberation of Palestine:
   a) *Al-Talib al-Thawri* (The Revolutionary Student) — cultural journal.
   b) *Sawt al-Jabhah* (The Voice of the Front) — political journal published in Lebanon.
   c) *Sada al-Thawra* (The Echo of the Revolution) — political journal published in Lebanon.

3. On behalf of the Democratic Popular Front for the Liberation of Palestine:
   a) *Sawt al-Fuqura'* (The Voice of the Poor) — published in southern Lebanon.
   b) *Al-Dimuqratiyya al-Sha'biyya* (Popular Democracy) — published in Lebanon.
   c) *Al-Thawri* (The Revolutionary) — published in Lebanon.
   d) *Al-Watan* (The Homeland) — published in Lebanon.

4. Publications of the Palestinian Trade Unions:
Sada al-Thawra (The Echo of the Revolution) — published in Lebanon, and deals with trade union affairs.

5. Functional Journals:
Shu'un Filastiniyyah (Palestinian Affairs) — ideological periodical dealing with the Palestinian problem; published by the Centre of Palestinian Studies since March 1971.

6. Foreign language publications:
   a) *Al-Thawra al-Filastiniyya* (The Palestinian Revolution) — an English-language monthly published by the United Propaganda Department of the PLO.
   b) *Fatah* — French periodical published by the Central Propaganda Department of Fatah.
   c) *As-Sa'iqa* (The Storm) — English periodical published by the Sa'iqa group since 1973.
   d) *Al-Nashra* (The Publication) — English periodical published by the Popular Front for the Liberation of Palestine since March 1973.

Palestinian News Agencies

1. *The Palestinian News Agency* — WAFA — started operations in Beirut in 1972, representing the Propaganda Department of the PLO; considered the official news agency of the PLO.

2. *Monitoring Israeli Broadcasts* — a news bulletin based on news monitored from Jerusalem, and published by the Research Centre of the PLO.

Palestinian Broadcasts in Arab Countries

In addition to their newspapers and news agencies, the PLO has maintained broadcasting stations in Egypt, Algeria, Yemen, Iraq and Lebanon.

In Lebanon, the Voice of Palestine broadcast daily news on the Palestinians in Lebanon, Syria and the "occupied lands." Its location was unknown; it was under PLO supervision.

Cinema and Television

Palestinian propaganda activity covered movies and television, too, especially after 1976. Their main cinema agencies:

1. The Department of Culture in the Propaganda and International Centre of the PLO; its most famous products were the films: "The Youth Camp" (1969) and "The Road to Palestine" (1974).

2. The movie department of the Popular Front for the Liberation of Palestine — produced the movies: "The Cold River" (1971) and "The Road of Revolution."

3. The Department of Palestinian Movies in Fatah, which later became the United Cinema Institution of the PLO. Their most famous movies were "With Spirit and Blood" (1970), "The Zionist Onslaught" (1972) and "They Cannot Survive" (1974).

4. The Cinema Department of the Democratic Front produced the movies "The Road" and "May and the Palestinians."

There have also been many Lebanese movies dealing with the Palestinian problem and defending the Palestinian cause; rather than dealing with the essence of guerrilla war, they generally only portrayed fedayeen operations.

The use of television by the Palestinians was rather limited, until they took over programmes on Lebanese television and the news programmes of Channel 7.

Measures Taken by the Palestinians to Improve their Propaganda

1. They openly bought local newspapers or gave them fictitious Lebanese names;
2. They bought off senior journalists by way of threats or bribes;
3. They published many Palestinian publications, dumping their dailies, weeklies and monthlies on the local and Arab markets;
4. They bought newspapers via agents.

1. Buying local newspapers:
   Every Palestinian organization obtained a special fund from Arab countries, to enable it to publish a newspaper or another publication. Following the 1967 defeat, the Arab regimes felt that the Palestinian organizations had snatched prestige from them, for they had become zero while the organizations took over the international scene by launching an effective propaganda campaign. With the view of limiting Palestinian domination, the Syrians established the pro-Syrian Sa'iqa, the Iraqis, the Arab Liberation Front, and Egypt financed the Front for the Liberation of Sinai. Those organizations bought existing journals like *Al-Hadaf*, which was purchased by the Popular Front of George Habash from Zuheir Aseiran. Thus, the Palestinians did not need a permit to publish newspapers because they could publish those they had bought. After 1973, the Lebanese authorities realized that the Palestinians and other Arab regimes who advocated "liberation," wielded a much more powerful

propaganda influence in Lebanon than the administration itself. For, at that point, even newspapers which had official permits to appear and Arab funding, sided with the Palestinians whenever they collided with the Lebanese government. Palestinian pressure amounted to actual domination of most Lebanese newspapers, not necessarily through buying them off, but also by forcing on independent journals a political line which suited Palestinian purposes.

2. Buying off senior journalists:
   a) Material temptations — One technique was to call the head of the foreign news department of a given newspaper and "tip him off" about a forthcoming operation against Israel. The official would acknowledge receipt of the full file of information, including all details and photographs. He would later be invited to a press conference where the "file" would be opened and the information shared with the rest of the correspondents. In this fashion, the Palestinians cultivated good relations with the senior journalists.

   b) Threats — Journalists who were not tempted by material tips were threatened and intimidated until they capitulated.

3. Dumping the markets:
   Palestinian publications and newspapers were distributed free of charge; they had an impact on their readers, even if the latter read only two or three percent of them. By 1973, most newspapers and information media in Lebanon were owned by either the Palestinians or other Arab regimes.

4. Buying newspapers via agents:
   Palestinians and Syrians, not content with dominating newspapers by temptations and threats, also made efforts to buy newspapers in Lebanon. Following are the newspapers which they took over via agents, and by means of Arab funding and intimidation (a list of 21 newspapers follows in the original article).

Palestinian Propaganda in Lebanon and the Western World

It is evident that under Palestinian domination, all Lebanese media have come to reflect Palestinian views first and foremost. Thus, Palestinian propaganda has succeeded, somewhat, in convincing western countries that the "oil crisis can be resolved only through the solution of the Palestinian problem," and that the presence of the PLO in Lebanon is a "revolutionary presence" aiming at liberating a land and not at occupying the land of others.

[Document 112]: Statement by Dory Chamoun

Dory Chamoun, son of former President Camille Chamoun of Lebanon, made the following statement at a news conference held at the Pierre Hotel in New York on 22 June 1982:

For most of us Lebanese, the Israeli invasion has been long overdue. Having failed politically and diplomatically to rid Lebanon of Syrian and Palestinian occupation, we became more and more convinced that Lebanon could only be freed by military action.

The fact that we Lebanese did not possess the necessary military clout meant that we were either doomed to remain occupied for a long period of time, or that someone else had to assume the role.

Due to the fact that most centres of activity for foreign correspondents are concentrated in West Beirut, they were compelled to play to the tune of the Palestinians, for two reasons:

1. Material temptation — lately, The Times (of London) published pictures of Palestinian children at Tel al-Za'tar as the "Children of the Lebanese War."[82] This shows to what extent the Palestinians have succeeded in tempting foreign correspondents to work for their cause.

2. Intimidation — often, the Palestinians threatened to kill foreign correspondents. Here are a few examples, cited in the western press:

    a) In Spring 1980, the journalist in charge of the Reuters office in Beirut was wounded by a shot in the back; a revolver with a silencer was used.
    b) The BBC correspondent in Beirut and his assistant were transferred to Cyprus following threats against their lives.
    c) The correspondent of the French newspaper "Le Figaro" left Beirut following threats on his life by the Syrians.
    d) In December 1981, a CBS correspondent left Beirut for fear about his safety.
    e) A senior Arab journalist left Beirut for London. He returned to Beirut for the funeral of his mother but was kidnapped on his way to the airport; his body was found in his car.[83] His murderers poured acid on his right hand, an ominous hint to all other journalists.

82. There have been no Palestinian children in Tel al-Za'tar since it was taken over by the Christian forces in 1976. The PLO apparently used old pictures of the massacre of 1976 to publicize the "plight of Palestinian children" caused by the June 1982 incursion of Israel into Lebanon.

83. Apparently refers to Salim al-Lawzi, one of the top journalists in Lebanon and the Arab world.

Because of the PLO's behaviour in Lebanon and their attacks on Israel, we knew that there would come a time when Israel would have to perform that surgical operation, which we had been unable to accomplish. We warned Palestinian and Arab leaders time and again, as far back as 1968, that PLO behaviour in Lebanon is unacceptable, and was going to bring about such action on the part of Israel — but to no avail. The reason we gave such warnings was not to safeguard the PLO, but to try and save Lebanon from war and destruction.

Our warnings also went to the Western world which was, at one time, prepared to see Lebanon disappear under the Palestinian and Syrian boot, not realizing that in so doing they were, in reality, making of Lebanon a gift to the Soviet Union. What more evidence is there to this than the Soviet reaction to the Israeli invasion of Lebanon, when Moscow protested and declared very solemnly that such an invasion was against Russian interests in the area.

Frankly, what worries us most is not the invasion as such — those who have suffered seven years of war and destruction can endure a few more days. We are worried about the outcome — will this finally mean freedom, security and the end of a nightmare, or will United States pressure once again force a compromise solution which will satisfy no one and just perpetuate the miseries of the inhabitants of the region?

The statement was followed by a question and answer period:

In answer to a question relating to the order of removal of foreign forces from Lebanon, Chamoun replied, "First the PLO, then the Syrians and finally Israel."

When questioned about the number of casualties, Chamoun answered that, according to his people's estimates, some 2,500-2,600 were killed and about 100,000 were homeless — although many of these were already returning to their homes.

Regarding his party's relations with Major Sa'ad Haddad, Chamoun suggested that Haddad should continue to serve in his present position. He added that Haddad is working towards the same goals as his own party, but because of the situation in Lebanon, they have been forced to work separately.

Questioned whether his party had given the green light to Israel before the Israel Defence Forces went into action, Chamoun answered that the Israelis did not need any green light to act, and that they had not asked for one.

Asked if he knew in advance about the Israeli action, Chamoun replied, "Of course; after all, the Israelis had been making their intentions known loudly and clearly for several months."

In the course of his answers, Chamoun made a point of separating himself from Israel and explaining that he was not a "puppet" of the Israelis. For example, when asked about a particular statement of Defence Minister Sharon, he replied that Sharon speaks in Israel's name, while he speaks in the name of Lebanon.

[Documents 113-122]: Some reactions in the world press

[Document 113]: *The New York Times*, 21 June 1982

For Christian Villagers, Happiness Amid Rubble

By DAVID K. SHIPLER
Special to The New York Times

DAMUR, Lebanon, June 19 — Abdallah Shaya, a 54-year-old gardener with a round, tanned face, found his house amid the rubble of Damur today. Unlike most of the stone and concrete buildings in the hillside village, it was intact, somehow spared the flying shrapnel from the bombs and shells that had ravaged the town and filled the streets with dust and chunks of rock.

"For seven years I have not passed this doorstep," he said as he stood outside, savoring the moment. Then he strode into his small dwelling and began to look around.

Damur, just south of Beirut, was a Christian village until January 1976, when its population fled an assault by Palestinian and leftist forces fighting in the Lebanese civil war. For nearly seven years, until the Israeli Army attacked and captured it last week, the town was inaccessible to its own people; the Palestine Liberation Organization made it a stronghold, using the churches as firing ranges and armories.

A huge new church, left unfinished by the fleeing Maronite Christians in 1976, is covered with spray-painted Palestinian nationalist slogans and plastered with posters of Al Fatah, the main P.L.O. arm, and other Palestinian factions.

On an inside wall where the altar was to have stood, two bull's eyes can be seen in faded paint, the stone in and around them roughened by bullet holes. Above them, where a cross would have hung, a triangular P.L.O. symbol is painted in the Palestinian nationalist colors of red, green, black and white, framing a silhouette of a rifle and a hammer. High in the belfry, a concrete cross has obviously been used as a target over the years, for it is chipped and gouged in a thousand places.

A mortar on wheels stands inside the church's big doors, along with a jeep and a military truck. Posters on the walls show the Star of David being shattered by a wedge drawn in the Palestinian colors. In a once-elegant old church next door, crates of ammunition and drums of fuel are stored.

One corner of the old building was hit by a bomb or an artillery shell during the Israeli attack, and its heavy stone blocks tumbled into a narrow street. But the new church was carefully and successfully avoided; a building just 30 feet away lies in complete ruins, evidently hit by an aerial strike that left the church unscathed.

Christians Tentatively Returning

After Israeli troops took Damur and drove the Palestinians out, Prime Minister Menachem Begin announced that the Christians, whom Israel has supported for several years, would be allowed to return and rebuild. And now the first few former residents have tentatively come to pick through the rubble and see what remains.

Nothing of Mr. Shaya's own things were left. The couches and chair askew in the living room, the dirty pots and pans, the women's makeup on a corner table, the plastic flowers, the beds with their charred mattresses and sheets as if a small fire had raged — these belonged to the Palestinian invaders, not to his family.

The floor was littered with fragments of glass. A large poster of Yasir Arafat, the P.L.O. leader, hung on the living room wall. Mr. Shaya, in tears and anger, grabbed it and tore it down, tearing it into shreds and throwing it onto the floor. A desk blotter, with a portrait of some leader he did not recognize, he could not tear, and so he bent it and sailed it out the door across a wall and out of sight.

"My family had lived here for 200 years, since the beginning of Damur," he said. "We worked in the orchards, grew lemons."

That pleasant, pastoral life ended in 1976. Since then, he said, "we have all been dead. If somebody doesn't have a home and doesn't have a village, what does he have to live for? Now we have started to live. My age is one hour old."

'What More Can I Say'

Mr. Shaya, who fled the Palestinians by sea to the northern port of Junieh and spent the intervening years living in a Christian suburb of Beirut, spoke in a loud voice that rang through the streets of the deserted town. He turned to an Israeli soldier. "What more can I say than thank you that you brought us back to our place," he said. "And God help you to get back to your place."

Walid Azzi, 27 years old, talked in similar images of death and life. "Outside Damur I feel myself like a dead man," he said. "But coming back here I am very happy."

What he found was not at all joyous, for his house was gone. "It is totally destroyed," he said. "Nothing remains, absolutely nothing. But we are happy anyway. We are returning to our village, our land. I was very happy. I took some earth and I made it so." To demonstrate, he grinned broadly, picked up some dust and sprinkled it on his head.

"I am very happy," he said. "I can't explain it. Just because our land is back to us."

And what of the future? "The Israelis are our friends," Mr. Azzi said, "and I hope they stay for some time with us. Our liberty is not sure. But maybe if the big countries make something for us, we will be sure."

Mr. Shaya saw it in simpler terms. "God will give all of us more years," he said, "and we will all come back and live in this village."

[Document 114]: ***The Jerusalem Post*****, 28 June 1982**

THE JERUSALEM POST Monday, June 28, 1982

Arms booty in Lebanon could equip 5 brigades

By YA'ACOV FRIEDLER
Jerusalem Post Reporter

HAIFA. — Enough light arms and ancilliary weapons to equip five infantry brigades, discovered in PLO bunkers in Lebanon, have been brought to a base in the north. A large quantity of heavy weapons has also been delivered.

"A thousand men and 150 trucks are working daily to bring in more captured arms and ammunition, and I estimate it will take four to five weeks more to complete the job," the deputy commander of the Logistics Corps, Tat-Aluf Meir Nitzan, told the press at the base yesterday.

On exhibit at the base are selected weapons including light arms, tanks, Katyusha-firing trucks, guns and mortars of different calibres and uses, and rocket launchers. There are also uniforms, military optics including Starlight Scopes for night sighting and training simulators. Nitzan hoped the exhibit would shortly be opened to the public "so everybody can see why we fought in Lebanon."

The ordnance officer said the amount of equipment captured is far above anything the PLO could possibly have made use of "and we know fairly exactly what their manpower potential is." This estimate was backed up by the number of men of foreign nationalities who were captured, showing that the terrorists were approaching the bottom of the barrel.

He declined to speculate for what or for whose use the huge quantity of weapons might have been prepared. He noted only that manuals in English and other foreign languages had been found with the arms.

Nitzan said the quantity of arms discovered so far is "ten times larger than the IDF had estimated" the PLO to possess and that it is too early to say how much more will be found, with new stores and dumps being discovered daily. He noted that the number and size of the dumps increased the further north one got from the border and he therefore expected that very substantial quantities may be stored in Beirut.

So far the weapons are predominantly of Russian or East Bloc manufacture, including North Korea, Vietnam and China, but also from Britain, U.S., Germany (including the latest G3 rifles and submachine guns), Belgium, France and Italy. There has not been a single Israeli-made weapon among the lot, he said.

Judging from the crates some of the weapons were packed in, they had been shipped directly as arms, while others had been marked as tractor parts or medical equipment and had been sent by devious routes. Some of the latest Russian-made Kalashnikov assault rifles already had numbers in Arabic on their sights.

In addition to the ordnance, a huge carpentry shop, a metal workshop and a PLO hospital had been found. "They had a big logistics back-up but their maintenance was poor," Nitzan said.

The dumps were discovered in villages, mainly near mosques, churches, schools and dispensaries so that the IDF would be unlikely to bombard them, "or if we did it could be displayed as propaganda of Israel harming civilians," Nitzan said.

In the cities most of the arms were found in cellars, up to four storeys underground, but also on the roofs of high-rise buildings. Sometimes the terrorists would force the residents to allow them to place dumps by their homes and in other cases "paid them rent of $100 per room per month."

The IDF has given priority to clearing the dumps in dwellings, for the safety of the residents, and is separating the weapons from the ammunition and explosives, which are being safely stored away. The PLO stores had been indiscriminately packed, presenting great danger to their vicinity, Nitzan noted.

A number of Russian T-62 tanks, all in full working order and captured from the Syrians, are also on display. They are a selection of the 500 tanks captured from the Syrians and the PLO.

[Document 115]: *The New York Times*, 30 June 1982

The New York Times June 30, 1982

Israel to Protest P.L.O.'s Use Of U.N. Refugee Installations

Special to The New York Times

JERUSALEM, June 29 — Israel intends to protest to the United Nations over the use of United Nations refugee installations in Lebanon for Palestinian military purposes, a senior Israeli official said today.

The Israeli Army has found extensive arms caches in Palestinian refugee camps and schools run by the United Nations Relief and Works Agency, known as Unrwa, which receives about 25 percent of its annual budget from the United States. The agency has been responsible since 1948 for providing assistance to Palestinian refugees and has received a total of $1 billion in American funds during its lifetime. The United States is the largest single contributor.

One modern vocational school near Sidon, visited last week, showed signs of having been used as a guerrilla training center. The dormitories were full of uniforms and propaganda posters, and ammunition was stored near classrooms.

In addition, according to an Israeli Army spokesman, a captured document shows that the United Nations Interim Force in Lebanon, the peacekeeping troops, provided intelligence information to the Palestine Liberation Organization about coming Israeli attacks.

'Top Secret' Document

The one-page document, written in Arabic and classified "Top Secret" was entitled "Operating Instruction No. 4 of the Palestine Nationalist Liberation Movement, al-Fatah," sent by the commander of the Kastel Forces, operations branch. It was dated May 26, 1981. According to an Israeli Army translation, it said:

"We received information on 11 May 1981 suggesting that the enemy is due to attack the positions in El Kasimiye, Arouzon and the region of Nabatiyeh, or one of the above mentioned positions. The source of this information is the international emergency force (Unifil)." The spokesman for the United Nations forces could not be reached for comment.

The findings are likely to be used bv Israel as arguments against acceptance of an expanded United Nations force to police southern Lebanon after an Israeli withdrawal. Officials here want something more dependable, such as an American-led multinational force, or a Christian Lebanese militia that would allow continual or periodic Israeli military presence or patrols.

The ranking official who told reporters of the coming protest did so on the condition that he not be identified. He said that "Unrwa allowed schools to be used as terrorist bases" and that in certain refugee camps administered by the relief agency, shelters and schools were used as huge arms depots. At the Ein Khilwan camp near Sidon, for example: "Above there was a U.N. flag, below a fortress. This places all activity of Unrwa in question."

The institution near Sidon, which the army has been showing to reporters, is called the Siblin Technical and Teacher Training Institute. It consists of modern, attractive buildings on a well-manicured campus several miles from the coast. A plaque shows that it was built in October 1963 and was funded by Sweden. "It is dedicated to the training of young Palestinian refugees in the fields of education and industry," the plaque reads.

Not far from the inscription is a room containing crates of rockets and boxes of rifle ammunition.

Across from the library is a dormitory strewn with military uniforms, apparently left by students who fled in haste as the Israeli armored columns advanced three weeks ago.

In one room, students had ingeniously fashioned a table out of the top of a wooden ammunition crate. The blue-painted door of a locker had been decorated with an assortment of photographs: Ingrid Bergman and other movie stars, Yasir Arafat and other Palestinian guerrilla leaders, Ayatollah Ruhollah Khomeini, two small children in battle fatigues making the "V" sign with their fingers. In the middle of the display, the student had drawn a big heart around the words, in English, "Love Story." An English-language textbook was on the floor.

[Document 116]: ***The Times*****, London, 19 June 1982**
The following is an excerpt from a Times *of London article, written from Sidon by Robert Fisk, entitled, "PLO Tactics Drew Israeli Raids."*

Several residents told the same story, although one middle-aged, middle-class woman, who owns some orange orchards, expressed their plight most dramatically.

"When the Israelis came," she said, "the Palestinian fighters took their guns and placed them next to our homes, next to apartment blocks and hospitals and schools.

"They thought this would protect them. We pleaded with them to take their guns away, but they refused. So when they fired at the Israelis, the planes came and bombed our homes."

The woman was telling the truth.

The director of one Sidon hospital still seemed to disbelieve his own words, as he described how the guerrillas deliberately set up their anti-aircraft guns around his clinic.

At their own Ein Hilwe camp, the Palestinians actually put their guns on the roof of the hospital. As another doctor put it, "The guerrillas knew what would happen. The Israeli planes came and bombed the hospital. Everyone there died — the sick, the wounded, the fighters with them."

This was also the fate of the elementary school off the Jezzine Road. The people clustered in the basement for protection — most of them refugees from Tyre — but the Palestinians put a gun mounted on a jeep beside the building. The vehicle lies there still, its gun barrels absurdly twisted by the explosions that followed. The Palestinians used the school for cover, so the Israelis employed equally savage retaliation. They bombed the school.

[Document 117]: ***The Jerusalem Post*, 24 June 1982**

UN school housed Arafat's school for terrorists

A picture of Yasser Arafat and a swastika are among the wall decoration in a room in the former terrorist central training school near Sidon. **See story at bottom of page.** (Rahamim Israeli)

By YOSEF GOELL, Post Reporter

SIDON. — What was apparently the central training school for Fatah terrorists in Lebanon was discovered several days ago by Israeli soldiers in a vocational training school run by the United Nations Relief and Works Agency.

The school, the Siblin Vocational Training Centre, sits on a mountaintop with a breathtaking view of the Mediterranean, several kilometres north of Sidon. It was founded as part of the UNRWA network of schools in June 1961, according to the plaque above the door of the administration building.

The impressive complex consists of a number of large three- and four-storey buildings on various levels of the mountain. The upper buildings seem to have served legitimate vocational-training functions. The lower buildings were devoted exclusively to the Fatah terrorist training school.

When reporters visited the school yesterday, Israel Defence Forces engineer corpsmen were busy defusing bombs, removing booby traps, and sorting out and loading the enormous quantity of weapons and ammunition found in the complex. It was their third day at the job.

There were crates of RPG (rocket-propelled grenade) launchers and missiles, Kalashnikov assault rifles, anti-tank and anti-aircraft missile launchers, hand grenades and an assortment of other weapons and explosives.

The officer in charge of de-activating the weapons and explosives said the large cache was mostly of Soviet and Eastern Bloc origin. But Chinese, Swedish, Belgian and NATO equipment, and American recoilless rifles, were also found.

The terrorist training centre had a modern audio-visual language laboratory, in every way the equal of the Hebrew University's language laboratory.

Most of the students' rooms contained eight double-decker beds and a double locker for each student. Clothing and personal possessions had been left behind in disarray, in what was apparently a hasty flight just ahead of the Israeli forces. The lockers contained books on business English, illustrated weapons manuals in Arabic, PLO propaganda material and, in one of them, a book of English poetry.

In a notebook labelled "Ahmed Salaimi Sayyed, 2nd year, 1980-84," was a handwritten letter that began:

"The English Broad Casting (sic) Co. 6 Mortimer St. London,W1. Dear Sirs, Please allow me to apply for the position of programme director with you."

It was not clear whether the letter was a copy of one actually sent or an exercise in business English that had been filed away for possible future use.

The Israel Defence Forces officer in charge said that one of the rooms in the building had been fitted out for Yasser Arafat's personal use as one of his scattered headquarters. Personal effects said to belong to the PLO chairman were on display, including his well-known Russian fur hat.

In another room, a picture of Arafat on the wall was flanked by a large black swastika on a red background.

Several dozen truckloads of weapons, ammunition and explosives had already been removed from the school by the time of yesterday's visit, and there were still many to come. Other arms caches were discovered in the general area, largely in private homes.

The unofficial IDF military governor of Sidon later said that the IDF had invited UNRWA to continue its activities in all its schools. None of the UNRWA staff of the Siblin school could be found to explain the double use that had been made of their vocational-training facilities over the years.

[Document 118]: ***Ha'aretz*, Tel Aviv, 29 July 1982**
The article, written by Oded Zarai, was entitled, "Trading on Palestine" (translated from Hebrew).

This is a short, smiling and self-confident brunette who belongs to the terrorist organization, Popular Front — General Command, headed by Ahmed Jibril, whom she has never seen in person. When she dared to ask, along with fellow-members of the organization, why the supreme commander had never visited southern Lebanon, nor reviewed the organization's base at Ein Hilwe, she was told that Jibril was "very busy in a far-away location, but his heart was always present with the fighters everywhere." When asked what had happened to the sacred slogan of the PLO, which was daily voiced by Arafat: "Revolution until victory!", she burst into laughter and said that in southern Lebanon the slogan had been reversed to read: "Revolution until the end of the month!" The meaning was simple: many members of the organization in the south "played" at revolution, but eagerly waited for the end of the month to get their pay check, which amounted to 400-1,500 Lebanese pounds ($80-300). Salaries were not determined according to one's seniority, affiliation or rank; they depended on the satisfaction of the boss with one's job. For example, the monthly income of a Fatah member from Sidon went up from 600 to 900 Lebanese pounds when he showed his superiors the way to the private safe of a rich local family where jewellery and ancient valuables had been treasured.

It turns out that the leaders of the terrorist organization in southern Lebanon never had any financial or personal problems. The accountants and pursers of the Fatah and the Popular Front never had any budgetary problems, because none of them depended on their salaries alone. Half the budgets of these organizations found their way to their private pockets. For example, the purser used to allocate 20,000 Lebanese pounds to purchase meat, but only half that sum was in fact budgeted to the unit, while the suppliers finally got, at best, only half the budgeted amount. The rest of the money was distributed among the commanders and the supply unit personnel. This sort of embezzlement was applied to other domains as well. For example, a local commander in a given PLO organization would decide to extend his "protection" to a neighbourhood, village, clan or rich family and collect fees in return. Thus, most commanders could afford to live with their families in posh areas of Sidon. The commanders used to mobilize Palestinian and Lebanese youth into their organizations, and entrust them with "security" tasks. These youth were expected to provide information about good-looking girls, expensive valuables, competitors from other organizations or Lebanese who had publicly shunned the PLO.

These PLO informants, who used to be poor and unemployed, overnight became the "aristocracy" of the PLO in southern Lebanon. They often wore uniforms and sported pistols, strolling the streets and terrorizing the local population.

One of these youths from Sidon, who adopted the slogan "Revolution until the end of the month!" said, 'What's wrong with accepting a salary of 600 Lebanese pounds a month in return for membership in the Fatah "Security Unit," and reporting about "suspects" among the population, and, at the same time, dealing in pornographic videotapes under the PLO's protective cover?' What is more, membership in the organization brought with it the automatic right to any girl one wanted, even those one would not have dared to approach before.

It is often thought that the PLO brutalized only Lebanese villages and towns. But it turns out that the same brutality occurred in the Palestinian camps in southern Lebanon and West Beirut. Hence, the irony in Arafat's insistence on guarantees for the safety of the Palestinian population in West Beirut after PLO evacuation. One could easily come across young pregnant girls, some of them under 18, not only in Sidon, Tyre and the Shi'ite villages of southern Lebanon, where PLO terrorists had raped them, but also in the Palestinian camps of Ein Hilwe, Rashidiye, Burb al-Shimeli and elsewhere. No wonder that in some of those places Palestinian notables are the most insistent in demanding that Lebanese sovereignty be restored to the entire country, including the Palestinian refugee camps. For the PLO's rule of terror was enforced in the camps no less than in the Lebanese towns and villages. In some cases, Palestinian families in the camps, who refused to send their children to the Fatah youth movement, were persecuted even more harshly than Lebanese families. Moreover, many Palestinian households lost their property, their relatives and their houses as a result of bloody conflicts within the camps between various PLO groups. The pro-Syrian Sa'iqa group often aimed cannon and machine gun fire into neighbourhoods where the Iraqi Arab Liberation Front had entrenched itself.

The PLO brought people from many nationalities into southern Lebanon, some of them "mobilized" by deceit. For example, when the PLO representative in San'a, Yemen, reported on a flow of unemployed Yemenite youth from the countryside to the city, the organization dispatched two special representatives to establish an "international development company," which sought candidates for very lucrative jobs. A week later, dozens of young Yemenites were flown from San'a to Damascus on behalf of that company, which existed only on paper. The next day, they were transferred to a Fatah training camp in West Beirut, after their belongings and money had been confiscated. They were unequivocally told, "You either stay here and starve, or live honourably under the wings of the Palestinian revolution." Many of those youths were trained, and then posted in southern Lebanon. They now curse the Palestinians, who mistreated them, insulted them and denigrated their Yemenite nationality; they were regarded as inferior creatures. They exclaim, "the PLO trades in Palestine, it does not liberate it. May Allah inflict his curse and wrath upon them!" In addition to the Yemenites, the PLO mobilized thousands of workers from other Arab and Islamic countries. There were electricians from Pakistan, engineers from Bangladesh, drivers and cooks from Iran, propagandists from Egypt, porters from Turkey, carpenters from India and Sri Lanka, mechanics and tailors from Iraq, and others. All of them ate poorly, hardly washed or changed their clothes...

[Document 119]: Newsweek, 2 August 1982

NEWSWEEK/AUGUST 2, 1982

Mideast Truth and Falsehood

GEORGE F. WILL

Lies are weapons and are today the PLO's most effective weapons. Newspapers that are fastidious about the truthfulness of grocery ads print anti-Israel ads filled with patent lies about Israeli-caused casualties. The New York Times ran a particularly Goebbels-like ad signed by, among others, Noam Chomsky, who has collaborated with a French author who claims the Holocaust never happened.

Lebanon is (in Hardy's words about Leipzig battlefield) "a miles-wide pant of pain." It has been since the PLO and Syrians invaded. It is today because the PLO is hiding behind the babies that Arafat is kissing for U.S. television cameras.

It is hard to prove but easy to believe that Israel, by aiding Lebanese Christians since 1975, has saved more civilian lives than have been lost in this war. But a television screen is easy to fill. A gaggle of Iranians did it for a year, while behind the cameras Teheran went about its business. Television in war is bound to suggest more generalized destruction than has occurred. Furthermore, had there been television at Antietam on America's bloodiest day (Sept. 17, 1862), this would be two nations. Americans then lived closer to the jagged edges of life, but even they might have preferred disunion to the price of union, had they seen the price, in color in their homes in the evening.

Not Chess or Surgery: If "wired democracies" are not to be disarmed by revulsion about televised wars, they must take this truth unperfumed: wars kill people; that is an immediate purpose of waging war. Many persons who preen themselves on their hatred of war do not hate it enough. They cannot: they know so little about it. They show this when they judge a military operation like Israel's unjust simply because it involves injustices. War is not chess or surgery. It is a leap into a realm of chance, desperation and improvisation. Confusion, unintended effects, undesired but unavoidable collateral effects—all these are expectable. It is morally immature to denounce a war because it has the general attributes of war.

It is said that a good man cannot save a nation because a good man will not do what is necessary. But that, too, is morally immature, confusing public and private duties. Begin's duties include understanding that the moral mathematics of Sadat's life ended with a positive sum because he followed military boldness with political boldness. Sadat, remembered as a peacemaker, first made war. In three weeks in 1973 Israel lost a portion of its population three times larger than the United States lost in eight years in Vietnam. Having failed to get to Jerusalem with Soviet tanks, Sadat went by Boeing 707. Begin's similar challenge is to know when he has reached the limit of his military options.

If the Begin-Sharon aim is to push all Palestinians off the West Bank and into Jordan, they risk a more irredentist Jordan. And the pushing would involve methods intolerable to most Israelis, unless they have lost their moral moorings. Begin's task is to use the threat or exercise of force to finish the PLO in Lebanon, and then make Jordan an offer it can't refuse, abandoning the chimera of "autonomy" and the dream of annexation.

> ***U.S. diplomacy, which is ineffectual without being innocuous, is resuscitating the PLO.***

The Reagan-Shultz aim is unclear. Shultz is off to a shaky start, allowing events to set for him a daunting debut: he is supposed to solve one of history's most intractable disputes. It is unhelpfully called "the Palestinian problem." It is actually the problem of Palestine. However laden the word "Palestinian" is with political connotations, it still is a classification more like "North American" than "American." It refers to a geographical origin, not a political association. The noun "Palestine" denotes a definable territory, that of the Palestine Mandate of 1923. Israel and Jordan disagree about the proper allocation of a portion of that remnant of the Ottoman Empire. Only they can come to an agreement that will tidy up the mess left by World War I. Neither Israel nor Jordan—both having fought the PLO, Jordan most bloodily—favors a PLO state on the West Bank, a state that would destabilize both Israel and Jordan, but Jordan first and Jordan most.

In the current crisis, PLO intransigence has grown proportionally with U.S. involvement, and now the United States is protecting the PLO. With words treated as though they are Cheerios, all alike, the U.S. aim has been described as evacuation, disengagement, peacemaking. The PLO had the capacity to injure but not destroy Israel, so if at the cost of military defeat it receives enhanced political status from the United States, it comes out ahead.

Maps: Israel has almost undone the mischievous work of the 1974 Rabat conference, which anointed the PLO the sole legitimate representative of Palestinians. This was an affront to Jordan. (Most Palestinians are Jordanian citizens, and most Jordanian citizens are Palestinians.) Today U.S. diplomacy, which is ineffectual without being innocuous, is resuscitating the PLO and preserving Jordan's excuse for not playing its indispensable role in any peace process worthy of the name. The PLO sits in West Beirut, holding perhaps 300,000 civilians hostage, issuing demands from behind the screen of Habib's mission.

Meanwhile, back in Foggy Bottom, the State Department may be short on realism, but has lots of maps, none of which shows any land that can conveniently be given to a "Palestinian entity." The map is even more full today than it was when Israel was shoe-horned into one-tenth of 1 percent of the land claimed by "the Arab world." That world consists of 21 nations with 175 million people and 7.5 million square miles. In the U.N. the PLO often enjoys the fervent support of 42 Muslim nations with 800 million people. But there is zero desire to make room for the PLO. So Israel is left to deal with the PLO, that creation of Arab hypocrisy and Western appeasement. And Israel still waits for Jordan and Saudi Arabia, two crucial nations of recent and problematic origins, to acknowledge Israel's legitimacy.

Persons far from the theater of menace and violence, persons making fine moral calibrations about Israel's conduct and fretting that Israel is "losing its soul," must hear Golda Meir's words: Jews are used to collective eulogies, but Israel will not die so that the world will speak well of it.

[Document 120]: *Chicago Defender*, 23 June 1982

LEBANON CHRISTIANS

Lebanon Christians are freed

As a result of Israel's successful military operation "Peace for Galilee," the Christian communities of Lebanon have been freed from the threats and attacks of the PLO, to which they have been relentlessly subjected for seven years. Predominantly Christian towns like Damour were returned to their control by the advancing Israel Defense Forces, and the Beaufort Castle, which served as a PLO terrorist stronghold, has reverted to them.

Units of Israel's Defense Forces have been received by Lebanese Christian communities with prayer, song and flowers.

Approximately half of Lebanon's population is Christian, with the remainder divided among a number of Moslem sects. More than one million Christians live in northern Lebanon and along the Lebanon-Israel border. The Lebanese civil war of 1975-76, sparked by the PLO, brought great tragedy to the country's Christian community, which suffered tens of thousands of casualities, dead and wounded, the destruction of their homes, churches, schools, hospitals, businesses and livelihood. Many Lebanese Christians have, since the civil war, been forced into exile or have become refugees at the hands of the PLO and the Syrian army, which since that time, has occupied Lebanon in the euphemistic guise of "peacekeeper".

The Christians in southern Lebanon, led by Major Saad Haddad, have consistently offered stiff resistance to PLO terrorists. While many in the western world might not have paid much attention to the tragic plight of Lebanese Christians, Israel, for humanitarian and strategic reasons, has provided Lebanese Christians its active support. The Lebanese Christians were stunned by the indifference and silence of the Christian world despite their numerous pleas for help. Major Haddad himself declared in Jerusalem that "The luck of the Christian community is that our southern neighbor is the Jewish State. Were it not for their help, our people would have endured indescribable suffering."

The events of the last week give the Christians of Lebanon a new opportunity to once again become a major factor in the life of their country. A Lebanon freed from PLO threats and intimidation and free from the presence and influence of the Syrian army could again become a truly independent country, a happy nation in which members of its dominant Christian community will be able to lead normal daily lives and be unhampered in the pursuit of their religious identity.

[Document 121]: F. Behrendt cartoons

These cartoons have appeared in various European newspapers in recent months.

"WE HAVE NOTHING TO DO WITH THE TERRORISTS!"
"BLACK SEPTEMBER"
"GREEN OCTOBER"
"BLUE NOVEMBER"
"SONS OF THE DESERT"
"BROTHERS OF REVENGE"
"COMMANDOS OF DEATH"

ISREAL MUST RETREAT... AND BECOME... A PLURALISTIC STATE
... LIKE LEBANON!

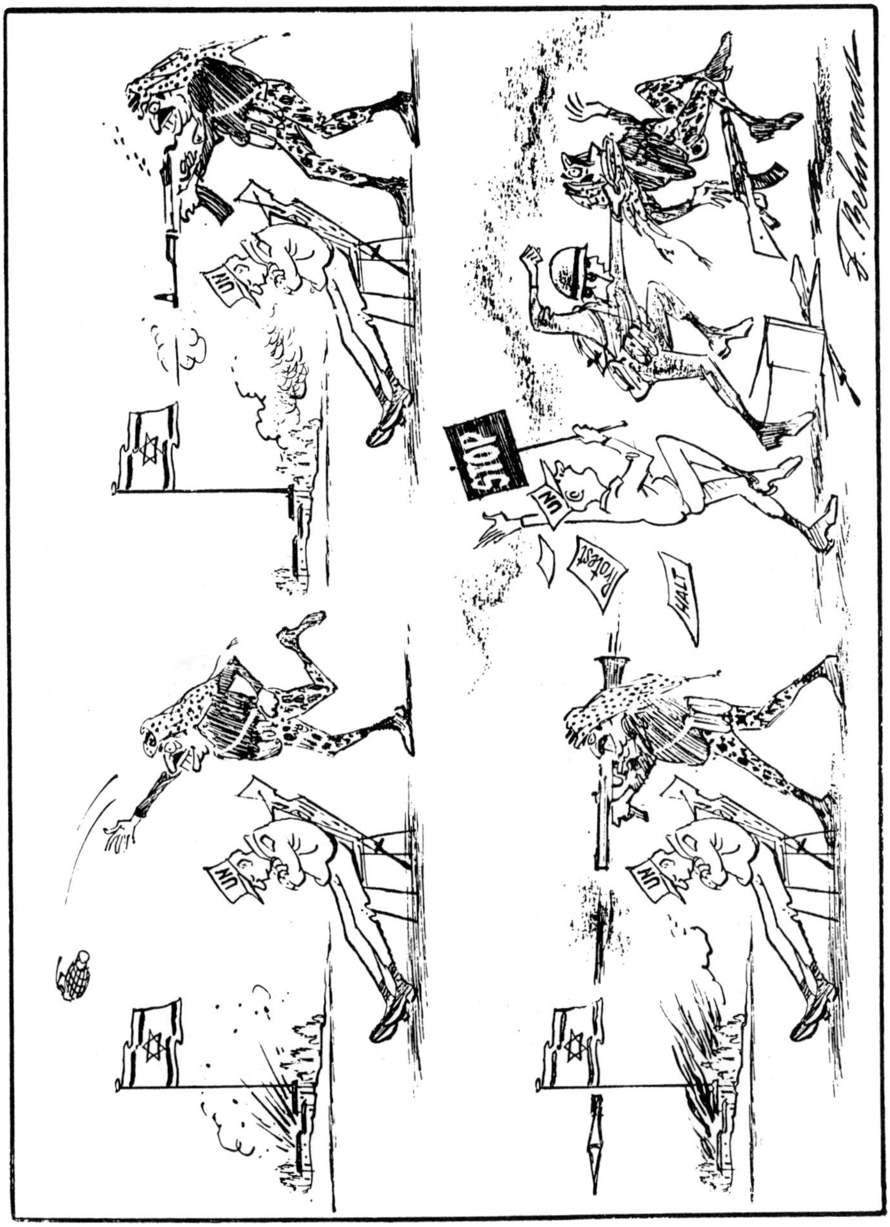
UN
UN
UN
UN
Protest
HALT

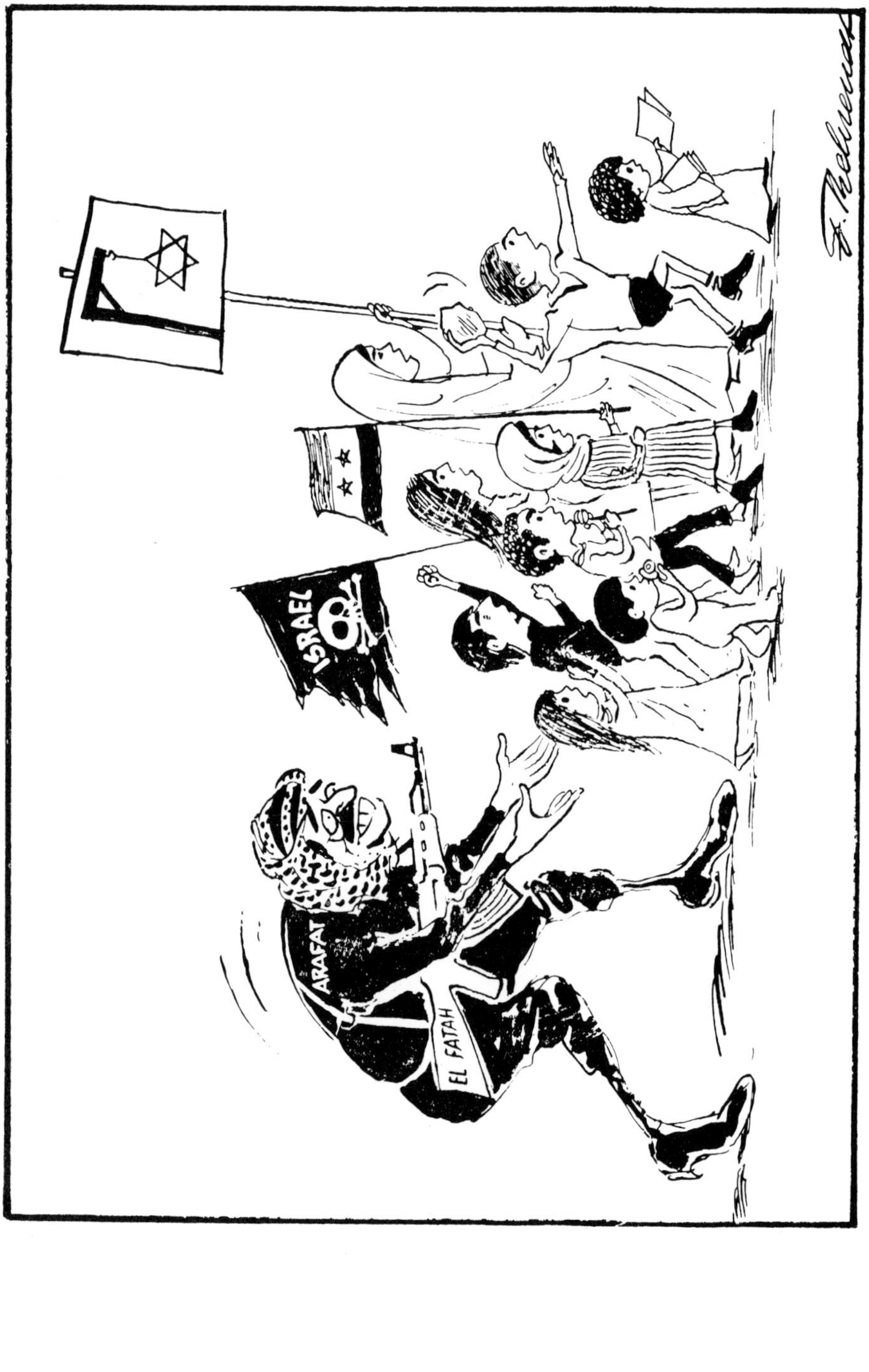

THE CHILDRENS' CRUSADE.

[Document 122]: "Dry Bones," 22 June 1982.

THE JERUSALEM POST June 22, 1982

Dry Bones